Making the World Safe

Making the World Safe

The American Red Cross and a Nation's Humanitarian Awakening

JULIA F. IRWIN

OXFORD
UNIVERSITY PRESS

OXFORD

UNIVERSITY PRESS

Oxford University Press is a department of the University of Oxford.
It furthers the University's objective of excellence in research, scholarship,
and education by publishing worldwide.

Oxford   New York
Auckland   Cape Town   Dar es Salaam   Hong Kong   Karachi
Kuala Lumpur   Madrid   Melbourne   Mexico City   Nairobi
New Delhi   Shanghai   Taipei   Toronto

With offices in
Argentina   Austria   Brazil   Chile   Czech Republic   France   Greece
Guatemala   Hungary   Italy   Japan   Poland   Portugal   Singapore
South Korea   Switzerland   Thailand   Turkey   Ukraine   Vietnam

Oxford is a registered trademark of Oxford University Press
in the UK and certain other countries.

Published in the United States of America by
Oxford University Press
198 Madison Avenue, New York, NY 10016

Library of Congress Cataloging-in-Publication Data
Irwin, Julia.
Making the world safe : the American Red Cross and a nation's
humanitarian awakening / Julia F. Irwin.
pages cm
Includes bibliographical references and index.
ISBN 978–0–19–976640–6 (hardcover); 978–0–19–061074–6 (paperback)
1. American Red Cross—History.   2. Humanitarianism—United States—History.
3. International relief—United States—History.   4. Economic assistance, American—History.
5. United States—Foreign relations.   I. Title.
HV577.I79 2013
361.7′6340973—dc23
2012041766

For Steve

CONTENTS

ACKNOWLEDGMENTS

I have heard tell that researching, writing, and revising a book can be a long, lonely, and tedious undertaking. For me, the process has been a satisfying, stimulating, dare I say pleasurable, experience. I would probably be singing a different tune if it were not for the immense intellectual and emotional support of mentors, colleagues, and friends, and the assistance of knowledgeable editors, archivists, librarians, and academic support staff. To all of these individuals, I am profoundly grateful.

This book began as a dissertation at Yale University, where it (and I) benefited from the inimitable guidance of John Harley Warner and Glenda Gilmore. John helped me to conceive of this project and to develop it at every stage of the process. His confidence in my work and his unflagging support were indispensable to me as I launched my scholarly career. From the moment I first began researching the American Red Cross in one of her seminars, Glenda took me under her wing. Since then, she has served as a devoted mentor, ardently and tirelessly committed to both my work and my professional development. Matthew Frye Jacobson and Naomi Rogers fundamentally influenced this project as well. Naomi's exhaustive comments helped me rethink my arguments and improve my prose, while Matt constantly helped me think about the topic from new and more creative angles. Kristin Hoganson, my external reviewer, gave me thoughtful and valuable criticism. Daniel J. Kevles steadfastly supported me throughout my time in graduate school. All of these individuals are model professors, and each has earned my enduring esteem.

These days, I feel extremely fortunate to have such smart and congenial colleagues as I do in the history department at the University of South Florida. As soon as I arrived in Tampa in the summer of 2010, they made me feel welcome. Since then, they have contributed to my development as both a researcher and a teacher in ways too numerous to count. My thanks go to Golfo Alexopolous, John Belohlavek, Giovanna Benadusi, Barbara Berglund, Kees Boterbloem, Brian

Connolly, Michael Decker, Jolie Dyl, Scott Ickes, David Johnson, Julie Langford, Bill Murray, Adriana Novoa, Fraser Ottanelli, Phil Levy, Franni Ramos, and Tamara Zwick, among others. Before moving to Florida, I also had the good experience of working at Southern Connecticut State University. All of my colleagues there—especially Christine Petto, Virginia Metaxas, Troy Paddock, Dick Gerber, and Steve Judd—made my transition from graduate student to professor a much smoother one. I am indebted to the SCSU History Department faculty for their support and encouragement during my time there.

Many people helped me conduct the research for this book. Over the years, I have relied on the knowledge and skill of many archivists and librarians. Susan Watson of the Hazel Braugh Archives Center, Matthew Schaefer of the Herbert Hoover Presidential Library, and Ken Rose of the Rockefeller Foundation Archives gave me their personal attention. I am also appreciative of the staffs of the National Archives and Records Administration; the Hoover Institution Archives; the Library of Congress; the American Heritage Center at the University of Wyoming; and the Archives and Special Collections divisions of Columbia, Georgetown, Yale, and Indiana Universities. At the University of South Florida, graduate students Brittany Vosler, Caitlin Alderson, Adam Howerton, Mary Kennedy, and Joey Tamargo and undergraduate Lauren Richardson all assisted me in tracking down new primary source materials as I revised my manuscript. Philip Siniscalco, a bright history major with a promising future, assisted me greatly in preparing the index.

Generous funding from a variety of sources subsidized my research and writing. The Program in the History of Medicine and Science and the department of history at Yale University both supported my graduate work, as did an Andrew W. Mellon Fellowship in Humanistic Studies from the Woodrow Wilson Fellowship Foundation. While I was a doctoral candidate, I received additional funding for research and travel from Yale in the form of a Smith-Richardson Foundation Fellowship and a John M. Olin Foundation Fellowship from International Securities Studies, a University Dissertation Grant, a John F. Enders Fellowship, and a Richard J. Franke Fellowship. After receiving my Ph.D., a travel grant from the Herbert Hoover Presidential Library, a summer writing grant from the University of South Florida Humanities Institute, and two dissertation prizes—the Edwin Small Prize from Yale University and the Betty M. Unterberger Prize from the Society for Historians of American Foreign Relations—all assisted me while I completed my revisions.

At academic conferences and other venues, I have had the opportunity to share my work and have benefited from the critiques and queries of many commentators, chairs, and audience members. In the course of writing this book, I gave papers to meetings of the Organization of American Historians, the Society for Historians of American Foreign Relations, the Society for Historians of the

Gilded Age and Progressive Era, the American Historical Association, and the American Association for the History of Medicine. I also presented portions of my research at the Berkshire Conference on Women's History, the Great Lakes History Conference, a Rockefeller Archives Center conference on "New Directions in the History of Nursing," and a conference on "Humanitarianism in Times of War" sponsored by the Historisches Institut, Justus-Liebig-Universität, Giessen, Germany. In each of these forums, I received diverse and insightful feedback. Colloquia presentations to the Program in the History of Medicine and Science and International Securities Studies, both at Yale University, and invited talks before the Brandeis University History Department and the History of International Organizations Network in Geneva, Switzerland, allowed me further opportunities to develop my ideas.

Editors and manuscript reviewers have helped me to strengthen my arguments and my writing. As I made the transition from dissertation to book, Susan Ferber at Oxford University Press lived up to her reputation as a first-class editor. Throughout the revision process, she was quick to answer my questions and address my concerns. Thanks to her sharp eye and her astute suggestions, I was able to clarify both my prose and my key points. Other members of the editorial team have been equally helpful, and I have appreciated all of their hard labor in the production process. Also at Oxford, two anonymous reviewers offered me a wealth of constructive revision suggestions. The book is a far better one because of them. Editors and anonymous referees at *The Journal of the Gilded Age and Progressive Era, Nursing History Review, The Bulletin of the History of Medicine, The History of Education Quarterly,* and *Endeavour* reviewed articles on topics related to this book and offered me invaluable critical feedback. I am especially grateful to Alan Lessoff, Patricia D'Antonio, Julie Fairman, and Branden Little for their editorial comments and positive encouragement, and to Kari McLeod, who graciously read the manuscript for style and clarity.

Becoming a historian was a career path I decided on a very long time ago, but it took the assistance of many individuals to make that possible. I am very appreciative of two teachers who inspired me early in my academic career to pursue history as a profession. Gary Kornblith, my undergraduate advisor at Oberlin College, and Bill Pope, my high school U.S. history teacher, nurtured my passion for history and continue to do so to this day. I would also be remiss not to thank the administrative assistants who have facilitated and organized so many aspects of my life and work over the past several years. Barbara McKay, Ewa Lech, Ramona Moore, Marcy Kaufman, Judy Drawdy, Theresa Lewis, Jennifer Dukes-Knight, and Maura Barrios have worked tirelessly to ensure that things run smoothly. I am grateful to them for all of the labor that they perform.

While I am indebted to those who have assisted me in my work, I am equally grateful for the companionship and camaraderie of many wonderful friends, individuals who have kept me grounded, happy, and well fed over the last few years. During my time in New Haven, I could not have asked for a better group of pals than Caitlin Casey, Lisa Covert, Helen Curry, Ziv Eisenberg, Alison Greene, David Huyssen, Eden Knudsen, Grace Leslie, Rebecca McKenna, Robin Morris, Brenda Santos, Dana Schaffer, Sam Schaffer, Dave Schuller, Kate Unterman, Jason Ward, and Kirsten Weld. In Tampa, I have developed fast ties with Gena Camoosa, Brian Connolly, Darcie Fontaine, Scott Ferguson, Michael LeVan, Amy Rust, Michael Spangler, James Turner, and Aaron Walker. At conferences, I have valued getting to know and learn from Brooke Blower, Chris Capozzola, David Ekbladh, David Engerman, Beth Linker, Marian Moser Jones, Erez Manela, Daniel Maul, Rob McGreevey, Christopher Nichols, Davide Rodogno, Ian Tyrrell, Jen Van Vleck, Tom Westerman, and many other historians from places far and wide. Emily Johnson and Sarah Wallace have always been and will always be there for me. Many of these friends have read and commented on my work, discussed ideas with me, or shared their professional advice. All have given me their constant encouragement and emotional support.

Family, too, has been central to my well-being. For my entire life, my parents have given me their unwavering love and support. Not only did they never question my decision to become a historian, they also encouraged me at every step. My dad, Lee Irwin, is always eager to discuss politics, academics, food, and a host of other topics. I deeply value the time we spend together dining, hiking, cooking, or just sitting around chatting. My mom, Ann Irwin, is nothing if not my number-one fan. Her constant praise and love keep me optimistic and self-assured. Ken, Jane, and Allison Prince are a warm, loving, and convivial second family. I consider myself very lucky to call them my in-laws. Jeff Prince and Zig Kantorosinski have become family to me as well, and have provided me with accommodations, delicious meals, and stimulating conversation during several research trips to Washington.

And then there is Steve Prince, my best friend and constant companion. When Steve and I met in a Civil War class in college, neither of us realized that it would mark the start of our relationship as both partners and colleagues in the historical profession. I'm awfully glad that it did. As this project evolved from an incoherent idea to a doctoral dissertation to a finished book, Steve never failed to give me his unbending intellectual and emotional support. I have certainly benefited from his keen and insightful comments on countless iterations of my work. However, I suspect that I have gained most from the innumerable informal conversations about history that we have held throughout the years: during seven-course dinners or over pizza and beer, on long jogs and longer car rides, while sitting on the couch playing Trivial Pursuit, or on the porch swing playing music. Steve's brilliant mind always keeps me on my toes; his good nature, humor, and affection make me feel as if I'm floating on air. To him—my summer love in the spring, fall, and winter—I dedicate this book.

Making the World Safe

Introduction:
A New Manifest Destiny

In the late summer of 1917, Edward T. Devine left his home in New York City and boarded a ship bound for the French war zone. In the months after the United States entered the First World War, a growing number of American men took the same trip "over there." But Devine was no wide-eyed draftee. Nor was he an average American. Edward Devine was one of the leading American social economists and a noted public intellectual. He had served as the executive secretary of New York's Charity Organization Society since 1896, was a professor at Columbia University, had been instrumental in founding the New York School of Philanthropy, and had spent a career engaged in urban reform initiatives. Yet, with total war raging across the Atlantic, Devine saw little choice but to put his professional commitments on hold.

Edward Devine did not go to Europe to take up arms. Rather than heading to the trenches to assist Allied forces, he used his professional expertise at the back of the line, aiding French civilians as the head of the Bureau of Refugees and Relief for the American Red Cross. Devine would not calculate his contribution to the Allied war effort by the number of mortars he fired, nor by the number of German and Austrian soldiers he killed. Instead, he would gauge his success by the number of women, children, and other noncombatants that he helped to feed, clothe, and house.

Devine never regarded humanitarian assistance as a lesser substitute for military service. In fact, he understood it as a vital complement to the armed intervention. He explained as much in a 1918 address to fellow aid workers in Paris. Speaking to scores of volunteers, Devine advanced his own interpretation of the famous appeal for American isolationism that George Washington made in his 1796 Farewell Address. "When Washington told us not to meddle in the affairs of Europe," Devine explained, "he meant of course not to meddle in their local quarrels and their rival ambitions; he did not mean that we should be provincial, isolated or indifferent to the welfare of other nations...Our manifest destiny is not indefinite expansion," he proclaimed, "but indefinitely expanding brotherhood."[1]

Devine's choice of words spoke volumes about his understanding of the role of humanitarian aid in American foreign relations. In evoking manifest destiny, Devine belied claims about the isolationist past of the United States. Indeed, he acknowledged a long history of American international involvement, a process that had increased greatly during his own lifetime. In recasting American manifest destiny as a project of "indefinitely expanding brotherhood," however, Devine offered an alternative means of engaging with the world. No longer could Americans remain detached from global political affairs; the Great War had made that much clear. Nor could they consider violent imperial conquest, religious proselytizing, and ruthless capitalist penetration as suitable forms of intervention. The new American internationalism required all Americans to accept a novel set of civic obligations, a common commitment of their minds and their money to improving the health and welfare of the wider world. Through the provision of emergency material aid and intellectual and technical expertise to civilians in Europe and throughout the world, Devine and many of his fellow Americans hoped to achieve one of the nation's principal avowed wartime goals. Together, they would make the world safe.

Making the World Safe is a history of American relief and assistance to foreign civilians in the early twentieth century. It traces how the U.S. government came to realize the value of overseas aid as a tool of statecraft and diplomacy. At the same time, it examines the lives of a cosmopolitan cadre of American civic leaders, philanthropists, and medical and social scientific professionals—individuals who embraced foreign assistance as a new way to participate in the international community. This book recounts how ordinary Americans understood, assessed, and reassessed the new global relief commitments that they were urged to make. It is, in sum, a study of how U.S. citizens and their government together defined foreign civilian aid as an American responsibility, of their efforts to carry out foreign relief and assistance projects at a heady moment in U.S. international history, and of the multiple political and cultural objectives they hoped their humanitarian interventions might achieve. It tells these stories by examining the pivotal role that one organization—a quasi-private, quasi-state organization called the American Red Cross—played in realizing this new commitment to civilian aid.[2]

*

In the late nineteenth and early twentieth centuries, the United States emerged as a key player on the world stage. Postbellum Americans grew more interested in international affairs. Increasingly, they traveled the world as businessmen, missionaries, and tourists. Recognizing the strategic and economic value of this privately led expansionism, the federal government promoted it by enacting favorable trade policies with certain regions, enlarging the navy, and increasing the size and strength of the diplomatic bureaucracy. By the end of the nineteenth century, fueled in large part by such private-public partnerships, the United States rivaled the great powers of Europe in terms of economic and cultural influence. It soon challenged them on political terms as well. Victory in the 1898 Spanish-American War resulted in American control of territories in the Caribbean and Pacific and established the country as an imperial nation. Less than two decades later, entry into the Great War embroiled the United States in the messy Old World politics that American policymakers had always vowed to avoid. In a period of unprecedented American expansion, citizens and government officials grappled with their nation's increasing prominence and power in the international sphere and debated how best to engage with the wider world.[3]

In these formative years of American global power, providing material relief and assistance overseas became a principal way for Americans to interact with the wider world and to provide a living demonstration of the country's new international identity. On missions to Asia, Africa, and the Middle East, American Protestants sought not only to save souls but also to improve lives materially through education, protective legislation, and social and sanitary reforms. Engineers and technical experts, philanthropists, and health professionals worked abroad to ameliorate disease, malnutrition, and other social problems with environmental reforms and medical aid. During the First World War and its aftermath, millions donated their time and their money to provide food, clothing, and other relief to European refugees, women, and children. Thousands traveled overseas to administer such aid. Many of these Americans believed that the United States had to behave as a benevolent world power, a nation ready and willing to direct its burgeoning material and intellectual resources toward the improvement of international health and welfare. By taking steps to reduce suffering in the world, these citizens aspired to live up to that ideal.

Rather than looking to the federal government to administer foreign assistance, Americans at this time tended to believe that bettering the world was a task best left to private enterprise. Churches and charities, not the state, took charge.[4] Though typically voluntary in character, their assistance nonetheless held profound political significance. Efforts to improve the lot of civilians helped foster global political and social order, thereby encouraging stable trade and reducing potential threats to U.S. security. At the same time, by projecting a positive image of the United States, relief served as effective propaganda.[5] In a period of largely informal internationalism, privately administered foreign aid represented an invaluable form of diplomacy. Well aware of the power of humanitarian relief, the federal government proved a ready and willing promoter.

Americans who elected to support or participate in foreign aid and assistance in these years could do so through a vast array of religious and secular charities, voluntary associations, and philanthropies. Some arose temporarily in response to immediate crises, while others enjoyed greater longevity.[6] At the turn of the twentieth century, however, one organization—the American Red Cross (ARC)—began to dominate the humanitarian landscape. By the Great War era, as the United States confronted the unprecedented social disaster of Europe's total war, the ARC would take the lead in administering civilian relief on the nation's behalf. In spite of the ARC's prominence in this field, historians of the early twentieth century have largely overlooked its efforts. Studies of U.S. international humanitarianism and reform have chronicled the work of a wide array of individuals and groups, including Protestant missionaries, colonial administrators, the Rockefeller Foundation, and Herbert Hoover's Great War–era charities. The ARC remains noticeably absent from these accounts.[7] Those who have examined the organization in any great detail have concentrated primarily on its position as an adjunct to the military or on its domestic disaster relief activities.[8] The ARC's work in overseas catastrophes and non-combatant war relief, such a gap would seem to indicate, was relatively inconsequential.

Far from peripheral, the ARC's international civilian assistance in the early twentieth century was wide-ranging and held major diplomatic and cultural significance. The organization's activities are central to the histories of both U.S. humanitarianism and U.S. foreign policy and, as such, merit further consideration from both fields. This book therefore tells the story of the private citizens and government officials who expanded the ARC's role in overseas civilian aid, analyzing how they used the ARC to achieve their international political and social objectives. It does not presume to offer an exhaustive history of the ARC; indeed, it explicitly ignores the ARC's extensive work in military and domestic relief. Rather, by integrating the ARC's civilian aid efforts into American social and diplomatic history, *Making the World Safe* illustrates the significance of voluntary foreign relief in American political and cultural relations with the world. This book traces the twin trajectories of the ARC's entry into foreign civilian aid and the fluctuating American interest in its voluntary international humanitarianism, beginning with the organization's earliest roots in the nineteenth century and concluding just after the end of the Second World War. Its primary focus, however, is on the years from 1914 through the early 1920s, the Great War era and the time in which the ARC's place in U.S. international affairs peaked.

*

The ARC's unique position vis-à-vis the U.S. government, U.S. society, and the international community makes it particularly valuable for understanding how foreign relief functioned as a facet of U.S. foreign relations. Established in 1881, the ARC was a privately funded and staffed relief organization, primarily dependent on volunteer labor. Yet the ARC differed in pronounced ways from other contemporary American voluntary associations. First, it formed part of the International Red Cross Movement. Like all other Red Cross societies, the International Committee of the Red Cross (ICRC) recognized the ARC as the designated agency to provide neutral wartime aid to soldiers on its nation's behalf. From its inception, however, the ARC also served a secondary purpose, distinct from the ICRC's founding mission. Its charge included aiding civilians during natural disasters, famine, political upheaval, and other moments of social unrest, both at home and overseas. Thus even as it benefited from its connection to the International Red Cross Movement, the ARC enjoyed significant autonomy, allowing it to serve American humanitarian goals beyond the sphere of military relief.

Second, in the early twentieth century, the ARC cultivated relationships with internationally minded leaders in politics, the military, business, and the social sciences—connections unparalleled by other voluntary relief associations. The organization benefited especially from its connections to the U.S. government, formalized by the Geneva Convention and, over time, by Congressional charters and ties to the White House and the State and War Departments. By 1911, the ARC had earned the designation of "the official volunteer aid department of the United States," a distinction that only grew sharper over the ensuing decade.[9] At the same time, the ARC began to forge strong ties to the American medical, social scientific, and philanthropic communities, whose more cosmopolitan members recognized its potential as a vehicle for carrying out reform and assistance projects abroad. Leading figures in corporate America, too, increasingly threw their support behind the organization and took part in its governance. Realizing that the social upheaval generated by disasters and war posed a threat to international production and trade, they appreciated the ARC's civilian aid as a means of restoring normal conditions. Such governmental and professional connections gave the ARC an incomparable level of political and cultural authority. Officially connected to the state but not fully part of it, simultaneously national and international in its identity, the ARC was well situated to achieve the diverse diplomatic and humanitarian objectives of the U.S. government and its citizens.

Although the ARC first began to play an important role in U.S. foreign affairs in the late nineteenth century, it was the Great War era that marked its most conspicuous and considerable involvement in this arena. From the start of the war in 1914, but particularly after the United States entered the conflict in 1917, the ARC garnered incredible popular and governmental support for its foreign relief work. Over one-third of the U.S. population joined the organization as members. American donors gave over $400 million in 1917 and 1918 alone, an enormous sum at that time. American physicians, social workers, nurses, and other professionals volunteered in droves, recognizing wartime service with the ARC as a way to extend their professional commitments across the Atlantic. Prominent bankers and businessmen took charge of the organization to ensure that its relief work was administered efficiently. President Woodrow Wilson and former president William Taft became indefatigable proponents, promoting the ARC to the exclusion of all other aid organizations and strengthening its partnership with the federal government further still. With such fervent popular and state backing, the ARC became America's largest and most influential wartime voluntary relief agency.

While the ARC of these years is often remembered for its service to soldiers at the front—an image popularized in the writings of ambulance drivers Ernest Hemingway and John Dos Passos and nurtured by subsequent generations of historians—a vast proportion of its resources in fact went toward civilian, not military, relief. During the war and its aftermath, the ARC organized assistance operations in over two dozen countries, mostly in areas where U.S. troops never deployed. In 1917 and 1918, during the years of U.S. armed involvement in the war, the ARC was the nation's principal provider of civilian relief. Its personnel provided food, housing, employment, and medical assistance to millions of refugees, women, children, and other noncombatants. Many went further, attempting to influence European welfare in the long-term through the orchestration of comprehensive health reform projects. Although the organization's leaders scaled back their assistance program after the Armistice, deeming wartime levels of relief outside the bounds of their appropriate peacetime responsibilities, hundreds of ARC personnel remained in Europe as late as 1923 to participate in relief and rebuilding projects.[10] Once the war concluded, many veteran ARC workers attempted to keep the potent public zeal for both the ARC and international humanitarianism alive. In part, they succeeded. The postwar ARC remained the "official volunteer aid department of the United States" and continued to play a leading role in American responses to international disasters. The widespread public enthusiasm for the ARC and its international humanitarian aid projects, however, proved in many ways a transitory phenomenon. Not until World War II would the American fervor for the ARC and its overseas assistance return. By the time it did, changes that had transpired in both the United States and the international community fundamentally altered the role the ARC and its voluntary civilian aid would play in the nation's foreign affairs.

As the United States expanded its position on the international stage—and especially as it faced the unprecedented crisis of the First World War—the ARC's voluntary civilian relief thus constituted a major part of the nation's foreign relations. The ARC's extensive program of foreign civilian assistance advanced both the strategic and social interests of the United States. On the one hand, the ARC promised to counteract the root causes of social and political instability while enhancing the image of the United States—both critical diplomatic goals. At the same time, through the provision of relief and assistance, American citizens found an unparalleled opportunity to interact with foreign civilians and to impart their ideas about health, charity, and social organization. Never simply a sideshow to U.S. diplomatic or military engagement, the ARC's overseas aid constituted an important route for Americans and their government to engage with the world beyond their borders.

*

While the ARC offers a critical window into the political, diplomatic, and cultural practices of U.S. foreign aid in the Great War era, it has as much to suggest about the workings of contemporary U.S. society and foreign relations more broadly. The ARC might have been part of the International Red Cross Movement, but far more than that, it was a product of the late nineteenth- and early twentieth-century United States. It embodied the political and cultural qualities characteristic of that period. Many wider currents in contemporary U.S. society informed the ARC's global actions, but three broad contextual strains prove especially salient for understanding the place the ARC occupied in the Great War–era United States: progressivism, missionary ideology and activity, and American cosmopolitan and internationalist thought. Through the history of ARC's foreign relief, this book tells the story of the American people at the turn of the last century, their approaches to social and political organization, and their contemporary ideas about their relation to the world.

To begin, the ARC that spread across the world during the Great War years was very much a creature of the Progressive Era United States. Admittedly, this designation risks obscuring more than it clarifies, but even a brief survey of the ARC's structure and ideology attests to the organization's convergence with many of the period's prevailing domestic trends. Following a major institutional reorganization in the first few years of the early twentieth century, a new generation took charge of the ARC, drawn from the ranks of the U.S. government and American corporate and philanthropic communities. These new leaders demonstrated a remarkable commitment to voluntary civic engagement and fiercely advocated service for the common good, hallmarks of contemporary theories of progressive democracy. Mirroring the impulses of the scientific management crusade, they labored to build the ARC into an organization known for its efficiency and accountability. These leaders also forged a strong association with the state, a form of reciprocal social organization quite typical of the time; the U.S. government relied on the ARC to administer American relief on its behalf, while the ARC depended on governmental boosterism.

Lastly, the ARC's leadership exhibited a robust faith in the power of professional expertise. At a time when physicians, social workers, nurses, and other welfare occupations were establishing their professional credentials and identities, ARC leaders appealed to leading figures from each of these fields to design and direct relief activities. Such an approach effectively denied untrained, amateur women, traditionally the lynchpins of American humanitarianism, any role in ARC leadership or decision making. On the other hand, overseas service with the ARC provided a valuable opportunity for female professionals to advance their careers or to assume leadership roles that would have been far less obtainable in the United States. But it was male professionals who arguably derived the greatest personal benefit, for ARC leaders typically appointed them to supervise aid activities and manage other personnel. In the process, the ARC played a central part in legitimizing humanitarian work as a career choice for American men. These welfare professionals, both male and female, left a profound mark on the ARC's approach to foreign aid. In the early twentieth-century United States, they first defined disaster relief as a professional enterprise, with the ARC and its staff assuming the mantle of the nation's premier disaster experts.

By the time the United States entered the Great War, the ARC's new leaders had built the organization into an association known for its social democratic spirit, its efficiency, its professionalism, and its expertise—distinct markers of its Progressive Era provenance. As a dominant and in many ways archetypal institution in the early twentieth-century United States, the ARC offers a focused way to examine U.S. civilians and government officials interacting within their domestic cultural milieu. As a major American organization in the world, moreover, it presents a chance to chart the international movement of key progressive individuals, institutions, and ideas.[11]

If progressivism provides the backdrop for thinking about the ARC's place in American culture both at home and abroad, two other conceptual factors help situate the organization with regard to U.S. international relations. First, the ARC's overseas assistance efforts formed part of a long and ongoing tradition of American missionary ideology and practice. The organization's formation and subsequent rise coincided with a surge in American Protestant overseas missionary activity and the development of a vast American moral empire. In key ways, the ARC's civilian relief efforts constituted part of this larger pattern of American cultural expansion and influence. Motivated by ideals of American exceptionalism and benevolence, the ARC's personnel assumed a corresponding obligation to aid the world. And yet they also diverged from the Protestant missionary tradition in profound ways. Deemphasizing avowedly religious motivations for their actions, the ARC's leaders tended to define their humanitarian missions in explicitly material and modernist terms. They employed a language of professional obligation and expressed a commitment to physical, rather than spiritual, uplift. Under the ARC's auspices, Christian universalism—at least on paper—started to give way to international humanitarianism. The organization's success reflects the beginnings of a trend toward the secularization of American missionary ideology, a pattern that grew stronger as the twentieth century progressed.[12]

Second, the ARC's explosion onto the world stage occurred in a period redolent with debate over the proper role for the United States in the world. In the early twentieth century, a growing number of Americans came to believe that the United States must become more involved with the international community in order to secure global peace and democracy. American internationalism was by no means a coherent worldview; U.S. citizens held wildly disparate opinions about how to exercise influence in the world. Some trumpeted a more powerful and forceful U.S. military as the answer, while others advocated participation in some sort of collective security apparatus. Many believed that expanding American investments and financial practices would generate economic and political stability in the world. Still others stressed the importance of nurturing personal connections with foreign individuals, of building a transnational community based on commitments to peace and global well-being. By offering U.S. citizens the opportunity to intervene in the world for the ostensibly liberal ends of improving health and welfare, the ARC's relief activities proved well suited to serve these diverse agendas. For those committed to peaceful, mutualist forms of global involvement, helping civilians seemed a viable alternative to more coercive or belligerent international engagement, a way to act in accordance with their cosmopolitan sensibilities. For those willing to exercise the power of the state, the military, or the market to secure American interests in the world, civilian relief appeared a ready complement to these other forms of intervention. And for those Americans who resisted and resented the state's expanding international role, privately administered aid generally appeared a more palatable way to engage with the world. In a moment of competing international visions, the ARC's civilian aid program won support across the political spectrum. Its success in navigating the deeply partisan waters of the early twentieth century points to the importance that diverse groups of Americans attributed to voluntary international humanitarian engagements.[13]

Moving beyond the realm of social and diplomatic ideas, the history of the ARC's civilian assistance efforts is at its heart a story about the American people—their relationship to the state and civil society, their participation in foreign aid enterprises, and their beliefs about the value of international humanitarianism. The internationally minded government officials and private citizens in the upper echelons of the ARC's leadership saw foreign aid as a way to secure their respective political and social objectives. Without the donations and support of American citizens, however, the ARC could not function; the organization's leaders therefore had to convince the American public of its importance as well. Together, U.S. government officials and ARC leaders labored to define support for the ARC and its foreign aid as a new American civic obligation and urged every American citizen to embrace this new international responsibility. During the Great War era, U.S. citizens joined the ARC in record numbers and declared an unprecedented commitment to overseas civilian aid. The millions of individuals who took part in the wartime ARC represented heterogeneous segments of the American body politic. They held disparate assumptions about the proper place of the United States in the world. They united, however, in support of the Red Cross and international humanitarian engagement. This enthusiasm for international civilian aid, though ultimately short-lived, suggests much about how early twentieth-century Americans thought of themselves and their responsibilities to the world community.

To understand the history of the ARC's civilian relief is thus to understand one of the major ways that U.S. citizens engaged with the world and with each other at a critical moment of American international history. To begin this story, Chapter 1 turns back to the early nineteenth century to chart the origins of American international humanitarianism, the rise of the International Red Cross Movement, and the creation of the organization that bridged the two: the American Red Cross. It then charts the ARC's steady growth through the late nineteenth and early twentieth centuries, focusing particularly on the organization's expanding international reach and the relationships that ARC leaders forged with American social scientists, philanthropists, and state officials. Together, these individuals built the ARC into an organization that would best serve their mutual interests in the field of international civilian aid.

The next two chapters examine the ARC's place in the United States in the Great War era. Chapter 2 focuses on the eight years prior to U.S. entry into the war. In these years, presidents William H. Taft and Woodrow Wilson became major supporters of the ARC, while their State Departments started relying on the organization's civilian aid in a number of conflicts and crises. Members of the business, social scientific, and philanthropic communities increasingly demonstrated their support as well. It was not until U.S. entry into the Great War, however, that the ARC's foreign assistance garnered wide enthusiasm among the American public. Chapter 3 explores the ARC's meteoric growth in the United States during 1917 and 1918. It analyzes how the ARC's leaders sold the ARC to the U.S. public and worked to define foreign assistance as a new wartime obligation. It also considers the extent to which individual Americans consented to this new set of international humanitarian responsibilities and discusses the varied meanings that they attributed to this foreign assistance.

The subsequent two chapters turn to the ARC's civilian relief efforts in Great War–era Europe. Chapter 4 examines the ARC's work in 1917 and 1918, the period of U.S. military involvement in the war. In these years, the ARC focused primarily on Western Europe. There, ARC workers not only provided material relief but also undertook major comprehensive health and welfare projects, including anti-epidemic campaigns, the construction of health demonstration centers, and the provision of nursing education to local women. Chapter 5 turns to the ARC's peacetime efforts on the continent, where personnel remained for more than four years after the Armistice. In the early postwar months, ARC leaders redirected the majority of their funds and personnel to Central and Eastern Europe, attempting to replicate many of the same approaches that their predecessors had developed during the war years. Declining public enthusiasm for the ARC, its foreign aid, and American international involvement more broadly, however, soon limited the organization's ability to administer generous assistance. Undeterred, the enduring proponents of American international humanitarian engagement worked to sustain their involvement in Europe. In an attempt to adapt to the hostile postwar climate, they refocused their efforts entirely on European children, the group they saw as most likely to win public support and most in need of their assistance. Both Chapter 4 and Chapter 5 call attention to the ways that the ARC served varied diplomatic and cultural agendas of the U.S. government and the American public. These chapters consider how U.S. diplomatic and military officials relied on the ARC to complement their larger goals of winning the war, preserving the peace, and achieving order and stability abroad. They also explore how American health and welfare professionals embraced assistance to achieve wholesale change in European society. Finally, they consider the ways that individual Americans, both in Europe and back in the United States, conceived of the ARC and its international humanitarian activities.

Chapter 6 moves out of postwar Europe to trace the humanitarian activities that the ARC pursued across the globe during the interwar years and in the aftermath of World War II. Focusing on ARC disaster response, development initiatives, international collaboration, and wartime relief, it demonstrates the ARC's continued role in U.S. international humanitarianism. At the same time, it also illustrates how changes in both the international system and the American state significantly altered the role that the ARC's civilian aid played in U.S. foreign relations. A brief epilogue reflects on the nature of the ARC's civilian aid as a form of U.S. foreign relations.

Together, these chapters tell the story of how Americans in the early twentieth century embraced a new Manifest Destiny for the United States and strove to infuse the ideal of "indefinitely expanding brotherhood" into their nation's foreign policy. To be sure, this approach to world affairs was never purely altruistic, and it was not without its problems. When U.S. citizens and government officials set out to aid and rebuild the world, they were driven, at least in part, by self-interest. In their encounters with aid recipients, moreover, American humanitarians inevitably engaged in an uneven power relationship. As benefactors in this dynamic, they held significant cultural, economic, and political clout over the foreign individuals and societies they pledged to assist, a fact that sometimes bred resentment and resistance. Yet at the same time, foreign aid efforts were neither entirely self-serving nor simply a veiled attempt at social control. In the early twentieth century, millions of Americans—from political leaders and social elites to everyday men, women, and their children—accepted the belief that they must work to alleviate overseas suffering. They advanced a benevolent and compassionate vision of their nation and its place in the world, a vision they labored to achieve through foreign aid activities. The implications of this international humanitarian awakening, with its inherent complexities and its positive and negative repercussions, are essential to the broader history of American foreign relations.

1

Making International Humanitarianism American

In the early years of his life, Ernest P. Bicknell probably did not envision his future as a globetrotter. Born in 1862 to a farming family in rural Indiana, Bicknell worked his way through Indiana University, graduated in 1887, and took a job at the Indiana State Board of Charities. In 1898, he became the general superintendent of the Chicago Bureau of Charities. Over the next ten years, he earned a national reputation as a leader in the period's scientific charity movement, known for his systematic efforts to reform philanthropy, corrections, public health, housing, and other municipal concerns. Bicknell's coming-of-age in the American Midwest coincided with a period of rising U.S. involvement and influence in world affairs. In the decades following the American Civil War, U.S. material and cultural exports, foreign investments, and military and naval power all increased meteorically. By the first decade of the twentieth century, the United States had acquired territories in the Caribbean and Pacific; asserted its hegemony in the Western Hemisphere; and emerged as a central player in Asian and European economic, political, and social affairs.

In 1908, Ernest Bicknell made a career change that destined him to play a central role in his country's expanding global involvement: he became the national director of the American Red Cross. By the time the First World War erupted in Europe in 1914, Bicknell and his colleagues had transformed the ARC into one of the nation's principal agencies for overseas civilian relief. When the United States entered the war three years later, many Americans recognized the ARC as the organization best suited to administer international aid on behalf of the U.S. government and its people. Bicknell's twenty-five-year career with the ARC took him to dozens of countries, where he provided assistance to the civilian victims of natural disasters, epidemics, and war. Thousands of other Americans joined him abroad as staff and volunteers. Millions of American donors funded their overseas activities. In their humanitarian endeavors, Bicknell and his fellow citizens served as informal ambassadors for the United States to the world.

At the same time, they reaped personal and professional benefits. Service with the ARC gave Bicknell and his colleagues an opportunity to not only see the world but also assist, reform, and rebuild it.[1]

By the Great War era, the ARC's overseas civilian relief activities would come to represent a critical part of U.S. foreign relations. Yet just as the young Ernest Bicknell would have been hard-pressed to predict his future work as an American international humanitarian, few in the post–Civil War United States foresaw the dominant role that overseas aid would play in American diplomacy and international engagement in the early twentieth century. The ARC's position as the United States' principal civilian relief agency, furthermore, was never foreordained. For either to occur required a fundamental shift in the way Americans conceived of both humanitarianism and their nation's position in the world.

This transformation of American sensibilities took place in the five decades following the Civil War. These years saw Americans alter their approaches to charitable assistance, missionary activity, and social reform. Throughout much of the nineteenth century, Evangelical Christianity had provided the mobilizing impulse for these American humanitarian activities, at home and abroad. This began to change as Americans embraced a new faith in the ability of professionals to solve social problems using new scientific methods. Although religious commitments continued to influence and inspire them, American humanitarians increasingly defined their work in non-sectarian and social scientific terms.[2] At the same time, they developed new expectations about an expanded role for the state in humanitarian activities. Confident in a galvanizing spirit of civic and religious voluntarism, most American humanitarians still presumed that the government would not dominate this field. Increasingly, however, they tended to regard cooperative relationships between the state and private actors as a better approach to fixing social problems.[3] Concurrent with these domestic shifts, Americans began to develop a greater awareness of the connectedness of the United States and the world community. They not only observed their nation's rising political power and global influence but also began to take part in international social movements and cultural exchanges. In the process, they forged new physical and emotional ties with the people and governments of other nations.[4]

From its inception, the ARC both reflected and contributed to these wider shifts in U.S. culture. The story of the ARC's creation and rise to national prominence in the late nineteenth and early twentieth centuries is simultaneously a story of how, due to changing domestic and global contexts, American politicians and citizens first began to see international civilian aid as an important element of U.S. relations with the world.[5] When founder Clara Barton established an American chapter of the International Red Cross in 1881, she linked the United States to a fledgling global humanitarian movement, organized to secure neutral aid for wounded soldiers at war, whatever their nationality, creed, or race.

Though it formed part of an international organization, the ARC immediately diverged from the ICRC's founding mission in order to serve the particular humanitarian interests of the United States. To win over the American people, Barton defined the mission of the American chapter broadly. Rather than limiting aid to wounded soldiers, she pledged to provide assistance in response to any calamity that produced human suffering. This early distinction helped define the ARC as an association ready to administer civilian relief on behalf of the United States, at home and abroad, in peace as well as in war.

The mere founding of the ARC did not guarantee its acceptance as the nation's primary overseas aid agency, nor did it generate widespread support for American international humanitarianism. Barton aspired to accomplish this pair of goals, but it took the next generation of leadership to achieve them. In the early twentieth century, a small group of Americans took charge of the ARC and reorganized it. They brought in social science professionals to manage and reform the organization, incorporating the principles of the period's scientific charity movement and practices of successful philanthropic trusts. Although they retained the ARC's status as a voluntary agency, these new leaders forged much stronger relationships with the federal government, most notably with Secretary of War William H. Taft. By the time Taft entered the White House in 1909, they had positioned the ARC as a key component of American statecraft and an avenue for all Americans to take part in overseas humanitarian endeavors.

Domestic and Global Genealogies

On May 12, 1881, twenty-two residents of the District of Columbia and its environs declared themselves members of an international movement for humanity and global civilization. On that evening, following the lead of a Civil War volunteer named Clara Barton, they signed a charter to form the American Association of the Red Cross. The assembled men and women pledged to build up an organization of volunteers, ready to provide relief in the wake of "war, pestilence, famine and other calamities," at home and abroad. They had created a national association to direct the humanitarian energies of the American people, but they understood their efforts as transnational in scope. Leaders of the ICRC in Geneva had already promised to support Barton's association. In signing the charter, American members committed to cooperate with all the other Red Cross societies of the world. They also vowed to lobby the U.S. government to ratify the 1864 Geneva Treaty and then, in accordance with its terms, recognize their society as the official relief agency of the United States.[6] As those founding members hoped, the International Red Cross Movement eventually gained traction in the United States. To succeed, however, it could not be transplanted wholesale into U.S. soil. The ARC's founders had to define their organization as a uniquely American association, one that adapted elements of the American humanitarian, reform, and missionary traditions to suit the increasingly global culture of the postbellum United States. To understand the ARC's beginnings thus requires expanding its origin story well before 1881 and well beyond Washington. Examining the ARC's historical roots, influences, and precedents— both domestic and foreign—puts its creation into context. Moreover, it explains how, from inauspicious beginnings, the organization became an internationally recognized relief society and a leading representative of the United States in the world.

Clara Barton's birth in 1821 provides a fitting starting point to trace the origins of an international humanitarian tradition in the United States. Born in Oxford, Massachusetts, Barton grew up in a region and a time energized by a broad array of moral reform movements. In the forty years before the Civil War, New Englanders and Midwesterners vigorously protested slavery, railed against alcohol and other vices, and called on town and business leaders to create better working and living conditions for all classes of people. This reform impulse stemmed in part from a response to the changing nature of antebellum American culture and society. As witnesses to the dehumanizing aspects of slavery and market capitalism and to the moral and physical hazards of industrialization and urbanization, these reformers developed a concern for the sufferings of other sentient beings. They felt new sympathies, new connections, and a novel moral responsibility to care even for distant individuals with whom they shared no personal connection. They declared it their moral duty to alleviate the pains of others and to convince their fellow citizens to do the same.[7]

Strains of religious and secular thought, which emphasized the need for human intervention to improve society and politics, provided the intellectual underpinning for this burst of humanitarian reform. As Evangelical revivals swept the Midwestern and Northeastern United States in the 1820s and 1830s, hundreds of thousands of Americans embraced the doctrines of the Second Great Awakening. The converted learned that they had a Christian duty to confront social injustices and to reform their underlying conditions. Personal salvation depended on doing spiritual work in the world. Inspired by this popular theology, hundreds of thousands joined in collective protest against perceived evils. They agitated their churches, their communities, and their political leaders to take stands against alcohol, sexual inequality, blasphemy, and—especially— slavery. For most antebellum reformers, the sacred and the worldly realms were inseparable.[8]

Influences outside the church and the revival tent also profoundly shaped the U.S. humanitarian tradition, most notably Enlightenment thought. At first glance, these two traditions appear incongruous. Enlightenment philosophy taught that through reason and rational thought, rather than Godly intervention, individuals could fix any societal problem. Yet Evangelical and Enlightenment rationales for social reform readily coexisted in that they shared a mutual faith in the power of human agency and the potential for universal human progress. Thus alongside religious tracts and moral suasion, antebellum American reformers touted scientific and technological interventions as the keys to improving society. The sanitary reform movement, which blossomed in the 1840s and 1850s, readily embraced these assumptions. In those years, medical and sanitary reformers began to see poor health and disease outbreaks not as acts of a vengeful God but as the results of poor hygiene, overcrowded living, and contaminated water and environments. To check these worldly evils, they campaigned for civic improvements to create water works and sewage systems, clean up refuse, and improve housing. Through human intervention, they aspired to curb the deleterious results of industrialization and urbanization.[9]

As the influence of Enlightenment philosophy makes clear, the roots of the American humanitarian reform tradition lay outside U.S. culture as well as within it. Antebellum Americans did not live in isolation from the rest of the world. They participated in transnational humanitarian causes and established relationships with like-minded reformers in Europe. In 1821, the year of Clara Barton's birth, vocal factions of the U.S. public urged President James Monroe to join Great Britain's intervention on behalf of Greek insurgents revolting against the Ottoman Empire. Even though the young U.S. government opted to remain outside the conflict, pledging in the 1823 Monroe Doctrine not to meddle with Europe's internal affairs, many members of the American public felt personal connections with afflicted peoples overseas.[10] Antebellum Americans also forged relationships with fellow European humanitarians, building networks that influenced their domestic reform efforts. Abolitionists and women's rights advocates shared concerns and tactics with fellow British activists, while sanitarians took much of their medical and hygienic knowledge from the scientific elite of London, Paris, Vienna, and Berlin. Clearly, antebellum American humanitarians were anything but isolated from the wider world.[11]

Even as American humanitarians imported inspiration and tactics from Europe, however, they invariably adapted those ideas to U.S. culture. The strains of religious and rationalist thought that motivated sanitarians, abolitionists, and other reformers meshed well with American republican traditions that emphasized concern for the collective well-being as a public obligation and a foundation of civic virtue. Antebellum American humanitarians and reformers were exemplary republicans. They joined together in a host of voluntary associations, benevolent societies, and political parties dedicated to improving the public weal and nurturing communal commitments. They formed groups dedicated to temperance, abolishing slavery, and uplifting morals; they also organized charitable aid societies. This strong civil society facilitated participation in humanitarian causes.[12]

Significantly, this strong spirit of civic voluntarism never precluded a desire for greater government involvement. With increasing frequency as the nineteenth century progressed, antebellum humanitarians exhorted local and national politicians to support their causes. By the 1850s, sanitary reformers in northern cities lobbied for the creation of city boards of health to secure municipal improvements and the passage of laws to improve the lot of the working classes and protect public safety. At the same time, many abolitionists expanded their moral suasion strategies into the realm of politics. They tried to achieve their goals through supporting the Free Soil and Republican Parties, petitioning, and pressuring Congress for stronger antislavery legislation. In the aftermath of natural disasters, too, they urged the state to step in to provide assistance. Thanks to this emerging culture of associationalism—a cooperative relationship between private individuals and their institutions of governance—antebellum humanitarians often enjoyed political support for their various causes.[13]

By the outbreak of the U.S. Civil War in 1861, a clear humanitarian tradition existed in the United States, rooted in a mixture of Evangelical, Enlightenment, and republican ideals. Coming of age in the four decades before the Civil War, Clara Barton would not escape its influence. Born to a family of Universalists and committed abolitionists, Barton learned from an early age that she had a moral responsibility to fight suffering and social injustice in the world. As an adult, she rejected organized religion but maintained a strong personal faith in God and the importance of moral action. She also took a deep interest in the social politics of her time and believed that private citizens and their governments must work together to achieve social reforms. Barton's early career demonstrated these commitments well. At the age of seventeen, she began work as a teacher in Massachusetts. There, she campaigned to improve the standards and facilities of her local schools. An adherent of public schooling, Barton later moved to New Jersey to establish and run a free school. In 1854, desiring a change, she moved to Washington, D.C., and obtained a job as a clerk at the U.S. Patent Office. In the nation's capital, she became acquainted with Republican Senators and Congressmen and grew engrossed with the fiery political debates over slavery then rippling through the country. Barton was still in Washington in April 1861, when news arrived of the firing on Fort Sumter.[14]

The Civil War provided a novel test for Barton and the humanitarian reform tradition in the United States. The violent conflict renewed concern for the pain and suffering of others. In response to this unprecedented national crisis, American women volunteered in droves. Their motives ran the gamut from Christian charity to a sense of patriotic duty to a belief in the powers of medicine and sanitary science to improve the health and well-being of soldiers. Both the Union and Confederate governments relied on these civilian relief efforts. In turn, private volunteers increasingly relied on the state and expected their governments to support them. This mutual dependence took its most formal shape in the U.S. Sanitary Commission. Just after the war began, a coalition of women's aid society members, physicians, religious officials, and other private citizens urged the Union government to sanction their relief work for wounded or ill Northern soldiers. Signed into law by Abraham Lincoln in June 1861, the Sanitary Commission worked alongside the War Department to organize and train nurses, maintain clean field hospitals, and collect donations to aid disabled soldiers and their families. In short, it channeled the religious and civic voluntarism of American women and medical men in service of the Union's wartime humanitarian needs.[15]

The history of the U.S. Sanitary Commission suggests some of the ways that the American humanitarian tradition had begun to change shape by the 1860s. Even as religious commitments continued to motivate American humanitarians during the Civil War, Americans at mid-century looked with greater frequency to new scientific breakthroughs as the keys to preventing and alleviating suffering. While approaches to humanitarianism and reform remained primarily voluntary and outside the state bureaucracy, the relationship that volunteers shared with the federal government grew stronger in the war years. This approach to social transformation continued to shape humanitarian activities in the Reconstruction period as well. Working through churches and new government agencies like the Freedmen's Bureau, thousands of Northerners headed to the former Confederacy to provide assistance. They went not only to provide immediate relief but also to modernize the prostrate South by teaching, building railroads, and encouraging new industry. By restructuring society and politics at large, these humanitarians hoped to alleviate the pains of racial discord and poverty. For them, the Reconstruction-era South represented a vital missionary field.[16]

As postbellum humanitarians considered how to redeem and reform the South, some of their compatriots set their sights on more distant locales. In the years following the Civil War, growing numbers of Americans embarked on religious and technical missions throughout the world. American Indian reservations became a prime target for American missionaries. Rejecting the U.S. military's efforts to exterminate native peoples, missionaries hoped instead to convert them to Christianity, capitalism, and the American way of life. Further afield, Evangelical Protestants focused their energies on China and the Middle East, where they labored to replace Confucian and Islamic religious traditions while teaching domestic skills and democratic values. Americans with expertise in agriculture, industry, and other scientific and technological fields followed the same routes as their religious counterparts, yet focused on material rather than

spiritual transformation. Most of these globally oriented humanitarians channeled their energies through such private institutions as churches, universities,
or businesses rather than state bureaucracy. In an era characterized by relatively
minor U.S. government involvement overseas, these American religious and
technical missionaries played a central role as ambassadors from the United
States to the world.[17]

Enmeshed in the American humanitarian tradition since birth, Clara Barton
played a central role in its evolution and global expansion during and after the
Civil War. As a frontline volunteer during the conflict, she delivered sanitary and
medical supplies to Union field hospitals and made attempts to identify dead
and wounded soldiers. Once hostilities ceased, Barton labored to locate missing soldiers and identify those killed in battle. Barton focused her attention on
domestic crises during the 1860s, but like many fellow American liberals, she
adopted a more cosmopolitan outlook in the postbellum years. Beginning in
1870, Barton would become a leading lobbyist for greater American involvement in international humanitarian movements. While traveling in Europe to
renew her health, she became aware of the International Committee of the Red
Cross. Barton volunteered with that organization during the Franco-Prussian
War, delivering medical and sanitary supplies to the battlefront just as she had
in the U.S. Civil War. During that time, she became deeply committed to this
international movement for humanity.[18]

The Red Cross Movement was only in its fledgling stages when Barton arrived
in Europe. The founders of the ICRC, Swiss citizens Henry Dunant and Gustave
Moynier, had organized it in the early 1860s to achieve two goals. First, they
desired the passage of a new set of international humanitarian laws to protect
ill and wounded soldiers at war. Second, they wanted to encourage the formation of national aid societies to provide neutral assistance to fallen troops. These
humanitarian aspirations represented a distinct reaction to the changing military,
diplomatic, and technological landscape of mid-nineteenth-century European
society. In this period of rising nationalism and belligerency, the weapons of war
became more deadly. Believing war inevitable, Dunant, Moynier, and their supporters hoped at least to diminish its horrors. In 1863, therefore, they convened
an international conference of like-minded humanitarians and formed the ICRC.
In 1864, the ICRC invited delegates from sixteen European nations to Geneva
to draft an international treaty, binding them to provide aid to wounded soldiers
in all future conflicts and to recognize the legal neutrality of both aid workers
and the wounded. The eleven original signatories to this Geneva Convention
also pledged to establish national Red Cross societies. Significantly, although the
ICRC claimed the power to grant official recognition to these national societies,
it did not assert any further authority over their operations. The ICRC encouraged their formation and served as a medium of communication between them,

but each national society maintained autonomy over its operations, bylaws, and charter. This relationship ensured that even as national Red Cross auxiliaries formed part of a larger international organization, they would invariably serve their own nation's needs.[19]

Both religious and utilitarian sensibilities motivated Dunant, Moynier, and the original supporters of the Geneva Convention to support this international humanitarian campaign. Dunant, an Evangelical Christian, saw such work as an expression of his faith in the worldly realm. The less pious Moynier, on the other hand, understood his efforts as more material in nature. He believed that through sanitary and technical interventions and international collaboration, rational human actors held the power to build a more civilized world. While ICRC founders may have been motivated by universalist religious and humanitarian sensibilities, many European state leaders elected to join the Red Cross Movement because they concluded that it served their own national interests. By designating a national association of willing volunteers to act on their behalf, policymakers realized, they could secure the protection of their own soldiers without much investment. At the same time, they could demonstrate their benevolence and concern to the public. Organized voluntary humanitarianism, thus conceived, served both nationalist and internationalist agendas.[20]

In 1864, the United States had the opportunity to take part in this international movement, by signing the Geneva Convention and creating its own Red Cross society. Nineteen nations went on to do so within two years, but the U.S. government demurred. Embroiled with the internal problems of the Civil War and national reconciliation, the administrations of Abraham Lincoln and Andrew Johnson were preoccupied with domestic concerns. Most Americans, moreover, deemed it prudent to avoid European treaties and alliances. Despite persistent lobbying by several members of the U.S. Sanitary Commission, Secretary of State William Seward declined to consider the Treaty. Citing precedents established by the Monroe Doctrine and other antebellum U.S. foreign policy, Seward argued that it was in the best interest of the United States to avoid entangling alliances, especially those related to war. His successor, Hamilton Fish, adhered to the same logic as the International Red Cross Movement spread through Europe in the 1870s.[21]

Upon her return to the United States in 1873, Clara Barton challenged this policy of non-engagement. Fresh from her experiences in Europe, she was determined to bring the United States into the International Red Cross Movement. In Washington, D.C., Barton began to lobby for U.S. ratification of the Geneva Treaty and to solicit support for an American Red Cross Society. She faced an uphill battle. Most Americans were far more concerned with the domestic turmoil of Reconstruction and pervasive political corruption than international issues. Undeterred, Barton lobbied government officials vigorously while also considering ways to win the support of the American public. Five years after returning from Europe, she found a solution. In 1878, Barton published a pamphlet called *The American Red Cross and the Geneva Convention*. The tract emphasized the moral importance of supporting international humanitarianism, but it also proposed a unique set of peacetime responsibilities for the proposed American association. Barton suggested that the ARC need not limit itself to foreign wars and conflicts but could respond to civilian suffering after natural disasters and other catastrophes as well. In proclaiming this set of duties, Barton created a role for the American association that went beyond the goals and aims of the International Red Cross Movement's founders. By expanding the association's reach to channel the voluntary energies of the American people in peacetime as well as during war, Barton hoped to garner the support of the American public and political officials.[22]

In 1881, Barton's lobbying efforts finally had their day. Armed with a letter from the ICRC's president, Gustave Moynier, Barton arranged meetings with newly elected President James Garfield and his secretary of state, James G. Blaine, to curry their support. Unlike their predecessors, Garfield and Blaine agreed to back Barton in her efforts to ratify the Geneva Convention and bring the Red Cross Movement to the United States. Blaine, especially, foresaw a greater role for the United States in global affairs and considered the country's historical commitment to non-entanglement outdated and immoral. As he put it concisely, "The Monroe Doctrine was not meant to ward off humanity."[23] In May 1881, buoyed by this official support, Barton and fifty-one others drafted the charter that created the American Association of the Red Cross. Having established a national Red Cross society, they increased their lobbying for U.S. acceptance of the Geneva Convention. In the spring of 1882, the U.S. Senate voted to ratify the Geneva Treaty and subsequently authorized the ARC to act as its official relief agency in time of war. The ICRC then recognized Barton's group as a formal national society. Nearly two decades after the founding of the International Red Cross Movement, the United States had taken a step toward greater participation in international humanitarian affairs.[24]

Yet it would be a mistake to describe this as a radical departure in either the nature of American foreign relations or its humanitarian tradition. Although the U.S. government had recognized the ARC as its official representative under the Geneva Convention, in practice it treated Barton's organization much like any other voluntary agency. The ARC's relationship to the state was minimal when compared to other Red Cross societies throughout the world; most significantly, it had no federal charter. Small and not widely known, the ARC competed with numerous civic and religious aid organizations for funds and national prestige. Since Barton's birth sixty years earlier, major changes in the way Americans thought about humanitarianism and global involvement had created an environment amenable to forming a branch of the International Red Cross Movement. Securing a more prominent and permanent place for the ARC in U.S. culture, however, would require further transformations in American understandings of the world and the part U.S. citizens and their government should play in it. A cultural sea change during the next quarter century would enable the ARC to become the leading player in U.S. international humanitarianism.

Gaining Influence in a New Era

During the late nineteenth and early twentieth centuries—amid a radical refashioning of ideas about charity, reform, and the global position of the United States—both international humanitarian sensibilities and the ARC's particular approach to foreign aid took firm hold in American culture. Clara Barton both relied on and helped produce this transformation. As she endeavored to gain support for the Red Cross Movement in the United States, participated in international Red Cross conferences, and provided civilian assistance in several foreign crises, Barton encouraged Americans to support international humanitarian ventures. At the same time, she benefited from their growing inclination to do so on their own. By the turn of the century, the ARC had become recognized, domestically and internationally, as an important U.S. voluntary association for overseas civilian assistance. As the ARC's visibility and global role increased, however, concern mounted over the way it was presenting the United States to the world. For an increasingly outward-looking United States, the nation's humanitarian reputation became a real priority.

Two major shifts in fin-de-siècle American culture account for this emergent international humanitarian sensibility at this particular moment. First, changing social, scientific, and religious ideas strengthened existing belief in the power of human intervention to improve society. In the late nineteenth century, a new generation of professional social workers, physicians, and nurses declared themselves more capable than amateur volunteers in administering charity. These health and welfare professionals argued that they could improve systemization and organization in social reform and relief efforts. Moreover, since they had greater knowledge of sanitary and social science, they could attack and prevent disease, poverty, and other social ills more effectively than reformers motivated by sympathy alone. The creation of municipal and state boards of health and charity, the organization of settlement houses, and the development of national professional organizations institutionalized these intellectual shifts.[25] Even as many humanitarians continued to derive inspiration from their faith, liberal interpretations of Protestant theology increasingly advised Christians that they had a spiritual obligation to materially improve the world around them and not simply to spread the good word. Inspired by these tenets of the Social Gospel, many Protestant reformers committed to improving the education, health, and living conditions of those around them. A growing number of Jewish and Catholic relief organizations likewise focused on improving the non-spiritual realm. Humanitarians from all faiths cast their social assistance in increasingly ecumenical terms.[26] Together, these changing scientific and religious beliefs about social interventions profoundly reshaped the humanitarian tradition in the United States around the dawn of the twentieth century.

Second, and coincident with these shifting ideas about social reform, the U.S. government and its people dramatically expanded their involvement and interest in world affairs. Revolutions in technology and communications, including the construction of faster ships, railroads, and telegraph lines, connected Americans more closely to world events and facilitated overseas travel. Already active in the years after the Civil War, the American foreign mission movement exploded in the 1880s and 1890s. At the same time, U.S. corporations began looking overseas for markets and sources of raw materials, thus widening the nation's investments and commercial interests in the Western Hemisphere, the Pacific, and Europe. By the 1890s, Republican Presidents Benjamin Harrison and William McKinley and their secretaries of state followed the lead of these private individuals to pursue expansionist and activist foreign policies. They took steps to modernize the U.S. Navy, drive European interests from the Caribbean and Central America, and insist on open trade policies in China. Under their watch, the United States became a major industrial power, competitive with Britain and Germany. After winning the Spanish-American War in 1898, the United States asserted formal political control over the Philippines and Puerto Rico and developed legal mechanisms to retain economic and political control over Cuba. By the turn of the century, the nation had become an imperial power and a potent political and economic rival of Europe.[27]

Even as the United States flexed its international muscle, intense debates erupted over the acquisition of foreign territories and the exercise of American power in the world. As these contests suggest, Americans were not only interested in imposing their influence on the world; many displayed a growing interest in cultivating international community and constructing a global liberal civilization. American liberal internationalists began looking for new ways to foster world cooperation, turning to arbitration and international law as a rational way to halt Great Power conflicts. They participated in intergovernmental global summits, such as the Hague Peace Conference of 1899, and meetings of international nongovernmental organizations like the Woman's Christian Temperance Union. They closely followed European discussions about democratic reforms, women's rights, and civil liberties and called for the United States to take an active part in these campaigns. Medical and social science professionals communicated with each other about how to improve the health of their cities and nations, how to increase democratic participation, and how experts might play a role in improving their societies. By the turn of the century, an unprecedented number of Americans believed in the need to engage in world affairs and demonstrate their nation's benevolent internationalism.[28]

Together, these changing ideas about humanitarianism and U.S. internationalism provided a fertile environment for an outward-looking, non-sectarian aid association like the ARC to represent the United States in its international humanitarian efforts. But before it could do so, Barton had to build the ARC's reputation and prove its usefulness and effectiveness to the U.S. public and government officials. By the time she established the ARC in 1881, the Red Cross societies in most European countries had developed into well-oiled national associations that were fully supported by their governments. The newly founded ARC did yet not enjoy these advantages. Having seen firsthand the benefits of this systematically organized, state-sponsored humanitarian aid in Europe, Barton strove to make the ARC an equal to its international peers. To achieve her goal of federal support, Barton would have to demonstrate the ARC's unique utility to the state. Although many of the world's other Red Cross societies included disaster relief among their activities by the 1880s, their primary service to the state— and the reason they garnered such extensive state support—rested in their role as medical auxiliaries to their national militaries. In the United States, a nation at peace, the ARC's charter mission to relieve civilians in times of natural disasters proved far more relevant than its charge to aid wounded soldiers at war. To build the ARC into a nationally recognized organization, therefore, Barton had little choice but to focus on civilian disaster relief operations rather than tending to battlefield wounded. Ironically, achieving international parity meant diverging from international trends. The focus on civilian relief during the ARC's formative years set a precedent for the centrality of such efforts in the future.[29]

Before the ARC could become an international civilian relief agency, it had to prove its ability to respond to domestic emergencies. In the 1880s, Barton thus worked to build up a network of Red Cross chapters in towns and cities throughout the country, ready to respond to disasters as soon as they occurred. To organize these affiliates, she appealed to skilled physicians and nurses, preferring their expert approaches to amateur relief efforts. Nevertheless, she often relied on any willing volunteers in order to provide rapid relief and to build the movement. As president of the ARC, Barton responded to a host of disasters within the United States. She oversaw the distribution of material aid and medical assistance to individuals affected by floods on the Mississippi and Ohio Rivers in 1883; a major earthquake in Charleston, South Carolina, in 1886; tornadoes in Illinois and yellow fever in Florida in 1888; and the catastrophic

Johnstown, Pennsylvania, flood of 1889. In each of these undertakings, Barton aimed to define Red Cross relief as systematic and professional, and thus worthy of national support. By the 1890s, the ARC still remained small in terms of membership and funds. Through wide aid efforts and skilled publicity, however, Barton had begun to establish its reputation for disaster relief.[30]

Barton believed in the importance of her domestic humanitarian work, but from the beginning she had global ambitions. As a recognized branch of the International Red Cross Movement, she understood, the ARC served as the official representative of the United States in a global humanitarian network. Barton maintained connections with other Red Cross societies in Europe and communicated frequently with ICRC founder Gustav Moynier about her society's work. She traveled to Europe as an official representative of the United States at International Red Cross Conferences: Geneva in 1884, Karlsruhe in 1887, and Vienna in 1897. By the 1890s, with the ARC's reputation at home more firmly established, Barton launched her first overseas relief operations in Russia, the Ottoman Empire, and Cuba. In each of these endeavors, Barton hoped that the U.S. government would formally designate the ARC to administer aid on its behalf. In its first two foreign missions, however, the ARC went abroad at the behest of other private agencies and without the official backing of the U.S. government. In 1891 and 1892, Iowa farmers and New York businessmen appealed to Barton to help them ship corn to Russia to relieve famine there. Then in the early months of 1896, the New York-based National Armenian Relief Committee asked Barton to go to Constantinople to assist Armenian Christians persecuted by the Ottoman Empire. In both cases, while working with existing philanthropies, Barton tried to define the ARC as the most appropriate vehicle to extend aid on behalf of the United States. Without government recognition, however, the ARC's international civilian relief work remained little different from that of other private agencies.[31]

The ARC's first major foray into international civilian relief as a formal representative of the U.S. government came in 1898, during Cuba's revolution against Spain. In the late 1890s, as news of Cuban political and social grievances started to saturate U.S. media, Americans began feeling a moral imperative to aid Cubans in some way.[32] In late 1897, in an effort to take action without declaring war, president William McKinley turned to humanitarian assistance. Recognizing the ARC's new national and international standing, he designated it as the U.S. government's official agent to distribute goods and funds donated by private American citizens. Officially sanctioned, Barton arrived in Havana with a full supply ship on February 9, 1898, six days before the explosion of the U.S.S. *Maine* and over two months before the United States officially declared war on Spain. In Cuba, she distributed food and medical supplies to civilians and established orphan asylums. After the United States declared war on Spain, the U.S. government named the ARC to act as the military's medical and sanitary auxiliary, as stipulated by the Geneva Convention. However, military officials, concerned that Red Cross volunteers might disrupt battlefield discipline, resented the ARC's assistance. The surgeon-general objected to Barton's efforts to send female nurses to aid troops, calling them "an encumbrance" to military operations.[33] Unlike its European counterparts, the ARC had not yet won acceptance as a medical auxiliary to the military. Although the War Department ultimately allowed Barton and her staff to assist some wounded soldiers, this situation resulted in much of their aid going toward Cuban *reconcentrados*, noncombatants imprisoned in Spanish concentration camps. Upon her return to the United States in November 1898, Barton continued this commitment to noncombatants, lobbying for funds to support some fifty thousand Cuban orphans. Experiences in Cuba solidified the ARC's national reputation for international civilian relief. The military may have resisted the ARC's assistance, but the McKinley administration relied on it to "exercise the noble purposes of its international organization" and to demonstrate the humanitarian concern of the United States for civilians abroad.[34]

By the time Barton returned from Cuba at the turn of the twentieth century, the United States had become a far more important player in global affairs than it had been in 1881, and many Americans were starting to recognize that humanitarian assistance might play an integral role in U.S. international relations. Moreover, they were beginning to see the ARC as potentially well suited to administer aid on behalf of the United States. The ARC's efforts over the previous two decades, coupled with its authority under international law to aid fellow signatories of the Geneva Convention, won over politicians and private citizens alike. To meet U.S. humanitarian commitments most effectively in this changed global context, policymakers decided to formalize the government's relationship with the ARC. In June 1900, nineteen years after the ARC's creation, the U.S. Congress finally granted it the charter that Barton had long petitioned for, thereby incorporating the ARC into the federal government. The charter named the ARC as the agency designated to "carry out the purposes" of the Geneva Convention in the United States. In addition to aiding soldiers at war, it charged the ARC with "carry[ing] on a system of national and international relief in time of peace" and promoting "measures of humanity and welfare of mankind." The federal government also required the ARC to submit annual financial and procedural reports, giving the government a measure of oversight over the organization. This charter defined the ARC as the official voluntary relief organization of the United States and created a unique private-federal partnership. After nearly twenty years, Barton had achieved her goal. The United States and the ARC stood together at the dawn of a new century, each prepared to take on new global responsibilities.[35]

As Barton and her supporters celebrated their successes, however, a growing chorus of critics voiced concern over the ARC's capacity to represent the
United States in the world. Such dissent had been mounting steadily throughout the 1890s. Alongside the acclaim that Barton had received for her work in
Russia, the Ottoman Empire, and Cuba had come a host of complaints about
her accounting, her record keeping, and her very approach to aid. In 1901, these
critiques erupted into a full-scale debate over Barton's qualifications to serve as
ARC president. The first signs of trouble occurred at the ARC annual meeting in December, where Barton's close friend, and ARC vice president Mary
Logan, "was greatly surprised to find that an element of discord had crept into
the society that threatened serious trouble for the organization and boded evil
for Miss Barton." A group of individuals in the ARC's Executive Committee
charged Barton with making decisions without their approval and with failing to account for funds spent. Barton, they asserted, was unfit to serve as the
president of the ARC.[36]

Mabel T. Boardman, a member of the ARC's Executive Committee since
the 1900 Congressional incorporation, led the campaign against Barton. Born
in 1860 in Cleveland, Ohio, Boardman had resided in Washington, D.C., since
the late 1880s. The daughter of a wealthy lawyer, Boardman never married and
involved herself in an array of philanthropic pursuits. By 1901, she had become
a prominent figure in Washington's Republican political and social circles and
wielded considerable influence in the capital. At the 1901 annual meeting, she
and twenty-two others, including former secretary of state John W. Foster and
former secretary of the Navy Hilary A. Herbert, seized control of the ARC. This
move left Barton, in her own words, a "powerless president, to be controlled by
them."[37] By the 1902 meeting, Barton's allies had harnessed their strength. They
elected Barton as the ARC's president for life and suspended Boardman and the
other dissident members.[38]

The infighting only escalated from there. Boardman and her allies brought
their appeal to President Theodore Roosevelt.[39] He subsequently "declined to
have his name connected with the organization" and "satisfied himself there was
something wrong with the management of the Red Cross."[40] He also rejected
Barton's request that he and his cabinet act as a board of consultation to the ARC,
instructing her "to have it publicly announced that the President and his cabinet
can not so serve." Roosevelt's refusal to endorse the ARC was just the evidence
that Boardman and her allies needed to show the threat that Barton's leadership
posed. Armed with this critique, they continued to push for Barton's resignation.
Barton appealed to the public, tried to make amends with her critics, and even
published an open letter to President Theodore Roosevelt to plead her case.[41]
Ultimately, confessing to friend and former secretary of state Richard Olney that
"the past two years have been hard—bitterly hard," Barton succumbed to the

pressure. On May 14, 1904, she tendered her resignation and left the organization she had founded.[42]

The three-year battle for control over the ARC represented, at its most fundamental level, an effort to reinvent the association for the twentieth-century United States. Barton and her detractors agreed on one thing: the ARC had a vital role to play in the nation and its foreign relations. They diverged on whether the ARC, in its state at the time, could perform those duties effectively. The problem according to critics was Barton's failure to incorporate modern approaches to humanitarian reform. Since the ARC's founding in 1881, the wider trends toward professionalization and organization of charity had accelerated greatly. Though Barton herself stressed the need for non-sectarian, professional, and systematized relief efforts, many of her opponents believed she had not succeeded in this regard. They protested that the octogenarian Barton wielded too much control over organizational decision making. They faulted her for her lack of formal training and for not including enough health and charity professionals or social elites in the ARC's governance. They accused her of poor accounting, record keeping, and planning. As Boardman and her allies realized, the ARC possessed neither the members nor the funds necessary to carry out extensive relief operations.[43] Barton, in short, had failed in her mission to make the ARC a professional and well-organized charity, one worthy of meeting the international humanitarian obligations of the United States.

If this status was important throughout much of the late nineteenth century, it had become even more significant since Theodore Roosevelt became president in 1901. Roosevelt, to a far greater extent than his predecessors, envisioned a major role for the United States in world affairs. As the Barton controversy unfolded from 1901 to 1904, Roosevelt and Secretary of State John Hay solidified U.S. control over the Philippines, took steps to reduce European influence in the Western Hemisphere during the Venezuela Crisis of 1902, exercised gunboat diplomacy to secure the Panama Canal Treaty, and began formulating principles of U.S. international police power over hemispheric affairs. In his foreign policy, Roosevelt assumed that the United States had a special obligation to ensure order and bring civilization to the world. He explained as much in his first address to Congress in 1901, when he declared, "We must henceforth recognize that we have international duties no less than international rights."[44] By bringing the most up-to-date approaches to social and political organization to the world, the United States would influence a new world order.[45]

Barton's detractors largely shared this worldview. They believed that the ARC could—and indeed must—fulfill U.S. international duties through overseas humanitarian assistance, but only if they assumed control of the organization, reorganized it, and increased its membership, funding, and prestige. Seeing their nation's expansionism as a positive development, they felt a special responsibility to consider how the ARC represented the United States to the world. In 1881, the ARC's founding members had joined an international movement for humanity and hoped to persuade Americans of its relevance. By 1904, a new generation of leaders had been convinced. Influenced by the evolving American reform tradition and eager to serve the nation's new international humanitarian obligations, they set out to reinvent the ARC for the twentieth century.

Readying the ARC for its New International Role

In January 1904, at the height of the Barton controversy, William Howard Taft returned to the United States after serving three years as civilian governor-general of the Philippines. In Washington, D.C., where Taft settled into his new post as secretary of war, Mabel Boardman became the driving force behind the ARC's reorganization. Representing U.S. humanitarianism faithfully to the world, she and other leaders believed, required appointing social science professionals to run the ARC, cultivating wide philanthropic and public backing, and securing the full confidence and endorsement of the federal government. Boardman and her allies aspired to succeed where Clara Barton had failed. Their vision for the ARC evidently appealed to the new secretary of war; in December 1905, Taft agreed to become the ARC's president. Over the next four years, throughout the remainder of Roosevelt's presidency, Taft presided over the ARC as it established firm connections with the federal government and the nation's philanthropic and social scientific communities. By the time Taft won the presidential election in 1908, the ARC's new leaders had reorganized the ARC and prepared it to take on wide-ranging international humanitarian activities on behalf of the United States.

Strengthening the ARC's relationship with the federal government represented the first step toward securing the association's special place in Progressive-Era foreign affairs. In December 1904, to mark its break with Barton, the ARC submitted a revised charter to Congress, which Theodore Roosevelt signed into law on January 5, 1905. Like its 1900 predecessor, the 1905 charter charged the ARC to provide aid to the sick and wounded during war, to act in accord with U.S. military and naval authorities, to "carry on a system of national and international relief in time of peace…and to devise and carry on measures for preventing the same." Though similar in many ways, the revised charter gave the U.S. government far more authority over the ARC. It required the ARC to submit a report to the U.S. War Department for an annual audit, further increasing governmental oversight. It also established an eighteen-member Central Committee to govern the association and gave the president of the United States the power to designate six of its seats. These

presidential appointments included the Central Committee chair and representatives from the Departments of State, War, Navy, Treasury, and Justice.
The charter thus secured the Presidential Board of Consultation that Roosevelt
had rejected just three years prior. Military authorities, who had largely dismissed ARC efforts in the Spanish-American War, became major players in
ARC affairs, as did other leading figures in national politics. Wide administrative involvement by members of the president's cabinet ensured a voice for the
federal government in privately administered humanitarian activities.[46]

The 1905 charter created the legal framework for a stronger and more official
government partnership, but it was the early and vigorous support of William H.
Taft that gave the ARC its most invaluable political connections. Taft knew little
about the International Red Cross Movement before 1905. That summer, he met
Mabel Boardman while on the steamship *Manchuria*, traveling to the Philippines
as part of an American goodwill tour. The pair developed a close and ultimately
lifelong friendship during the four months they were on board.[47] Taft, meanwhile,
became a major proponent of the ARC. Committed to an active role for the United
States in promoting world peace, international cooperation, and global stability,
he recognized humanitarian assistance as an important tenet of his philosophy
on U.S. foreign relations.[48] Upon their return, at Boardman's urging, Taft became
the president of the ARC, thus filling the vacancy created by Barton's departure.
Because the 1905 charter put control in the hands of the Central Committee, the
position of president was now largely honorary. Nonetheless, Taft's role as the
organization's figurehead demonstrated firm political support for the ARC and
its efforts. With his connections to the military, U.S. corporate and financial elites,
and the Republican Party—then in control of the White House and both Houses
of Congress—Taft worked to generate wide support for the newly reorganized
ARC. He helped Boardman secure an office for the ARC in the Department of
War building in downtown Washington and urged prominent Wall Street financiers and Washington Republicans to join its governing board. Shortly after its
reorganization, the ARC had attained significant political support.[49]

The first tangible benefit from these new political connections came on
April 18, 1906, when an earthquake and ensuing fire devastated San Francisco.
Just days after the quake, Roosevelt issued an appeal to the people of the
United States urging them to direct their donations to the ARC, "the national
organization best fitted to undertake such relief work." In addition to cement-
ing the ARC's status as a federally endorsed philanthropy, Roosevelt emphasized its accountability, efficiency, and expertise. He promised Americans
that by contributing money solely to the Red Cross, they could be sure that
"this work may be well systematized" and "wisely administered." Such praise
represented a substantial change from Roosevelt's 1903 refusal to connect his
name to the ARC.[50]

Connection with the federal government gave the ARC a political stamp of approval, but ARC leaders also desired a closer association with professional social scientists to demonstrate the organization's rational and modern approach to humanitarian assistance. The San Francisco earthquake gave them this opportunity. Upon hearing that Edward T. Devine, the executive secretary of the Charity Organization Society of New York and a professor of social economy at Columbia University, had volunteered to assist in relief work in San Francisco, Boardman and other leaders jumped at the chance to appoint him as their representative. Devine was an exemplary figure in the scientific charity movement. His consent to represent the ARC in San Francisco marked an important step toward the organization's scientific and expert management of humanitarian assistance.[51] This relationship also piqued the interest of social scientists nationwide, including the secretary of the Chicago Bureau of Associated Charities, Ernest P. Bicknell. By 1906, Bicknell, had established a national reputation in the field of organized charity. He published widely in professional journals and worked with such figures as Jane Addams, Julia Lathrop, and sociology faculty at the University of Chicago. After the quake, Bicknell took a leave of absence from his post to assist Devine and the ARC in their relief efforts. When Devine left San Francisco to return to New York, the ARC appointed Bicknell as his replacement.[52]

Out of the New York Charity Organization Society and the Chicago Bureau of Associated Charities came the philosophical and methodological influences to redefine the ARC's humanitarian assistance as a social scientific undertaking. Although catastrophic events were by nature temporary and unpredictable, full-time professionals committed to scientific, methodical planning promised to make the response to disasters more effective. By the early twentieth century, state and municipal boards of charity, settlement houses, and other social welfare institutions all employed full-time, academically trained professionals. If the ARC wanted to ensure professional disaster relief, Bicknell counseled, it could not "depend on chance help for its leadership." To be an effective national society, the ARC required a permanent executive, ready to respond to disasters at a moment's notice and armed with "the most valuable studies and reports in existence on methods and measures of relief in war and in great calamities."[53]

Not only did the ARC readily receive Bicknell's call for a permanent, informed manager to represent the Central Committee, but they also looked to Bicknell to take the position. As one member explained, "There is no one in whom the Red Cross has more confidence than in Mr. Bicknell."[54] In February 1907, the ARC offered Bicknell the new position of national director. He initially turned it down, but a felicitous financial contribution changed his mind. In 1908, the newly organized Russell Sage Foundation pledged to cover his salary for the first three years. Bicknell accepted the offer, confident that "the Red Cross would inaugurate its new policy by showing the world that it intends to carry on its works here after in a thoroughgoing, scientific manner."[55] American social scientists applauded this embrace of the principles and key figures of scientific charity, a move that, in their minds, greatly enhanced the ARC's standing. As the journal *Charities and the Commons* editorialized, "The choice of Ernest P. Bicknell to lead the American Red Cross movement seems almost as inevitable as the operation of the law of natural selection."[56] Although the Central Committee continued to make decisions about how to run the organization, Bicknell became the organization's public face and provided a solid connection to American social scientific circles.

At the same time, the Russell Sage Foundation's financial support established an important link to the philanthropic community. Its board members, including John Glenn, Robert W. de Forest, and Cleveland Dodge, were nationally known figures in the fields of philanthropy and social reform. They recognized the potential for the ARC to become a leading humanitarian agency and wanted to encourage its development.[57] These men saw supporting the ARC as an opportunity to reform the field of emergency relief according to social scientific methods. In addition to financing Bicknell's salary, they therefore contributed an additional $20,000 to launch the ARC Endowment Fund. Like the U.S. government, board members also wanted to exercise greater control over the ARC's administration; they considered their oversight essential to achieving their larger goals. Their philanthropy came with stringent requirements. In order for the ARC to be most effective in its work, they demanded that ARC leaders take steps to "affiliate the Red Cross and local Associated Charities and Charity Organization Societies throughout the United States." They also required that the ARC include some of the Russell Sage Foundation's own members in the ARC's governance. Finally, the Foundation's leaders insisted that the ARC must reorganize further to best serve the diverse fields of military, national, and international relief. ARC leaders gladly consented to these stipulations, sacrificing institutional autonomy for the support of a major philanthropy and the guaranteed income of a new endowment.[58]

Thus within just a few short years of the ARC's reorganization, a new generation of leaders had forged close relationships with the federal government and with American social scientific and philanthropic communities. At the ARC's annual meeting in December 1908, the first held since Ernest Bicknell joined the organization as national director, three key organizational decisions welded these connections tighter still. Since 1905, Taft had recognized the benefits that the government accrued from a strong relationship with the ARC, just as ARC leaders understood the prestige that his association conferred on their organization. Therefore in December, only weeks after Taft's election to the White House, ARC leaders unanimously reelected him president of their association, an honor he readily accepted. The incoming president of the United States was now president of the nation's Red Cross society.[59] At the same meeting, Russell Sage Foundation board member Robert W. de Forest assumed the newly created position of vice president, fulfilling one of the conditions of the Foundation's donation. De Forest, a founder of the New York Charity Organization Society and New York School of Philanthropy and a leading figure in philanthropic and reform causes, lent the organization another layer of cultural esteem. To satisfy the Russell Sage Foundation's other funding requirements, the ARC's leaders also created specialized Boards for War Relief, National Relief, and International Relief. With the formation of its International Relief Board, the ARC established a body specifically designated to administer overseas civilian assistance on behalf of the U.S. government. Following Taft's inauguration, his assistant secretary of state, an experienced diplomat named Huntington Wilson, became its first chair. From that point forward, the State Department would become a major player in the ARC's operations, offering its services to foreign governments that accepted or requested American humanitarian assistance and helping to coordinate its expanding roster of activities abroad. Together, these three changes in the ARC's leadership and organizational structure would profoundly shape its work in the years to come.[60]

By the end of 1908, the ARC had developed the infrastructural foundations necessary to administer professionally organized international civilian relief on behalf of the United States. Clara Barton had started this process in the nineteenth century, when she brought the United States into the International Red Cross Movement while adapting its mission to the particular humanitarian and diplomatic traditions of the United States. Over the next quarter century, a period of significant shifts in American ideas about humanitarianism and international engagement, Barton and the next generation of ARC leaders reorganized their society and forged new connections with key political and cultural authorities of the Progressive-Era United States. While the ARC remained small in terms of funding and membership, most of the elements were in place for it to begin playing a much larger role in the world. During the next fifteen years, as the United States engaged in global events to an extent theretofore unprecedented, the ARC and its international civilian relief efforts would become essential to the nation's foreign relations.

2

Humanitarian Preparedness

On March 27, 1915, the District of Columbia witnessed a striking moment of bipartisanship. That afternoon, President Woodrow Wilson and former president William H. Taft laid the cornerstone of a new national memorial at 17th Street Northwest dedicated to the women of both the North and South who had alleviated suffering on the battlefields of the U.S. Civil War (figure 2.1). This would be no small monument. Nor was it intended solely as a testament to past humanitarianism. The cornerstone formed the base of an $800,000 marble building, funded by a $400,000 Congressional appropriation and large donations from the Rockefeller and Russell Sage Foundations. Once complete, this living monument would serve as the national headquarters of the ARC. After Wilson spread the first layer of mortar, he passed the trowel to Taft. Wilson then set the symbolic stone in place, while Taft addressed the assembled crowds. The ARC deserved such a grand institutional home, Taft explained, because it provided "the people of the United States a certain and effective means of relieving human misery in their own country and in the world."[1] Given the revolution that had rocked Mexico since 1910 and the great conflict that had erupted in Europe the previous summer, ensuring the ARC's ability to administer overseas assistance with certainty and effectiveness struck both Taft and Wilson as a vital national concern.

Just over two years later, on May 12, 1917, Taft and Wilson reunited in the same spot to commemorate the building's opening. By then, the ARC's capacity to carry out international humanitarian activities had assumed even greater importance; one month earlier, the United States had declared war on Germany and entered the First World War. This time, it was Wilson who addressed the audience. In the face of this unprecedented crisis, he proclaimed, there was "no time for amateurs." The Red Cross, he asserted, would therefore "be our instrument to do the work of alleviation and of mercy which will attend this struggle."[2] Wilson, like Taft, recognized the ARC as a critical public instrument, the voluntary association best suited to provide foreign aid in the name of the United States to a world at war. Whatever their political and personal differences, the

Figure 2.1 William H. Taft and Woodrow Wilson shake hands at the ceremony commemorating the laying of the cornerstone of the American Red Cross Headquarters. 1915. Harris and Ewing Photograph Collection, Library of Congress.

two presidents wholly concurred on the centrality of ARC civilian aid to U.S. foreign affairs.

In the eight years from the start of Taft's presidency to the beginning of Wilson's second term in office, from early 1909 to early 1917, the ARC built upon the foundations laid at the turn of the century to become a principal agency for U.S. overseas civilian relief. The broad social trends that had facilitated the ARC's rise in previous decades—increased U.S. engagement with the world, rising social scientific influence, and expanding government-private partnerships—all accelerated in these years, helping to influence this outcome. During Taft's presidency, from 1909 to 1913, the State Department started relying on the ARC to administer civilian aid in areas of key strategic concern, and assisted in coordinating and planning the organization's overseas aid operations. Prominent American medical professionals, social scientists, and engineers became leaders in these ARC foreign aid missions, conferring on those endeavors a greater sense of cultural prestige. In Europe, Central America, and Asia, ARC civilian aid offered both American policymakers and public figures a way to take part in contemporary world affairs. During Wilson's first term, the Mexican Revolution and the Great War in Europe created new opportunities for the ARC to expand its role abroad. These years saw the State Department broaden its involvement in the ARC's international aid to an even greater extent. Military authorities now looked to the ARC to assist soldiers and sailors, but the military also began to see value in the organization's noncombatant and civilian relief operations. Outside the government, ever greater numbers of health and welfare professionals joined the ARC in its missions abroad. The Russell Sage Foundation maintained its earlier connections to the ARC, but other leading philanthropists also began to take note. Most notably, the Rockefeller Foundation became a major funder of ARC projects and a promoter of its international civilian relief. As tensions in Europe escalated, prominent U.S. financial and business leaders also joined in ARC governance and decision making. They reshaped the organization in accordance with contemporary corporate principles and practices so that it could best serve the needs of a nation readying itself for war.

Internationally minded politicians and cosmopolitan members of the philanthropic and social scientific communities had begun to appreciate the diplomatic and social significance of ARC foreign aid, yet the American public proved slower to follow suit. When Taft entered the White House in 1909, the ARC still lacked the personnel, the membership base, and the capital to respond to international humanitarian needs as effectively as its leaders and proponents wished. Over the next eight years, the ARC's leaders and the Taft and Wilson administrations took a number of steps to build public support and put the ARC on more stable financial footing. Though they had made some progress by early 1917, the ARC's membership statistics and financial stability still paled in comparison to sister societies around the world. It would take U.S. entry into the conflict to truly fuel popular support.

Nonetheless, the years from 1909 to 1917 marked an important period of growth for the ARC. This rapid ascendancy suggests the importance of integrating the ARC and its international civilian relief activities into existing narratives of the period's foreign relations. Taft and Wilson, along with growing proportions of the American public, believed that the expansion of U.S. influence in the world promised to achieve global stability and to nurture international liberal civilization. Putting this liberal internationalist philosophy into practice took various forms, from loans and financial advising, to military interventions and occupations, to arbitration and "cooling-off" treaties to prevent war.[3] Although both presidents developed larger diplomatic and military apparatuses to perform some of these tasks, they also relied heavily on associational partnerships with private citizens and voluntary organizations to carry out American foreign policy. Taft depended on bankers and financiers to act as his dollar diplomats, while Wilson expected leaders in banking, business, agriculture, and labor to mobilize the nation for war. These figures, in turn, willingly committed their services to the state, recognizing the personal benefits of such a partnership. This associational form of social organization, so typical of the Progressive-Era United States, shaped American approaches to world affairs.[4]

Of equal importance to this history was the bond that both administrations formed with the ARC and, by extension, with the social scientists, philanthropists, and social and political elites who ran it. Taft, Wilson, and their administrations understood international civilian assistance as crucial to their larger foreign policy goals of promoting global peace, international order, and liberal civilization. Rather than creating a state mechanism to administer aid, they turned to a key institution of civil society, the ARC, to administer the nation's foreign relief and to serve their diplomatic needs. For most of the ARC's leaders, steeped in a culture of associationalism and sharing a similar liberal internationalist worldview, this relationship made utmost sense at the time. To be sure, not all of the ARC's leaders concurred with Taft and Wilson's foreign policy approaches. Many individuals—better characterized as progressive internationalists—favored more thoroughly multilateral, cooperative, or peaceful forms of interaction with the world community than either president pursued.[5] They converged, however, on the belief that the United States should take part in relieving world suffering. For liberal and progressive internationalists alike, the ARC—with its unique national and international political position—appeared to be an institution particularly well suited to achieving the nation's international humanitarian goals. In the eight years preceding U.S. entry into World War I, a wide consensus on the value of the ARC's overseas aid developed among many cosmopolitan Americans, both inside and outside the government. As a form of peacetime diplomacy and a complement to military intervention, they believed, its voluntary civilian aid had a fundamental role to play for a nation expanding its place in the world.

"Bread Instead of Bullets": International Civilian Aid during the Taft Presidency

When William Howard Taft traded his legal career for a political one in 1900, he became part of a government committed to the belief that the United States must increase its role in world affairs in order to promote international liberal civilization. As governor-general of the Philippines from 1900 to 1904 and then secretary of war until his own election to the U.S. presidency, Taft had been a key figure in this pursuit. As president, he vowed to continue a foreign policy agenda based on the "promotion of peace and international morality" and the encouragement of global progress and stability.[6] In relations with Europe and some of the more powerful nations of South America and Asia, he and Secretary of State Philander Knox pursued arbitration treaties and encouraged the international justice efforts of the Hague Tribunal. In relations with politically weaker nations, on the other hand, the pair built their policy around financial lending and advising, an approach known as "dollar diplomacy." Pledging to eschew Theodore Roosevelt's penchant for military intervention by substituting "dollars for bullets," they sought to create international order by developing the economies and reducing the debts of Caribbean, Central American, and Asian nations. To carry out this program, they formed partnerships with private bankers and financiers willing to devote their expertise to the administration's efforts. While critics faulted the policy for its paternalistic approach to other nations, for bolstering the power of banking interests and financial trusts, and for ultimately failing to deter military intervention, Taft and his supporters understood this partnership with American bankers as central to his larger goal of world peace, stability, and cooperation.[7]

Just as central to Taft's foreign affairs program—and related in both goals and form—was his administration's vigorous promotion of the international civilian relief activities of the ARC. During his time in office, while a series of retired U.S. military figures chaired the organization's governing Central Committee, Taft's close friend and confidante Mabel Boardman continued to behave as the organization's de facto leader and took charge of much of its day-to-day decision making. She and national director Ernest Bicknell together oversaw the ARC as it expanded its international reach to record levels. They dispatched aid to Italy, China, Nicaragua, and a host of other sites. Relying on prominent U.S. health and welfare professionals to carry out its growing roster of foreign interventions, the ARC gave emergency aid following natural disasters and political upheaval, and enacted reform measures to prevent future disasters and social unrest. ARC leaders also hosted an International Red Cross Conference in 1912, the first held in the United States, thereby demonstrating their nation's commitment to a wider global humanitarian movement.

On each of these endeavors, Taft and his administration gave the ARC substantial support. As president of the ARC, Taft spoke frequently on behalf of the organization. Knox and the State Department coordinated the ARC's efforts abroad, offering its aid to foreign governments and, in some cases, requesting that the ARC send assistance. As chair of the ARC's newly created International Relief Board, Assistant Secretary of State Huntington Wilson facilitated communication and collaboration between the two bodies. Foreign aid and assistance, Taft and his cabinet realized, could do much to bolster their vision of U.S. internationalism and to advance the global peace and stability they coveted. The ARC's professional humanitarians served the interests of the Taft administration in several ways. By relying on a privately administered organization to carry out overseas assistance on its behalf, the Taft administration accrued the benefits of assistance without making official commitments. ARC aid also served as valuable public diplomacy by characterizing the nation's citizens as selfless and globally concerned. The ARC, in short, served the varied internationalist ambitions of U.S. citizens and their government officials.

*

The first test of the new International Relief Board's capacity to represent the humanitarian spirit of the U.S. government and its people came less than two months after Taft's election to the White House and just weeks after his reelection as ARC president. On December 28, 1908, an earthquake and consequent tsunami devastated the area surrounding the Straits of Messina in southern Italy. The disaster killed over one hundred thousand people and left five hundred thousand homeless in mainland Calabria to the east and Sicily to the west. Upon hearing the news, Taft cabled the Italian government and the Italian Red Cross to "tender...profound sympathy."[8] He pledged that contributions from the United States would be forthcoming. And indeed they were. Over the next few months, the American public donated nearly $1 million to the ARC for these endeavors; the funds were channeled to Italy through the State Department. The U.S. Congress, in a move without much precedent, also allocated $800,000 in public funds—a clear sign of the U.S. government's sudden interest in and support for American foreign relief endeavors. When the Italian government promptly accepted the offer of aid, ARC leaders named the U.S. ambassador to Italy and the U.S. vice-consul at Milan as its special representatives. These two representatives, along with several other men, arrived five days after the quake with a steamer filled with relief supplies. In the United States, the ARC focused on fundraising and dispatched its new national director, Ernest Bicknell, to the scene. Over the next several months, Bicknell oversaw the distribution of food, arranged housing, and administered other forms of relief. By the time the ARC turned over relief operations to the Italian government in late November 1909, eleven months after the earthquake occurred, the ARC's new leaders had executed their first major foray into international civilian relief.[9]

This aid to Italy carried important political implications for all involved. By the early twentieth century, Italy had begun to occupy a more prominent place in U.S. diplomatic designs, both because of the millions of emigrants who left the country for the United States every year and due to its rising importance as a European power.[10] ARC leaders touted the diplomatic value of humanitarian assistance, which demonstrated U.S. concern for Italy. At the same time, they saw the potential to accomplish something more; civilian assistance could be used as a tool for long-term social reform in the area around the Straits of Messina. In this region, home to a large proportion of America's new immigrants, addressing the perceived threat of pauperization, dependency, and idleness represented a fundamental goal of U.S. assistance.[11] To counteract these presumed tendencies, Bicknell and his colleagues first put in place a system to investigate Italians who applied for material assistance to determine if they deserved relief. ARC staff then focused on creating jobs. They put 1,200 Italians to work and, applying the tenets of scientific management—Taylorism—to their relief, organized them into gangs with each laborer assigned to a particular task. These aid recipients constructed thousands of sixteen-by-twenty-foot cottages to house refugee families and built colonies to house orphans. Celebrating the merits of their approach to charity, ARC leaders assured American donors that all funds had "gone quickly and efficiently to the places where it was most needed" and furthered "a carefully considered and well matured plan of permanent rehabilitation."[12] The ARC pledged not only to restore southern Italy but also to improve it morally and materially.[13]

Such assistance promised to benefit both the Italian recipients of aid and the American social scientists responsible for administering it. For Bicknell, here was a clear opportunity for critical investigation and social scientific research and experimentation. Bicknell seized the chance to collect quantitative and qualitative data about relief activities in Italy. "My mission is to study this matter," he explained. Through their work in southern Italy, "the most valuable field for investigation that ever existed for Red Cross experts," Bicknell and his colleagues developed a firmer understanding of how the ARC could best aid the world, how it could accomplish something far greater and longer lasting than the mere provision of relief supplies.[14] The approach to disaster assistance developed in southern Italy, characterized by a mixture of professionally organized emergency relief and constructive reform efforts and administered in close coordination with the State Department, would underpin future ARC efforts for foreign civilians.

As Bicknell administered the ARC's assistance in southern Italy, Taft settled into the first few months of his presidential administration. The ARC's work in Italy convinced him and his cabinet of the diplomatic and stabilizing potential of foreign assistance. Philander Knox, noting that "the international activities of the American Red Cross can not but be a factor in international relations and good feeling," began encouraging individuals who wanted to contribute to foreign aid to do so through the ARC, a "centralized, appropriate, and highly efficient channel."[15] The State Department, in turn, agreed to promote any ARC foreign assistance through the U.S. diplomatic and consular service. Even as they endorsed the ARC's civilian relief work, both Taft and Knox worried that the organization's small size hindered its ability to serve the United States effectively in this regard. When the earthquake struck Messina in late 1908, the ARC had a paid staff of just three and a national membership of just over ten thousand. While the U.S. public donated over $1,000,000 to the disaster, the ARC's permanent endowment amounted to only $50,000. By comparison, Austria, France, Germany, Italy, and Japan all boasted endowments and membership fig- ures in the millions. Given Taft's confidence in the superior civilization of the United States, he saw the nation's failure to measure up to "the other first pow- ers" as quite an embarrassment.[16]

In December 1909, Taft took steps to remedy this discrepancy. Noting the ARC's status as the "authorized official organization of the United States for volunteer aid" and commending "the standing of this remarkable organization throughout the world... and its beneficent influence for peace and goodwill in international relief work," Taft named a committee to raise a $2 million ARC endowment. He put Secretary of the Treasury Franklin MacVeagh in charge of the campaign. Prominent diplomats and bankers—including the former assis- tant secretary of state Robert Bacon; Lloyd Griscom, the ambassador to Italy; and Henry P. Davison, a senior partner at J. P. Morgan and Company—rounded out the committee. Relying on a partnership of public officials and private citi- zens, Taft set out to put the ARC "on a permanent and efficient basis... prepared at all times to carry out the purposes for which it has been created." The commit- tee could not succeed, of course, unless U.S. citizens supported its efforts with their donations. Taft therefore made a patriotic appeal, calling on "the public spirited men and women of the United States" to back their Red Cross society by funding it and becoming members.[17] Ensuring the United States could com- pete with other leading powers on international humanitarianism was becoming an obligation of citizens and a priority of the government—trends that would increase significantly in the years to come.

Over the next several years of Taft's presidency, as ARC leaders worked to build the organization's membership and its permanent endowment, its International Relief Board continued to send money and relief supplies in response to natural disasters throughout the world. It offered aid in response to earthquakes in Portugal and Costa Rica, floods in Mexico, famine in Japan and Russia, and—replicating Clara Barton's efforts two decades earlier— persecuted Armenian Christians in the Ottoman Empire.[18] At the same time, Boardman and other ARC leaders began moving in new directions. Specifically, they began to regard long-term, constructive foreign assistance projects as suitable fields for their international humanitarian interventions. With an eye toward preventing future disasters rather than waiting until the damage was done, the ARC began sending financial resources and expert personnel to areas of strategic interest to the Taft administration. Humanitarian assistance gave Americans a sense of con- trol over these regions, their populations, and their economies, a prerequisite for stable trade and improved diplomatic relations.

China, a nation that piqued multifaceted American diplomatic, business, and humanitarian interests, became the ARC's most important target in these early constructive assistance projects. China had long occupied an important place in U.S. foreign relations. Since the nineteenth century, American missionaries, financiers, and military personnel all worked to expand their influence and markets in China. By the turn of the twentieth century, the United States faced tensions in the region on a number of fronts. Several European powers and Japan had begun scrambling to partition China, prompting Secretary of State John Hay to insist on an "Open Door" policy in regard to Chinese commerce. Despite U.S. efforts to prevent formal imperialism, U.S. encroachment bred resentment among Chinese nationalists. Discriminatory U.S. immigration policy, codified in the 1882 Chinese Exclusion Act, further fueled animosity. The 1900 Boxer Uprising and a 1904–05 boycott of U.S. goods made it clear that both Chinese citizens and the Chinese government objected to U.S. policies. Growing unrest against the imperial Ch'ing Dynasty, culminating in the 1911 Chinese Revolution, cemented China as a key area of diplomatic concern for the Taft administration.[19] As these political tensions mounted, reports of widespread famine and epidemic pneumonic plague in China began to reach the United States. Hunger and disease threatened the lives of tens of millions of Chinese civilians. Many Americans lamented the humanitarian catastrophe. Others, particularly potential investors, questioned China's stability as a trading partner. Taft administration officials feared that these events might fuel further internal unrest or prompt European powers to intervene.[20]

Ending China's recurring famines and disease outbreaks served each of these diverse international agendas, promising to strengthen the country's financial and political stability, demonstrate U.S. concern, and improve Chinese perceptions of the United States.[21] By the time Taft became president, Boardman and other ARC leaders had already begun to raise funds for famine relief. In 1907, they coordinated with several private U.S. aid organizations then operating in China, including the *Christian Herald* and Central China Famine Fund, and began distributing aid on their behalf. Although these groups initially welcomed the ARC's cooperation, hoping its size and esteem would help them achieve their own goals, the ARC's increasing largesse soon bred resentment. Louis Klopsch, the head of the *Christian Herald*, complained that the ARC had not given his organization the credit it deserved. Moreover, he criticized the ARC's nonsectarian aid policy, arguing that "the benefit this money will bring is not half so great as the benefit of the influence on the minds of the people, in knowing that they are being cared for by a Christian people."[22] As such a critique suggests, the ARC's claim to represent the international humanitarian sensibilities of the United States was hardly uncontested. Even as the organization garnered increased support from the state and many cosmopolitan Americans, its approach to aid alienated other international humanitarians. Nonetheless, ARC leaders maintained their involvement in famine relief and sent hundreds of thousands of dollars to

U.S. consuls and aid organizations each year. More laudatory American observers reported that these contributions had improved relations between the United States and China. Lebbeus R. Wilfley, a judge of the U.S. Court for China, noted that the ARC's assistance had "made a profound impression upon the Chinese people and was interpreted by them as an unmistakable evidence of the generosity and friendship of our people."[23] Though some American civilians questioned the ARC's claim to represent the United States and its international interests, others praised it as an ideal form of voluntary diplomacy.

While food relief may have offered diplomatic and altruistic benefits, it failed to prevent the root causes of famine. By 1911, the ARC had committed over $600,000, yet starvation persisted. As revolutionary uprisings against the imperial government rippled across Chinese provinces in that year, U.S. observers grew increasingly anxious to find a way to permanently curb the unrest. Such concern prompted one of the ARC's partner aid organizations, the Central China Famine Fund, to consider how "to induce the Government to administer its relief along more scientific lines."[24] Bicknell and other ARC leaders likewise began considering what would constitute a more "scientific" approach to aid. One of the reasons for the lack of food, they recognized, stemmed from recurrent flooding in China's Huai River Valley and the consequent destruction of crops. Controlling this natural phenomenon through technological intervention, they recognized, provided a logical way to prevent a prime cause of China's starvation.

Thus as an answer to China's ongoing humanitarian and political crises, the ARC's directors began to refocus their efforts on preventing the causes of famine. In 1911, the State Department offered the Chinese government the services of a corps of U.S. engineers, funded by the ARC, to study flood prevention in China's Huai River Valley and devise a flood conservancy project.[25] When China's imperial government accepted, the ARC sent a prominent American engineer, C. D. Jameson, to lead the survey mission.[26] After several months in China, Jameson issued a report reaffirming the inefficiency of food relief. He recommended that the ARC instead make a much larger commitment to drainage, flood prevention, and land reclamation. Such a project, Jameson promised, would result in "the elimination of the suffering, starvation and degeneration of several millions of people" and substantively reduce "unrest and lawlessness."[27] This idea won the support of the State Department, which advised U.S. representatives in Peking that it would readily endorse a conservancy project executed by the ARC. The Chinese government, too, expressed its interest. Ultimately, however, the ARC's leaders decided that funding the project went too far beyond both the limits of its charter and the budget of the International Relief Board. While the ARC and State Department did help China secure international loans and expert assistance to carry out the project on its own during the early years of Woodrow

Wilson's presidency, the ARC in these years was not yet prepared to commit to long-term assistance projects.[28] Nonetheless, the move toward preventive work suggested the new direction that the organization began taking on the eve of the First World War.

Further indicative of this expanded reach was another ARC foray into preventive aid in China, this time focused on medical assistance. In early 1911, as the ARC Huai River survey project got underway, pneumonic plague ravaged Manchuria. Desperate to quell this additional cause of social unrest, the Ch'ing government appealed to foreign governments to send medical experts to investigate the causes of the epidemic and suggest preventive measures. In the United States, Philander Knox turned to the ARC to secure and fund a medical expert.[29] ARC leaders chose Richard P. Strong, a Harvard specialist in tropical diseases and then head of the U.S. Biological Laboratory in the Philippines. For three months in the spring of 1911, Strong worked from a makeshift laboratory to study plague among infected Chinese patients. In April, he represented the United States and the ARC at an international plague conference of the eleven nations that had committed to Chinese plague research. Strong's efforts, like Jameson's, seemed to have good diplomatic effect. "Several prominent Chinese officials," reported the U.S. minister to Peking, "commented on the splendid representation of the American Government and the Red Cross Society... and expressed the highest appreciation."[30] Focused on investigation, prevention, and the exchange of knowledge rather than the mere alleviation of suffering, Strong's intervention in China further demonstrated the ARC's evolving approach to humanitarian interventions.[31]

In Manchuria and the Huai River Valley, as in the Straits of Messina region, the ARC joined expert assistance and rational planning to reduce the harmful effects of natural phenomena. In the process, preventive assistance became naturalized as a rational alternative to repeated emergencies and a new form of cultural diplomacy. Although sponsoring a conservancy project and plague research hardly fit the ARC's founding mission to relieve suffering in times of war and disaster, it represented, in Taft's words, a "modern and scientific" approach to humanitarian assistance that demonstrated American altruism and goodwill. "The Red Cross had represented to the people of China the disinterested, helpful friendship of the people of America, above suspicion and above reproach," Taft would later declare. "Back of it lay no ulterior motive that threatened the integrity of their Empire, and no selfish purpose that endangered their welfare."[32] In Taft's mind, the ARC's voluntary humanitarian aid offered visible proof of his own internationalist ideology, evidence that the global involvement of American experts was both a benevolent undertaking and a path to instilling order in the world.

While China and Italy represented key areas of strategic concern, the diplomatic potential for aid was perhaps nowhere more obvious than in Nicaragua, a nation of critical political and military interest during the Taft presidency. In 1909, Taft and his State Department began aiding a group of conservative rebels in Nicaragua working to overthrow the country's president, Jose Santos Zelaya. Regarding Zelaya as fiscally and politically irresponsible, the Taft administration deemed his removal necessary to protect U.S. capital investments and economic stability. When Zelaya's government executed two Americans for supporting the resistance in late 1909, the two countries broke diplomatic relations and the Taft administration threatened to invade. Zelaya quickly resigned, but the revolution continued. In the spring of 1910, Taft sent four hundred Marines to the country, ostensibly to protect U.S. interests but with the ulterior motive of swaying the rebellion in favor of Zelaya's key opponent, Juan Estrada. The rebellion eventually turned in Estrada's favor, but State Department officials doubted his commitment to U.S. interests. By 1911, the State Department had helped to install a new president favorable to Taft's dollar diplomacy, the Conservative Adolfo Díaz. Political unrest continued, however. Anti-American and anti-Diaz sentiments motivated oppositional forces to revolt, throwing the country into a violent civil war. In late August 1912, Taft sent in another occupying force of 2,700 Marines to quash the rebellion. Although Taft pledged that U.S. involvement in Nicaragua "help[ed] the cause of international peace and indicates progress in civilization," many Nicaraguans doubted his promises.[33]

As a response to Nicaraguan resentment of American military and financial interventions, U.S. officials turned to humanitarian assistance to win local hearts and minds. In December 1909, at the height of tensions with Zelaya, Philander Knox asked the ARC to help relieve captured soldiers from Zelaya's army. The ARC ultimately gave $10,000 to provide blankets, clothing, and food for nearly two thousand prisoners. "'Bread, instead of bullets,' is the watchword of the State Department," ARC leaders explained, adding that "the prospects of food and medical attention will win over more men from the government ranks than any other plan that could be adopted."[34] Juan Estrada, then desirous of U.S. support, understood the diplomatic intent. Praising "the unequivocal proof of humanity which the Navy Department of the United States and the American Red Cross Society have tendered the people of Nicaragua," Estrada thanked Philander Knox for humanitarian actions, reporting that they had "awakened in us the feeling of deepest affection and sympathy and will without doubt contribute to the establishment of solid ties of fraternity."[35] While Knox saw aid as a way to win hearts and minds, Estrada recognized the need to express appreciation for American assistance if he wanted to remain on good terms with the United States. Both Nicaraguan and U.S. officials acknowledged the diplomatic significance of ARC aid.

As the events that unfolded over the next three years belied Estrada's words, the U.S. government continued to rely on ARC aid to offset criticisms of its more aggressive interventions and to instill order among Nicaraguan civilians. In the summer of 1912, U.S. officials in Nicaragua began reporting widespread hunger due to a combination of political upheaval and drought-induced crop failure. After Taft deployed Marines in August to quash insurrectionist resistance, State and War Department officials grew even more concerned with quelling rumbling stomachs, prompting Knox to inquire whether the ARC could send food supplies for noncombatants.[36] Eager to comply, ARC leaders donated thousands of pounds of beans and cornmeal for distribution. American occupying forces quickly opened railroads to distribute ARC supplies in Managua, Granada, Léon, and other key cities. "The prompt and generous action of the American Red Cross," the U.S. minister to Nicaragua reported, "has won expressions of deep appreciation from those who have been helped and has created the kindliest feelings among all classes of people in Nicaragua."[37] While Nicaraguan insurrectionists surely disagreed with this assessment, the logic certainly appealed to State Department officials and military leaders. In Nicaragua, as in Italy and China, ARC civilian assistance proved its diplomatic value.

*

During Taft's four years in the White House, ARC international civilian relief became ever more central to U.S. foreign relations. Through humanitarian activities, such American health and technical professionals as Bicknell, Strong, and Jameson found a chance to test their methods abroad. Concurrently, as State Department officials recognized, these projects held the potential to demonstrate American benevolence, improve diplomatic relationships, and stabilize political and economic conditions. "In these days when the spirit of humanity and helpfulness more and more ignores boundaries," Philander Knox explained, "international aid in case of foreign disasters is especially appropriate and is of very real value, I believe, in promoting that international good will with the fostering of which the diplomacy of the United States is so much engaged."[38] The ARC's civilian aid served the desires of the liberal internationalist state and its citizens, earning the organization a unique and special status in U.S. society. In 1911, Taft made this much clear. The ARC, he declared, was not simply "a private association created by certain persons for benevolent purposes," but rather "the official volunteer aid department of the United States."[39]

While the ARC strengthened its relationship with the U.S. government and society, it remained part of the larger International Red Cross Movement. Even in this capacity, however, the ARC served important American interests. Through its participation in this global humanitarian organization, the ARC positioned the United States as an equal to the other major world powers. In May 1912, the ARC hosted the Ninth International Red Cross conference in Washington,

D.C., the first such meeting held outside of Europe. Both ARC leaders and the U.S. government recognized the profound symbolic importance of the meeting. Congress allocated $20,000 to the gathering, and the Department of State appointed several of the delegates who represented the American society. Taft hosted an opening reception on the White House lawn, while the former secretary of state Elihu Root gave the opening address. The ARC's leaders took great care in planning the meeting. Organizers built an exhibition pavilion to demonstrate modern American methods of relief and included Ernest Bicknell, Edward Devine, and other noted professional humanitarians on the program. The site chosen for the conference, the Palace of the Pan-American Union, revealed an unmistakable effort to link the ARC to America's growing role in the Western hemisphere, an area that had figured prominently in the nation's statecraft over the past several decades.[40]

In this elaborate conference, the ARC brought together representatives from thirty-two nations to discuss international humanitarian issues, but leaders also used the occasion to showcase the ARC's many achievements since its 1905 reorganization. The assembled delegates learned, for example, that the American social scientific community fully endorsed the ARC. Addressing the conference, social economist and former ARC volunteer Edward T. Devine lauded the ARC "for securing wise administration of emergency relief," its efforts "based on the belief that a 'trained personnel' is essential." Noting that such "system and order inspires confidence," Devine gave his stamp of approval to the ARC's work and proclaimed its ability to solve global affairs.[41] That a renowned figure in the scientific charity movement chose the words *system*, *order*, and *confidence* to describe the ARC suggested to other nations that the United States, through its Red Cross society, could be trusted to bring aid anywhere it might be called.[42]

In addition to showcasing social scientists' enthusiasm, the conference also illustrated to representatives from other nations how much the U.S. government had come to value its Red Cross society in recent years. The Taft administration hoped that by hosting an International Red Cross Conference, the United States could assert its status as one of the world's "civilized" nations and take the lead in promoting greater international collaboration. This project convinced at least one attendee, a member of the Turkish delegation, to envision the potential for the conference to forge a "future world in which all civilized nations will be seen joined." Such efforts had failed before, he admitted, "but the United States of America will *not* fail, because it is…a great nation that desires to see the world united in eternal peace."[43] This message—that the citizens of the United States, through their Red Cross, stood prepared to guide the world community in peaceful international cooperation—was exactly what conference organizers and the State Department had hoped to inspire. By electing to play a more active role in the greater Red Cross movement, the ARC offered proof of the internationalist leanings of the U.S. government and its citizens.

Foreign representatives to the International Red Cross Conference may have discovered the esteem that the U.S. government and the social scientific community held for the ARC, but they would have been less impressed had they looked to the U.S. public for the same. Since Taft came into office, Americans had proven increasingly willing to fund specific ARC appeals but not to support it on a permanent basis. In 1912, national membership still hovered at around ten thousand. Although Taft's endowment committee had made some progress, the ARC's permanent funds remained well below $1 million, far from their target. Compared to its international counterparts, the ARC remained quite underdeveloped.[44] By the time Taft lost the 1912 presidential election to Woodrow Wilson, the ARC had come a long way toward convincing government officials and cosmopolitan elites of its importance. It would take U.S. involvement in an unprecedented global crisis, however, before it could win substantial public support as well.

Aiding a World at War, 1913–1917

On March 4, 1913, the day Woodrow Wilson took the inaugural oath of the executive office, he also assumed the presidency of the ARC. Taft had served in the honorary position since 1905, but he voluntarily resigned upon his defeat, "with the hope that President Wilson might accept it and use the union of the two offices in the same way I have attempted to use it, for the benefit of the public of the United States and of the world at large."[45] Taft would not be disappointed. Nor would he be displaced. During Wilson's first term in office, Taft remained a central figure in the ARC's governance. For several years, his close friend Mabel Boardman continued to serve as the de facto leader of the organization, keeping Taft personally connected and invested. As the United States drew closer to entering the war in Europe, however, Taft and other ARC leaders grew concerned that the organization was not prepared to carry out either civilian or military relief on the scale required. In late 1915, in an attempt to rectify this situation, Taft briefly took charge of the ARC before turning the chairmanship over to a handpicked successor, a corporate manager chosen to infuse modern business principles into ARC operations. By the time the United States entered the First World War in 1917, Taft and Wilson, the former political rivals, were working closely to prepare the ARC for its new responsibilities and to advance their mutual international goals.

Such bipartisan cooperation and concern for the ARC has much to suggest about Taft, Wilson, and their shared worldview. Though they differed over how to achieve their objectives, Taft and Wilson largely agreed on the role the United States must play in the world. Both believed that the central aim of U.S. foreign policy should be the active promotion of international peace and order. Both proved willing to secure that outcome through military intervention, yet both also sought to develop multilateral institutions of arbitration and diplomacy. The United States, they concurred, must take the lead in creating a new, more stable international system. By alleviating physical suffering—both a result and a cause of global unrest and turmoil—the ARC's foreign assistance projects promised to assist in this endeavor. For Wilson and Taft, and for growing numbers of internationally minded Americans, overseas civilian assistance was an activity that transcended partisan politics.[46]

The two central foreign policy crises of Wilson's first term in office—the Mexican Revolution and the Great War—tested ARC civilian assistance in new ways. In their response to these events, ARC leaders continued along much the same trajectory as they had during crises in the previous four years, experimenting with social scientific approaches to civilian relief in collaboration with the government and leading philanthropists. In both Mexico and Europe, Bicknell and other staff members devised preventive and constructive aid programs, intended to ensure professional, efficient relief. With the continued involvement of the Russell Sage Foundation and the new support of the Rockefeller Foundation, the organization deepened its ties to the American philanthropic community. The State Department likewise continued to increase its involvement in ARC affairs. Wilson's first secretary of state, avowed pacifist William Jennings Bryan, welcomed international humanitarianism as a form of U.S. engagement. Though his successor Robert Lansing diverged from Bryan in many respects, the two shared a vision of the ARC as a force for peaceful internationalism. Indeed, before becoming secretary of state, Lansing served as the chair of the ARC's International Relief Board. Connections between the ARC, the government, and the philanthropic and social scientific communities only grew stronger in response to the decade's new emergencies.

As the United States drew closer to war in both hemispheres, many began to call the ARC's professed neutrality into question. Both U.S. citizens and the international community could not help but observe the ARC's growing involvement in the world and its increasing ties to the federal government. This led many to wonder whether humanitarian intervention in foreign conflicts, though avowedly a neutral act, in fact invariably constituted a political action. During Wilson's first term in office, the diplomatic potential of international civilian assistance grew clearer to all concerned. As it did, the nature of this type of foreign relations increasingly became a matter for debate.

*

By the time Woodrow Wilson became president of the United States and its Red Cross society in 1913, the Mexican Revolution had come to occupy a major area of U.S. international concern. During his first term in office, Wilson tried to sway the course of the revolution through both diplomatic suasion and military intervention. As he did, his State Department called on the ARC to introduce order, improve social conditions, and demonstrate American goodwill. Though fairly limited in scope, ARC assistance to Mexican civilians represented an important aspect of the United States' wider reaction to the revolution. Moreover, the ARC's brief involvement in Mexico, from April 1914 to October 1915, tested its ability to minister to civilian suffering in a large-scale war and therefore provided an important prologue to its far greater intervention in the Great War in Europe. Public discussions about that intervention, finally, mirrored much wider debates over the ARC's right to intervene and raised concerns about the political nature of U.S. humanitarian assistance.[47]

Though ostensibly an internal conflict, the Mexican Revolution involved the United States through economic ties, military interventions, and humanitarian actions. The revolution began in late 1910, two years into Taft's presidency, when liberal Democrat Francisco Madero called his fellow citizens to mount an armed insurrection against longtime dictator Porfirio Díaz. Uprisings soon spread to more than a dozen Mexican states. By May 1911, Díaz had ceded power to a provisional government led by Madero, but the revolution was far from over. Taft and Knox feared Madero's leftist tendencies and saw him as a threat to U.S. investments. In late February 1913, Díaz loyalists, assisted by Taft's ambassador to Mexico, overthrew Madero and assassinated him. The conservative general Victoriano Huerta then assumed power. In reaction, moderate reformers such as Venustiano Carranza and revolutionaries with more radical demands, such as Francisco "Pancho" Villa and Emiliano Zapata, united against Huerta's forces for control of Mexico.[48]

When Wilson became president just weeks later, he responded to the continuing revolution with a mix of fascination and concern. To a far greater extent than Taft, Wilson understood and sympathized with the democratic sentiments motivating Mexico's revolutionaries. He, too, scorned Huerta and considered his rule illegitimate. Yet Wilson also doubted the capacity of any of the revolutionary factions to establish a working democratic government without U.S. help. When on April 9, 1914, Huerta's forces arrested several U.S. sailors in Tampico, Wilson used the relatively minor incident and affront to U.S. honor as a justification for intervention. On April 21, 1914, Wilson deployed several hundred U.S. Marines and sailors to Veracruz, beginning an occupation that would last until November.[49]

The U.S. military intervention in the Mexican Revolution created an opportunity and a demand for ARC involvement. Until 1914, the ARC's response to the war had been limited to assisting U.S. citizens living in Mexico and relieving refugees and soldiers who crossed the border into the United States.[50]

The 1914 occupation of Veracruz changed the dynamic. Two days after the invasion, hoping to soothe anti-American sentiments and improve social conditions, the U.S. rear admiral in Veracruz requested that the ARC send an experienced relief agent to care for wounded soldiers and refugees. Charles Jenkinson, an ARC regional director who had been assisting U.S. citizens in Mexico City, arrived on May 6 as a special representative of both the ARC and State Department. Though called to aid soldiers, Jenkinson focused his energies primarily on civilian relief. At the request of the U.S. commanding general, Jenkinson distributed corn, beans, canned milk, and other supplies to those "families as might be destitute as a result of presence of American forces."[51] Military officials hoped that food aid would reduce resentment among Mexican civilians and restore order, as it had in Nicaragua several years prior. In an effort to achieve those goals, however, Jenkinson soon took on far grander tasks. Working in concert with the U.S. occupying forces and Army sanitary officials, he began to implement an array of hygienic and moral reforms. As the ARC had done in Italy in 1909, Jenkinson set up an inspection system to ensure that all aid applications met ARC criteria, in order to prevent pauperism and idleness among aid recipients. Beyond providing material relief, he funded vaccination clinics and city sanitation campaigns. At the request of U.S. military officials, he worked to track down Mexicans with tuberculosis and educate them about preventing the spread of the disease. When the U.S. military rounded up suspected prostitutes, it relied on Jenkinson's ARC office to examine and treat them. The ARC involvement in Veracruz lasted only until September 1914, but by that time its initial relief efforts had expanded into an attempt at nation building, medical surveillance, and social control. With the invitation and cooperation of U.S. occupying forces, Jenkinson used material aid and coercive relief policies to shape a future Mexico more in line with American ideals. Just as U.S. military intervention aimed to sway the political course of the Revolution, humanitarian assistance aspired to influence cultural changes among Mexican citizens.[52]

While Jenkinson carried out his work in Veracruz, U.S. humanitarian and political focus shifted to Mexico's capital city. By the summer of 1914, the revolution had spiraled in new directions. Forces opposed to Huerta had steadily gained the upper hand, and in July 1914, Huerta surrendered and fled. On August 15, Carranza's troops occupied Mexico City; five days later, Carranza declared himself president. Not everyone consented. Although Carranza, Villa, and Zapata had been united in opposition to Huerta, they disagreed deeply over the proper form for Mexico's new government. In the months after Carranza's forces took the capital, Villa's and Zapata's factions allied against him and began fighting for control. Wilson, worried that Carranza might threaten U.S. investments in Mexico, initially sided with Villa but opted to deny formal recognition until a clear winner emerged. The prolonged fighting and political unrest had profound effects for civilians throughout Mexico, but particularly in Mexico City. Food and water supplies grew scarce or prohibitively expensive, while the prevalence of typhus, smallpox, and other epidemics increased. In the spring of 1915, unable to respond to these conditions itself, the Mexican Red Cross appealed to the ARC for assistance.[53]

The request to expand its intervention beyond Veracruz raised questions about the ARC's legitimate role in foreign conflicts and its obligations as a representative of the U.S. government and people. Ernest Bicknell, Mabel Boardman, and other ARC leaders recognized the severity of the humanitarian crisis and reported on it widely to the American public.[54] Still, they debated whether the terms of the Geneva Convention permitted them to expand the intervention without government invitation. Because the Wilson administration had not recognized either side, ARC leaders feared that their involvement might imperil U.S. claims of neutrality.[55] In late May 1915, with reports of hunger, disease, and unrest in Mexico City continuing to mount, Secretary of State William Jennings Bryan ultimately decided to put these concerns aside and requested that the ARC become involved. Boardman agreed but, still concerned with issues of legality, only on the condition that aid be limited to noncombatants. With the ARC now formally involved, Wilson subsequently issued an appeal to the American public, calling on them to contribute money and supplies specifically to the American Red Cross to aid Mexican civilians in "an impartial spirit of brotherhood."[56] Lacking formal consent or invitation from any of the leaders of the revolutionary factions, the ARC thus began sending funds and food to U.S. consuls stationed throughout Mexico.

One month later, ARC representative Charles O'Connor arrived in Mexico City, the area of key strategic and humanitarian concern. O'Connor set up eight stations to distribute soup and dried corn and beans. In collaboration with the Mexican Red Cross, the local American Relief Committee, churches, and other charities, he implemented the now familiar ARC system of investigation, intended to ensure that only those deemed truly in need received food and to reduce the perceived threat of dependency. The sheer demand, however, made such oversight attempts difficult. At peak distribution, the ARC was providing food to nearly fifteen thousand families per day. Still, the situation seemed little improved. By August, O'Connor had come to doubt the ARC's capacity to relieve Mexican famine given the tumultuous state of political affairs.[57]

The ARC's intervention in Mexico would last less than four months, its brief duration dictated by the complex political and diplomatic situation. By the summer of 1915, Carranza began to gain the upper hand, prompting Wilson to consider shifting support to him and away from Villa. Fighting continued apace, with control over Mexico City shifting hands four times during O'Connor's time there. This upheaval contributed further to food scarcity and mounting food prices in the capital. As O'Connor labored to provide relief, he struggled to prove his and the ARC's commitment to neutrality. O'Connor saw his motivations as purely humanitarian and above the politics of the revolution. Denying "sympathy with any faction," he blamed the Carrancistas, the Villistas, and the Zapatistas equally for the "desolation and destruction for which they are responsible."[58] Nonetheless, rumors swirled about his allegiances. Many Mexicans, he reported, saw him as just "another spy of President Wilson" and believed that he "came to represent the United States government and had some political mission here."[59] Despite his assurances to the contrary, many Mexicans saw O'Connor's presence as merely a pretext for another U.S. military intervention. The actions of other Americans living in Mexico City did little to dispel such doubts. By July, some of these residents had called on the Wilson administration to launch a full-out military intervention in Mexico. O'Connor may have seen himself as an apolitical actor, concerned only with feeding the starving, but his physical presence in Mexico City inevitably raised the specter of further U.S. interventionism and complicated an already difficult undertaking. As O'Connor quickly understood, "the less the Red Cross appears to represent the U.S. government, the better it can do its work."[60]

O'Connor's struggles reflected a much larger set of disagreements over the right and responsibility of the United States to influence the course of the Mexican Revolution. On the one hand, whether they agreed with deploying U.S. military forces or not, many U.S. citizens shared with Wilson the belief that they had a moral obligation to intervene in Mexico and assist its civilians. It was following this logic that a new player on the philanthropic scene, the Rockefeller Foundation, endorsed the ARC's civilian relief work with a $25,000 donation and a declaration that "the relief of destitution in Mexico is a duty so far as we are concerned, it is also a duty that should fall upon the American public."[61] The American public likewise contributed thousands of dollars to food relief.[62] While some Mexicans welcomed and benefited from this assistance, others proved quite skeptical of U.S. intentions. Many also resented the symbolic nature of U.S. aid, namely the impression that Mexico depended on the United States for its survival. These concerns certainly resonated for Carranza as he worked to consolidate power. In late September, regarding ARC assistance as another form of U.S. meddling and a threat to his claims to legitimate, independent governance, Carranza announced to the State Department that further U.S. relief work was "unnecessary and inexpedient." Although U.S. consuls reported that hundreds of thousands of civilians might starve without food aid, the State Department complied with Carranza's request and asked the ARC to recall O'Connor.[63]

In the autumn of 1915, international diplomacy trumped international humanitarian concern in the Wilson administration's decision. The agreement to withdraw O'Connor occurred at a critical time in U.S.-Mexico relations. Just weeks later, on October 19, 1915, Wilson recognized Carranza as the de facto leader of Mexico. Wilson had come to believe that Carranza would emerge victorious and wanted to both distance the United States from the revolution and support the winning side. In this context, respect for Carranza's request to withdraw American aid proved more important to Wilsonian diplomacy than continued assistance.[64] Still, the conflict had not ended, nor was the U.S. involvement with Mexico complete. In 1916 and 1917, Wilson sent General John J. Pershing and ten thousand U.S. troops into Mexico in an attempt to capture Villa and his forces. During this time, ARC leaders appealed to U.S. citizens to maintain their humanitarian support. They published sensational articles and press releases that called attention to "distressing conditions" caused by widespread hunger and unrest.[65] Concerned U.S. citizens called on the ARC to intervene and the ARC leaders made several offers of aid, yet the Carranza government persistently refused assistance.[66] Thus while Ernest Bicknell, speaking for the ARC in May 1917, declared that "we are not indifferent to the unhappy conditions of many of the people of Mexico," he understood that the priorities of the Wilson administration and U.S. donors, together with the political desires of the Carranza government, made further ARC commitment in Mexico impossible.[67] Humanitarian assistance was simply too politically charged.

The ARC's declining interest in Mexico was in part a resignation to Carranza's resistance, but it also resulted from a new diplomatic and humanitarian crisis that had begun to capture U.S. attention. In the years that the ARC had been involved in Mexico, the nations of Europe had propelled headfirst into the Great War. Increasingly—and especially as the United States edged closer to entering the war in 1916 and early 1917—ARC leaders shifted their attention and resources to Europe to devise a response to that crisis. By the time the U.S. military pulled out of Mexico in February 1917 to turn its attention to Europe, the ARC had already charted a similar course. As ARC leaders began their foray into relief efforts for European civilians, the questions of neutrality and international obligation that they had wrestled with in Mexico again influenced the nature of their relief efforts.

*

On June 28, 1914, while the United States struggled to manage its occupation of Veracruz, an event halfway around the world marked the beginning of a war of unprecedented proportions. On that day, Serbian nationalist Gavrilo Princip assassinated Archduke Franz Ferdinand of Austria-Hungary, setting off a chain of diplomatic reprisals and war declarations that soon embroiled the continent in the Great War. As they watched these events unfold, many Americans regarded the conflict as evidence of the failures of Old World politics and diplomacy.

Woodrow Wilson certainly did. When he declared U.S. neutrality on August 19, 1914, the majority of U.S. citizens supported his call to remain impartial—in action if not in thought.[68]

A commitment to political neutrality, however, was never an outright disavowal of U.S. involvement in the war.[69] Entering the conflict may have been out of the question, but privately administered relief for European noncombatants was another matter entirely. It stood to demonstrate U.S. concern for suffering civilians worldwide, to affirm the U.S. commitment to international peace and civilization, and to prove—in Wilson's words—the American "spirit of absolute disinterestedness."[70] Whether they favored neutrality or armed intervention, this was a project that many U.S. citizens could support. From 1914 to 1917, during the period of official U.S. neutrality, Americans therefore contributed to an impressive range of charities for noncombatants, from Herbert Hoover's Commission for Relief in Belgium to the American War Relief Clearing House to the American Committee for Near East Relief. In these years, the ARC gradually entered the field of European civilian relief. This move was not without hurdles. As in revolutionary Mexico, the ARC's professed neutrality became a matter for debate. So too did its readiness for simultaneous large-scale civilian and military interventions. Nonetheless, by the eve of U.S. entry into the war, ARC leaders had positioned their organization as one of the nation's foremost agencies for aiding Europe's noncombatants.

William Jennings Bryan, a secretary of state dedicated firmly to U.S. neutrality and the promotion of peace, wasted little time involving the ARC in the Great War. Bryan, however, did not immediately call on the ARC to assist civilians. Rather, soon after the fighting erupted, he arranged with the ARC's leaders to provide medical relief to the sick and wounded soldiers of all belligerent nations, the sphere of humanitarian activity expressly reserved for Red Cross Societies by the Geneva Convention. Because the ARC did not distinguish between the Central Powers and the Entente, Bryan considered such efforts well in keeping with the U.S. declaration of neutrality. As he understood it, such assistance was "purely charitable and in the interest of humanity."[71] On September 12, 1914, a ship flying Red Cross flags and christened the *Red Cross* sailed out of New York City's harbor. On board were eleven units composed of three surgeons and twelve nurses each, armed with surgical equipment and hospital supplies and bound for seven belligerent nations in Europe that had accepted the ARC's offer of aid. The State Department did much to assist this enterprise. To ensure that "the efforts of Americans in the interest of suffering humanity may be as effective and creditable as possible," Bryan advised "every diplomatic and consular officer of the United States" to give the ARC representatives their "earnest and sympathetic support."[72] Moreover, Bryan and his staff endeavored to ensure that ARC supplies "not be declared contraband" by the belligerent governments "but be free and be expedited everywhere."[73] Neither the Allied naval blockade nor political conditions on the continent, Bryan asserted, must limit the American ability to provide medical assistance. Less than three months after the assassination of Archduke Franz Ferdinand precipitated the Great War, the ARC and State Department had deployed a voluntary medical force to care for wounded soldiers and to demonstrate America's neutral humanitarian concern.[74]

Although the first offer of ARC aid to Europe took the form of military relief, State Department officials and ARC leaders were equally concerned with the dire conditions affecting civilians. Reports of hunger, homelessness, and epidemic disease saturated American media and diplomatic correspondence. Robert Lansing, a counselor for the State Department and chair of the ARC's International Relief Board, testified that never before 1914 had the "calls for active service been so many and so far-reaching."[75] ARC leaders discussed the possibility of aiding noncombatants, but they realized they lacked the funds necessary to stage an effective response. In the fall of 1914, recognizing this dilemma, Wilson proposed committing federal funds to the ARC for noncombatants. This proposal, however, generated significant concern from within the State Department. While the Geneva Convention clearly protected the ARC's right to aid wounded soldiers, it said nothing about noncombatants. Civilian relief may have been an element of the ARC's charter, but it was not a sphere of aid protected by international law. Providing state funds to the ARC risked complicating the matter all the more. As Lansing warned, it would invite "charges of partiality which would seriously interfere with the friendly relations which it now has with the governments of all the countries at war."[76] ARC leaders shared these apprehensions. In 1914, neutrality was contested terrain; the United States had to tread carefully to avoid becoming embroiled in world turmoil. Declaring that noncombatant relief "cannot be impartially administered" and citing the organization's limited funding, small endowment, and tiny staff as clear impediments to staging an effective response, Boardman and other leaders voted in December 1914 to restrict relief work to wounded soldiers and to leave all noncombatant relief to other voluntary aid societies.[77]

And yet, in spite of this official decision, ARC leaders soon began making minor forays into the field of civilian relief. The prodding of a prominent newcomer on the philanthropic stage, the Rockefeller Foundation, first prompted the ARC to dabble in this arena. Though only incorporated in 1913, the Rockefeller Foundation had quickly become an influential institution in international medical relief.[78] Much like his counterparts at the Russell Sage Foundation during the previous decade, Rockefeller Foundation secretary Jerome Greene took great interest in the ARC's potential for international relief work. He hoped to encourage its entry into the field of European civilian aid. Shortly after the ARC launched its relief ship, Greene and his fellow Rockefeller Foundation trustees invited Ernest Bicknell to join their War Relief Commission in Europe, a group organized to investigate civilian conditions on the ground. They also agreed to assume all expenses related to the trip. Bicknell well understood the benefits the ARC might accrue by uniting with the Rockefeller Foundation. As he explained to ARC vice president and Russell Sage trustee Robert W. de Forest, the ARC would be "tremendously strengthened" and able "to command large sums of money for relief purposes" if the Rockefeller Foundation could "be led to look to, and depend upon, the Red Cross as the adequate and satisfactory channel for the expenditure of its relief contributions."[79] Concurring with this logic, the ARC Central Committee granted Bicknell a paid leave of absence from his post of national director so he could join the Rockefeller Foundation. From late 1914 to late 1915, he traveled throughout England, Belgium, Holland, France, Poland, Germany, Serbia, and Russia to observe the effects of war on noncombatants. Bicknell valued the chance it afforded him to make "a very thorough study of conditions."[80] Moreover, he successfully utilized the opportunity to win the respect of the Rockefeller Foundation's trustees who—as Greene confided to Bicknell—soon came to "feel very great confidence in [his] judgment."[81] Bicknell's surveys allowed the ARC to prepare for its own civilian relief efforts, while his involvement with the Rockefeller Foundation fostered lasting connections between the two organizations and secured philanthropic patronage for the ARC's international ambitions.[82]

As the Rockefeller Foundation pressed the ARC to take on civilian assistance activities, the State Department began urging the same. While Bryan and Lansing continued to disapprove of providing federal funds to the ARC, they acknowledged that its civilian assistance could achieve important diplomatic outcomes. Of major concern to U.S. government officials was an outbreak of typhus in Serbia. In the winter of 1914 and 1915, the State Department received dozens of reports of appalling conditions and high mortality among Serbians, then under attack by Central Powers forces. The American consul in Saloniki, Greece, wrote to Bryan that there had been forty-eight thousand proven cases of typhus in Serbia over the past few months, with mortality rates as high as eight hundred per day. The epidemic threatened to further destabilize an already volatile and disorderly region of Europe.[83] Aware of both the humanitarian and political threat typhus posed, Bryan called on the ARC to control it.[84] Funding for the endeavor came from the Rockefeller Foundation in the form of a $145,000 appropriation, proof of the value of the ARC's new philanthropic connections. With this government and private support, ARC leaders organized a sanitary commission to the Balkans and invited the renowned Harvard epidemiologist and tropical disease specialist Richard P. Strong to direct it. As a former director of the government biological laboratory in the Philippines and a member of the ARC expedition to control pneumonic plague in Manchuria, Strong had earned a reputation for controlling disease in sites of U.S. strategic interest. His leadership expanded this pattern to Eastern Europe. The sanitary commission sailed for the Balkan States on March 17, 1915. To fight typhus, they erected disinfection stations, dispensaries, and mobile sanitary trains in the region. Although Strong returned to the United States in early October, the ARC remained an important presence in Eastern Europe. Several ARC representatives stayed in Serbia to organize a hospital for women and children and to establish other civilian relief operations. They also commenced a food distribution program, modeled on the work of the Commission for Relief in Belgium, to prevent starvation among civilians in occupied Serbia.[85]

Within less than a year of the outbreak of war in Europe, the ARC had thus taken some limited steps into the field of noncombatant relief. By aiding civilians, such prominent experts as Bicknell and Strong sought to emphasize the compassion and the neutrality of the United States. As early as 1915, however, such claims of U.S. impartiality and antimilitarism became more difficult to substantiate. In May of that year, the German sinking of the British ship *Lusitania* and consequent death of 128 U.S. citizens invited Wilson's strong rebuke. In June, citing Wilson's apparent favoritism toward the British and French over the Central Powers, Bryan resigned as secretary of state. His successor, Robert Lansing, rebuffed Bryan's neutrality and began putting pressure on Wilson to intervene on the side of the Entente. Growing proportions of the U.S. public began to favor the British and French cause as well. Even if they did not support entering the war, many Americans began to call for greater preparedness. Groups such as the National Security League and the League to Enforce Peace, a group headed by William H. Taft, agitated for an expanded Army and Navy to better defend U.S. interests. Although Wilson continued to formally insist on neutrality, he too began to express his growing support for "reasonable preparedness." In June 1916, he made this commitment official when he signed the National Defense Act, which provided for expanding the military and Navy in the event that the United States entered the conflict.[86]

Despite these trends, many Americans did object to their nation's increased militancy and its apparent move away from neutrality. This did not mean that they wholly objected to some form of involvement in Europe's bloody war.[87] Even as the United States began preparing for the possibility of war, many Americans continued to endorse impartial civilian assistance as a viable, non-military mode of intervention. Increasingly, both government officials and private citizens pushed the ARC to reconsider its 1914 decision to limit aid to soldiers. Not only must ARC leaders enter this sphere of relief, such proponents argued, but they must take the lead in these efforts as well. In late 1915, Rockefeller Foundation officials asked ARC leaders to give "most considerate and sympathetic attention" to taking on civilian assistance, stressing that "modern war necessitates not only the care of the wounded, but noncombatant relief on a large scale." Not content to have the ARC play a minor role in civilian relief, they wanted it to become "the one organization for relief purposes, par excellence, through which all other agencies...would work."[88] Popular progressive Democrat and soon-to-be secretary of war Newton Baker concurred. Baker, a self-proclaimed pacifist, shared Wilson's desire to keep the United States out of war and to end the conflict peacefully. He also shared the administration's commitment to foreign aid. Writing to Boardman in February 1916, just weeks before his appointment to Wilson's cabinet, Baker "expressed the hope and belief that the Red Cross would now advance into the relief of non-combatants as its pioneering field." Reporting that he was "deeply distressed by the limitations which the Red Cross felt obligated to put upon its activities" Baker "grieve[d] that America has been denied the privilege of feeding the hungry women and children of Europe, comforting the destitute and nursing the sick." Moreover, he lamented that the preponderance of competing "nationalistic appeals" for aid had resulted in waste and inefficiency, preventing the U.S. public from giving as generously as it might have had humanitarianism "been centered in one great, neutral, and honored agency like the Red Cross."[89] Baker, like Rockefeller Foundation officials, saw the ARC as the agency most able and most suited to lead the nation's civilian relief work.

ARC officials did not object to the idea that their organization should oversee all U.S. aid efforts for noncombatants; indeed, most agreed wholeheartedly with this proposal.[90] Yet the ARC's small size and limited funds continued to hamper its ability to take on a major civilian aid program. When war broke out in 1914, these factors had been instrumental in the decision to leave civilian relief to the hands of other voluntary organizations. More than a year later, the situation had not changed substantially. At the end of 1915, the ARC counted just 22,500 national members. The ARC had raised over $700,000 for Europe and Mexico, but leaders recognized that to adequately administer relief to both European civilians and soldiers would require millions more.[91] Fiscal concerns had already prompted ARC leaders to withdraw their medical units in Europe earlier that year.[92] Committing to a large-scale civilian relief program seemed wholly impossible. A central problem, as ARC leaders and their allies saw it, was that dozens of other relief agencies now competed with the ARC for funds. As Boardman explained to the State Department, "Such great demands have been made during the past 11 months on the people of the United States in an endeavor to relieve distressed conditions that for some time there has been a marked decrease in the funds and other donations sent to the American Red Cross."[93] If the ARC wanted to take the lead in European civilian relief, ARC leaders believed, they had to do more to set their organization apart from the competition. In order to secure the membership and funds they would need to meet both the military and civilian relief obligations of the United States, they would need to convince the public to recognize the ARC as the leading authority in international civilian relief and the one clear representative of the U.S. government and its citizens.

As they set out to build membership, raise funds, and define the ARC's centrality in the field of civilian relief, the ARC's leaders and their allies in the Wilson administration adopted the logic and language of the growing U.S. preparedness movement.[94] Just as military preparedness advocates demanded a larger, better supplied, and better funded Army and Navy, they argued, so the nation needed a professional and fiscally stable agency to carry out overseas relief. Achieving this goal meant another round of organizational changes for the nation's official voluntary aid agency. Since 1904, Mabel Boardman had behaved in many respects as the ARC's de facto leader. Although retired Civil War general George Davis had served as the official chair of the organization since 1906, few would have objected to Bicknell's later recollection that Boardman "was the chief... the voice of authority in the country at large as well as inside the organization."[95] When Davis resigned from his post in the summer of 1915 due to ill health, Boardman assumed the role as acting chair of the ARC's governing Executive Committee.

With diplomatic tensions over Mexican aid mounting and calls for civilian aid in Europe increasing, however, many of the ARC's other leaders began to question Boardman's capability to respond. In October 1915, the other members of the ARC's Executive Committee reported to Wilson that the rapid expansion of the ARC's current relief infrastructure had produced "waste, overlapping and inefficiency," as well as "increasing confusion both in the public mind and in the work itself." Humanitarian preparedness, they argued, required a more streamlined organization and a more professional leadership, ready to respond to Wilson's call at a moment's notice. These critical ARC leaders included Russell Sage Foundation principal Robert W. de Forest; Secretary of the Interior Franklin K. Lane; surgeon generals of the Army and Navy, William C. Gorgas and William C. Braisted; and Charles D. Norton, vice president of the First National Bank. When key voices from the military, philanthropic, and financial worlds complained, Wilson listened. As president of the United States, Wilson held the authority to appoint the ARC chairman. The members of the ARC Executive Council urged him to select "a man of national reputation, so that the policies and methods announced by the Red Cross go to the public with the weight of a name known throughout the country."[96] Wilson's close friend Cleveland Dodge had the perfect suggestion. "The one best man for the chairmanship of the Executive Committee," he offered, "by reason of his long familiarity with and interest in Red Cross matters and his position and standing throughout the entire country," was William H. Taft.[97]

Wilson readily accepted this recommendation and, on October 28, 1915, asked his former rival for the White House to chair the nation's Red Cross society.[98] Before agreeing, Taft discussed the matter with Boardman. In no uncertain terms, he advised her to relinquish her authority. Boardman may have successfully managed the ARC in peacetime, but Taft and others concerned with the international situation deemed her incapable of effectively overseeing the ARC during war. Though Boardman initially resisted, she eventually consented to Taft's counsel and agreed to let him replace her.[99] Although Boardman remained an influential member of the ARC's governance, especially active in fundraising and publicity, leadership of the ARC had become a man's job.

Wilson's appointment of Taft as ARC chair illustrated the high level of consensus that American liberal internationalists held on the importance of American international humanitarianism. While they differed in the details of how to achieve their goals, Taft and Wilson shared a commitment to the U.S. promotion of world peace and international stability and cooperation. Both shared the belief that the ARC's civilian assistance was a vital means to secure those goals. As Taft explained to an audience at Clark University in 1915, "Through the medium of the Red Cross a new era may dawn upon this war-weary world—an era not of national rights, but an era of international duties and international service." Taft reasoned further that a reduction in militarism could not occur "until the foundations of international relationships are built upon the rock of international friendship and good will," something the ARC's overseas aid would help to create.[100] Such sentiments struck a chord with Wilson, who likewise defined the ARC as the clearest embodiment of the entire United States and its humanitarian concern for Europe, an organization that "represents the sympathy of us all."[101] Despite political differences, Wilson recognized Taft as an able and effective leader in the movement for international cooperation and stability, an obvious choice to help prepare the ARC for its expanded role in the war.

In late 1915 and early 1916, ARC leaders took two further steps to prepare their organization to be the nation's primary civilian relief agency. First, they divided the organization's operations into two distinct departments, one of military relief and one of civil relief. Colonel Jefferson Kean, a member of the U.S. Army Medical Corps, directed the former, while national director Ernest Bicknell took charge of all efforts for noncombatants. Second, they abruptly brought in a new chair to replace Taft. Given the intense lobbying on his behalf, this move appears surprising at first. Taft's diplomatic and political experience, after all, made him an obvious choice to lead the ARC. In fact, even though he agreed to chair the ARC, Taft himself doubted that these qualifications alone were sufficient. To ensure real accountability and efficiency of the organization, he argued, the ARC needed "to be readjusted and reframed on modern corporate business principles." As agitation for U.S. intervention in Europe escalated in 1916, Taft thus looked to the U.S. business community to complete the ARC's transformation. Taft recruited Eliot Wadsworth, managing partner of the Boston consulting firm Stone & Webster, as his replacement. In addition to being a product of "the modern school of corporate managers," Wadsworth had also served with Ernest Bicknell in Europe as part of the Rockefeller Foundation's War Relief Commission. Wadsworth's "service in applying his knowledge and experience...to the business organization of the Red Cross," Taft emphasized, "is exactly what we wish." Presaging the influx of dollar-a-year men—elite American business executives whom Wilson tapped to manage war industries for a token salary—to Washington, Wadsworth retired from his professional work and devoted himself to the management of the ARC without income. At no cost, the ARC managed "to secure a corporate reorganization of the most approved modern plan."[102] Taft, for his part, consented to serve as vice chair. The ARC, newly restructured, stood ready to become a leading figure in the field of civilian relief.

Following this reorganization, the ARC's new leaders began looking for ways to increase their involvement in civilian relief activities. The immediate lack of financial resources, however, forced Taft, Wadsworth, and their colleagues to maintain their reliance on other U.S. voluntary agencies to organize most of the relief efforts for noncombatants. Unable to establish a large independent presence in Europe right away but still hoping to make their growing involvement in the field known, they began to formally designate other private agencies to administer relief on the ARC's behalf. They named the Paris-based American Relief Clearing House for France and Her Allies as the official representative of the ARC in Europe. They also gave official endorsement to such agencies as Herbert Hoover's Commission for Relief in Belgium and the Serbian Agricultural Relief Committee. By establishing official ties with these existing agencies and their work, the ARC gained an important foothold in civilian relief before it could build its own aid infrastructure in Europe.[103]

At the same time, ARC leaders did begin to expand their own international civilian relief efforts. As they did so, ARC leaders proclaimed their capacity to impartially and effectively administer noncombatant assistance on behalf of the United States. By 1916, however, wider national debates over American neutrality and the changing geopolitical context conspired to test those claims. Beginning in September 1915, the British Government started restricting permits on ARC relief supplies bound for Central Powers nations, limiting what humanitarian items could get past the Allied blockade of Europe.[104] In March 1916, Britain announced that it would prohibit all such relief shipments and "treat them as contraband of war." Lansing, Taft, and Walter Hines Page, the U.S. ambassador to England, tried to negotiate, but to no avail. The State Department ultimately assented to Britain's demands and ceased coordinating shipments of ARC aid to Germany.[105] This decision raised the ire of many U.S. citizens, who argued that it made the ARC nothing more than a tool for the pro-Allied cause. "At the very time when President Wilson claims to stand before the world as the upholder of humanity and international law," one such critic railed, the acquiescence to British demands represented "an act of the most cold-blooded inhumanity…in absolute abrogation of the most solemn compact of international law."[106] Others tarred the ARC with being "instrumental in prolonging the Great War" by furnishing aid "to only one side of the belligerents."[107] Faced with these charges, ARC leaders struggled to affirm the ARC's neutrality. They explained that the ARC was committed to "the relief of suffering wherever it is able to do so" and asserted that "our duty to suffering humanity lies to all that we can reach and has nothing to do with the causes of the belligerents."[108] As much as ARC leaders may have believed in and emphasized the ARC's impartiality, the international politics of war and the diplomatic decisions of the Wilson administration invariably limited their potential field of civilian relief operations and raised doubts about their ability to act without favoritism.

These larger issues of neutrality and geopolitics impinged on the ARC's fledgling civilian relief efforts in other areas as well. In January 1916, the State Department offered to send a small ARC commission to distribute food and medical supplies within the Ottoman Empire, an effort to prevent the deaths of hundreds of thousands of Armenian Christians then being subjected, in the State Department's words, to the Turkish government's campaign "to exterminate by starvation."[109] The Turkish government consented to the offer of ARC aid, contingent on the ARC's promise to work with the Turkish Red Crescent Society and to "conduct relief work for civilians of all races."[110] Although the State Department accepted this stipulation, the planned aid distribution immediately hit several snags. First, the Allied blockade of Ottoman Empire ports prevented the ARC from distributing its relief supplies as widely as proposed. Then, as U.S. diplomatic officials tried to convince France and Britain to make an exception for material aid, the Turkish government reneged on its earlier acceptance of American aid. "If [the] Turkish government is not attempting to starve inhabitants," a skeptical Robert Lansing wondered, "what are its objections, if any, to sending relief supplies?"[111] ARC relief eventually entered Syria and Lebanon in late November 1916, but only after months of negotiations with both sides.[112] The politics of war also hindered relief work in Serbia, where staff of the ARC Sanitary Commission had been operating since early 1915. In the fall of 1916, the occupying Austro-Hungarian government demanded that the State Department terminate further ARC operations there. Arguing that the U.S. inability to challenge Entente blockade regulations had kept the ARC from delivering the aid it promised, Austro-Hungarian military authorities asserted that they would provide for civilians in occupied territories without outside aid.[113] Lacking permission to remain yet still desiring to continue their work, ARC workers relocated headquarters to Saloniki, Greece, where they provided assistance to Serbian refugees and other civilians for the duration of the war.[114]

By early 1917, the ARC had moved into the field of civilian relief. In spite of the organization's official commitment to providing neutral assistance, it was clear that neither the Central Powers nor the Entente—nor, for that matter, many members of the U.S. public—regarded its work as either impartial or apolitical. Such issues significantly hindered the ARC's ability to relieve noncombatants in Europe and raised concerns at home about its true allegiances. The importance of the ARC's professed neutrality, however, soon became a moot point. The U.S. declaration of war in April 1917 changed the dynamic profoundly, restricting the ARC's civilian efforts exclusively to the Allies and ushering in a new phase of the ARC's international humanitarian intervention.

The Eve of War

By the eve of U.S. entry into the First World War, the turn-of-the-century drive to make the ARC an efficient and professional organization and a clear representative of American international humanitarianism was almost complete. During Taft's presidency and Wilson's first term in office, the ARC had deepened its connections with the White House, State Department, and War Department; with prominent philanthropists, social scientists, and medical professionals; and with corporate America. ARC leaders and their allies had done much to set their organization apart from other private charities and to position themselves as prepared to take charge of the nation's international civilian aid efforts. At the ARC's December 1916 annual meeting, the assembled delegates passed a resolution affirming this commitment. Declaring that "the obligation of neutrality is not incompatible with unselfish generosity toward those who suffer" and that the prosperity of the United States "places a peculiar obligation upon our people to give generously" for the "mitigation of the sufferings of non-combatants," the ARC's leaders resolved to "take the lead in a new and energetic movement" for overseas relief. In so doing, they pledged to make the United States "better entitled to that gratitude and goodwill from the nations of the world."[115] Rockefeller Foundation trustees gave their clear nod of approval to the ARC's aspirations to preeminence in the field of noncombatant assistance, declaring their "decision in favor of turning the war work over to the American Red Cross" rather than competing with it.[116] Like the Red Cross societies of Europe and Japan, the ARC had become the recognized voluntary civilian relief organization of the United States government and many of its cosmopolitan citizens.

But one more ingredient was required for the ARC to truly rival its sister organizations: public backing. Since the outbreak of war in Europe and the U.S. intervention in the Mexican Revolution, increasing numbers of U.S. citizens had come to support the ARC's efforts. Indeed, in 1916 alone, membership rose from 22,500 to over 286,000. In that year, the ARC's endowment had finally passed $1 million, thanks in large part to the ARC's new corporate connections—the J. P. Morgan and the Busch families had each contributed over $100,000 to the cause.[117] In spite of this growth, the ARC still lacked the popular support that leaders deemed necessary to carry out the organization's new commitments to European civilians. Until large proportions of the U.S. public came to see the ARC as their preferred choice for civilian aid, leaders could not hope to secure the funds necessary to relieve Europe. On the eve of U.S. entry into the war in Europe, the ARC had won the support of the government and the philanthropic community, had reformed its organization, and had started to build momentum among the public. This final stage was fully realized once the United States entered the fray.

Significantly, in the process of rivaling its sister societies during the period of U.S. neutrality, the ARC had diverged more than ever from the International Red Cross Movement's founding purpose to aid the battlefield wounded. The U.S. government and military did, in accordance with the Geneva Convention, recognize the ARC as the official agency to administer aid to injured and ill soldiers and prisoners of war on behalf of the United States. Yet, as the increasing emphasis on emergency relief and preventive reform efforts for noncombatants indicates, both government officials and private citizens regarded assisting foreign civilians as an equally critical part of the ARC's responsibilities, an indispensable aspect of U.S. political and culture engagement with the world. To suit their own nation's particular global interests, ARC leaders modified the specifics of the ICRC's international humanitarian vision. As this adaptation suggests, the ARC may have been part of the International Red Cross Movement, but its primary allegiance was always to the United States. The consequences of this fact, too, became clearer as the United States and its Red Cross society plunged into the Great War.

3

Mobilizing a Volunteer Army

An organization without a history could not hope to have much of a future. Mabel Boardman recognized as much in 1915 when she published her history of the ARC, *Under the Red Cross Flag at Home and Abroad*. In its pages, Boardman lauded the ARC for its efforts in the preceding few decades to improve global well-being and foster world cooperation. Through its overseas relief, she wrote, the ARC was "laying foundation stone after foundation stone in the great structure of international brotherhood yet to be built." Even as she emphasized this enormous potential, however, Boardman lamented that the organization was "lacking still the size and development it must attain before it is a worthy representative of these United States of America."[1] The ARC had won the affections of the U.S. government and many prominent social scientific professionals, philanthropists, and financiers; yet only with broad participation and popular support could it effectively serve and symbolize the American commitment to alleviating civilian suffering abroad.

U.S. entry into the First World War provided the conditions necessary to achieve this goal. In the two years between Wilson's reelection and the end of the Great War in November 1918, the American Red Cross grew at an explosive rate. By the early months of 1919, roughly one-third of the U.S. population—twenty-two million adults and eleven million children—had joined their national Red Cross society. Many millions worked for the ARC in the United States, while thousands traveled to Europe as ARC staff and volunteers. Collectively, the U.S. public had raised over $400 million for its domestic and overseas war activities and had built up an endowment of nearly $2,500,000. The support and confidence of the public at large provided the final ingredient necessary to define the ARC as the nation's preferred instrument for overseas civilian relief.[2] Aiding European civilians represented only one of the ARC's wartime activities; in 1917 and 1918, the organization also provided extensive assistance to U.S. and Allied troops, wounded soldiers, and prisoners of war. But in these years, noncombatant relief represented a central part of the ARC's operations, as fundamental as military assistance to its humanitarian mission.

By war's end, moreover, millions of ordinary Americans had come to recognize aiding foreign civilians through the ARC as an essential element of their wartime responsibilities.

The wartime zeal for the ARC's efforts to help European civilians and the simultaneous mainstreaming of international humanitarian sensibilities constituted a major departure in U.S. foreign affairs. To an extent never before matched in U.S. history, Americans in the Great War years voluntarily elected to give their time and money to ameliorate the suffering of unknown children, women, and men in distant lands. That millions made this choice is a fact, yet the statistics themselves fail to explain the public's extraordinary enthusiasm. Widespread enrollment in the ARC was not inevitable. Americans heard plenty of competing requests for their time and money, both from other voluntary organizations and from Uncle Sam himself. Nor was it foreordained that U.S. citizens would prove eager or even willing to contribute vast sums of money to European civilians. After all, they had plenty of domestic concerns on their minds. Furthermore, despite increasingly cosmopolitan attitudes among some segments of the U.S. population, many Americans continued to believe that their nation was best served by avoiding involvement in European affairs. For these reasons, the success of the ARC's wartime international civilian aid program was by no means guaranteed.

How, then, to account for this rapid swelling of popular support? In part, the public interest in ARC civilian aid should be understood as a popularization of the ethos of international humanitarian concern that had been emerging in U.S. culture since the nineteenth century. Witnessing the sheer brutality of Europe's total war and its devastating human effects was enough to convince many members of the American public that they must come to Europe's aid. Equally important to the story, however, is the active role that ARC leaders and members of the Wilson administration took in securing this outcome. These individuals attributed great diplomatic and strategic importance to foreign aid; they therefore concluded that building public enthusiasm for the ARC's civilian relief operations was best not left to chance or passive process.

Immediately after the United States entered the war, Wilson, with the full approval of ARC leaders, appointed prominent U.S. business, financial, philanthropic, and political leaders to run the ARC for the duration of the conflict. Just as he charged the Committee on Public Information, the official U.S. propaganda agency, with selling war to the American public, Wilson called on the these men—known collectively as the ARC War Council—to generate public support for the ARC's overseas relief activities and to define them as part of the broader U.S. war effort. One early decision made crafting the latter half of this message easier; after the United States joined the conflict, the War Council ruled against offering any further aid to civilians in Central Powers nations. Still, the

War Council's members had to overturn both the public's indifference and its sus-picion of involvement in European affairs. They had to convince U.S. citizens that giving their money and time to help an Italian mother or a Russian child thou-sands of miles away was, in fact, a vital national interest. As business and financial leaders, the War Council's members orchestrated their appeals in the way they knew best. To overcome parsimony and apathy, they turned to publicity and mass media. Using multiple rhetorical and visual strategies—including magazines and speeches, posters and spectacles—they constructed a public image for the ARC's civilian aid projects and disseminated it throughout the country.[3]

These public messages delineated a novel set of responsibilities for all U.S. citizens, casting active support for the ARC's civilian aid as nothing less than a new patriotic obligation. Good Americans had a responsibility to support U.S. troops, but this alone was insufficient. To be truly loyal, Americans now had a civic duty to commit their money and voluntary labor to Allied civilian relief as well. The War Council told Americans that they must make sacrifices for the peoples of all democratic nations, just as they would for their fellow citizens. They were to fund efforts to improve European health and welfare as enthusi-astically as they knitted bandages for the doughboys, to care about the Allied home front as much as the front lines. Supporting the ARC's international civil-ian assistance stood to bolster other Allied societies, demonstrate the strength and the sympathy of the entire United States, and prove the nation's standing as a benevolent, liberal world power. If they backed the U.S. war effort, patriotic Americans must prop up the nation's relief mission as well.[4]

That, at least, was the message. Whether U.S. citizens actually understood sup-porting ARC civilian relief as their civic duty was another matter entirely. Many certainly did. A public commitment to aiding foreign noncombatants through the ARC increased discernibly in 1917 and 1918. Millions of Americans acted upon this responsibility by making donations, volunteering at home, or the ulti-mate act of serving overseas. Even so, levels of devotion varied widely. Some gave large amounts of time and money, others little more than a one-time donation of pocket change. The individual meanings that ARC supporters attributed to their assistance differed in key ways as well. Many donors and volunteers believed deeply in their duty to relieve overseas suffering, but a host of other incentives simultaneously motivated people to support and work for the ARC. Fear of European unrest, a chance to advance in one's career, or a simple fascination with Europe and the Great War all influenced American decisions in this regard. Although it enjoyed much support, the ARC certainly did not lack critics. Some resented its domineering position, others its compliance with the Wilson admin-istration and its larger foreign affairs agenda, and still others its overall approach to aid. Just as Americans were divided over the war and its meanings, so too did they differ in their views of the ARC and its civilian relief.[5]

Thus in spite of the War Council's efforts to construct and disseminate the concept of international civilian aid as a patriotic obligation, the idea never achieved total consensus in U.S. society. Nonetheless, the burst of international humanitarian sentiments suggests the extent to which the Wilsonian state, the ARC's leaders, and large proportions of the American public found convergence over their presumed responsibility to aid Allied noncombatants. For a brief moment in 1917 and 1918, international humanitarianism became an American obligation.

Wilsonian Ideology and Strategy and the Work of the ARC War Council

On March 5, 1917, the day that Woodrow Wilson gave his second inaugural address, he and his fellow Americans had a lot on their minds. Wilson had campaigned for reelection the previous November based on his success in keeping the United States out of the Great War. Just four months later, U.S. entry into the conflict appeared imminent. For years, Britain, France, Russia, and Italy had implored the United States to intervene on their behalf. Wilson and Secretary of State Robert Lansing had resisted these pleas, but a deteriorating relationship with Germany had caused the administration to reevaluate its neutrality pledge. In January 1917, Germany announced that it would commence unrestricted submarine warfare. The next month, the British government intercepted the Zimmermann Telegram, which proposed a German-Mexican alliance against the United States. While Wilson had offered to act as mediator on numerous occasions, a persistent refusal by leaders on both sides of the conflict had led him to doubt his ability to negotiate peace without armed intervention. As Wilson considered the possibility of sending U.S. troops to Europe, Russians in Petrograd revolted and staged a successful coup against Tsar Nicholas II, the February Revolution. In the revolution's aftermath, a provisional government headed by Aleksandr Kerensky and composed of liberal and socialist factions took control of the Russian state. As Wilson watched these events unfold, he decided he had no choice but to renege on his campaign pledge. On April 2, he asked Congress to declare war against the Central Powers.[6]

By the time the United States entered the war, the conflict had already raged for over two and a half years. Though millions had died in the trenches, it was clear that the battlefield was not the only site of suffering. Civilians on the home front experienced material deprivations and the wholesale destruction of traditional family and social support networks. In France, Italy, Palestine, Belgium, and Greece, millions of refugees had fled their homes to escape fighting. Families of soldiers lacked money and material resources for basic survival; nor could

they find employment. Children, the elderly, and the ill suffered from malnourishment and lacked medical care. Epidemic disease and political unrest contributed further to this war-induced social instability. Overwhelmed, European
private charities and state institutions lacked the resources to stage an effective
response. In many areas, riots and strikes signaled mounting popular opposition to the war. Clearly, the war powerfully and profoundly affected those living
behind the lines.[7]

From the moment the United States entered the Great War, the Wilson
administration understood that assisting these civilians would serve as an essential complement to its armed intervention. There were several interrelated reasons for this. One was ideological and closely linked to Wilson's broader liberal
internationalist worldview. Wilson's professed justification for entering the conflict centered on his sense of the global humanitarian responsibility of the United
States. In requesting the declaration of war, Wilson defined it as a "fight...for
the ultimate peace of the world and for the liberation of its peoples," a crusade
to secure individual rights, freedoms, and welfare, and to establish a firm foundation for universal democratic government. Because the German government
had "thrown aside all considerations of humanity and of right," the United
States was obligated and privileged to intervene against it. But this could not
be accomplished with guns and soldiers alone. Americans had to demonstrate
their compassion as well as their military might. They had to prove that they had
"no selfish ends to serve," that they desired "no conquest, no dominion."[8] The
American people, as Wilson went on to declare in his Fourteen Points Address
in January 1918, were committed only to ensuring "that the world be made fit
and safe to live in."[9] Generous noncombatant aid would serve as an example of
these Wilsonian ideals in action, an effort to secure peace and global welfare
without seeking personal gain.[10]

In addition to its ideological significance, providing civilian aid appeared crucial to achieving America's strategic objectives, both in the short and long term.
For three years, the Great War had uprooted families, disrupted food supplies,
destroyed homes and communities, and impaired mental and physical health. If
ignored, such widespread civilian upheaval risked generating social unrest and
depleting the morale of soldiers who feared for the well-being of their families.
These conditions clearly posed a threat to the Allied war effort. Just as significantly, they imperiled Wilson's postwar goals. The success of Wilson's internationalist vision depended on the readiness and willingness of like-minded
nations to advance the ideals of liberal democratic governance and capitalist
economic order. This, in turn, required not only an Allied victory but also the
existence of orderly, industrious postwar societies that would be prepared to put
Wilson's plans into action. It demanded that Allied noncombatants be healthy
and well fed, that children receive educations, that workers remain productive,

and that an ideal home life be preserved. In order to secure world democracy, the Wilson administration reasoned, the United States needed to do more than join Allied troops on the battlefield. It had to provide relief to people living behind the lines. The fate of international civilians, both in the immediate moment and in the long term, was in the nation's self-interest.[11]

Finally, and related to both Wilsonian ideology and strategy, civilian aid stood to serve as valuable propaganda. Although the physical provision of relief was important, so too was the message of American involvement that it transmitted. A visible demonstration of American investment and concern offered a potent way to win Allied hearts and minds. To be most effective as propaganda, however, civilian relief had to remain a voluntary enterprise. By relying on private citizens to administer aid, the Wilson administration could present assistance as tangible proof of Americans' selflessness and righteousness and could define the United States as a benevolent nation, prepared to revitalize the world thanks to its intellectual and material resources and the generous spirit of its citizens. Democratic government, in this rendering, produced compassionate and inspired citizens who solved the world's problems without burdensome state oversight. Privately administered civilian assistance would demonstrate the sincerity of American alliance and the superiority of America's political and cultural values.

The ability for voluntary organizations to provide civilian assistance thus had obvious value for the wartime United States. Given its importance, Wilson saw the need to increase his administration's involvement with the nation's voluntary relief organizations to ensure that they best served the government's interests. Similar logic had already prompted him to establish the Council of National Defense, a body that brought together Wilson's cabinet secretaries with a nonpartisan advisory committee of leaders in labor, industry, finance, and health to coordinate the state's various wartime needs with the private sector. The United States' entrance into the conflict would stimulate the creation of a host of wartime agencies, groups such as the Committee on Public Information and the Food Administration, each staffed with private citizens and charged with voluntarily assisting the nation's war efforts. In a wartime climate, the already thriving associational state of the prewar years grew even more powerful.[12]

At the earliest stages of this state mobilization of U.S. voluntarism, Wilson turned his attention to the ARC. By 1917, the ARC's leaders had succeeded in positioning their organization as the recognized face of American humanitarianism. Privately funded and staffed, yet tied to the government in myriad ways, the ARC appeared to Wilson to be the obvious choice to lead the nation's civilian relief efforts. The idea of making this status official had arisen even before the United States joined the conflict. In January 1917, the secretary of the Rockefeller Foundation, Jerome Greene, urged Wilson to invite "the most influential business and professional men in the country to meet him at the White

House" to devise plans for coordinating American war relief under the auspices of the ARC.[13] In February, leaders of principal American relief organizations, including Herbert Hoover of the Commission for Relief in Belgium, John R. Mott of the YMCA, and Cleveland Dodge of Near East Relief, met with ARC chair Eliot Wadsworth to "discuss a better consolidation and furthering of relief effort abroad" and to take steps toward "the formation of a great national relief fund...to be raised primarily for the American Red Cross."[14] With the U.S. declaration of war, Wilson elected to move forward with these plans. On April 6, 1917, the day that Congress voted to enter the Great War, Wilson issued his Statement on the Coordination of Relief that publicly established a de facto monopoly status for the ARC among U.S. voluntary aid organizations. Explaining that "a multiplicity of relief agencies tends to bring about confusion, duplication, delay and waste," Wilson argued that the only way to make foreign relief work "thoroughly efficient" was for it to be "coordinated and concentrated under one organization." That organization, of course, was the American Red Cross. With this statement, Wilson designated the ARC as the one organization charged with coordinating all of the nation's humanitarian assistance. It was an organization "broad enough to embrace all efforts for the relief of our soldiers and sailors, the care of their families, and for the assistance of any other non-combatants who may require aid."[15] The ARC was now, without a doubt, the nation's official voluntary agency for both military and civilian relief.

Association with the wartime state dramatically elevated the ARC's position among aid agencies, but it also entailed several major changes for the organization. First, in the interest of serving the needs of the wartime United States, ARC leaders altered their previous stance on neutrality. In the weeks after the United States entered the war, ARC staff reported many puzzled inquiries regarding the agency's neutral stance. To resolve the matter, ARC leaders called on William H. Taft, the organization's legal expert in residence. Taft affirmed that the ARC would remain neutral with regard to sick and wounded prisoners of war, a fundamental tenet of the Geneva Treaty. He reasoned, however, that this specific principle did not demand "political indifference" on the part of ARC leaders. Nor, significantly, did it obligate the ARC to provide "aid and comfort" to the enemy.[16] The Geneva Convention might require Red Cross impartiality on the battlefield, but it said nothing about civilians. With the United States at war, ARC leaders had no interest in trying to succor civilians in Central Powers nations. As ARC Executive Council member Charles Norton explained it bluntly, "We do not propose to be tried for treason."[17] With the end of U.S. political neutrality thus came an official end of the ARC's willingness to consider aiding any belligerent noncombatants. Now in the service of the U.S. government and devoted to winning the war in favor of the Allies, ARC leaders restricted civilian aid to the Entente.[18]

In addition to affecting the ARC's ideas about neutrality, the shift from peacetime to wartime occasioned yet another restructuring of the ARC's leadership. In late April 1917, Taft suggested that Wilson form a new body to conduct ARC operations now that the United States was at war. On May 10, 1917, following several conferences with Taft and other members of the ARC Executive Committee, Wilson named a seven-man war council, composed of leaders in finance and industry, to take over the ARC. As with the U.S. Railroad Administration, Shipping Board, and other key industries, Wilson appointed these men to ensure that the nation's humanitarian assistance was administered effectively and efficiently. He entrusted the War Council with "the duty of responding to the extraordinary demands which the present war will make upon the services of the Red Cross in the field and in civilian relief." The best way to "impart greatest efficiency and energy to this relief work," he asserted, was "to concentrate it in the hands of a single experienced organization which has been recognized by law and by international convention as the public instrument for such purposes."[19] With the creation of the ARC War Council, Wilson effectively harnessed voluntary assistance as a weapon in the nation's war arsenal.

The composition of the ARC War Council illustrated the associational, bipartisan approach that Wilson and Taft deemed essential to staging the nation's humanitarian response. Wilson retained both Taft and the ARC's new chair, businessman Eliot Wadsworth, as members of the War Council but, at the suggestion of Taft and Cleveland Dodge, he appointed Henry P. Davison to lead it. Davison had worked his way up through the banking world to become a senior partner at J. P. Morgan and Company in 1909. Although Davison was both a Republican and a Wall Street man—characteristics that might have engendered Wilson's scorn—Taft convinced Wilson that Davison's expertise in business and finance qualified him to lead an unprecedented fundraising drive to support the ARC's new expenses. The other four members of the War Council brought further political and social connections and business acumen to the organization. They included Harvey D. Gibson, the President of the Liberty National Bank of New York; Cornelius N. Bliss, a Republican politician, businessman, and philanthropist; John D. Ryan, the president of the Anaconda Copper Mining Company; and Charles D. Norton, the vice president of the First National Bank in New York. Together, these seven men would oversee the ARC for the duration of the conflict.[20]

Wilson relied on these men to administer the nation's aid according to corporate principles and bureaucratic management and to make the ARC "the one great agency for relief." To achieve this goal, they spearheaded several major initiatives. First, to extend their oversight nationwide, the War Council divided the ARC into thirteen regional divisions, each split further into several hundred chapters. Local leaders answered to regional directors, who in turn reported directly to the War Council, creating an efficient and orderly chain of command. Second, to oversee the work of other American relief agencies and volunteers, the War Council established a Committee on Co-Operation that concentrated the relief work of other aid organizations "under the protectorate of the Red Cross." This move allowed groups such as the National League for Women's Service, the American Friends Reconstruction Unit, the Salvation Army, the Circle for Negro War Relief, and the American Relief Clearing House to channel all their resources to the ARC while still preserving their individual identities and collecting funds under their own names.[21]

In addition to directing the daily operations of the ARC and administering the work of other aid agencies, Wilson charged the War Council with raising funds and membership. Here the personal connections of War Council members proved extremely valuable. Relying on the wartime culture of civic voluntarism, Davison appealed to leading financiers such as J. P. Morgan, Jacob H. Schiff, and Cornelius Bliss to make "a personal canvass of every man in the Wall Street district" for funds.[22] The Rockefeller Foundation, a longtime ARC supporter, gave $5 million in 1917 and another three million the following year; other leading philanthropists and corporate figures followed suit.[23] While they wooed financial and philanthropic elites, War Council members also made the wider public a top priority. To raise money and encourage Americans to join the ARC, they organized December membership drives and Spring Red Cross Week fundraising campaigns in 1917 and 1918. Hoping to encourage the spirit of voluntary giving, the War Council asked leaders of every local chapter to appoint the "most efficient men in the community and give them full power" to run these drives.[24] Such an approach worked quite well. Although some considered Davison exceedingly optimistic when he set $100 million as the target of the first Red Cross Week drive, collections in 1917 eventually exceeded $114 million. The 1918 drive proved even more successful, with an estimated forty-three million Americans contributing $169.5 million in only seven days. By the end of the war, the ARC's endowment, a constant concern during the previous decade, neared $2.5 million. Membership soared as well. From a base of 238,000 members in December 1916, ARC rosters increased to 6,385,000 by June 1917. One year later, over 22 million U.S. adults had paid at least one dollar to join the local chapter of their national Red Cross society.[25] In a population of roughly 100 million, this was an extraordinary feat. It was also an extraordinary thing to manage. Davison therefore hired "a great New York trust company to handle the money end of the business" and tapped the secretary of the treasury, William Gibbs McAdoo, to serve as treasurer of the War Fund. Under Davison's leadership and in the feverish environment of war, the federal government, corporate and philanthropic elites, and the American public joined to make the ARC the nation's most powerful relief organization.[26]

The War Council's leaders and their allies in the Wilson administration saw building a well-funded ARC with a large popular base as crucial to achieving Wilson's ideological and strategic objectives in the war. As Davison noted following the second War Fund drive, the existence of a strong ARC would help the Allies not simply to win the war but "to win it worthily and greatly" and to "carry a deepened assurance of sympathy and support to all the armies and civilians fighting the battle of democracy."[27] But beyond serving the interests of Wilsonian statecraft, they also believed that a burgeoning Red Cross movement portended important benefits for U.S. society. The ARC, they believed, served as an important mechanism for promoting American voluntarism and civic engagement. As Wilson explained to the public in 1918, the ARC was so important because it brought Americans together "with a great eagerness to find out the most serviceable thing to do." Under its auspices, "the people of the United States are being drawn together into a great intimate family whose heart is being used . . . for the service of civilians where they suffer."[28] Mobilizing the public behind the ARC's civilian aid promised not only international returns, but also domestic ones.

Because of the ARC's presumed potential to unify Americans in service and present them in a positive light to the world, War Council leaders realized that it made little sense to restrict their reach to the continental United States. Thousands of U.S. citizens resided abroad as employees of the State Department, the U.S. military, and various American corporations. These individuals and their dependents represented an untapped source of financial and material contributions to the ARC's war effort. To secure their membership and donations, Davison established an Insular and Foreign Division (IFD) and appointed Otis H. Cutler, a prominent New York financier, to lead it. In cooperation with the U.S. State Department and the Bureau of Insular Affairs, the IFD appealed to consular officials and prominent citizens to organize and lead foreign branches in areas of American interest around the globe. By November 1918, the IFD included one hundred thousand adult members, scattered throughout 150 chapters in twenty-six countries.[29]

The ARC gained funds and support from these IFD members while promising important civic benefits in return. War Council leaders feared that U.S. citizens who lived far from the heart of American society might lose sight of what it meant to be properly American. The IFD's importance thus rested not in "the value of the goods or the number of dollars involved," as Davison argued, "but rather the effect such a relationship must have upon the American who has been so long away from home that he may have begun to believe himself a 'man without a country.'" Through the IFD, distant Americans joined their compatriots at home in mobilizing for the war effort, ensuring that they did not lose sight of their patriotic obligations. "The American in a foreign land has been, at least in spirit, brought home and made to realize a new sense of responsibility and obligation," Davison explained to Woodrow Wilson. "The result of it is that he is a better man, has a better standing in his own community, and the spirit now permeating our country is carried effectively into the remote community in which this man lives."[30] If this process was valuable for those who were already citizens, then it surely had a role to play in nurturing civic values, patriotic duty, and democratic participation among the indigenous populations of U.S. territories and protectorates. Following this logic, Cutler included all residents of U.S. territories and protectorates as full ARC members. By supporting the ARC, these individuals were to learn their civic responsibilities and thereby become more fit for eventual self-government. "In Porto Rico and Hawaii, in the Philippines and Guam and the Virgin Islands," Davison cheered, "men, women, and little children found a new meaning to their American citizenship."[31] Civilians in these areas worked alongside American citizens to knit bandages, collect material goods, and raise funds for U.S. and Allied soldiers in faraway Europe. U.S. chapter workers embraced the labor of these new pools of able-bodied volunteers as they lauded the more civilizing benefits of service. With its potential to Americanize indigenous populations and re-Americanize U.S. citizens abroad, it was no surprise that, by the end of the war, the IFD had "planted the outposts of the American Red Cross around the world."[32]

Given the fervor with which American men and women joined the ARC throughout the world, it was only a matter of time before they mobilized their children. Soon after the United States entered the conflict, War Council leaders began discussing the desirability of a Junior division, to be affiliated with the nation's schools. Through such a partnership, the ARC could engage students in humanitarian assistance through in-class activities, thus teaching youth about their responsibilities to the international community as part of the curriculum. Davison tapped prominent figures in U.S. education and children's work to design the Junior Red Cross (JRC), including Henry Noble MacCracken, the president of Vassar College; Julia Lathrop, the head of the U.S. Children's Bureau; and Anna Hedges Talbot, a New York vocational school director and reformer. On September 2, 1917, Davison invited the 22 million schoolchildren of the United States to join the newly organized JRC.[33]

The JRC's proposed activities for the schools, which included raising money and producing relief supplies for Allied civilians, garnered substantial public support from high-ranking political and educational leaders. The commissioner of the Bureau of Education and the secretary of the interior both endorsed it, as did the president of the National Education Association.[34] It was Woodrow Wilson's appeal, however, that gave the JRC its most welcome publicity. On September 18, speaking as the president of both the United States and the ARC, Wilson addressed a proclamation directly "to the school children of the United States." The JRC "will bring to you opportunities of service in your community and to other communities all over the world," Wilson asserted. "It will teach you how to save in order that suffering children elsewhere may have the chance to live." In making this appeal, Wilson underscored both the JRC's immediate work of engaging American children in foreign aid and its forward-looking policy of nurturing the international humanitarian commitments of future generations.[35] With these goals and endorsements, the JRC found a warm welcome in many schools. By the November 1918 Armistice, it counted eleven million schoolchildren engaged in foreign service activities in their classrooms. Juniors helped produce over 371,500,000 relief articles for U.S. and Allied soldiers and refugees, valued at nearly $94 million. JRC activities had "opened fields of service to boys as well as to girls," instilling in them a commitment to civic participation and international humanitarianism.[36] The schoolchildren of America now counted as committed members of the humanitarian army of the ARC.

In 1917 and 1918, in a climate of wartime patriotism, the War Council succeeded in realizing the wildest dreams of earlier ARC leaders. They convinced vast numbers of U.S. adults and youth, at home and overseas, to support their national Red Cross society and fund it generously. The War Council strengthened the organization's relationship with leading philanthropists, financial elites, and government officials. With the help of the Wilson administration, War Council leaders publicly pronounced the ARC to be the nation's foremost civilian aid agency, the organization best equipped to coordinate and carry out voluntary noncombatant assistance for the United States. In the process, they modified their earlier commitment to neutrality, limiting their assistance only to those civilians allied with the American cause. With the United States at war, the ARC was mobilized not to address the suffering of international humanity, but to serve the particular ideological and strategic objectives of the wartime state.

Defining International Relief as an American Patriotic Duty

William Taft interrupted his otherwise jovial 1917 Christmas letter to Mabel Boardman to transmit a glum message from his daughter. "Helen is with us for the Christmas holidays," he wrote, "and she is quite disposed to criticise the publicity of the Red Cross. She thinks that we haven't made clear to the public what we have been sending the money to France for."[37] Helen Taft's disparagement surely came as a blow to her father, one of the ARC's most ardent disciples, but she raised a valid question: Why should Americans support international civilian relief? Why should she, or any other U.S. citizen, send money to relieve noncombatants in France? Or in Italy, Russia, or Serbia, for that matter? It was this set of doubts, which millions of other U.S. citizens shared with Helen Taft, that the ARC's wartime leaders had to efface. It was not enough to persuade Americans to become members of the ARC or support its efforts for the U.S. and Allied militaries. Given the critical importance that civilian aid had assumed for the Wilson administration, all objections to it had to be silenced. War Council leaders had to convince the public to support their efforts for European non-combatants generously and willingly. They had to replace public suspicion and indifference toward Europe with a new international humanitarian sensibility.

Throughout the First World War, but especially after U.S. entry in 1917, ARC media and publicity helped to construct and popularize this mentality as it endeavored to sell civilian relief to the American public. Although a variety of governmental and nongovernmental agencies collectively contributed to the cultural production of this ideology through their own publicity, the ARC's wartime leaders played a leading role. In the Great War years, they undertook a concerted publicity campaign, flooding the American cultural landscape with two distinct yet intertwined messages. First, they advanced the idea that all loyal U.S. citizens had a civic duty to support their nation's civilian relief efforts. To be a good American citizen now demanded more than showing concern for one's compatriots; it required coming to the aid of fellow democratic citizens wherever in the world they happened to reside.[38] Second, they declared that such assistance was best administered by the ARC, an exceptional aid organization that uniquely embodied the humanitarian values of the U.S. government and the American people. Supporting the ARC's civilian aid efforts, such media emphasized, represented the most effective way for Americans to live up to their new global responsibilities (figure 3.1). With these twin messages, ARC leaders offered Americans a new missionary ethos primed to inspire a nation at war for civilization. Such ideas proved valuable not only to the ARC as it tried to raise funds and build membership, but also to the Wilson administration as it labored to mobilize U.S. society for the war effort.[39]

To define support for the ARC's civilian aid as an American patriotic obligation, War Council leaders did not have to start from scratch. They drew on the longstanding traditions of Christian fraternalism, civilizing mission, and republican humanism that had motivated earlier generations of Americans to ease the suffering of others. They also built on contemporary discourses of social democracy and progressivism, which emphasized reforming public life for the greater good and were grounded in cosmopolitanism and liberal internationalism, worldviews that prized global interdependence and peaceful interaction. They appealed as well to a wider culture of wartime voluntarism and sacrifice. Finally, they tapped into a widespread conviction of the Great War era—one increasingly shared by many internationally minded Americans—that with "civilization itself seeming to be in the balance," the United States had no choice but to respond in some way.[40] Since

Figure 3.1 A wartime poster defines support for the American Red Cross as an
American patriotic obligation. Artist Grant Gordon, ca. 1914–1918. World War I Posters
Collection, Library of Congress.

the earliest days of war, more conservative internationalists such as Theodore
Roosevelt implored the United States to intervene militarily, stressing war's moral
and masculine virtues. Initially, a large coalition of pacifists, religious leaders, and
liberal and progressive intellectuals opposed this course. By the time the United
States entered the conflict, however, many of these earlier critics agreed that U.S.
military intervention was vital. Leading Protestant and Catholic voices promoted
armed involvement in terms of personal redemption and moral crusade. Public
intellectuals John Dewey and Walter Lippmann argued that mobilizing for war
would nurture social cohesion and civic engagement at home, all while inculcat-
ing a more peaceful and internationally connected world order. While such ardent
pacifists as Randolph Bourne and Jane Addams maintained their objections to U.S.
militancy throughout the war, they concurred that U.S. citizens must participate
in international affairs by joining transnational movements for social justice and
peace. Whatever their stance on U.S. military intervention, these cosmopolitan
Americans agreed that they had a special responsibility—as U.S. citizens and as
citizens of the world—to protect European civilization, democracy, and humanity. To be sure, many of their compatriots disagreed. However, these isolationist

and non-interventionist mentalities became increasingly marginalized as amoral or immoral stances. In the Great War era, the desire to take part in European affairs became mainstream in a way it never had before.[41]

Together, these wider cultural currents fused in the Great War era drive to encourage a patriotic commitment to the ARC's civilian assistance. Crafting this set of ideas, though, was only part of the process. To spread its message widely, the War Council embraced the modern art of public persuasion, adopting novel techniques from corporate advertising to elicit support. Employing diverse forms of mass media, including magazines, posters, films, political speeches, and public spectacles, wartime leaders built a publicity machine to define the ARC as a national movement for international humanity. During World War I, they saturated the American wartime landscape with Red Cross publicity.

War Council leaders did not act alone in their campaign. They sought out political, religious, and cultural authorities across partisan and doctrinal lines to convince their followers that the ARC was the representative of all good, loyal Americans. They urged church leaders "to promote the campaign by pulpit notices" and sent pamphlets to thousands of local unions asking labor leaders to appeal to their members. They hired speakers "of national importance, including college presidents, editors, preachers, and other distinguished men" to speak about the ARC; tapped personnel returning from Europe to join the Chautauqua lecture circuit and bring firsthand accounts of the value of ARC assistance activities; and recruited students "from the senior classes of Yale, Harvard, and Columbia" to bring the message to their communities.[42] To demonstrate that international humanitarianism transcended domestic politics, they relied largely on the ARC's own Republican and Democratic leadership. From his post on the War Council, Republican William Taft championed both the national and international obligation to support the ARC. In stump speeches, Taft reminded Americans that "the movement which you represent is a part—and a very important part—of the great work of preparation that the American people now have to do in carrying on the war."[43] To reach larger segments of the population, he also arranged with the editor of the widely circulated *Ladies' Home Journal* to create a Red Cross department and to put him in full editorial control. Through monthly columns, Taft spread the ARC's messages widely.[44] As president of both the United States and the ARC, the Progressive Democrat Woodrow Wilson paralleled Taft in his indefatigable promotion of the organization. In speeches, press releases, and news articles, Wilson explained how Americans demonstrated their patriotism and international humanitarian concern through ARC participation. "But a small proportion of our people can have the opportunity to serve upon the actual field of battle," he declared in 1917, "but all men, women, and children alike may serve and serve effectively by ... giving to your Red Cross."[45] Americans had a "duty," he proclaimed a year later, to show Europe not only "the real quality

of our power...but the real quality of our purpose and ourselves."[46] Such public accord on the political and humanitarian significance of overseas assistance
helped present the ARC and its efforts as a national responsibility and a national
good. Americans might disagree over the merits of armed intervention, but their
cultural and political leaders defined a place for the ARC's voluntary international
assistance in any field of foreign relations.

The spoken and written endorsements of esteemed public figures were
invaluable, but effectively promoting the ARC and its civilian aid required
more than their words. Wartime leaders therefore utilized many other forms of
mass media in their efforts to persuade the public. Recognizing that "big businesses have been built around a popular slogan," the War Council distributed
books of ARC jingles to incorporate into campaigns. Such gems as "Show me
your Red Cross membership button and I'll tell you what kind of an American
you are" and "The language of the American Red Cross is universal" succinctly
defined international humanitarianism as a patriotic duty.[47] Books such as
Red Cross Stories for Children and *The Children of France and the Red Cross* provided longer narratives of the ARC's international mission for young and old
Americans alike. So, too, did the new medium of motion pictures, with films
such as *To the Aid of Poland* and *Italy's Sons of the Sea* demonstrating ARC civilian
relief in action.[48] Parades and pageants offered an especially visible and public

Figure 3.2 American Red Cross nurses parade in Washington, D.C., creating quite the
public spectacle. 1917. Harris and Ewing Collection, Library of Congress.

demonstration of the ARC and its growing prominence in U.S. culture (figure 3.2). May 18, 1918, marked the pinnacle of such spectacles. On that day, the chairman of the ARC's Division of Parades coordinated two thousand processions to march simultaneously in the United States, the "greatest demonstration in [the] history of [this] country," according to Davison. At the head of the largest of these, a seventy-thousand-person march down Fifth Avenue in New York City, was none other than Woodrow Wilson.[49] With such spectacles, the ARC became an omnipresent symbol in American wartime culture.

Alongside these cultural productions, cheap magazines and newspapers represented an effective and affordable way to reach mass national audiences.[50] The War Council called on editors at leading newspapers and magazines to publicize the ARC as a patriotic service. Davison made frequent appeals to editors at U.S. newspapers, asking that they "give such preference and display as may be practicable, to news, editorials, and 'feature stuff' as it comes to you from day to day...regarding the activities and needs of the Red Cross."[51] The ARC also reached out to mass-circulated periodicals. Taking a cue from Taft's successful *Ladies' Home Journal* column, the War Council established a Bureau of Magazines "for the purpose of directing and coordinating the relations between authors and the leading magazines so far as Red Cross subjects are concerned."[52] For its 1918 Christmas membership drive, the ARC discovered an entirely new field for publicity, outside the "so called magazines of the first class," and sent stories, photos, and cartoons to "second grade magazines, trade papers, business papers, and house organs," reaching an estimated circulation base of over twenty-five million Americans.[53] Government agencies assisted ARC leaders greatly in their quest to flood print media. Journalist George Creel, head of the wartime Committee on Public Information (CPI), worked closely with Davison to put "the advertising interests of the United States on a basis of war co-operation."[54] The CPI's Division of Advertising assisted the ARC by securing free and reduced-cost advertisements and features for it in commercial publications. At the same time, the CPI's daily *Official Bulletin* frequently published pieces that detailed the ARC's activities, helping to establish the organization's legitimacy and importance to the wartime state. *The Stars and Stripes*, the official newspaper of the American Expeditionary Forces, likewise gave a good deal of space to the ARC to spread its messages among the troops. These government organs gave the War Council a forum for appeals to volunteers and donors, a space to call on Americans to "respond in a way which will electrify the world."[55]

But it was in the pages of its own mass-market magazine that ARC leaders most clearly articulated their organizational mission and ideals to the American public. This project originated long before the War Council's formation, and even before the outbreak of war in Europe. In 1913, ARC leaders had hired journalist Austin Cunningham to edit and revamp their quarterly *Bulletin,* hoping to convert what was a rather dry institutional journal into something with more popular appeal. Marking this change, Cunningham rechristened it *The American National Red Cross Magazine* and set out to create "an interesting, instructive, attractively illustrated humanitarian publication," ready to compete with other contemporary mass-market periodicals such as *Ladies' Home Journal, Good Housekeeping,* and *The Saturday Evening Post.*[56] From 1914 to 1918, as the United States began readying its military and eventually went to war, ARC leaders increasingly directed more resources toward *Red Cross Magazine,* enlarging both its page counts and its page sizes several times. *Red Cross Magazine* included progressively more images, as well as color illustrations beginning in September 1917. Cunningham commissioned articles and images from noted progressive journalists and photographers such as Ida Tarbell, William Allen White, and Lewis Hine. In short, he followed national trends and appealed to national tastes in the attempt to foster American interest in international affairs and in the ARC's assistance activities. Realizing that "the magazine is one of the most powerful agencies in forwarding the objects for which the American Red Cross stands," the ARC's leaders easily rationalized the costs of an increasingly glamorous publication.[57]

Through the pages of *Red Cross Magazine,* wartime leaders aspired to chronicle—indeed, to create the very language of—a unique and vital movement of international humanitarianism, unparalleled in U.S. history. They conceived of the magazine as an informative and inspirational journal capable of uniting the American reading public in support of civilian aid. In some respects, they mirrored trends in other internationally oriented publications, most notably *National Geographic.*[58] Like that periodical, *Red Cross Magazine* relied on exotic images and stories to attract subscribers. *Red Cross Magazine* editors, however, professed to give viewers something greater than shock or entertainment value. Instead, they promised Americans exclusive, firsthand accounts of the world at war and of the dire conditions necessitating U.S. assistance. Their stories purported to provide a real, unbiased account of U.S. foreign affairs while educating Americans about the international community with which they had so recently become entwined. Because Americans "hear strange names of strange countries," editors explained, "we try to reflect through the Red Cross eyes what is going on in these different places."[59] *Red Cross Magazine* pledged to provide a socially conscious contribution to knowledge about the world at large and to record how Americans were helping to shape that international order. A narrative of the ARC's international ventures as they unfolded, it entreated U.S. citizens to join that history in the making. With millions of subscribers by 1918, *Red Cross Magazine* proved an

incredibly effective tool for selling both the ARC and its message of international humanitarian patriotism.

As with all other ARC publicity, the magazine had two principal tasks: to
persuade U.S. citizens of the ARC's exceptionalism among aid organizations
and to convince them of their responsibility to support foreign civilian assistance. To achieve the former, *Red Cross Magazine* relied on several different
narratives. First, its articles celebrated the ARC for its role in nurturing social
democratic and international commitments, for uniting Americans with different backgrounds and beliefs through their voluntary concern for Allied civilians.
The ARC "embraces as many types and classes of men, women, and children
as our great western Melting-Pot produces," Cunningham wrote.[60] Testifying to
the ARC's support among all economic classes, he reported that funding "has
come from little boys who earned a few cents shoveling snow in an Idaho town.
It has come from a group of Indian maidens who pooled their nickels and dimes
on an Oklahoma reservation. It has come from wealthy philanthropists in many
parts of the United States."[61] Other articles lauded the ARC's potential to bridge
Americans across ethnic lines. One piece reported that in the Lower East Side of
Manhattan, an area that contained "the greatest mixture of races on earth," the
Red Cross had "captured the interest and imagination" of immigrants representing over a dozen different nationalities, "a wonderful bit of testimony to the fact
that the Red Cross is helping to weld us into one nation."[62] The ARC, according
to such messages, brought all Americans together and nurtured a shared commitment to the nation and its international responsibilities.

Demonstrating the efficiency and accountability of ARC assistance was a second focus. Through *Red Cross Magazine* articles, readers learned that the many
business leaders who worked for the ARC during the war were dollar-a-year volunteers, committed to service above profit. With their backgrounds in corporate
leadership, these men would reduce administrative expenses, improve efficiency, and raise the funds necessary to provide generous assistance. *Red Cross
Magazine* articles likened the ARC to a "big business machine," its thousands of
coordinated activities resembling an intricate array of "cams and cogs and ped-
als and shafts." In this metaphor, the ARC was a complex but well-oiled apparatus, one that "turned out its product with such precision and rapidity."[63] That
product, of course, was overseas civilian aid. *Red Cross Magazine* articles were
also quick to note that "a gradually increasing efficiency is making itself manifest
throughout all the Red Cross work in Europe...and the cost of inefficiency has
been reduced to insignificance by organized work."[64] The ARC's skill at efficient,
expert management of overseas relief further exemplified its preeminent status
among aid organizations.

Efforts to describe the ARC's moral and humanitarian exceptionalism represented a final theme, one that relied heavily on gendered images and rhetoric.

Red Cross Magazine made use of both feminine and masculine constructions, combining them in striking ways. The ARC was at once caring, loving, and nurturing, as well as a rational, masculine, and powerful force. Promotional material had long depicted the ARC as "The Greatest Mother in the World," but wartime leaders revised this image by emphasizing her strength, power, and efficiency (figure 3.3). Referring to this icon, one *Red Cross Magazine* piece avowed, "No mother is more loving, more unselfish, more ready to take upon her well-burdened shoulders additional tasks or burdens," nor "more efficient to succor the helpless." The Greatest Mother in the World was surely a compassionate figure, but she was also brave, professional, and intelligent.[65] While the magazine often presented the Red Cross as a woman, it also emphasized the masculine side of humanitarian assistance. Since reorganizing in 1904, ARC leaders had sought to project an image of the organization as an efficient enterprise led by social scientific experts and businessmen. The appointment of the War Council and other key male leaders, together with the service of thousands of American men as ambulance drivers, physicians, and dollar-a-year volunteers, gave ARC media makers a large stock of publicity material to solidify this impression. *Red Cross*

Figure 3.3 A wartime poster depicts the American Red Cross as the Greatest Mother in the World, a strong and confident figure. Artist Cornelius Hicks, 1917. World War I Posters Collection, Library of Congress.

Magazine articles introduced readers to Taft, Davison, and Bicknell to showcase manly leadership. Photographs depicted men at work behind battle lines, bearing stretchers and dressing wounds even as they risked gas attacks and mortar fire. An article entitled "What a Man Can Do" focused on men ineligible for military service, suggested that those who stayed behind could still contribute to the common fight by taking part in the ARC. Urging doctors, carpenters, firemen, and mechanics to enlist in the cause, the *Magazine* ensured male readers, "Your help is needed and your help is wanted." By defining humanitarian service as an appropriately masculine activity, the ARC gave American men the opportunity to live up to their patriotic duties.[66]

Red Cross Magazine espoused the ARC's exceptional status among aid organizations by touting the ARC's unifying character, efficiency, and rational empathy, but this was just one part of the challenge; it also had to win support for foreign civilian assistance. To do so, editors defined international concern and sympathy as particularly American characteristics. Austin Cunningham trumpeted this message frequently, noting that "humanitarianism and generosity, to say nothing of self-sacrifice" were traits "abundantly possessed by the American people."[67] To make sure the message of duty to nation was clear, the magazine sprinkled Woodrow Wilson's statements on the ARC liberally throughout its pages. Wherever "Red Cross men and women go," Wilson's words informed *Red Cross Magazine* readers, "they are carrying the message that Americans cannot rest without seeking to relieve such suffering."[68] Through ARC participation, readers learned, Americans emphasized their voluntary spirit and humanitarian concern to the world.

To firmly convince Americans of the importance of foreign civilian aid, the magazine also had to create a genuine concern for peoples across the sea. Here, Cunningham offered readers visual and textual proof of suffering and salvation overseas, relying on the ARC's Foreign News Service, part of its publicity department, to provide this evidence. To forge bonds with aid recipients, he appealed to both negative and positive American sympathies. Many pieces offered detailed, graphic accounts of civilian suffering in Europe. Articles such as "The Greatest Horror in History" documented sickness, homelessness, and famine in Europe and the Near East, trying to sway American readers by appalling them.[69] At the same time, *Red Cross Magazine* counterposed these with such stories as "Look Out for the Children," which presented Europeans in a far more positive light— proud, virtuous, and heroic in spite of the war.[70] Such articles publicized the dire European need for aid while casting Allied civilians as worthy of U.S. assistance. Photography was an important tool in crafting this narrative of worthy victimhood. It purported to show Americans the truth about European conditions and offer visible proof of the successful outcomes of humanitarian assistance. ARC publicity directors urged European field workers to send as many photographs

of "the conditions of misery" as possible, "in order to be able to paint this picture of want so that the American people will appreciate the need."[71] They also
turned to such prominent figures in social photography as Lewis Hine to volunteer their eyes and their cameras to the cause. Hine's photographs of civilians
in the Balkans, France, and Belgium portrayed aid recipients as suffering, yet
dignified; they were in need of American assistance, yet worthy to receive it.[72]
Using sympathetic representations of European civilians and emotive tugs on
American heartstrings, the ARC tried to manufacture American empathy for
civilians abroad.[73]

Although *Red Cross Magazine* claimed to show Americans the objective reality of European suffering, this form of media clearly relied on subjective, coded
language and imagery in its attempts to persuade. The gendered publicity that
cast the ARC as a strong, nurturing mother coexisted with a very different set
of feminized representations of European civilians, depicting them as weak,
suffering, and victimized. Further contributing to this characterization was the
magazine's persistent attention to youth. Images and stories of children occupied
a key place in the appeals because children immediately represented neutral victims, entitled to help from the generous citizens of the United States.[74] These
children, according to *Red Cross Magazine* pieces, were at risk of becoming a lost
generation. To circumvent this fate, U.S. readers learned, they had an obligation
to intervene, to destroy the nationalist tendencies that had undermined peaceful cooperation. The Great War "was fought for the children, for the future of
the race which they typify," *Red Cross Magazine* explained.[75] By aiding children,
American readers learned, they would take part in "the great work of healing the
spirit of the nations, of purging men's hearts of hate and suspicion and revenge,
and of freeing their minds from the bondage of narrow nationalism and selfish
materialism."[76] In response to a war that divided families and orphaned thousands, the ARC positioned itself and the United States more broadly as protec-
tors of childhood and family, saviors of the Europe of the day, and preservers of
Europe's future. Only by actively supporting this project, readers learned, could
U.S. citizens pledge their commitment to Allied societies and therein fulfill their
new patriotic duties.

The magazine thus appealed to American sympathies, emotions, and moral
commitments through its visual and narrative representations of foreign civilian suffering, feeding voyeuristic appetites while avowing the U.S. responsibility
to aid weaker beings via the ARC. If wartime leaders used *Red Cross Magazine*
to construct and disseminate the complex narrative of international humanitarian patriotism, they distilled its messages most succinctly into one final piece
of mass media, the now iconic ARC publicity poster. Using stunning visual
imagery and few, if any, words, ARC posters plainly defined support for voluntary humanitarian assistance as a patriotic act. As did *Red Cross Magazine*, ARC

posters appealed to public concern through images of worthy victims, including women, children, and wounded soldiers. They relied on a similarly gendered, missionary logic that cast strong and generous American humanitarians as the saviors of suffering mothers, emasculated men, and starving babies. One particularly poignant poster depicted these European civilians reaching out to the United States, a glowing beacon of hope, for aid (figure 3.4). To be a loyal American, to be "one of US," the poster explained, demanded aiding these sufferers by contributing to the ARC. Such publicity went beyond merely asking the public for help; it made saving suffering Europe a requirement for U.S. loyalty. Another poster clearly demonstrated that good Americans were not only expected to keep the armed forces fighting, they were also expected to "keep this hand of mercy at work" by giving their money to civilians in war-torn nations (figure 3.5). Supporting assistance was an obligation as critical as supporting war. Through these and numerous other posters, War Council leaders complemented *Red Cross Magazine's* attempts to define U.S. aid as a moral imperative and a civic duty in popular discourse.

In an attempt to generate American enthusiasm for overseas relief and its place in the larger war effort, the ARC's wartime leaders thus took a leading role in crafting and presenting a new patriotic obligation, one that defined aiding Allied civilians through the ARC as an American civic duty. The ideology was fresh, yet many of its fundamental premises—a faith in American global responsibility and moral authority, a belief in the imperative to uplift and protect threatened

Figure 3.4 A wartime poster presents relieving foreign civilians as an American patriotic obligation. Artist L. N. Britton, 1917. World War I Posters Collection, Library of Congress.

Figure 3.5 A wartime poster portrays support for Allied civilian relief as an essential complement to supporting the war effort. Artist P. G. Morgan, 1918. World War I Posters Collection, Library of Congress.

populations—echoed longstanding concepts of American exceptionalism and American mission. To persuade effectively, ARC publicity relied on a variety of existing cultural tropes and assumptions. Nevertheless, War Council leaders defined the ARC's mission as a thoroughly modern and unique one. They emphasized the ARC's corporate masculine leadership, heralded the progressive efficiency and efficacy of their assistance while affirming its essential humanity and benevolence, and relied on photography and firsthand reporting to assume the burden of proof. As they sold their organization and its relief to the American public, the War Council's leaders aspired to do nothing less than inculcate a new international humanitarian sensibility among the U.S. public.

Millions of Members, Millions of Meanings

The ARC's wartime leaders may have been skilled publicity makers, but they ultimately had no control over whether Americans consented to the new international humanitarian obligations put before them. Nor could they force U.S.

citizens to support the ARC and its foreign aid projects. To understand the status of both the ARC and its institutional ideology in the wartime United States therefore requires looking beyond the War Council and its messages to examine how the public regarded the ARC and its civilian assistance activities. The War Council's narratives no doubt played a part in convincing many Americans to support the ARC's activities, but they were never the sole motivating factor. Many Americans proved uninterested, wary, or openly critical of ARC foreign aid. Even though no universal consensus on the ARC ever existed, Americans could not help but grapple with its ubiquitous messages. In their personal considerations of these narratives, U.S. citizens altered, translated, and appropriated the War Council's carefully crafted publicity. They came to their own understandings about the importance of voluntary overseas aid and its role in U.S. foreign affairs.

As evidenced by the ARC's membership and funding statistics, the War Council's publicity clearly did resonate across much of the United States. Indeed, the speed and intensity with which Americans threw their support behind the ARC left contemporary observers searching for explanations. In his analysis of the ARC's "sudden blossoming…into an organization of stupendous magnitude," journalist and author H. Addington Bruce advanced a psychological justification for this "remarkable social phenomenon." Bruce attributed part of the ARC's popularity to the power of suggestion and "psychic contagion," yet maintained that the idea of foreign aid must also "have accorded with deep seated and intense desires" of the American public. Growing awareness of suffering prior to U.S. entry into war, he reasoned, had awakened the "gregarious instinct" in the collective subconscious, a psychological factor that compelled U.S. citizens to care for "not merely the safety of America, but the safety of civilization itself." Once the United States joined the fray, he concluded, this "conjoint influence of instinct and of organized campaigning in behalf of the Red Cross" caused the burst of public support.[77] Addison was not the only one grappling with the ARC's new power. War Council chair Henry Davison privately pondered it. Davison was "convinced of the fact that the people liked the idea of giving to the Red Cross," yet he had a hard time pinpointing the precise reasons why. Ultimately, as he explained to Taft, he believed that Americans liked donating to the ARC because they understood that "in so giving, their sense of responsibility [was] discharged."[78] In their minds and their actions, Davison reasoned, millions of U.S. citizens had come to regard funding the ARC's foreign relief as a way to fulfill new patriotic and moral obligations.

Bruce and Davison offer valid partial explanations, but public zeal must also be attributed to the ease of supporting the ARC and its mission. The fact that U.S. citizens accepted foreign assistance as their responsibility need not imply that international humanitarian patriotism was an exclusive ideology. It

could—and did—coexist among a variety of other political and cultural traditions. Many Americans found it easy to embrace, at least in part, because a commitment to voluntary civilian aid reinforced their other values and ideals. Hawks
and doves debated armed involvement, but they agreed on humanitarian interventions. Those opposed to extensive state or military commitments could readily approve of an army of volunteers representing U.S. interests abroad. Ardent
nationalists could see that civilian aid would help the U.S. win the war and could
assume, with paternalistic conviction, that the United States had a special role to
play in uplifting the world. Those committed to more cosmopolitan worldviews,
on the other hand, could regard human assistance as an enterprise that transcended national boundaries. By supporting foreign relief, Americans bolstered
their other philosophical and political commitments.

Supporting the ARC did not preclude support for other aid agencies, nor
did it require Americans to forsake other loyalties. Wilson's April 1917 appeal
to coordinate the relief work of other aid organizations under the ARC was
intended to foster cooperation and eliminate competition for resources, not
destroy other outlets of voluntarism. Americans who donated to the Salvation
Army, the American Relief Clearing House, or any other group "under the protectorate of the Red Cross" simultaneously supported the ARC in its ventures.
The ARC's professed secular humanism further enhanced its inclusiveness,
allowing it to attract Protestants, Jews, Catholics, and the nonreligious alike.
For a nation that prized voluntarism and associational relations between private
agencies and the state, the ARC's organizational structure and social position
also proved quite appealing. With its claims to nonpartisanship, universalism,
and efficiently executed assistance, in short, the ARC proved a good fit in U.S.
Great War–era culture.

The ease of supporting the ARC and its mission, together with the War
Council's media barrage and the Wilson administration's endorsements, convinced many Americans to regard the ARC as the face of American aid and, by
extension, to accept their international humanitarian commitments. Rockefeller
Foundation trustee Jerome D. Greene joined Wilson and the War Council in
declaring the ARC "the one great agency for relief." He urged all existing aid
organizations to "combine the common interests of all under the flag of the Red
Cross" and forecast an "awakening of the American people to a fuller realization
of their duty to respond generously to the needs of non-combatants."[79] Writers
in *The New Republic* extolled the ARC's virtues as well, noting that the organization "affords civilian patriotic feeling an immediate and a wholesome outlet in
essentially philanthropic work, and so converts it into a valuable preparation for
the healing ministrations of peace." The ARC, the journal concluded, "is perhaps
the most salutary existing expression of that better nationalism which is not easy
to keep alive in the poisonous atmosphere of war."[80] James Cardinal Gibbons of

Baltimore, a leading voice in Catholic circles, praised the JRC for teaching youth "those lessons of unselfish love and service which must be part of the education of every child if this republic is to endure as a Christian nation, and remain the haven of Freedom."[81] These prominent supporters reified the War Council's own rhetoric and further cemented the ARC's position as the nation's leading voluntary relief agency.

Many ordinary citizens agreed, and expressed their appreciation through personal letters to ARC leaders and their associates. Caroline Van Dyke of Louisiana, for instance, wrote *Red Cross Magazine* editors to laud "the universal extent of the American Red Cross beneficence."[82] While the ARC's voluntary nature won support from many corners, some enthusiastic supporters so valued the ARC that they wanted it formalized as an official branch of the government. One citizen, writing the State Department, urged as much, calling on Secretary Lansing to put the ARC "under the command of the Secretary of State." Given the ARC's significant international role, he asserted, "every patriotic citizen in the United States...would rather see the nation's Red Cross work committed to a volunteer army commanded by the President."[83] Throughout the United States, such expressions of zeal demonstrated public acceptance of the War Council's messages.

But not all Americans were so enthusiastic. Even those who joined or funded the ARC did not necessarily agree fully with the War Council's narratives. Many who opted to support the ARC did so because they appreciated its efforts for U.S. troops; assistance for foreign civilians was but a secondary concern, if a concern at all. In a wartime culture that expected civilians to make voluntary sacrifices and champion Wilson's war aims, many others undoubtedly felt pressured or coerced into backing the ARC. The 1917 federal prosecution and conviction of Wisconsin resident Louis Nagler, charged under the Espionage Act for criticizing the ARC War Council, more than likely scared a number of would-be critics into toeing the line.[84] Even with the very real pressure to take part in and endorse the ARC, many Americans did not do so. Twenty-two million adults and eleven million schoolchildren officially joined the ARC, but that left roughly seventy million nonmembers. Levels of participation varied widely by region. Midwestern and western states drew the largest numbers of active supporters, followed closely by New England. Southern states, especially those in the Deep South, reported the lowest enrollments, typically less than ten percent of the population.[85] A host of cultural impulses begin to account for this resistance. Throughout the war, many Americans tenaciously adhered to a policy of nonengagement in Europe's affairs in any capacity. Others, especially those of German or Irish descent, either opposed the ARC's abandonment of neutral assistance or supported the Central Powers. Some worried that U.S. aid to Europe would take American minds off social reform initiatives at home. Others, simply put, prioritized their own pocketbooks. The specifics of local political culture, including levels of support for the war, Wilson, and international engagements, all influenced the War Council's ability to successfully persuade and win support for ARC civilian aid.

Many rejected the ARC passively by not joining or funding it, but more active opponents made their voices heard on a number of issues. Some critics protested the organization's monopolization of relief. A 1916 *Chicago Tribune* editorial entitled "The Red Cross Octopus" set a precedent for such critiques even before the United States had entered the war. "The Red Cross society stands among us as an organization whose success in collecting money is only equaled by its tenacity in holding it," the article seethed. "The society has organization, political power, and ability to keep others out of the field of helpfulness. It, unfortunately, does not occupy that field."[86] Such critiques mounted following the U.S. entry into the war and the subsequent increase in government support for the ARC. Executives at the American Fund for the French Wounded, for instance, strenuously objected to Woodrow Wilson's call to coordinate relief activities and vowed to "resist the effort to force them into the Red Cross."[87] Clearly, not everyone accepted the notion that the ARC deserved to be prized above all other aid agencies.

Others faulted the ways that wartime leaders spent American money. In late 1917, the War Council received complaints from a number of U.S. citizens over the ARC's experimentation on animals in its infectious disease research in Europe. Regarding these antivivisectionists as a threat to "humanitarian and humane" purposes, ARC leaders tarred them as disloyal, asserting that any attempt to slow down medical research "is in reality giving aid and comfort to the enemy."[88] Though written off as anti-American, complaints like these pointed to a lack of concord on the War Council's use of public donations. Another more common—and less easily dismissed—critique about the use of funds concerned the War Council's payment of salaries to Red Cross war workers. In an effort to attract and compensate expert workers, the War Council greatly expanded its staff of paid personnel. Some received full salaries, others small stipends for living expenses. Regardless, the payments made to "volunteer employees" invited the scorn of many U.S. citizens. Ultimately, the dissent prompted the ARC's treasurer, U.S. Comptroller John Skelton Williams, to weigh in. Arguing that many "are only too glad to contribute their services freely and without compensation of any sort except the knowledge that they are doing good," Williams counseled War Council leaders to reduce their expenditures. The money in ARC coffers, he argued, represents "great self-sacrifice and privation on the part of the generous men and women and children who have given it." Entrusted with these funds, the ARC's leaders had an obligation to spend them with the utmost probity and accountability.[89] In spite of the War

Council's pledge that it oversaw relief efficiently and professionally, its actions left many unconvinced.

As the ARC grew in size and prominence, rumors about its activities increasingly began to circulate. Some of the most common accusations blamed the ARC for contributing to the moral degradation of American women. Writing "with regard to the perils" purported to greet volunteers in France, one Massachusetts woman told ARC leaders that she had "been informed that they cannot escape being mutilated by the Germans, and that every week nurses are brought home to this country either crippled for life, or pregnant; and that it is hushed up by the Government." Another concerned citizen from North Carolina wrote that she heard from a Quaker preacher that "800 or more red Cross Nurses had been sent back to this Country to become the Mother of bastard children." Others inquired about the "immorality... believed to exist among the nurses" and whether it was true that "every nurse was a damn whore." ARC leaders took these rumors seriously and tried to negate them. "There is no question but that it is German or Pacifist propaganda, and absolutely without foundation," read one characteristic response. "Please do not hesitate to deny as vigorously as possible similar rumors if you hear them."[90] Though the War Council did its best to reject such stories, many Americans remained suspicious about the organization and its overseas activities.

Some dissenters supported the ARC's efforts in theory but objected to its seeming abandonment of neutrality. A self-professed "humble member of the Red Cross" wrote Wilson "to register an emphatic protest against a shameful perversion of the purposes of the Red Cross." The writer condemned the War Council's decision to aid only Allied civilians, which he saw as "barbarous and inhuman," "un-Christian and un-American in spirit." He called on Wilson to reaffirm the ARC's "neutral, impartial, humanitarian, and international character" and requested "the immediate elimination of Mr. Davison from the War Council."[91] Trying to quell concerns such as these, Davison, Taft, and their colleagues wrote frequent letters of defense. They strove to convince Americans that "with the position of war between the United States and Germany, the position of the American Red Cross toward Germany changed at once."[92] Many U.S. citizens, however, rejected this justification and lamented that ARC leaders had forsaken their organization's founding principles.

The most radical critics condemned not just the ARC's abandonment of neutrality but the very existence of international humanitarian relief. Socialist and surgeon James P. Warbasse blasted the ARC as no less than an "accomplice in keeping warfare alive." ARC physicians, nurses, and other volunteers "should not beguile us with the claim that they are non-combatants and inspired only by love of humanity," Warbasse proclaimed, for their "sentimentalism, combined with a confused ethical sense which calls for impartiality, results in the promotion of war." If Americans really wanted to assert their neutrality and humanity, he argued, they "would employ their energies to end the war" rather than doing anything to assist the Allied cause or mitigate the conflict's horrors.[93] For Warbasse and others vehemently opposed to war, civilian aid appeared nothing less than another tool in the militarist's arsenal.

Thus, even as the responsibility to support foreign aid became a familiar part of the public discourse in American culture, opponents critiqued the War Council's narratives on a number of grounds. Wartime leaders worked to suppress unflattering portrayals as quickly as possible while touting the truth of their own publicity, but even those who supported the ARC did not adopt its messages in a straightforward manner. Americans chose to back the ARC for myriad personal reasons. This was the case for the millions of Americans who made only minimal sacrifices to the organization such as giving a dollar, knitting a sweater, or attending a Red Cross parade. It was just as true for the thousands of Americans who made the highest possible commitment to the ARC: traveling to Europe to administer civilian assistance.

What It Meant to Go Over There

After the United States entered the Great War, thousands of American men and women began crossing the Atlantic to serve as ARC staff and volunteers. As they carried out civilian assistance in France, Italy, Serbia, Russia, and other Allied nations, these Americans were supposed to represent the humanitarian face of the Wilson administration and the benevolence of the U.S. public. War Council leaders therefore tried to ensure that all personnel had been inspired by the logic of international humanitarian patriotism and understood the profound nature of their commitment. Realizing that the employment "of any but thoroughly serious and reliable" volunteers was "likely to bring discredit to the organization," the War Council required prospective personnel to provide letters of recommendation from Americans "of well-known standing and reputation." They appealed to nationally known professionals in health, medicine, and social science to lead its relief efforts and recruited graduates from the best colleges and universities to staff its canteens, ambulance corps, and other relief units.[94] The War Council's leaders took great care in constructing its volunteer army, just as they had its institutional publicity.

On the whole, the U.S. citizens who served with the ARC in Europe represented some of its most ardent disciples, those most likely to embrace the organization's professed ideals. They had, after all, made a significant commitment to the ARC and its mission. Even so, numerous factors simultaneously influenced each individual who decided to live and work in Europe. ARC workers desired not only to assist Europe, but also to see it, to experience it, and to play some part in the epic struggle. Those who volunteered for overseas relief work cut across a wide swath of the American populace and held a wide spectrum of political, economic, and social views. They were men and women of various ages and from all parts of the country. Many were college-educated members of health and welfare professions, but there were also lawyers, factory workers, secretaries, and retirees. The ARC's leaders may have crafted a coherent, if multifaceted, institutional ideology and tried to make sure its personnel adhered to it, but the heterogeneity and sheer size of the organization's volunteer army ensured that not all workers possessed the same level of commitment to the ARC's international humanitarian ideals.

Among those most poised to accept the ARC's institutional ideology were cosmopolitan and progressively oriented members of the American medical and social scientific professions. Though often divided over U.S. military intervention, hundreds of physicians, nurses, and social workers chose to serve with the ARC because of how they understood the war and its social effects. Trained in contemporary theories of hygiene, sanitation, and quantitative social work, the members of these professions regarded individual and community welfare as inextricably linked. They tended to prize preventive and constructive measures to improve individual and community well-being. Committed to social scientific approaches to solving civic problems, they insisted on expert planning and oversight. In the prewar United States, they had lobbied for improved housing and nutrition, labor reforms, prenatal and child health care, visiting nurse services, and aid for dependent mothers. As they did so, they had engaged in transatlantic conversations with fellow reformers in France, Italy, and Britain; the United States' allies in the Great War had been its progressive peers and mentors in the decades preceding the conflict. The outbreak of war, however, provoked great concern among many American health and welfare professionals for the fate of these international reform efforts. War threatened to cripple the civil societies of like-minded nations, leaving them ill prepared to protect their citizens and rebuild their communities. In this context, many American health and welfare professionals understood their participation in war relief as a means to sustain the progressive reform tradition in Western Europe. In addition, they hoped to get a chance to nurture similar reform movements in areas further east. Volunteering to help European civilians was but an extension of their social and political commitments to the international community.[95]

As professionals in public health and social welfare considered how to commit their expertise to the wartime cause, the ARC's leaders did their best to attract them. The War Council recognized the dedication of these individuals and the value of their skills, and thus appealed to noted social professionals to design and lead European civilian relief activities. Especially desirable were those with "special technical experience such as physicians with special experience in tuberculosis or child welfare, trained nurses with health experience, [and] social workers with general experience."[96] To encourage their service, ARC leaders presented civilian relief as a professionally satisfying activity. War work consisted of more than "handing black steaming coffee to refugees trooping past a station canteen or distributing raisins and apples at the point of destination or fixing up straw beds and food stations for people."[97] Relieving Europe, like reforming sanitary and social conditions in American cities, demanded expert leadership to ensure efficient administration and up-to-date methods. Service with the ARC was not a pause in one's career but a complementary venture that presented "an extraordinary opportunity for constructive advance in the whole social field."[98] The War Council promised professional volunteers personal benefit from helping Allied civilians to support themselves, reconstruct their cities and villages, and improve their health and social conditions.

For many progressive health and welfare professionals, it took little convincing. By 1917, the ARC had established its commitment to scientific assistance; had ample funds to support relief work; and had the clear support of the federal government, philanthropic organizations, and the U.S. public. With promises of vast resources and professional opportunities, ARC service presented an unparalleled career opportunity. Furthermore, according to its clearly articulated institutional mission, the ARC seemed to share many of the same political and social commitments as would-be personnel. Following U.S. entry into World War I, hundreds of social workers, physicians, nurses, and public health officers therefore joined its ranks. These progressive professionals represented a special segment of the volunteer army, for they were the architects, directors, and staunchest advocates of the ARC's civilian assistance projects. Many of the individuals who directed civilian relief activities had a history of involvement in ARC international activities. The head of the ARC's Division of Civilian Relief, Ernest Bicknell, spent most of the war directing civilian relief efforts in occupied Belgium, while social economist Edward Devine headed the ARC's Bureau of Refugees in France. Serving alongside and under these veterans were scores of physicians, nurses, social workers, and other professionals. As they left behind their careers in hospitals and dispensaries, tenements and settlement houses, universities and city boards of charity, the individuals who organized civilian relief in Europe carried their worldviews and professional commitments with them.

Homer Folks, as the director of Civilian Relief in France, was arguably the most influential of these professional ARC workers. Like Bicknell and Devine, Folks embraced his new international humanitarian commitments because they accorded closely with his broader worldview. Folks had served as the director of the New York State Charities Aid Association since 1893. In that position, he involved himself in a wide array of progressive causes, from municipal reform to the promotion of widow's pensions to antituberculosis and mental health campaigns. Particularly interested in child welfare, Folks had fought for juvenile court and child labor reforms, served as the vice-chair of the White House Conference on the Care of Dependent Children in 1909, and helped to develop the United States Children's Bureau in 1912. For nearly a quarter of a century, he had devoted his career to scientific charity, social work, child welfare, and public health. Hoping that he would approach Europe's diverse civilian relief needs in the same way as he had tackled social problems in Progressive-Era New York, the War Council called on Folks to oversee its civilian assistance efforts in France.[99]

In the summer of 1917, as Folks contemplated whether to accept this offer, he sought advice from a friend. "If the organization of the American Red Cross can put you into that field for so important a line of work," his friend counseled, "it would seem to me to be the call of duty and an opportunity not to be neglected."[100] Believing firmly in his international humanitarian responsibilities, Folks concluded that he had no choice but to accept the ARC's offer. He arrived in France in July and became director of the Department of Civil Affairs in August. In Europe, he became an ardent and vocal proponent of the War Council's narratives. If Woodrow Wilson had entered the war to save civilization, Folks reasoned in a 1918 speech, then there was no threat "more grave nor more significant" to that goal than the demise of Allied European civil societies. Soldiers and humanitarians, he declared, were "engaged in two sides of the same task." While soldiers were "fighting for the survival of liberty and democracy," humanitarians were "working for the conservation of the human resources of the allied nations to enjoy that liberty and democracy."[101] Military intervention would help to win the present war, but only by intervening to preserve Allied health and welfare could Folks and his fellow Americans ensure liberal Europe's postwar viability and sustain the coming peace. Clearly, Folks found much to agree with in the ARC's wartime messages.

The sense of obligation to improve international well-being motivated many of Folks's fellow health and welfare professionals. Lulu Hunt Peters, a physician from Los Angeles who served in Serbia, affirmed that, above all, she "came over here to make their lives happier" and she would "do [her] duty."[102] Edward Devine concurred with this sentiment. Moreover, he saw participation in the ARC as a way for himself and others who were disqualified from military service to profess their commitment to both the U.S. armed intervention and the American humanitarian intervention. Devine articulated this point to a group of ARC workers in France. "We are for the most part not eligible for that high service; we are women, old men, and physical defectives," Devine stated. "That is not our fault, and we are here primarily to demonstrate that it is also not our misfortune or the misfortune of the cause in which our hearts are enlisted. We are here on war work, on serious, practical, necessary war work."[103] As Devine saw it, overseas assistance was not an inferior substitute for military service, but a vital complement to it. Significantly, this logic failed to fully persuade the Wilson administration. While many conscientious objectors hoped that service with the ARC might serve as a suitable alternative to military service, Wilson and Secretary of War Newton Baker ultimately decided that it would not suffice as a replacement. Afraid that too broad a definition might "have the effect of encouraging further 'conscientious' objecting," they refused to allow ARC work to substitute for combat service.[104] Official policy aside, many proud ARC volunteers such as Peters and Devine continued to see working for the ARC as counterpart to military service.

Many health and welfare professionals believed that they fulfilled their international humanitarian obligations through ARC work, yet this did not prevent them from simultaneously realizing other, more personal benefits. With its noted personnel, ample funding, federal support, and absence of bureaucratic hindrance, the ARC proved an ideal employer. As Homer Folks explained, "We have had sufficient funds, substantial freedom in the use of them, absence of the countless limitations and traditions attached to governmental work, and ... I have in my department four or five of the very best physicians in the United States, together with quantities of specialists of every sort and description, all of whom I order about from place to place with the utmost freedom." Furthermore, he reported that there was "everywhere a most receptive attitude and a very widespread interest in the subjects we are dealing with."[105] Folks may have believed in the moral value of the international humanitarian work in which he engaged, but he also valued the career opportunity. Service conferred professional benefits.

This chance to develop professionally while aiding Europe proved particularly valuable to female personnel in fields such as nursing, medicine, and social work. In the early twentieth-century United States, women in these careers had struggled mightily to achieve autonomy and respect.[106] The ARC offered many of them a chance to not only practice their professions but also prove their capabilities. While California physician Clelia Duel Mosher, a volunteer bound for France, pledged to "come and do [her] part no matter what it cost [her] personally," she also made sure to inform the ARC that her "seven years' working in preventive medicine would especially fit [her] for this work." Her time in Europe did not disappoint. Reflecting later on her experiences assisting French refugees, she admitted that "every bit of experience, judgment and knowledge ... was called upon" as part of her ARC service.[107] Working in the ARC allowed Mosher and her fellow professional women to develop their skills; to carry their ideas and practices to Europe; and to enjoy challenging, innovative, and personally satisfying career opportunities. Simultaneously, by providing visible proof of the

ARC's claims to benevolent yet professional leadership, these women reinforced the messages of the War Council's publicity.

Although many of the health and welfare professionals who oversaw civilian aid activities in Europe closely adhered to the ARC's institutional ideology, not all personnel were as committed to that logic. For some, the primary reason for volunteering was not to help foreign civilians specifically, but because they saw it as a quicker and easier way to take part in the war effort. John Stewart Van der Veer, assigned to Camp Pike, Arkansas, for officers' training camp in 1918, recalled that his "desire to see action on the front became an obsession." Van der Veer requested transfer overseas, only to see his efforts thwarted several times. "Constitutionally unable to weather prolonged frustration," he resigned from his commission under the advisement of his army doctor, who worried that the sheer frustration at not being allowed to go overseas might result in a nervous condition. Van der Veer then joined the ARC in Italy, and in less than a month found himself "doing something that took on the nature of a dream."[108] At fifty-eight years old, former mayor of Chicago Carter H. Harrison also found it difficult to obtain a wartime position. Although he offered his service to the government "in any capacity," Harrison complained that "unless one belonged to a learned profession, was a technical expert, or closely hooked up with 'Big Business,' he could expect short shrift." The ARC, however, readily enlisted Harrison to work with refugees in Toul, France. Eager to join the war effort in any capacity, he sailed in 1918 as a full volunteer, receiving no salary and paying all of his own expenses.[109]

The ARC provided many of the nonprofessional women who left the United States to serve in Europe an opportunity to play an active part in the war. Alice W. Wellington, the secretary of the ARC-affiliated Smith College Relief Unit, invited her fellow alumnae "to do a patriotic and humane service" for the people of Europe. Because "our men must help drive out the invader," she contended, American women must "help restore the humble lives so ruthlessly shattered."[110] Wellington defined women's humanitarianism as of equal importance to men's military service, but others imagined themselves in a supporting role. Florence M. Marshall, for one, argued that the women who worked in France played an important part in the ARC because they could take up jobs that required little or no training "and thus release men for more important positions."[111] The ARC gave women a position in the war effort, but these female personnel often deferred to male superiors. For them, service demanded subservience.

Like women, other marginalized U.S. citizens saw joining the ARC as a way to participate in the war and demonstrate their patriotic commitment to the government. ARC media had made this message clear. Racism and nativism, however, often thwarted those efforts. In 1918, Charles E. Mason, a trustee for the Tuskegee Institute, complained to War Council leaders that African Americans

had been barred from overseas service with the ARC. Although the national organization had no segregation policy in place, it did not prevent local chapters from
employing discrimination in hiring or appointing volunteers. "The President has
instilled in us all the belief that the present war is one for democracy," Mason
asserted. "It is almost criminal that all classes in this country cannot share in
the relief work which is being done as they would like to."[112] Other prominent
African Americans added their critiques to the chorus. Tuskegee Institute president Robert R. Moton pointed out that the ARC's refusal to confront institutionalized racism had created "indifference on the part of colored people" to the
organization.[113] Mason and Moton understood service with the ARC, like the
military, as a way for African Americans to prove their patriotism and gain the
benefits of citizenship. Yet although ARC leaders pledged to deliver aid without
regard to race or creed, they proved unwilling to demand that these same stipula-
tions be extended to would-be volunteers. War Council leaders refused to upset
the status quo, calculating popular support from white Americans to be more
important than fighting for racial advancement. As in so many other spheres of
American life, Jim Crow drastically limited the opportunities of would-be ARC
workers.[114]

Immigrants also understood ARC involvement as a way to demonstrate
their loyalties, but just as racial prejudices limited the opportunities for African
Americans to serve, wartime suspicions of foreigners hindered immigrants'
attempts. When Charles D. Malaguti, a naturalized U.S. citizen born in Italy,
applied to serve overseas with the ARC, he learned that the State Department
had not yet ruled on whether aliens or even naturalized citizens would be allowed
to fill such positions. Malaguti "is intensely patriotic... and feels very keenly the
hesitation on the part of the Red Cross Society," one of his advocates ensured
the State Department. Nevertheless, his background raised suspicions about
his American loyalties.[115] Individuals from Central Powers countries met even
fiercer scrutiny. In 1917, representatives from the Allied governments asked the
U.S. State Department to prevent individuals of German, Austro-Hungarian,
Bulgarian, or Turkish birth or parentage from serving overseas with the ARC.
Although Henry Davison ultimately succeeded in resisting this policy, the State
Department's willingness to consider this request worried U.S. citizens who
wanted to serve abroad.[116] One nurse wrote to Woodrow Wilson to express trep-
idation that she would be barred from volunteering. Her father, she explained,
arrived in the United States when he was six months old and "fought in the Civil
War on the side of the Union," while her Polish mother had arrived in the United
States at the age of thirteen after fleeing the Kaiser in Germany. The nurse asked
Wilson to "kindly advise me whether, in view of the above facts, my German
parentage will bar me from service?" A male American citizen, born to a German
father, understood the contradictions well. "It certainly seems strange that the

government will let me serve the country as a soldier," he wrote to Robert Lansing, "but not as a Red Cross worker."[117]

These and scores of other petitioners wanted to join the ARC to demonstrate their patriotism, but in the wartime United States, a nation fractured by racial and ethnic stereotypes and fears, contemporary prejudices threatened to thwart their attempts to serve. Indeed, many Americans saw the issue from the opposite perspective and criticized the War Council for its overly liberal stance on the issue. "Are the lives of French, British, Belgian and American soldiers to be sacrificed or put in jeopardy in order that the feelings of those who not long ago were among the Kaiser's upholders in this country might be spared a little hurt?" wrote one critic, adding, "There are other ways open to former pro-Germans to serve the common cause which are not open to suspicion."[118] Those most affected by these contemporary biases hoped that by serving in the ARC, they might prove their loyalty and their Americanness. Those who doubted the loyalty of immigrants, on the other hand, worried that these so-called hyphenated Americans would manipulate overseas assistance for their own treacherous purposes. With the world at war, humanitarian assistance became deeply embroiled in much broader American cultural and political debates.

For all the Americans who joined the ARC—or tried to—because of patriotic, altruistic, or professional interests, many undoubtedly signed up simply because they had a thirst for adventure and travel. In the early twentieth century, U.S. civilians journeyed increasingly to Europe for business and pleasure, their transport eased by faster ships and reduced costs. The war slowed this tourist boom substantially. In July 1915, the *New York Times* reported that only 170,000 American tourists had traveled to Europe during the previous twelve months, half the number that would normally be expected and "the smallest number of departures for Europe in a generation."[119] As restrictions on foreign travel tightened following U.S. entry into war, overseas service offered Americans a chance to see the world and, as a volunteer from North Dakota planned, "make the most of … a golden opportunity to improve my mind through travel."[120] The ARC gave her and thousands like her a chance to see the world firsthand. Such personal pleasures, together with humanitarian zeal, patriotic commitment, and professional callings, formed the multifaceted set of reasons that compelled Americans to go abroad in an ARC uniform.

Crossing the Ocean

On November 30, 1917, New York librarian Helen Grannis set sail for a ten-day Atlantic crossing to Europe. The boat ride marked the first stage in her service as an ARC volunteer, a period to reflect on what lay in store, to meet fellow ARC workers, and to learn the rules and culture that would soon govern her life. Various activities punctuated the voyage, including inoculations, daily French and Italian classes, evening card games, and opportunities to socialize with sailors. As Europe neared, Grannis took a moment to reflect on the excitement that she sensed among all her fellow volunteers. "There is a most enthusiastic crowd on board," she wrote in her diary, "All going for something—even though their idea of it may be rather vague."[121]

As Grannis observed, national enthusiasm for the ARC failed to produce a national consensus on the country's international humanitarian mission. The wartime ARC enjoyed a clear groundswell of popular support, as did a belief in the importance of overseas civilian aid. Nonetheless, Americans differed widely in their reasons for coming to Europe's aid, and many chose not to. Despite the War Council's efforts to build universal American support for the ARC and its overseas aid, a gap persisted between official ideology and public understanding. ARC leaders and their proponents hoped that they had sparked a permanent change in public sentiment. Only time would tell, however, whether this was a permanent shift or a temporary effect of wartime fervor. Over the next six years, as Americans like Helen Grannis went to Europe to put international humanitarian ideals into practice, they would test the limits of this new vision of American statecraft.

4

Relieving Europe

On June 3, 1917, Ernest Bicknell boarded the ship *La Touraine* in New York City's harbor and set sail for Paris. Less than two months after the United States entered the Great War, the ARC War Council had appointed him, along with seventeen other men, as the first representatives of the ARC Commission to France. They went, as Bicknell confided to his journal, "to blaze the way into a field of activity for which neither the members of the group nor indeed the Red Cross itself had the guidance of experience or precedent." On June 12, 1917, the same day that General John Pershing arrived in the City of Lights to command the American Expeditionary Forces, the men reached Paris and began to organize relief activities.[1] Two weeks later, on June 29, a dozen American physicians, public health experts, and bacteriologists boarded a train in New York City and headed west. Led by Frank Billings, a noted University of Chicago physician, this ARC Commission to Russia planned to provide medical and food aid to civilians in the aftermath of the February Revolution. After crossing the United States by rail and the Pacific Ocean by ship, the party arrived at the Pacific port of Vladivostok, Russia. There, they boarded the imperial train of the former Tsar and set off on the Trans-Siberian Railroad. On August 7, they arrived in Petrograd, the home of Russia's new democratic provisional government.[2] Within months of the United States' entry into the European conflict, the War Council had launched a two-front humanitarian offensive. Through the distribution of food, clothing, and expert medical advice, they intended to demonstrate America's commitment to the peoples of Allied Europe.

The diplomatic and humanitarian promises of the ARC, envisioned at length in the wartime United States, were put to the test through the widespread provision of civilian assistance among the Allies of the Great War. The June 1917 deployment of small commissions to France and Russia marked only the beginning of this venture. In less than two years, the War Council established commissions and civilian relief operations in twenty-five countries, dispatching thousands of American personnel as far as Italy, Belgium, Serbia, and the Near East. "Carrying a message of comfort and cheer," Henry Davison explained, they were "helping especially to care for the refugees driven away from their homes, to care for the children, and to provide for the sick and needy."[3] While the War Council first called on ARC personnel to focus on acute needs such as food, shelter, and medical aid, the heads of the ARC's Departments of Civil Relief quickly expanded the scope of the mission. In collaboration with European state and private agencies and U.S. philanthropies, ARC personnel launched campaigns against epidemic disease, public health and nursing education programs, child health initiatives, and an array of other comprehensive reform efforts. By war's end, the quest to relieve European civilians had morphed into a humanitarian undertaking of massive proportions.

This extensive program of noncombatant relief was central to the ARC's European designs, and to Great War–era foreign relations more broadly, for several reasons. Leaders in the War Council, the Wilson administration, and the State and War Departments regarded civilian aid as a crucial component of the U.S. commitment to Allied Europe, due to its strategic and ideological importance. Keeping Allied societies stable, maintaining high morale, visibly demonstrating U.S. involvement, and nurturing a strong postwar international community were fundamental to achieving their larger designs for Europe. Even as the ARC's civilian aid projects benefitted the Wilson administration's wartime agenda, they meant something loftier to many of the cosmopolitan health and welfare professionals who designed and oversaw them. For these individuals, the goal was not only to win the war and preserve the peace but also to sustain international social reform efforts and make lasting improvements to European public welfare. The thousands of Americans who volunteered overseas to aid civilians, meanwhile, invariably came to their own conclusions about what their assistance meant. In the process of working abroad, they developed new understandings about European peoples and European society. Some saw themselves as peers to Europeans, there to lend a helping hand, while others assumed a responsibility to guide and tutor aid recipients, to school them in the presumed benefits of American methods and ideals. Americans thus rationalized and conceptualized their nation's humanitarian mission in diverse ways as they carried it out in Europe.

Although they may have differed in their understandings of civilian aid, War Council leaders, Wilson administration officials, and ARC workers clearly saw a special place for it in the ARC's wartime efforts, a fact made all the more clear when considering noncombatant assistance against the organization's concurrent military relief activities. From April 1917 to early 1919, working closely with the War Department and American Expeditionary Forces, the War Council sent tens of thousands of nurses, physicians, ambulance drivers, and other lay volunteers to aid U.S. and Allied soldiers, the battlefield wounded, and prisoners of war.[4] To a large degree, civilian assistance remained distinct from this enterprise.

Civilian and military relief operated as independent spheres within the ARC's own bureaucracy. While the U.S. military exercised significant authority over ARC personnel involved in aiding the armed forces, those assigned to work with noncombatants retained relative autonomy. Civilian assistance also rivaled military relief in financial terms. In many assisted regions, particularly those to which U.S. troops never deployed, appropriations for foreign civilians matched or even surpassed those made to soldiers. As the special attention paid to Allied refugees, women, and children demonstrates, the U.S. government and private citizens attached an immense and specific value to the task of aiding noncombatants.

The particular importance that the United States attributed to civilian relief also stands out when comparing the ARC's wartime work to that of its fellow Red Cross societies. In making civilian aid such a central part of their broader humanitarian intervention, the ARC's leaders deviated greatly from the founding traditions and contemporary activities of the International Red Cross Movement. Established in 1864 to provide neutral aid to the battlefield wounded, the ICRC in Geneva had since expanded its official sphere of responsibilities to include sailors and prisoners of war. Still, its focus remained overwhelmingly on military relief. Although ICRC leaders did initiate limited efforts to aid civilians during the Great War, they restricted their attention to those interned in occupied or enemy territories, mostly ignoring noncombatants in their home countries. Military relief also took priority among the national Red Cross societies of France, Great Britain, Germany, and other belligerent countries. During the war years, these organizations served principally as the voluntary medical auxiliaries of their nations' armed forces. While many of these Red Cross societies did offer some aid to civilians in their home countries, the need to fulfill their primary obligation to the military effectively limited the funding, supplies, and personnel available for noncombatant relief. Other major players in the International Red Cross Movement thus paid some attention to civilians, but none paralleled the ARC in the extent of its relief efforts for those behind the lines. The Geneva Conventions did not designate assistance to noncombatants as a responsibility of Red Cross societies, yet the ARC War Council leaders made them a major priority.[5]

The centrality of the ARC's wartime civilian aid program to the broader U.S. intervention is telling, for it has much to suggest about how U.S. citizens and government officials understood their relationship and their responsibility to European society in the Great War years. Through the wide-scale administration of noncombatant relief, Americans proclaimed an exceptional role for their country in ensuring international health, well-being, and stability. They imagined themselves friends, caregivers, and even saviors of the democracies of Europe, and a vital bulwark against both Central Powers autocracy and Bolshevik revolution. Through the ARC, Americans aspired to demonstrate their alliance and their compassion, while making Europe a better place—according to their standards, at least. The story of ARC wartime civilian relief efforts, in short, provides important insights into how Americans negotiated and reconceptualized their position relative to Europe during the last two years of the Great War. It also casts light on the shifting power dynamics at play in this process. Above all, Americans believed, they must make Europe safe.

Mapping Civilian Assistance in Wartime Europe

From June 1917 to February 28, 1919, the ARC War Council established a dense network of assistance for the civilians of Allied governments in Europe and the Near East. War Council leaders did not create this aid infrastructure alone, nor did they start from scratch. Since the first ARC relief ship sailed to Europe in September 1914, the State Department and its consular officials had coordinated the ARC's growing range of activities in Europe. By the time the United States entered the war, ending the ARC's efforts among Central Powers nations, most Allied countries had already accepted offers of ARC assistance and the organization had established a significant presence on the continent. Efforts during the period of U.S. neutrality, however, had focused primarily on military assistance. While ARC leaders had made several notable forays into civilian aid by the spring of 1917, including food and medical relief to Serbia and the Ottoman Empire, the ARC's limited finances had led them to rely primarily on other U.S. and European voluntary agencies to organize most of the relief efforts for noncombatants. Groups such as Herbert Hoover's Commission for Relief in Belgium and the Serbian Agricultural Relief Committee administered civilian aid on behalf of the ARC or with its full endorsement.

Following U.S. entry into the conflict and Wilson's subsequent designation of the ARC as the nation's chosen voluntary agency, War Council leaders quickly expanded upon the ARC's fledgling commitment to European civilian relief, finally accomplishing what the State Department, the ARC's leaders, and the ARC's proponents had been calling for throughout the period of U.S. neutrality. With U.S. entry into the war, however, came a new factor affecting ARC decision making: the U.S. military would play a major and influential role in determining how the ARC's relief was organized on the European continent. Although military officials had long been involved in the ARC's institutional hierarchy and decision making, they assumed an unprecedented level of control over many aspects of its operations when the United States went to war. On June 20, 1917, shortly after they had all arrived in Paris, General John Pershing assembled his adjutant general, several AEF officers, and the head of the ARC Commission to France (Grayson Murphy) to determine the ARC's relationship to the military. What transpired would ultimately prove quite favorable to both sides. A West Point graduate and senior vice president at the Guaranty Trust Company, Murphy was a colleague of Henry Davison and an ardent supporter of U.S war aims. Both he and Pershing saw an important role for the ARC in the war effort. Hoping "to insure conformity between the operations of the American Red Cross and the policies of the Commander-in-Chief," Pershing named Murphy as a member of his staff.[6] His general staff then went on to define the ARC as one of four official "welfare societies associated with the A.E.F.," a special status shared only by the Y.M.C.A., the Knights of Columbus, and the Salvation Army. Yet among those organizations, the AEF declared a unique role for the ARC. Resolving that "relief work for the benefit of the civil population seems essentially within the scope of the Red Cross as the recognized international relief agency," the AEF announced that "the Red Cross will provide for the relief work" and relegated "amusement and recreation of the troops" to the other three associations.[7] Translating Woodrow Wilson's domestic favoritism into military policy, Pershing and his general staff named the ARC as the AEF's chosen agency for relief. Together, Pershing and Murphy determined how the ARC could best serve military needs and how the AEF, in turn, might support the ARC's humanitarian efforts.

This new level of collaboration between the ARC and the U.S. military affected all of the ARC's activities, yet those personnel involved in military relief felt its consequences far more than their counterparts in the field of civilian assistance. Formal efforts to distinguish between these two areas of relief dated to late 1908, when the ARC's leaders had first split military and civilian activities into separate spheres within the institutional bureaucracy. These divisions continued on the ground in Europe, where Pershing and Murphy decided it best to divide the ARC's operations into two broad departments, one devoted to military affairs and the other to civil affairs. Officially, the AEF vowed "a policy of non-interference in the internal activities" of the ARC and declared it would not "attempt to direct their administration in the same sense as it directed the administration of the various military services."[8] Both Murphy and Pershing readily concurred, however, that the military must be able to exercise control over the ARC's military relief activities if the ARC was to be of use to the armed forces. Agreeing that all "work with the American Army would be carried on in strict accordance with the views of the army," Murphy ceded a good deal of authority over the Department of Military Affairs to the AEF. Personnel at the Department of Civil Affairs, on the other hand, enjoyed far more independence and far less oversight. While Murphy also pledged that work "with the civilian population" would "be carried on in accordance with the plans of the Commander-in-Chief," the AEF played very little direct role in work related to noncombatants in actual practice.[9]

This wartime relationship with the AEF, forged in the earliest days of the U.S. armed intervention, held important implications for the form that the ARC's civilian aid operations would take in France and, later, throughout Europe. By naming the ARC as the designated relief society of the U.S. military, the AEF further reinforced the ARC's already dominant position among American aid agencies. Yet because Pershing granted the Department of Civil Affairs significant autonomy in its operations, ARC personnel retained significant flexibility in the planning and design of noncombatant relief. ARC workers, in short, enjoyed significant support to implement civilian relief in Europe as they saw fit.

Having determined the relationship between the ARC and the AEF and the bureaucratic division of the ARC's two spheres of relief, the leaders of the Commission to France began to develop their civilian program. Activities for noncombatants commenced shortly after the June arrival of the first seventeen volunteers. Ernest Bicknell, the long-time director of ARC civilian relief work in the United States, took provisional command of this area. He promptly organized investigation trips to explore civilian conditions across France and began to determine a course of action.[10] By August, the New York social worker Homer Folks had arrived to become the permanent head of the Department of Civil Affairs. From his post in Paris, Folks devised plans to address France's diverse and immense civilian needs. Folks did not work from a blank slate. He expanded activities rapidly by building upon the work of other American and French aid societies. To promote both cooperation and efficiency, his strategy involved working with existing relief agencies where he could, while looking for ways to eliminate redundant activities.[11] Folks collaborated with a number of French medical professionals, charities, and social welfare institutions, many of which shared his vision for relief but lacked the resources to tackle the issue independently.[12] He also exploited the existing U.S. relief infrastructure in France. Many voluntary aid organizations in the United States, including such groups as American Friends Service Committee and the Secours National, had been sending cash and material aid to civilians in France for years before Folks arrived. At the same time, Americans living in Europe had organized many of their own charities. The author Edith Wharton, for instance, had established the American Hostels for Refugees, the Wharton Children of Flanders Charity, and the Tuberculeux de la Guerre organization, among others. By far the largest of these voluntary organizations was the American Relief Clearing House for France and Her Allies. Established in 1914 by U.S. ambassador Myron T. Herrick and American banker Henry Harjes, the American Relief Clearing House coordinated the distribution of cash and supplies that various American individuals and groups donated to French civilians. Before the United States entered the war, it had also served as the official representative of the ARC in France. With the ARC now positioned as the official U.S. relief agency, Folks and the Department of Civil Affairs set out to absorb the work of these organizations.[13]

The ARC may have had the full support of U.S. political and military leaders, but the move to centralize all American aid work under its umbrella proved a thorny issue, testing the willingness of Americans to accept the ARC as their nation's official relief agency. Some, including the American Relief Clearing House, quickly turned over their funds and activities to Folks, agreeing that the "whole American relief work in Europe should be carried on under one agency, the Red Cross" and accepting Henry Davison's promise that through the ARC, their work "shall not only be maintained but strengthened."[14] Others proved more skeptical. Edith Wharton initially agreed to merge her charities, "in the full conviction that the Red Cross had come here with the intention of facilitating the efforts of American war-workers in France," but her impression of the ARC soon shifted. She criticized the Commission to France for managing her charities poorly and alleged that the organization failed "to show proper consideration to our tubercular patients."[15] Although Folks and other ARC leaders dismissed Wharton's criticisms as "very small affairs," it was clear that the ARC's growing power and special status had the potential to breed resentment among those it displaced.[16] Yet as Wharton and other critics learned, they had little say in the matter. Armed with the support of the president of the United States and the commander of the AEF, and under the direction of influential U.S. bankers and social experts, the ARC maintained the upper hand in its relations with private American charities for French relief. By September 1917, Folks had largely solidified the ARC's status as the principal American charity for civilians in Paris and throughout France.

As he built upon the efforts of French and American humanitarians, Folks also crafted his own relief activities. The War Council had chosen Folks to address French civilian needs as he had tackled social problems in urban New York, and he did not disappoint. Within weeks of his arrival, he had initiated Department of Civil Affairs projects throughout Paris and across much of France. ARC workers provided food and shelter for refugees, established workrooms for civilian women, funded hospitals and health clinics, and opened orphanages and child-feeding stations. They also launched more comprehensive projects, including a national antituberculosis campaign, educational initiatives to reduce infant mortality and childhood disease, and courses to teach nursing and sanitary science principles to French women. Stressing the importance of a coherent and logical structure for all this relief work, Folks reorganized the department's activities into specialized bureaus and sought out Americans trained in public health, medicine, and social science to direct and staff them. Prominent U.S. health and welfare professionals soon filled the ranks of the Department of Civil Affairs, making its staff a veritable *Who's Who* list of American progressive reformers. Social economist Edward Devine led the Bureau of Refugees, while William Palmer Lucas, a physician and professor of pediatrics at the University of California, headed the Bureau of Needy Children and Infant Mortality. In charge of the Bureau for the Care and Prevention of Tuberculosis was William Charles White, the future medical research director of the National Tuberculosis Association. Paul U. Kellogg, editor of the progressive social work journal *The Survey*, agreed to manage the Editorial Bureau and ARC publicity.[17] Working under them were dozens of American doctors, nurses, and social workers. By the time U.S. soldiers joined in the final Allied military offensive in the fall of 1918, the French Department of Civil Affairs had grown to include a staff of fourteen hundred Americans operating in over one thousand French towns and cities. Together, these Americans executed the U.S. humanitarian intervention in France, by far the largest of the ARC's wartime aid endeavors.[18]

France may have been the first and most extensive of the ARC's civilian efforts but, shortly after the ARC's June 1917 arrival, civilian conditions in other Allied countries prompted ARC leaders in Washington to dispatch additional commissions to Europe. In each site to which the War Council sent personnel, the program that Folks developed in France provided the basic model for civilian work. "It might almost be said," Henry Davison explained, "that the work in each country was simply a duplication, in a smaller way, of the work done in France."[19] While the ultimate shape and scope of civilian operations in each nation varied depending on local needs, conditions, and resource availability, the types of projects and the approach to organizing the ARC relief infrastructure proved largely comparable. The overarching goal, moreover, remained consistent for each site of relief. By sending ARC workers across Europe, ARC leaders hoped to serve America's diplomatic needs while expressing its humanitarian concern.

Just weeks after they dispatched the Commission to France, War Council leaders sent a similar commission to Russia. Russia, like France, represented both a critical ally and a nation crippled by widespread civilian deprivations. The Great War, though, was not Russia's only challenge. Since March 1917, Americans had observed Russia's democratic revolution and the ensuing events with great fascination. Many progressive Americans embraced the revolution and its political potential. Herbert Croly, the editor of the *New Republic*, described it as a "magnificent" yet "portentous" event, a prelude to further democratic revolutions.[20] Woodrow Wilson, heralding it as a defeat against autocracy and a victory for republicanism, quickly extended official recognition to the provisional government of Aleksandr Kerensky. Even as they held hope for the revolution, however, many Americans worried about conditions on the ground. A widespread famine, coupled with popular dissent against Russia's involvement in the Great War, had fueled much of the unrest that motivated the uprising in Petrograd. If the new Russian government failed to restore order, any potential for democratic progress might be lost. Moreover, Russia's tenuous commitment to the Allied war effort risked faltering if civilian support evaporated further.[21] In this light, the decision to send ARC personnel to Moscow and Petrograd represented an attempt to demonstrate American support for the Russian people while encouraging their commitment to the war effort. Welcomed in August 1917 by the Russian minister of foreign affairs and the Russian Red Cross, the members of the ARC Commission to Russia soon set to work, pledging "cooperation in all of the relief work in Russia with all of the public relief organizations of Russia." ARC representatives began distributing "milk and other necessary foods, clothing and shoes" and considered enlisting "a qualified member in social welfare work" to improve the efficiency and effectiveness of the aid distribution.[22] As in France, ARC personnel set out to create a collaborative aid infrastructure, capable of providing for Russia's relief needs in a professional manner.

In August 1917, as the Commissions to Russia and France began their work, Belgium's king and its minister of the interior requested that the ARC send personnel and relief supplies to the area of their country that remained unoccupied. The ARC was neither the first nor the best-known American charity to assist Belgium. Since the early months of the war, Herbert Hoover's Commission for Relief in Belgium had distributed millions of dollars worth of food and material aid to civilians there.[23] Following U.S. entry into the war, however, the Belgian government began to call on the United States to increase its humanitarian commitment. In a personal appeal to Woodrow Wilson, Belgium's King Albert declared that "the imports of foodstuffs have been inadequate" and warned that Belgians faced "hardship and suffering" and "actual famine," "appalling" rates of infant mortality, and an upsurge in tuberculosis that was "threatening the future of the race."[24] Desirous of more assistance, Belgium's leaders called on the official U.S. relief agency to assist their cause as well. In early September, with Folks well in control of French relief, Ernest Bicknell left France and headed north to serve as the commissioner for Belgium, a post he held for the duration of the war. To execute their civilian relief venture in free Belgium, Bicknell and his staff formed partnerships with local agencies, granting funds and supplies to roughly 150 different organizations. Focused especially on relief work for children and refugees, they aimed to supplement Hoover's long-standing commitment to Belgium.[25]

France, Belgium, and Russia took priority in ARC relief planning until a disastrous military defeat in Italy captured the War Council's attention. On October 25, 1917, the Austrian military broke through Italy's northeastern alpine front at Caporetto, forcing five hundred thousand civilian refugees to flee south. Shortly thereafter, several members of the Commission to France headed east to distribute the contents of twenty-four train cars filled with blankets, clothing, surgical instruments, and other supplies. From there, the humanitarian intervention in Italy quickly escalated. Paul Kellogg, Edward Devine, and Ernest Bicknell immediately took leave from their positions in France and Belgium to survey conditions in Italy and make recommendations for future work.[26] On December 20, twenty-seven men arrived in Rome to lead a permanent ARC Commission to Italy. Chester Aldrich, an architect who had designed settlement houses in New York's Italian immigrant neighborhoods, served as Homer Folks's equivalent in the Department of Civil Affairs. Like Folks, he expanded the ARC's relief work rapidly throughout the country. By the summer of 1918, Aldrich and his staff had established orphanages, feeding programs, health clinics, hygiene and nursing education for women, and other forms of civilian relief and assistance in 142 towns and villages. Working with over 1,000 Italian volunteers and paid staff, 210 American personnel directly assisted over 48,000 civilians each week. Although the Commission to Italy also offered military assistance, civilian relief activities received the major share of attention, with roughly two-thirds of ARC funds directed to noncombatants. By war's end in November 1918, Italy would be second only to France in terms of the dollars spent and material relief afforded to those on the home front.[27]

The ARC moved not only into Italy, but further east as well. Already in Saloniki, Greece, where ARC personnel had set up headquarters following their 1916 ouster from Serbia proper by Central Powers occupying forces, a Commission to Serbia under the command of Pennsylvania physician Edward Ryan continued to provide food, housing, and medical relief to thousands of Serbian refugees for the duration of the war.[28] The ARC also expanded its efforts in the Balkans to Rumania, where a small commission of U.S. physicians, financiers, and nurses— led by lawyer and philanthropist Bernard Flexner—arrived to distribute food and medical supplies in September 1917.[29] In the Ottoman Empire, which had received limited civilian assistance from the ARC during the period of neutrality, the U.S. declaration of war and the ARC's subsequent decision to withdraw from Central Powers nations compelled War Council leaders to end their assistance. However, War Council leaders continued to intervene indirectly, channeling millions of dollars to the American Committee for Armenian and Syrian Relief to aid civilians on the ARC's behalf. In March 1918, after the British occupied Jerusalem, the War Council deployed its own ARC commission to the Near East to work alongside the American Committee and British occupying forces. Led by John Finley, an educator and editor, the ARC Commission to Palestine and the Near East was composed primarily of health professionals who undertook projects to combat cholera, typhus, malaria, and famine. Greatly expanding the ARC's 1916 efforts to aid civilians in the Ottoman Empire, an eventual 144 American personnel established relief operations in Port Said, Aleppo, Beirut, and over fifty other towns and cities in the Near East.[30]

By the end of the Great War in November 1918, the initial work of a few ARC staff in Paris had thus grown into a vast infrastructure of relief for the civilians of the Allied nations.[31] This expansion was not a passive process, nor was it inevitable. A combination of factors—including diplomatic and military interests, humanitarian concern, and geopolitical realities—together informed the War Council's decisions about where to send personnel and the level of resources to devote to noncombatant relief at any particular site. During the war, France received the lion's share of appropriations and personnel, followed by Italy.[32] While the presence of the U.S. military in these nations partly explains the ARC's significant role in these nations, it fails to account fully for the vast amount of funding and supplies that the War Council made available for noncombatants there. The explanation lies in the fact that these countries held clear strategic value for the United States. American policymakers regarded these nations as critical to winning the war and ensuring the peace. The ARC's leaders therefore made civilians in these nations a top priority. Strategic interests, of course, were never the sole factors determining the distribution of resources. Actual need informed the War Council's decisions as well. Thus even though England certainly rivaled France in terms of strategic importance, British civilians faced nowhere near the level of deprivation and social upheaval as their continental allies. The absence of occupying forces and the relative adequacy of food and social services obviated the need for the War Council to provide civilian relief there. Although a small ARC commission did deploy to England, its members focused only on American and British soldiers and sailors.[33] On the other hand, while the Balkans and the Near East arguably paled in comparison to the Great Powers in terms of their strategic value, the effects of war on civilians in those areas generated significant humanitarian concern. Reports of famine and epidemic disease, coupled with appeals for aid by U.S. lobbying groups and from the assisted nations themselves, did much to convince War Council leaders to expand relief eastward.

Perhaps the most salient factor determining the distribution of civilian aid, however, was the influence that broader wartime geopolitics brought to bear on ARC operations. Most obviously, the War Council's ruling against offering aid to Central Powers nations prevented War Council leaders from aiding civilians in any region occupied by the enemy. The presence of Central Powers forces in both Belgium and Serbia caused War Council leaders to restrict their personnel to the small areas of those nations that remained free. Not until the British took Palestine did the ARC recommence its intervention in the Near East. The defeat of Rumania in spring 1918, on the other hand, brought an end to the ARC's work in that country.

While armies of occupation limited aid to Belgium, the Balkans, and the Near East, radical shifts in the political situation in Russia ultimately prompted War Council leaders to cut off assistance there. From the time they arrived in Petrograd in August 1917, the members of the ARC Commission to Democratic Russia had distributed over $1 million in food, medical supplies, and other material aid.[34] The State Department and ARC had begun discussing the expansion of humanitarian work when on November 7, 1917, Vladimir Lenin led a successful armed coup in Petrograd, declaring Bolshevik control of Russia and marking the start of the Russian Civil War. Wilson, backed by many Americans, deplored this new phase of the revolution and threw his full support behind the anti-Bolshevik coalition.[35] In Russia, ARC personnel knew only that "all information seems to point to a long period of disorganization."[36] Commission leader Frank Billings opted to return to the United States, but his deputy Raymond Robins—a vocal supporter of the Bolsheviks—remained in Petrograd and took charge of the Commission's operations.[37] Difficulties, however, fast multiplied. In March 1918, Robins and the Commission fled to Moscow following the German advance on Petrograd.[38] Just two months later, Henry Davison recalled Robins in reaction to mounting concern among State Department Officials and War Council leaders over his pro-Bolshevik stance. Although Davison was initially "very reluctant...to withdraw [the] entire Red Cross commission," he voiced doubts about the "likelihood [of] continuing service."[39] The Allied invasion of Russia in July 1918 put an end to his indecision. In September, with Russia and the United States now in a state of war, the U.S. consul general in Moscow decided ordered ARC personnel to evacuate, thus bringing the Commission to Russia's tumultuous intervention a close. Conceived in June 1917 as a way to succor a democratic ally, the ARC Commission to Russia lost both its welcome and its purpose in the wake of the Bolshevik Revolution.[40] The new specter of Communist Russia over Eastern Europe, meanwhile, provide an additional, powerful motivation for expanding relief to that region; indeed, War Council leaders would begin to direct substantially more resources there during the last few months of the war.

In myriad ways, the politics of war and revolution thus dramatically affected the shape of the ARC's wartime operations. The experiences of the Commission to Russia, and the development of the ARC's relief infrastructure as a whole, point to the complicated forces at play in the War Council's efforts to organize noncombatant relief operations in Europe. Strategy, sympathy, and geopolitical reality conspired to determine the map of ARC civilian aid in Europe.

The Diplomatic and International Humanitarian Potentials of Civilian Assistance

The thousands of ARC personnel who worked across Allied Europe in 1917 and 1918 embodied dual, often contradictory, impulses of Great War–era U.S. foreign policy. In the process of administering civilian relief, they simultaneously served the national and the internationalist interests of U.S. citizens and government officials. Civilian aid, as many Red Cross workers understood (and often appreciated), was a crucial piece of the Wilson administration's broader war strategy, a way to maintain stability among Allied nations while projecting American commitment to them. At the same time, many ARC personnel saw themselves as more than mere pawns to the U.S. and Allied war effort. For more cosmopolitan Americans, civilian assistance represented a way to uphold prewar transatlantic social reform efforts and to improve European welfare. These Americans understood aiding Europe as an opportunity to forge lasting personal connections, a necessary step toward overcoming the nationalist mentalities that had produced war in the first place. A more focused consideration of the form of ARC civilian assistance projects and the diverse meanings that Americans attributed to them has much to suggest about how U.S. citizens and government officials conceived of their position relative to Europe during the war years and the ways that ARC civilian aid factored into this relationship.

*

In a number of key respects, the deployment of funding, supplies, and personnel to Allied Europe constituted a conscious act of diplomacy. By improving the physical and psychological conditions of beleaguered civilians, ARC aid aimed to secure an Allied victory and lay the foundations for a postwar Europe more favorable to the United States. More specifically, the strategic benefits of civilian relief were threefold. First, civilian relief worked as valuable public diplomacy by demonstrating the sincerity of the American alliance. It showed Allied Europeans that the United States had come to help them and that the nation intended to make good on its pledge of assistance. This task was necessary to strengthen wartime alliances, but it was equally essential to nurture the permanent friendships that would be required for a lasting peace. Second, improving civilian material conditions promised to boost morale among both noncombatants and their loved ones at the front, thus keeping Allied societies invested in the war effort. Finally, by reducing hunger, homelessness, and economic insecurity, relief offered a means of imposing order on social chaos and restoring normalcy to European civilians—a concept measured by how closely aid recipients adhered to the values and cultural assumptions of the ARC's largely middle-class, professional workforce. By making civilians industrious, virtuous, healthy, and above all orderly—all while providing visible proof of Wilsonian wartime rhetoric in action—the ARC's Departments of Civil Affairs aimed to serve the strategic interests of the Wilson administration, the State Department, and the AEF.

American policymakers, military strategists, and ARC leaders understood full well that civilian relief efforts could serve as valuable publicity for the United

States. Any steps taken to improve the conditions of noncombatants stood to project American compassion and concern. The "essence of our value," as Commission to France leader Grayson Murphy put it, was the ability to show civilians "that American sympathy and loyalty are expressed not in words but in acts."[41] In Kerensky's Petrograd, likewise, American aid promised to "stir the imagination of all of Russia" and "to keep clearly before the Russians the fact that the United States, through the Red Cross, wanted to help them."[42] The potential propaganda value of civilian assistance extended beyond those receiving assistance to their relatives in the fighting forces. "If the soldiers at the front feel that their families are attended to and their fleeing women and old men are made happy and comfortable by American effort," ARC leaders reasoned, "they will be more likely to give their best work in repelling the enemy."[43] Broadcasting the particular nature of ARC assistance—a mission funded by private donations and staffed by volunteer citizens—formed an important part of this narrative. It contributed to an impression of the United States as a land of concerned, committed friends rather than an abstract foreign government (figure 4.1).

Figure 4.1 An ARC poster in France attempts to demonstrate to French civilians the veracity of American concern and compassion. Artist Waldo Peirce, 1918. World War I Posters Collection, Library of Congress.

In addition to creating a positive impression of U.S. involvement, civilian relief defused the widespread criticism that the United States had failed to fulfill its responsibilities as an ally. From 1914 to 1917, the United States had resisted the pressure to intervene in Europe. When Congress finally declared war in April 1917, the nation's standing army comprised only 140,000 men. It would take months for the military to mobilize, train, and equip troops for active combat, but in the meantime, the provision of foreign aid could offer tangible proof of U.S. concern.[44] In France, private humanitarian assistance served as a visible vanguard to the military effort. Relief was "of immediate importance to the conduct of the war," social reformer and ARC volunteer Paul Kellogg explained, for it helped "make the French people at large feel that we are doing our part even though Americans may not be in the trenches this fall and winter."[45] ARC workers thus labored "to make the French acutely conscious of the reality of the American alliance by concrete acts of war-relief."[46] This message took on greater strategic weight in Italy, where no American forces arrived until late July 1918, and became more important still in the multiple Allied nations to which U.S. troops never deployed. Through well-choreographed demonstrations of their nation's humanitarian concern, ARC workers sought to convince Allied civilians of the United States' sincere commitment to the war.[47]

Recognizing the valuable cultural diplomacy inherent in ARC assistance, both the Wilson administration and ARC leaders took active steps to make the message as obvious as possible. All relief, as ARC leaders stressed, needed to possess "an American character pronounced enough to constantly remind everyone connected with it that this help comes from America."[48] To achieve this goal, ARC workers hung up U.S. flags, distributed photographs of Woodrow Wilson, and otherwise heavily advertised the origins of their aid whenever they distributed relief (figure 4.2). One early policy decision by the AEF aided this publicity campaign enormously and demonstrated the clear benefits that the ARC accrued from its military connections. In the summer of 1917, the War Department proposed that ARC personnel be granted military ranks and the right to wear military dress. Although Pershing initially opposed this measure, conferences with War Department and ARC officials quickly convinced him "that some sort of militarization was probably desirable."[49] In October 1917, therefore, he issued a general order that gave ARC commission members "assimilated rank but without military authority, obligation, pay, or allowances."[50] It also permitted Red Cross workers the right to wear the U.S. Army uniform. Military officials rationalized this change in protocol as a way to facilitate ARC work on the battlefield. The decision to include ARC civilian relief workers, however, served little practical purpose other than to give the visual impression U.S. troops had arrived to help (figure 4.3). With this decision, Ernest Bicknell, Homer Folks, and other heads of ARC Departments of Civil Affairs achieved the rank of Colonel overnight.

Figure 4.2 American Red Cross workers prominently display the American flag to advertise a food distribution in Anguillara, Italy. ca. 1918. American National Red Cross Collection, Library of Congress.

Figure 4.3 Leaders of the ARC Commission to France, in military uniform, stand outside ARC headquarters in Paris. ca. 1918. American National Red Cross Collection, Library of Congress.

Majors and lieutenants clad in khaki fatigues filled the ARC ranks, visually suggesting America's military intervention every time they served a meal or helped a refugee find a bed for the night.

Because ARC workers represented not only the organization but indeed the entire United States, ARC leaders took great care to instruct them on how to behave properly. "In carrying out the immediate work of relief," commission leaders instructed their staffs, ARC personnel had to demonstrate to Allied civilians "the fact that America is with them in winning this war and is ready to give every man and every resource it possesses to attain that object."[51] Try as they might, however, ARC leaders could not always control the actions of individual ARC workers, a fact that threatened to undermine their careful attempts to craft the ARC's public image. Throughout Europe, ARC administrators cringed at the liquor guzzling, rabble-rousing, and noncompliance. The head of the Commission to France, for instance, lamented that the ARC was "seriously troubled by many instances of insubordination...of drunkenness and riotous behavior," a trend that he believed threatened "the good name of the American Red Cross and the general standing of the Americans."[52] Though they did their best to publicly define the ARC's aid as symbol of American compassion, leaders never had full control over their organization's public face.

Nonetheless, civilian relief served as a potent expression of American alliance and concern. But despite its value as propaganda, aid would amount to little strategic benefit unless ARC workers took active steps to counteract the social dislocations that bred disorder and discontent. In addition to visibly demonstrating their sympathies, ARC personnel had to actually feed and shelter civilians and work to improve their economic security. As they did, ARC workers acted according to their own deeply held philosophies about charity, relief, and culture. Relieving Allied Europe became a quest to instill order by adhering to American conceptions of proper wartime aid and ideal social organization. In all of their efforts, ARC personnel persisted with the task of showing Allied Europe that the United States was on hand with aid.

In their mission to relieve Europe and circumvent Allied unrest, ARC Departments of Civil Affairs made feeding hungry civilians a top priority. Ernest Bicknell explained the strategic importance of fighting hunger when he warned of the danger of food shortages in Naples, Italy. There, Bicknell explained, "a large, poor, disorderly population" had become "desperate" for food, causing them to "go out in the street and parade around and shout and get ugly."[53] In Naples and throughout Europe, food seemed the surest way to improve civilian morale, to not only quell rumbling bellies but also quash rumbling political unrest. Across Allied Europe, ARC workers set up canteens and food distribution points where personnel rationed milk, beans, rice, lard, tinned meats, and canned soups to civilians. Tens of thousands of Europeans received food, both uncooked and prepared, each day. Wherever they went, ARC workers took great care to indicate the origins of the assistance. "Served always under the American flag," wrote one ARC worker, "that sustaining mixture of rice, beans, and beef was the original herald of American friendship."[54] Food promised to nourish European civilians as it nurtured Allied-American alliances.

ARC workers deemed the provision of housing for displaced civilians another critical element in the quest to restore and preserve Allied stability. In Paris, Florence, Saloniki, and other large cities where refugees congregated, ARC workers scrambled to find sufficient and adequate temporary housing. In liberated war zones, personnel repaired damaged buildings and distributed furniture, clothing, and other household needs at reduced prices so that returning civilians could rebuild their lives. These basic foundations must be restored, aid workers stressed, to provide a normal, orderly life for refugees.[55] The mere provision of shelter, however, did not go far enough. ARC personnel also saw a role for positive aesthetics in counteracting civilian discontent. They therefore worked to make refugee housing not just functional but also attractive. It boosted "the morale of the refugees to make the difference between a hovel and a home," ARC literature explained, "to make the difference between constant grumbling and even bitterness on the one hand, and contentment on the other."[56] To ensure social order while winning civilian hearts and minds, ARC personnel did what they could to restore some semblance of normal home life.

For many ARC workers, the ultimate goal—and the most effective way to secure social stability in the long term—was to restore economic self-sufficiency. Although ARC leaders recognized the importance of temporary food and shelter, most also emphasized that "nothing should be undertaken that involves the continued support of healthy persons, men or women, in idleness."[57] Making citizens productive, self-supporting, and industrious was paramount. To do this, ARC staff required aid recipients to participate in productive labor whenever possible and set up work assistance programs to facilitate that outcome. "Anything that we can do to help refugees get back on farms or help them to earn a livelihood on jobs to which they are accustomed," leaders proclaimed, "is well worth our while."[58] Across the continent, the ARC hired thousands of local civilians to staff its canteens, offices, and other relief sites. ARC personnel distributed farm equipment and seeds to promote agricultural work, measuring success by the numbers of gardens planted and cultivated.[59] They also established hundreds of *ouvroirs*, or workrooms, where civilians sewed clothes and shoes for refugees, knitted bandages for soldiers, and even crafted U.S. flags for the ARC cause.[60]

This gainful employment served multifaceted American interests, both practical and ideological. It created a local source of supplies by providing materials needed for ARC military and civilian relief work. It kept potentially rowdy noncombatants occupied and off the streets. Finally, as one ARC worker explained, it taught civilians "to be self-supporting," helping "prepare them for normal conditions of living."[61] As such a rationalization suggests, ARC personnel saw work relief not only as a way to restore economic order but also as a means to inculcate self-discipline. Work promised yet another moral benefit to women. Throughout Europe, ARC leaders warned, thousands of women "had been compelled to forsake their homes and were wandering alone and without support in the great centers." The wide provision of ouvroirs and canteen service posts, personnel reasoned, provided a "means of lessening the danger which lies in wait"— in other words, preventing women's presumed descent into prostitution and sexual deviance.[62] By keeping women off the streets, ARC workers pledged to protect them from such moral threats while schooling them in the virtue of paid labor.

While most ARC civilian aid promised to achieve the twin strategic benefits of creating social stability and demonstrating American concern, these outcomes did not always coexist easily. The propaganda value of aid sometimes trumped other goals, particularly the promotion of self-sufficiency, leading to institutional tensions over the fundamental purpose of the ARC's relief. These disagreements were particularly acute with regard to the issue of monetary aid. In addition to creating jobs and providing food and housing, the ARC also gave out substantial sums of hard cash. Perhaps the most monumental of these financial relief undertakings occurred in April 1918, when the Commission to Italy organized a large-scale cash distribution to assist the families of soldiers. Giving cash handouts without any accountability for how recipients spent the money defied contemporary theories of scientific charity. Personnel in Italy argued, however, that any "objections the professional expert in relief might raise in theory is silenced in this instance by the results obtained."[63] For two weeks in April 1918, the Department of Civil Affairs distributed 6,850,000 Lire (about US$1 million) to Italian civilians. Dozens of representatives visited 8,323 different towns and villages and distributed cash to a reported 318,000 families of Italian soldiers and others whom local governments approved as worthy of aid.[64]

Cash distributions, in Italy and elsewhere, were clearly designed for their publicity potential. "Staging our visits," reported one representative, "was of prime importance."[65] ARC workers planned their visits with local leaders ahead of time to ensure well-publicized receptions. As they rode into towns wearing American military uniforms, they met staged local receptions and crowds of people. Along with cash, aid recipients received flags and other trinkets, as well as postcards that pictured the U.S. and Italian flags woven together or a portrait of Woodrow Wilson (figure 4.4). ARC workers then asked each family to send these to their husbands and fathers at the front. Personnel argued that it was easy "to imagine the effect upon a soldier's spirits to learn that his family has been cared for," maintaining that soldiers would be more efficient fighters if they were not anxious about their families.[66] For Ernest Bicknell, a committed adherent

Figure 4.4 Italian children given an American flag to hold while receiving ARC supplies. ca. 1918. American National Red Cross Collection, Library of Congress.

to the philosophies of scientific assistance, these methods raised grave concern. "As each family will receive a very trifling sum, my first inclination would be to regard the project as an admirable method of wasting money," he complained. Although he criticized the blatant propaganda, Bicknell ultimately opted to trust in the judgment of the ARC personnel in Italy. "I hope that this distribution will be justified by the results," he wrote, adding, "If the Italian people are as easily pleased and 'bucked up' as they are said to be, it may be that the results will be worth the cost." Those who organized the cash distribution certainly declared this to be the case. They reported that they had been "received everywhere with the greatest enthusiasm, not because of the money received ... but because of the pledge of America's actual participation in the war."[67] Others put it more bluntly, cheering that "no better propaganda could have been done" and praising the cash distribution for countering the socialist and pacifist tendencies of "a wavering population."[68] The members of the Commission to Italy justified their deviance from proper, professional methods of relief by declaring their success in showcasing the American alliance. This outcome mattered as much as, if not more than, the material relief afforded and the broader social improvements attained.

Wartime civilian relief was thus in many ways a deliberate, carefully scripted public diplomacy that had clear benefits for the United States. By shoring up the material and psychological well-being of Allied societies, aid intended to ensure that Europe's democratic civilian populations stayed physically and men-tally invested in winning the war while developing a lasting appreciation for the United States. At the same time, it aimed to build a commitment to produc-tive labor, encourage an idealized home life and other moral behaviors, and foster social stability—all values accorded a central place in most contempo-rary American middle-class worldviews. In so doing, relief promised to lay the groundwork for a more orderly and democratic postwar world, an environment fertile for Wilson's peacetime visions to take hold. Visible proof of American alliance mattered enormously in this calculus. If civilians did not realize that aid came from the United States, its morale and diplomatic effects would be lost. Throughout Allied Europe, ARC civilian aid wore its origins on its khaki-colored sleeves.

*

Although ARC civilian relief served clear U.S. national interests, it would be a mistake to characterize it as purely propaganda or solely in the service of the Wilsonian state. For many of the American social workers, physicians, nurses, and other personnel who designed and administered ARC civilian aid projects, the overarching goal was not just to bolster the U.S. wartime cause, but to ensure that the war did not impair European health, welfare, and social reform efforts. Fulfilling this objective and taking part in an international quest to better human well-being had motivated many ARC personnel to go to Europe in the first place. Once there, they continued to act with these same convictions in mind. Thanks to the ARC's vast war fund and the AEF's ruling that work "done by the Civil Affairs Department of the Red Cross...is not connected with the work for American troops," these more cosmopolitan civilian relief workers enjoyed substantial resources and autonomy to design and implement their assistance in a manner consistent with their ambitions.[69] Although they prioritized food, shelter, economic aid, and other emergency material assistance, ARC workers soon began to initiate long-term projects to improve public health, increase local medical and hygienic knowledge, and ensure positive childhood development. In their minds, all such activities legitimately fell under the banner of "wartime relief." In pursuing these projects, ARC workers did act alone. They forged new partnerships with like-minded reformers and agencies in Europe, built on earlier collaborative efforts with the Rockefeller Foundation, and expanded the existing efforts of other U.S. charities. Throughout Allied Europe—particularly in France and Italy, the largest relief sites—ARC workers and their allies labored to ensure that civilians survived the present crisis and permanently thrived. Many ARC workers, in short, imagined themselves to be taking part in a shared international crusade for better health. Nonetheless, as they interacted with fellow reformers and the objects of their assistance, they could not escape the fact that an uneven power dynamic inevitably underlay their relationships with European aid recipients. A genuinely mutual international exchange proved an elusive goal.

Homer Folks, Ernest Bicknell, Paul Kellogg, Edward Devine, and their fellow U.S. health and welfare professionals had known about the social dislocations of war before they ever left home, yet only upon seeing Europe firsthand did they realize the full magnitude of the problem. Two and a half years of war had sapped the financial and human resources devoted to social welfare and halted many European reform initiatives. Devine lamented that French hospitals, orphanages, reformatories, asylums, and charities, "the whole vast network of organized philanthropy, whether official, semi-official, or voluntary" had been "profoundly affected by the war." To complicate the situation further, French reformers had abandoned social experiments such as improved housing, public health education, prenatal and infant health programs, and playgrounds. As Devine understood, the war decreased wealth, health, food, and living standards and created "an actual slackening of the effort to prevent these evils, even as they exist in normal times."[70] Things were no better in Italy, as Kellogg, Bicknell, and Devine discovered on their seven-week inspection tour of that country in the fall of 1917. Kellogg marveled at the destructiveness of war and its effects on both land and civilians. He described Venice, a northern city in disarray after the Battle of Caporetto, as "Coney Island raised to the Nth power, or better the World Fair City at Chicago, built solid and weakened with age." Even in Naples and Messina, in the southern toe of Italy and far from the battlefields, he recorded "bitter evidence of the reach and spread of the misery caused by the invasion." The war had uprooted civilian life, yet Kellogg maintained, "The issue of this war, tremendous as it is, is less than the issue with which we shall be confronted at its close."[71] In Italy and France, and in the roughly two dozen other nations to which the War Council sent aid, American health and welfare professionals concurred that they must tackle every dimension of this social emergency.

Even as they worried about the extent of the humanitarian disaster, ARC workers also recognized their overseas service as a once-in-a-lifetime chance to join like-minded reformers in addressing international health issues. Here though, a constant tension lingered over how they must engage with Europeans, as equals or as guides. Many truly imagined themselves as partners in a global humanitarian crusade. While Homer Folks regretted being "absent from America during the most interesting period of her history," he consoled himself with his faith that his efforts were "an international enterprise in spirit and we are all taking part in it on both sides of the water."[72] In Folks's mind, ARC work was to be a purely cooperative enterprise. In France, he explained, "We aim not to set up distinctly American enterprises. We aim to work in French steps, in institutions they set up."[73] Edward Devine echoed these internationalist sentiments. "The distress and the suffering of the war itself, and the tremendous burden of recon-struction that will come after the war is over," he asserted, "can only be met by the concerted generosity and the statesmanship of the entire world."[74] One ARC nurse in Italy went a step further, noting that she and her colleagues were "work-ing in a country whose civilization is older, and in many respects more advanced than our own." With this realization, she concluded that Americans "had a good deal to learn and to receive as well as to give."[75] For many ARC workers, time in Europe offered a valuable chance for shared exchange.

And yet, even as ARC workers tended to emphasize the cooperative nature of their assistance, they frequently assumed a leadership role in aid projects. Devine may have declared that relief work "must be born by all the great nations," but he also believed that the United States had a special obligation to contribute to the cause "because of the great prosperity that has come to us by the war itself, and... because we have ourselves been relieved of the disasters, distress and hardship."[76] Paul Kellogg went further, assuming that the war had presented Americans with a unique opportunity to influence European society in accor-dance with their own values and ideas. By giving "some of the most experienced executives in social work in America... the resources and free rein to bend to the tasks in hand," he explained, the ARC had provided them with the chance to engage in nothing less than a project of "nation-wide social engineering." Through their work, American humanitarians would be "making social history, carrying forward demonstrations in human conservation which may prove of value to the whole world."[77] While such mentalities underlay ARC efforts in Western Europe, they proved even stronger among ARC workers in areas like Russia, Eastern Europe, and the Near East, regions that Americans generally considered less advanced or developed than their western European counter-parts.[78] ARC personnel may have pledged to assist fellow social reformers but, as Devine's and Kellogg's comments suggest, many also felt a potent duty to uplift Europeans and instruct them in the particular value of American approaches to health and welfare. This set of tensions manifested itself throughout the ARC's time in Europe.

Whether they saw themselves as leading the way or as joining Europeans as equal partners, ARC workers generally agreed that they must confront the social dislocations of war in much the same way as they had tackled health and welfare problems back in the United States. For this reason, ARC civilian relief bore a striking resemblance to contemporary American social reform campaigns. In their emergency relief work for civilians, ARC personnel emphasized the impor-tance of maintaining the most basic tenets of professional social work, insisting on careful planning and expert oversight. In spite of the war, Department of Civil Affairs leaders expected "that certain minimum standards should be observed—such as home visiting, keeping of accounts, cooperation with other agencies engaged in similar work."[79] To verify the efficiency and accountability of civilian relief activities, ARC Departments of Civil Affairs sent traveling inspectors to examine all ARC relief sites. To ensure that aid recipients deserved assistance and did not become dependent on charity, they refused to distribute material aid randomly. Only families deemed truly in need, either by ARC inspectors or by trusted local authorities, were deemed eligible to receive food, housing, and clothing rations. In an attempt to provide safe and sanitary housing, ARC inspectors limited the number of people living and sleeping in each house and made sure there were appropriate facilities for cooking, bathing, and outdoor play for children. By implementing relief according to their own best practices, ARC personnel attempted to control it and to mold it in a way they saw fit.[80]

Maintaining the professional standards of emergency relief was important, but if ARC personnel were to really "make social history," they believed, they must take far bolder steps. Across Europe, ARC Departments of Civil Relief therefore moved well beyond the provision of basic material needs and took steps to minister to more extensive and comprehensive civilian health needs. In Allied cities, towns, and rural areas, from France to Italy to Belgium to Russia, ARC personnel established hundreds of clinics and dispensaries and dozens of hospitals, all specifically for civilians. In areas where epidemics of typhus, malaria, and cholera raged, including the Near East and Serbia, ARC workers treated ill individuals while undertaking broad environmental and sanitary reform projects. While the Departments of Civil Affairs provided such medical aid to all noncombatants, they demonstrated particular concern for children. Many ARC clinics and hospitals specialized in infant and childhood illnesses, while other institutions offered preventive health measures to make sure that children developed properly and stayed healthy in the first place. ARC personnel provided school lunches and erected special stations to distribute milk and cocoa—health foods of the day—to European youngsters. They operated or funded scores of orphanages, playgrounds, fresh air camps, and industrial schools across the continent. In each of these ways, ARC personnel hoped to better the long-term health and welfare outcomes of European civilians by providing them with the social services that the war had staunched.[81]

While this mission to make relief a more comprehensive endeavor underlay ARC efforts across the continent, its most dramatic examples occurred in France and Italy. Because these countries received the most resources from the War Council, they were also the sites where ARC personnel found the greatest latitude to experiment with radical new approaches to relief. So it was from his office in the Department of Civil Affairs in Paris that Homer Folks "set in motion some very large things...which will have substantial results long after we have all gone home."[82] In Italy, Chester Aldrich followed in his colleague's footsteps in a number of these ventures. Together, these two men and their staffs radically expanded the range of activities considered to fall within the bounds of war relief, justifying all such work as part of the global struggle for better health. As they did, they provided the models and precedents for ARC leaders to follow in other regions of Europe, both during the war years and in the years to come.

A campaign against tuberculosis marked the ARC's first move toward comprehensive long-term relief and the first attempt to permanently influence European welfare. Since the late nineteenth century, tuberculosis, a leading cause of death in all industrial nations, had become the target of an all-out public health crusade in Western Europe and the United States. The Great War, however, had largely brought those campaigns to a halt. A decrease in resources for fighting the disease, a lack of civilian access to medical care, widespread malnourishment, and overcrowding among troops and refugees all threatened to cause an upsurge in morbidity and mortality rates. Without active intervention, decades of effort to control tuberculosis risked being reversed in the course of several years.[83] Preventing the resurgence of tuberculosis by rekindling French antituberculosis activities was thus a project that appealed mightily to Homer Folks. Through the ARC, he found a chance to do just that. Shortly after the United States entered the war, leaders of the Rockefeller Foundation called on the ARC War Council to join them in a joint antituberculosis campaign in France. Wickliffe Rose and George Vincent, directors of the Foundation's International Health Board, pledged $8 million to fund the project and looked to the ARC to administer it on the ground.[84] In July 1917, shortly after he arrived in France, Homer Folks set to work. In designing this venture, his Department of Civil Affairs worked closely with a commission of French physicians, health officials, and other citizens—all appointed by the French government. Noted figures in the American antituberculosis movement joined them, boosting the campaign's prestige. Its directors included Livingston Farrand, the chair of the National Association for the Study and Prevention of Tuberculosis, and William Charles White, a professor of medicine at the University of Pittsburgh. The war had presented these U.S. health professionals with "an unprecedented opportunity to promote scientific public health work in France," and they jumped at the chance.[85] In France, ARC workers and their allies took steps to increase the number of hospital beds for civilians. They erected regional clinics for examinations and outpatient care. They lobbied for new laws to require reporting tuberculosis cases. Mobile dispensaries and motion picture projectors carried treatments and educational messages to all parts of the country. All of these efforts mirrored tactics used in both the United States and Western European nations before the war. Such activities soon captured the attention of health reformers beyond France. In November 1917, at the request of the Italian Red Cross and the Italian government, Farrand and White launched a parallel campaign in Italy.[86] In both countries, ARC personnel and their allies revived European antituberculosis work while aiming to lay "the basis of its future lasting effort."[87]

The antituberculosis campaigns marked only the beginning of the ARC's comprehensive relief initiatives. To create the foot soldiers for French and Italian tuberculosis campaigns and other public health initiatives, ARC personnel launched programs to educate civilian women in the principles of public health and nursing. Both the French and Italian Departments of Civil Affairs opened formal training schools in major cities that taught local women to be public health educators. Through a four-month series of lectures and demonstrations, American and European physicians and nurses instructed students about child welfare, hygiene, nutrition, obstetrical nursing, common diseases, and sanitation. To reach an even greater number of civilians, ARC personnel also offered shorter, more basic classes on hygiene and health education to interested women in Paris, Lyon, Florence, Milan, and other urban centers. ARC personnel regarded these European laywomen as especially valuable because they understood local language, culture, and prejudices. Although only a fraction of European women might take their courses, ARC workers assumed that those pupils would return to their hometowns to educate others, thereby disseminating contemporary public health methods and beliefs throughout the countryside. This army of trained women promised to assist ARC personnel in their goal of improving health standards on the continent. Through their classes, ARC leaders hoped to permanently influence the ways French and Italian women understood and influenced child health in their nations.[88]

While ARC staff trained civilian women to carry biomedical and hygienic ideas to remote French and Italian towns and villages, they also established model institutions of healthy and hygienic living to present these concepts in a more choreographed manner. This project began in earnest in September 1917, when Folks requested a $1 million appropriation from the ARC War Council to construct two permanent demonstration sites in France. One was rural, in the Department of the Eure-et-Loir in north-central France, and the other urban, in the nineteenth arrondissement, a working-class ward in Paris. Staffed by American and French personnel, each proposed center was to include a tuberculosis dispensary, an infant welfare and milk station, a prenatal dispensary, and a bacteriological laboratory. They were also to provide relief funds for families that had been affected economically by illness, arrange for the inspection and improvement of housing conditions, and work to prevent contagious diseases. The health centers aimed to bring together dozens of contemporary ideas about health and welfare under one roof, packaged and ready to present to French civilians. Through them, it seemed, the Department of Civil Affairs was turning the war zone into a veritable settlement house.[89]

The scope of the proposed health centers went far beyond any previous type of wartime assistance and raised questions about whether such activities should legitimately be categorized as war relief. War Council chair Henry Davison had his doubts. In early 1918, he considered cutting the million-dollar appropriation. "All our energies must now be bent toward the winning of the war," he reasoned, "and it is felt that this does not directly contribute to that end."[90] In response, Folks and his allies countered that such work would in fact "have immediate and substantial military value." They rationalized education and preventive public health work as well within the bounds of war relief because these projects boosted France's overall vitality and its long-term stability.[91] Ultimately, influential voices at the Rockefeller Foundation settled the matter. In May 1918, after visiting with Folks in person, IHB director George Vincent expressed his full support for Folks's plan. Health education work among civilians had an "immediate and vital bearing on war efficiency," Vincent declared, "To limit work to hospital and other direct service to soldiers would seriously weaken America's aid to her allies. The full program," he concluded, "is essential."[92] Convinced, Davison subsequently approved the million-dollar appropriation. By 1918, public health education had become as much a part of ARC civilian assistance as the provision of food and housing. As Folks and other ARC workers saw it, this was their chance to leave "a permanent impression upon the public health situation" in Europe.[93]

Buoyed by the success of these sites, Folks and his colleagues soon conceived of other demonstration projects, this time targeting infant and child health specifically. Wartime conditions in Europe had produced declines in birth rates and high rates of infant and childhood disease and mortality, all while stalling prewar efforts to improve child health and to educate mothers about proper child hygiene.[94] Compelled by the logic that "unless the babies of these years were saved there would be no children in the years to come, no nation of the future," and that "saving France cannot be done without saving her young life," ARC workers vowed to join their French counterparts in combating these setbacks through treatment and education.[95] Even as they planned to collaborate with French colleagues, however, ARC personnel also hoped to provide instruction to them. As members of the ARC Bureau of Needy Children and Infant Mortality put it, the goal was "to combine the French ideas and French methods of dealing with the child welfare problem, with a practical demonstration of certain very important and fundamental ideas that had as yet hardly been attempted in France."[96] Successfully navigating between assistance and oversight, ARC staff believed, was critical if they were to achieve real improvements in the French child health situation.

The mission to improve the long-term welfare of French children through public education began in April 1918 in Lyons, France, when a group of ARC personnel and French child health professionals joined to open the Exposition d'Enfance, a large fair designed to showcase modern methods of child health and welfare. Held in a grand hall requisitioned by the mayor of Lyons, the Exposition housed a cinema and a lecture room capable of accommodating one thousand French civilians who came to hear about health topics. A number of smaller sites demonstrated specific ideas about health and hygiene. From inside a glass demonstration house, American and French doctors and nurses showed audiences in twice daily shows how to properly wash and dress babies, while in the Jardin d'enfants, an American physical education expert taught children daily exercises (figure 4.5). A children's hospital, modeled on a modern American institution, alerted French visitors to the types of institutions they might build for their children. Dietary experts gave advice on general nutrition and on how to sterilize milk; gleaming dental chairs and oversized toothbrushes taught visitors about oral hygiene. Posters throughout the Exposition alerted visitors to the dangers of alcoholism to unborn babies, the death rates of tuberculosis throughout the world, and to French laws relating to child welfare (figure 4.6). Child health expositions proved wildly popular, first in Lyons but

Figure 4.5 Peering through glass windows, mothers and children watch a demonstration on infant health at an American Red Cross Child Welfare Exposition in France. ca. 1918. American National Red Cross Collection, Library of Congress.

Figure 4.6 An ARC poster in France advertises the health demands of French infants, including "to be nourished regularly," "healthy relatives," "mother's milk," and "to be protected from flies." Artist Jacques Carlu, ca. 1918. World War I Posters Collection, Library of Congress.

soon throughout France and Italy. The Lyons Baby Show opened to a crowd of twelve hundred people. Over the three weeks that it ran, average daily attendance reached nine thousand. Based on this success, the French Department of Civil Affairs established six other large expositions. They also organized smaller traveling shows to carry the message to other French cities and, eventually, to Italian ones as well.[97]

The overarching goal of these expositions was to ensure the immediate and long-term health of Europe's future democratic citizens, by encouraging existing French efforts and introducing new methods, fresh from the United States. Admittedly, many of these displays broadcast child welfare ideals that were as accepted among French medical professionals as they were among their American colleagues. Yet ARC workers also assumed that only with "American scientific spirit, American public health organization, and American sympathy," as Folks proclaimed at the opening of the Lyons exposition, could the United States best help Allied Europe improve its health.[98] Folks's words spoke volumes to the power dynamics at play. ARC personnel were not merely trying to share scientific or public health ideals—a theoretically universal concept—but to offer Europe the benefits of distinctly *American* approaches to child health. In the Expositions d'Enfance, as in so much of their work, ARC personnel tread a fine line between assisting Europeans and trying to uplift them.

ARC epidemic campaigns, courses for women, health centers, and baby shows all aimed to improve the physical health of European civilians while, at the same time, trying to inculcate new behaviors among them. In Italy, efforts to achieve both of these goals were most fully realized when ARC leaders decided to build a model city. In late February 1918, Venetian consul B. Harvey Carroll and Chester Aldrich, the director of the Department of Civil Affairs in Italy, came up with a plan to construct a colony outside Pisa for two thousand Venetian refugees. The endeavor, Carroll contended, would make a ready appeal "to the American press and to the American public" and would serve "as a concrete example of what America can do when she bows her neck to it."[99] The pair soon persuaded interested Italian parties to support the enterprise. On May 1, ARC and Italian workers broke ground on thirty acres of formerly private property that the Italian government requisitioned for the project. More than simply refugee housing, ARC leaders imagined the Pisa Village as a "modern American city" and a way to showcase ideas of health and welfare in Italy. Designers followed contemporary theories of hygienic housing, such as ensuring an abundance of light and air in each home. The planned living space included eighty concrete homes, divided into several apartments of two to four rooms each. The village also included a small garden, offices, shops, a community kitchen, a church, workrooms, schools, a hospital, and a concrete replica of Venice's famous Piazza San Marco—"all that makes for the happiness and safety of the family."[100] The ARC advertised the village to Italian refugees as a place where they could reestablish their lives and their communities, support themselves through employment rather than charity, and raise their families in a stable and orderly climate. The Pisa Village, as conceptualized, was to be a lasting testament to the United States' innovative approaches to humanitarian assistance and a permanent model for Italian social reformers to follow. Yet, as it turned out, the Pisa Village was not even a temporary fix to the refugee situation. The November 1918 Armistice occurred prior to the village's completion, making it possible for refugees to return to their homes in the north. Members of the Italian Department of Civil Affairs never had the chance to test this most ambitious of attempts at comprehensive reform and social engineering (a fact that did not prevent War Council leaders from advertising it widely in the United States).[101] If nothing else, the ARC's efforts outside Pisa indicated just how all encompassing wartime aid had become by the time the conflict ended.

*

In 1917 and 1918, driven by international humanitarian commitments and by the desire to put their professional training to use during a momentous period in world history, the ARC's personnel thus expanded the definition of civilian relief to include a wide array of health and welfare interventions. Officially, ARC leadership instructed staff in each nation to offer assistance "not in the American way," but "in a way which would be satisfactory to the people of that country."[102] In certain respects, ARC workers lived up to this charge. Personnel worked alongside local individuals and agencies to administer relief. Because their presence in any country required the authorization of the assisted government, an implied consent existed for their activities. In general, ARC personnel assumed that they were taking part in a much broader project of enhancing international welfare. Yet no matter how cosmopolitan they imagined themselves to be, ARC workers could not avoid the fact that, as middle-class experts and American administrators of humanitarian aid, they inevitably had the upper hand in an unbalanced relationship. ARC workers consistently attempted to influence and shape European peoples and societies according to their own standards and assumptions, seeing this as necessary if they were to leave a lasting imprint on the continent. The power dynamics intrinsic to foreign assistance assured that it could never be the truly international, egalitarian enterprise that so many ARC personnel proclaimed it to be.

Furthermore, even though many of the ARC's personnel understood their efforts as an international social justice issue—something larger than mere national interest—their comprehensive relief activities invariably served the Wilson administration's needs as well. By targeting immediate health outcomes among the Allies, ARC workers helped to promote social stability and build support for the United States. By taking steps to buttress the long-term health of Allied civilians, they worked to ensure that the citizens of Europe's democratic nations would be fit and prepared to implement Wilsons' liberal internationalist visions once the war came to an end. For many ARC personnel, of course, serving both national and internationalist interests was never contradictory. True victory in a total war for global civilization, they believed, demanded more than just defeating Central Powers forces. It meant taking every possible measure to reduce human suffering and to perfect international society.

Assessing the Significance of Wartime Civilian Relief

At eleven o'clock in the morning of November 11, 1918, the Armistice termi-
nating hostilities between Germany and the Allied Powers went into effect.
Buoyed by the hope that the Great War had been a war to end all wars, ARC
personnel joined Allied civilians in a celebration to surpass all other celebra-
tions. "The news of the signing of the armistice was received in Paris on Monday
a little after eleven in the morning and for two days we have been living through
excitement and joy and celebration such as I never expect to see again," wrote
one worker to her family, "You have probably read all about it in the papers
but *nothing* can really describe it."[103] Clelia Mosher, a physician from California,
attempted to convey the experience to her mother. "I will try to tell you the
story of this time as well as I can," she wrote, "tho' it must be totally inadequate
as an expression of what I have lived through in these two wonderful days." As
Mosher understood, neither her mother nor anyone else in the United States
could truly empathize with the revelry, for "one needs to live thro' those terrible
days of doubt and suspense to put the real joy into this celebration of the cessa-
tion of the terrible war."[104]

With the conclusion of conflict, the ARC's wartime raison d'être—to relieve
Allied noncombatants—ceased as well. Just as ARC workers like Mosher tried
to put the war into perspective and describe it to their friends and families back
home, they also used the moment as an opportunity to take stock of what their
aid work had accomplished. Yet even before the Armistice—indeed, ever since
the first wartime commissions arrived in June 1917—ARC workers had engaged
in a continual process of evaluating, reevaluating, and attempting to explain the
significance of civilian relief. During their time in Europe, many became convinced of the importance of their service, while others expressed reservations
about the utility and purpose of the humanitarian intervention. Those observing
ARC work from the outside, meanwhile, formed their own opinions of its value.
Collectively, these varied appraisals contributed to broader popular discourses
and understandings about the place of humanitarianism in U.S. foreign relations
and the nature of American responsibility to Allied Europe.

According to its most ardent proponents, ARC wartime relief succeeded in
its goal of projecting the authenticity of American humanity and concern, demonstrating the U.S. commitment to Allied civilians as it forged lasting bonds
between them. Almost universally, leaders within the upper echelons of the
organization trumpeted the organization's accomplishments in this regard. As
War Council chair Henry Davison heralded, "The gratitude the people feel for
what the American people are doing through the Red Cross is beyond description…America is today a rainbow," he explained, toward which Europe "looks
as the sign of comfort, hope, and victory."[105] Ernest Bicknell reported that he,

personally, had "found it impossible to escape the rush of affectionate emotion" that Europeans poured upon him and other Americans.[106] Mabel Boardman, visiting France and Italy in 1918, marveled at the extent of civilian relief operations in both countries, clearly realizing that "the original purpose of the Red Cross," to work among the battlefield wounded, had "become a secondary matter."[107] Many personnel outside the administrative hierarchy echoed the glowing assessments of their superiors, frequently affirming their international humanitarian obligations and the necessity of their involvement in Europe. "These civilian victims need relief as much as soldiers," wrote one ARC worker in France upon seeing the results of wartime devastation. "Thank God we are over pretending to be neutral and took our part like men and women!"[108] Other personnel extolled the ARC for its achievement in forging bonds between the United States and its allies. A worker in Italy understood its relief as "one of the connecting links between the hearts of the Italian *contadini* and those of the millions of generous ones back home," while another credited the organization with having "established and affirmed a link of brotherhood between the two Nations which now, no doubt, will strengthen the already existing friendship by a lasting alliance."[109] For ARC leaders and many ARC workers, the organization's on-the-ground effects confirmed the rhetorical promises of the War Council's institutional ideology.

Many ARC personnel, so convinced of their obligation to relieve their international compatriots and of the ARC's special role in this mission, labored to persuade their fellow citizens of the same. "If American donors could see how much Italians appreciated their gifts," one man noted, "it would give some idea of the appreciation which the valiant and suffering people of Italy feel for every token of affection and help which reaches them from their allies of the United States."[110] Clelia Mosher likewise defended the importance of American giving to her sister. "If you could see what your money is doing, how it is putting heart into the people here," she wrote, "you would realize how worth while it is."[111] ARC workers further justified their assistance by highlighting the dignity and worth of European aid recipients. "These refugees are not paupers," one ARC worker wrote. "It is no discredit for a woman with little children to be in need of help when her husband is earning soldier's wages at the front and the family home, business, and property is gone."[112] Another woman, describing refugees to a friend, explained that they were "refined, decent people ... just the type of people you would find in a small New England town."[113] By advancing such positive impressions of the recipients of civilian relief, American personnel rationalized the ARC's intervention as a legitimate charitable undertaking for international peers, one that their friends and family had a clear obligation to support. In so doing, they reinforced the War Council's scripted public messages.

It was not only insiders who appreciated and proclaimed the ARC's value. Both European and American observers extolled its work in private correspondence and official statements. Felix Frankfurter, assistant to secretary of war Newton Baker, celebrated the ARC as "one of the most important agencies in affecting the morale" of civilians, affirming that "the relation of the civil to the military morale is evident," while U.S. ambassador to Italy Thomas Nelson Page confided to Wilson that the ARC was not only "doing a great work here" but that it also had "undoubtedly, an excellent effect as propaganda."[114] Other State Department officials in Europe joined Page in lauding the "very favorable effect" that the ARC projects had on public opinion.[115] European leaders confirmed these reports. French president Raymond Poincaré thanked the ARC for demonstrating "to the widows, to the orphans of France, a beneficence and generosity, the memory of which shall never vanish from our hearts," and Italian premier Vittorio Orlando commended its "highly effective, intelligent help," rendered "with true spirit of unity and brotherhood."[116] So, too, did General Pershing. "Our people may well be proud of the record of the Red Cross," he reported to Henry Davison. "In giving prompt and efficient relief the Red Cross has won the eternal gratitude of millions of people. The Armies of France, from commanders down, testify to the great good it has accomplished."[117] Raymond Fosdick, chair of the Commission on Training Camp Activities, sung similar praises. "The civilian relief work of the Red Cross is perhaps its best organized branch," Fosdick concluded in a report to the AEF. "I believe that this practical, homely assistance, which the American people, through the Red Cross, are bringing to the French in the hour of adversity, will have a lasting effect upon the relationship between the two countries." So complimentary was Fosdick, in fact, that he recommended to the AEF that "the time has come when ALL relief work abroad which is not carried on by or through the Red Cross should be prevented in every way possible so as to eliminate the inefficiency and waste which inevitably accompany the management of small, competing enterprises."[118] Given the ARC's clear success as America's principle civilian relief agency, he argued, its special status among aid organizations deserved to be made permanent. For many outside observers, both American and European, the ARC had proven its worth and lived up to War Council leaders' claims.

Enthusiasm was widespread, but it was by no means universal. For all those in Europe who believed that the ARC had put its ideological promises into action, others proved quite skeptical of the association's intentions and its effectiveness. Some condemned ARC assistance as nothing more than a crass attempt to win public affection. "We are here for propaganda it seems," complained John Dos Passos, a twenty-one-year-old ARC volunteer in Italy. "We will be used in the most conspicuous way possible—we must show Italy that America is behind them...We are here to help cajole the poor devils of Italians into fighting."[119] Others criticized the ARC's domination of relief. Raymond Fosdick may have supported the ARC's "policy of combination and co-ordination," but it bred resentment from Edith Wharton and many other philanthropists who found themselves displaced by the sprawling ARC relief infrastructure. ARC claims to efficient, accountable spending faced occasional reports to the contrary, with some ARC workers testifying to widespread "graft and loose handling of finances."[120] Diplomatic hurdles also arose from time to time during the ARC's stay in Europe, most obviously with regard to the organization's brief but turbulent relationship with the Bolshevik government. Finally, individual ARC workers sometimes invoked the ire of both their colleagues and aid recipients. Carter Harrison, an ARC volunteer in France, complained that "favoritism was shown in the assignment of personal friends, business associates and bearers of letters from friends and associates," allowing "every chap with a pull in the J. P. Morgan realms of high finance" to claim the best positions.[121] Perhaps the most egregious of these examples was that of Edward Ryan, the ARC commissioner to Serbia. Toward the end of the war, the War Council began receiving reports that accused Ryan of being "overbearing, intolerant, high-handed, and incompetent," leaving "his staff demoralized, and his work, as a result, inefficient." In late September 1918, hoping to forestall further complaints, ARC leaders relieved Ryan of his post.[122] ARC wartime civilian relief did enjoy considerable acclaim, but never unanimous approval.

Such criticisms, however, do not belie the fact that from June 1917 to November 1918, ARC civilian relief represented a fundamental and overwhelmingly popular part of U.S. involvement in the Great War. It complemented governmental wartime strategy. It also provided a nonmilitary mechanism for U.S. citizens to engage with Europe, whether as firsthand participants or as audiences for the stories and reports that ARC personnel relayed back to the United States. Through the ARC, Americans had found a means to fulfill their new international humanitarian obligations. This had been the War Council's promise, the message that its leaders had worked so hard to construct and disseminate in the wartime United States. In the seventeen months that ARC commissions worked in wartime Europe, the ideological premises that underpinned the War Council's public messages and its institutional ideology appeared quite secure. But had this been simply a wartime phenomenon? Or could the international humanitarian ethos and this new type of U.S. foreign involvement remain sustainable in the postwar period? After the Armistice, ARC leaders in Europe and the United States began taking steps to disband the wartime commissions. On March 1, 1919, Wilson dissolved the War Council, restoring the ARC to peacetime leadership. By that point, most of the thousands of Americans who had worked for the ARC had returned to the United States. The end of the war, however, did not bring an end to Europe's humanitarian crises. Even as the ARC shifted to a peacetime footing, its postwar leaders began planning for a prolonged intervention in Europe, hoping to address the myriad social problems left in the wake of war. In the years after the Armistice, the ARC's international humanitarianism would again be put to the test, this time in an entirely new field of foreign relations.

5

Rebuilding Europe

On November 16, 1918, five days after the signing of the Armistice, an ARC worker in Paris wrote a letter to his family in the United States, the first line of which summed up that heady moment concisely: "Since I wrote you last Saturday—well,—it's a different world." The abrupt conclusion of World War I changed everything in Europe. ARC workers could not help but wonder what it meant for them. "Everybody's plans are uncertain now of course," explained another to her family. "Nobody knows anything about future plans for what we'll allow."[1] She did not have to speculate for long. Though they had yet to settle on the details, ARC leaders had already begun to envision a role for their civilian assistance in postwar Europe. It was in the service of planning this peacetime program that, on Armistice Day itself, Homer Folks turned direction of the French Department of Civil Affairs over to Ernest Bicknell to embark "on the new mission with which the American Red Cross has charged me—that of making a study of the needs of the civilian populations in the European countries in which the American Red Cross has commissions, or is likely to be asked to do work in the near future."[2] Barely pausing to participate in the revelry that swept through Paris that day, Folks left France and headed east on a survey trip of Italy, Greece, Serbia, Rumania, and Russia. Over the next few months, he visited dozens of cities, towns, and villages, where he met with local government leaders, public health officials, and physicians. The trip, he hoped, would "help the A.R.C. to make its appropriations" while providing "an accurate statement of civilian conditions in Europe resulting from the war." Such data, Folks contended, "may be a real contribution toward a mutual understanding between America and these various countries, and toward one phase of the data which should be taken into account at the peace negotiations."[3] The war may have ended, but Folks and his colleagues remained convinced of the enduring diplomatic and social potential of American civilian assistance. During the next four years, a period surging with debate over the ideal level and form of U.S. engagement with Europe, these proponents of U.S. international humanitarianism fought against countervailing tides to sustain the ARC's intervention into European health and welfare.

Though scholarship on post–World War I American foreign relations most often centers on the fierce fights over U.S. participation in the League of Nations, the transatlantic turn against Woodrow Wilson and his internationalist visions, and the ascendancy of American economic and cultural power in Europe under Wilson's Republican successors, the American response to European civilian distress represents a central piece of this history.[4] More than four years of war had resulted in a profound and continuing humanitarian crisis in Europe. The conflict left millions undernourished, homeless, and orphaned. Rates of typhus, tuberculosis, malaria, and other diseases surged. These dire conditions threatened lives across the continent, but especially in Central and Eastern Europe. There, long-standing economic disparities, the sudden breakdown of old governing structures, the wartime disruption of normal agricultural production, and the effects of the wartime Allied blockade (which lasted into the spring of 1919) converged to produce widespread starvation and illness. In Russia, both the ongoing civil war and the concurrent Allied military intervention against the Bolshevik government exacerbated human suffering further still.[5]

For several years after the Armistice, Americans grappled with how to respond to this situation. In the early postwar months, many American policymakers and private citizens regarded relieving Europe as essential. Some assumed a moral responsibility to do so; others feared that without their aid, widespread hunger and illness would breed social disorder and Bolshevism, threatening an already tenuous peace. As the proponents of foreign aid recognized, adequately responding to both the effects of this human catastrophe and its underlying causes could take years and would require significant resources. But for a variety of reasons, mirroring the wider U.S. political and cultural "return to normalcy" (to borrow Warren G. Harding's 1920 campaign pledge), American popular and political enthusiasm for a major postwar humanitarian intervention quickly eroded. Some called on the United States to rein in its foreign commitments, whether formal or nongovernmental; some balked at the idea of aiding the former Central Powers and the new U.S. adversary, Communist Russia; and many Americans simply lost interest in assisting the world beyond their borders, now that the war no longer compelled their attention. Regardless of where they came down on the matter, the question of how—or whether—to respond to Europe's persistent social dislocations was one of the major foreign policy considerations of the postwar United States.

This foregoing narrative of American aid to Europe in the Great War's wake draws primarily from studies of the U.S. response to famine, particularly the work of Herbert Hoover's American Relief Administration (ARA). Without question, Hoover's relief efforts were the largest and most ambitious of the United States' postwar aid endeavors in Europe. In the first six months of 1919 alone, his ARA oversaw the administration of billions of dollars in food aid and other reconstruction assistance across the continent. While both federal and public willingness to support his efforts declined significantly by the end of that year, Hoover continued to oversee child-feeding efforts throughout Eastern Europe and Russia—in spite of significant American political opposition—until 1923.[6] Yet the ARA, though grand in scope, was not the only channel through which the United States negotiated and waged its humanitarian response. In the aftermath of war, the ARC continued to operate in Europe as well, administering a wide range of medical and health-related relief activities across the continent. Far smaller in scale than Hoover's better-known efforts, yet just as salient for understanding the diplomacy and culture of U.S. foreign assistance in these years, the ARC's civilian health and welfare efforts form an essential part of this broader story of American postwar international humanitarianism.

Given the ARC's dominant role in wartime civilian assistance, the organization seemed a likely candidate to lead the U.S. postwar aid program; the fact that it quickly ceded its position as America's foremost foreign aid agency might therefore come as a surprise. From the outset, however, ARC leaders deemed the monumental task of feeding European civilians as beyond their capabilities. In the weeks following the Armistice, as the ARC's leaders reorganized for peace, they determined to play a more limited—yet no less crucial—role in tackling Europe's ongoing humanitarian concerns. Willfully surrendering the task of food relief to Herbert Hoover and the ARA, ARC leaders directed their energies primarily toward health and medical assistance, doing so through two distinct channels. First, War Council chair Henry Davison took the lead in organizing a new international confederation, the League of Red Cross Societies (LRCS), which aimed to coordinate the efforts of all national Red Cross societies around peacetime public health activities. This association got off the ground quickly, but the ARC's new peacetime leaders in the United States and in Europe did not wait to see whether it would take hold. Profoundly concerned with both humanitarian suffering and political unrest in the Balkan States and Russia, they embarked on a second path, redirecting the bulk of their attention and resources away from Western Europe and toward these areas. Building upon activities and precedents established in wartime France and Italy and working in harmony with ARA personnel, they took up a concerted program of reconstruction and medical assistance. In both of these ways, the ARC's leaders tried to define a new role for their assistance in postwar Europe and to help resolve the novel social and diplomatic concerns facing the continent.

Riding a tide of wartime popularity, the ARC appeared well positioned to pursue these specific relief activities, continuing its humanitarian intervention on behalf of the United States. For a number of reasons, however, the ARC's postwar efforts soon proved less successful and popular than their wartime antecedents. The two years after the Armistice witnessed a rapid decline in American enthusiasm for the ARC and its foreign relief projects, dashing the War Council's earlier goal to foster a permanent sense of international humanitarian obligation among the U.S. public. At the same time, disagreements arose over the organization's proper peacetime role. While some desired to sustain and expand the ARC's international efforts, others criticized the scope of its postwar projects, urging retrenchment and a return to a more limited position in the world. On the ground in Europe, the proponents of postwar ARC aid ran into further problems. Davison's drive to lead the International Red Cross Movement in new directions bred resentment among the heads of the ICRC in Geneva, while ARC efforts in Russia and Eastern Europe generated criticisms of their own. There, European government officials, health professionals, and civilians objected to the continued American presence and to ARC workers' assumptions of superiority. ARC fieldworkers, meanwhile, grew frustrated with their inability to effect immediate change on the ground. The declining support for aid at home, the growing irritation with American interference abroad, and a mounting disenchantment among ARC personnel over their inability to fundamentally transform European society undermined the plans of those who desired to maintain a more significant presence in Europe. By 1920, ARC assistance, overwhelmingly popular in the war years, had lost much of its luster on both sides of the Atlantic.

Though the prevailing winds may have blown against the ARC and its European relief activities in these years, the shift was by no means absolute. A number of ARC leaders and workers remained fiercely devoted to the international humanitarian sentiments that had guided them during the war years. Even as inadequate funding and growing discord led ARC leaders to terminate their general postwar program in mid-1920, these individuals labored to retain the organization's presence in postwar Europe. Ultimately, they found it possible to do so for several more years by restricting their efforts to the one segment of the European population they judged most likely to garner sympathy and support. From late 1919 through 1923, ARC leaders devoted their remaining resources to European children. Opting for a more limited focus on youth allowed ARC leaders to maintain some involvement in European welfare, even as they found it necessary to scale back their more extensive postwar plans. Echoing the efforts of their wartime predecessors, ARC workers administered two separate child health and welfare programs, conceptually united by their missions to influence European social welfare in the long term. As in prior relief endeavors, these child health projects once again found ARC personnel engaged in a constant struggle to balance their expressed commitment to join their European colleagues in a shared crusade with their desire to shape Europe in accord with their own ideals and assumptions. Though some tried to change the dynamic, old habits died hard.

The ARC's postwar relief efforts in Europe are significant not simply as part of the history of U.S. humanitarian assistance but for what they reflect about much wider contemporary ideas and debates on American international engagement and the new position of the United States vis-à-vis Europe. Just as Europeans negotiated the new political, economic, and social clout wielded on the continent by the U.S. government, American businesses, and American culture, they also contended with the enduring presence of the ARC and the power dynamics inherent in its assistance programs.[7] And, just as Americans debated and disputed the merits of U.S. political internationalism, so too did they quarrel over the validity of the nation's international humanitarian mission. While the large majority of Americans cast aside the cosmopolitan sensibilities that had motivated them to assist Europeans in 1917 and 1918, a good many remained convinced that they must continue to play a part in bettering the state of European social affairs.[8] Such contests over the ARC and its aid shed important light on the complex nature of U.S. relations with Europe during the tumultuous years of postwar reconstruction. Americans did not immediately or universally accept the call to "return to normalcy" once the war concluded. Many continued to believe that they had an obligation to continue making the world safe.

Reorganizing for the Peacetime World

On December 13, 1918, Woodrow Wilson arrived in France to represent the United States at the Paris Peace Conference. Before joining the talks, he spent over a month touring the capital cities of Western Europe; he was greeted with ebullient fanfare at every stop. Back in Paris on January 18, 1919, the day formal negotiations commenced, Wilson described the conference as more than a purely diplomatic meeting. This was a critical moment in history, a chance to "lift from the shoulders of humanity the frightful weight which is pressing on them."[9] Achieving this goal, Wilson well understood, would require more than successful negotiations and a signed peace treaty. It demanded overcoming the social upheaval that the war had wrought. Wilson's allies in the ARC certainly agreed with this assessment. During the roughly six months that Wilson spent overseas working to negotiate the peace, ARC leaders in both the United States and Europe reorganized their association and began to redesign their approaches to civilian assistance. In so doing, they aspired to continue serving the diplomatic and humanitarian interests of the Wilsonian state while acknowledging the novel needs and challenges of the peacetime context. By the time Wilson returned to the United States in the summer of 1919, the ARC's new peacetime leaders had delineated a new role for their organization in the field of European health and medicine.

*

In theory, the ARC's extensive civilian relief efforts during the Great War era had positioned the association to remain the foremost player in American postwar aid as well. Even before the Armistice, many ARC workers believed that the organization stood to accomplish great things in this regard. While journalist Paul Kellogg admitted in September 1918 that "the part which the American Red Cross can and will be able to play in permanent reconstruction remains to be seen," he hoped that he and his colleagues could plan "a post war work as vigorous and meaningful as that which it has engineered while the war is on." As a result of the war, Kellogg explained, humanitarian assistance had been transformed into a tool of progress, had "broadened—as charitable relief in our own domestic life long since broadened—into a constructive program of social work and engineering." By prolonging their commitment to comprehensive overseas aid, Americans could continue to "play their part in the household affairs" of Europe.[10] Many supporters outside the ARC agreed with Kellogg's assessment. George Creel, head of the Committee on Public Information, reasoned that Europe's "instant and tremendous need can only be met through [the ARC], an organization that has donated funds at its disposal and is without the checks that impede government activities." While Creel voiced his own utmost confidence in the ARC and its voluntary humanitarianism, he also believed that a robust postwar ARC program "would appeal directly to the generous sympathies of America."[11] Subsequent events appeared to confirm his predictions. The ARC's annual membership drive, held in mid-December 1918, brought in the largest number of ARC members in the organization's history, with over twenty million adults joining the cause. Public opinion, it seemed, provided a mandate for a continued program of ARC international humanitarianism.[12]

Perhaps most significantly, Woodrow Wilson himself saw great promise in the ARC and its potential postwar role and took steps to encourage it personally. In late November 1918, Wilson's close confidante and the ARC's national secretary, Stockton Axson, advised the president that he must do what he could to "secure a great future to the Red Cross." Axson lauded the ARC for its wartime work. Nonetheless, he admitted that it would be "impossible for the people of America indefinitely to continue to carry alone the burden of relief and welfare work among the peoples of the world." The ARC, he argued, must prolong its own international health and welfare efforts, but its leaders must simultaneously encourage other Red Cross societies to join it, thereby putting the ARC's wartime efforts on a permanent global footing.[13] Wilson firmly agreed with Axson's assessment and in early December 1918, just before leaving for Paris, took up the issue with War Council chair Henry Davison. Explaining that he greatly valued the ARC and did "not want to see it contract," Wilson urged Davison to find a way to maintain the ARC's wartime assistance activities in the new peacetime environment, both through its own infrastructure and by encouraging the collaboration of other partners in the International Red Cross Movement. Quite taken with this idea, Davison pledged to continue the discussion in the coming weeks, once he and Wilson had both arrived in Paris.[14]

With the endorsement of the president and the public at large, the ARC was well positioned to lead the nation's postwar aid efforts. And yet, in spite of the far-reaching enthusiasm, Davison and his fellow ARC leaders ultimately opted to scale back their efforts in Europe. This decision was much to the chagrin of Herbert Hoover. As the director of the Commission for Relief in Belgium and the U.S. food administrator from 1917 to 1918, Hoover boasted a long résumé of humanitarian service. During the war, he had also developed an abiding respect for the ARC and its vast civilian relief operations. Recognizing the humanitarian and strategic importance of quelling European hunger, Hoover departed for Europe immediately after hostilities concluded to organize food relief operations. Naturally, he appealed to Davison and the ARC to join him in this undertaking. Despite the pressure from Hoover, Wilson, and much of the American public to maintain an extensive relief program in Europe, Davison declined. In early January 1919, he informed Hoover that he and his colleagues had determined it "imprudent and unwise" to undertake such a major relief program. While Davison imagined "there would be much work for voluntary organizations to do in supplementing that work of the governments," he and the War Council's other leaders had come to the decision that the "full force of the distress . . . was incalculable, and that it could only be coped with by the governments." Deeming the work too great and anticipating that the massive outlays of funding that had supported wartime work would not last, he consented only "to assist in meeting such emergencies as in our judgment we are warranted in endeavoring to do."[15]

The ARC's decision to limit its postwar aid efforts marked a definite shift in the nature of U.S. foreign civilian relief. With the ARC no longer willing to serve as the nation's principal relief agency, Wilson turned to Hoover to officially administer the nation's postwar aid program. In Paris, he appointed Hoover director general of relief in Europe and a member of the Supreme Economic Council. On February 24, 1919, Wilson issued an executive order to create the American Relief Administration (ARA), the nation's first fully governmental foreign aid organization, and named Hoover to lead it. Breaking with its usual reluctance to fund voluntary relief agencies, the U.S. Congress subsequently appropriated some $363 million to supplement private donations and help fund the ARA's work. Over the next few months, Hoover and the ARA distributed over $1 billion in food and other aid throughout Europe. After the ARA's federal mandate expired at the end of June 1919, Hoover reorganized it as a privatized charity, renamed the ARA's European Children's Fund. Under the ARA's auspices, Hoover continued to orchestrate one of the nation's largest international relief undertakings in history. The ARC, the principal instrument of U.S. foreign assistance in the war years, had taken a clearly subordinate position to a new humanitarian agency in the field.[16]

Although the ARC's leaders declared it beyond their peacetime capacities to feed Europe, they did not plan to withdraw from Europe entirely. On the contrary, they sought to maintain a significant international presence, only in a more limited and focused manner. With Hoover and the ARA in charge of food relief, ARC leaders turned their attention to other crucial areas of need. They prioritized activities intended to foster better European health, but they would also pursue other related reconstruction efforts as they saw fit. Significantly, ARA and ARC leaders saw themselves not as rivals in the field but as partners in the crusade to tackle Europe's humanitarian crisis. From the beginning, Hoover assured the ARC, "I do not wish to transgress on the field of the Red Cross." ARC leaders, in turn, promised Hoover that they had no objections to his food relief program and would in fact "be very glad indeed to see this great need met ... at the earliest possible moment."[17] In Europe, they instructed ARC personnel to avoid "competition or friction of any sort" and to cooperate with the ARA to the greatest extent possible, "with a view to full realization of not only the letter but the spirit of the program."[18] Understanding the ARC's important complementary work, Wilson's advisers at the Paris Peace Conference established an official relationship with the ARC's representatives in Europe as well.[19] Together, the ARA and ARC set out to address Europe's postwar humanitarian crisis. The former focused on feeding; the latter on improving health, curing disease, and restoring order in European societies.

*

Having dispensed with the significant matter of food aid, the Wilson administration and the ARC's leaders began to dismantle their wartime relief infrastructure and put the organization on a peacetime footing. In the United States, Henry Davison and fellow wartime leaders chose March 1, 1919, as the date to disband the War Council and restore the ARC to its prewar leadership structure. Although Wilson invited Davison to stay on as chair of the ARC, Davison demurred; nonetheless, he significantly influenced the shape of the postwar ARC. The ARC, in Davison's estimation, could be the "greatest humanitarian agency in world," but in order "to insure such position," he stressed, "the best men in America should be selected for job." In his mind, this meant retaining many of the ARC's wartime leaders, a suggestion to which both Woodrow Wilson and William Taft proved "equally cordial."[20] Together, these three men largely handpicked the ARC's postwar leadership, ensuring a great deal of ideological continuity as the ARC shifted to its peacetime work. Davison and three other War Council members assumed positions on the seven-member governing Executive Committee, allowing them a great deal of authority over daily decision making. Frederick P. Keppel, former dean of Columbia University and third assistant secretary of state during the war, became director of foreign operations, with longtime ARC leader Ernest Bicknell as his deputy. Wilson maintained his largely honorific role as ARC president, while Taft and Robert Weeks de Forest shared the position of vice president. Collectively, these appointments symbolized both the state's and philanthropic community's continued approval of the ARC's international activities.

Wilson's pick for chair of the ARC, the organization's highest leadership role, solidified the institutional commitment to sustaining the ARC's intervention in European health issues. He selected Livingston Farrand, a prominent figure in antituberculosis work and president of the University of Colorado. During the war, Farrand had led the joint ARC and Rockefeller Foundation antituberculosis campaigns in France and Italy. By 1919, he had become supremely confident in the ARC's international potential in the field of public health. "For the first time in the history of the world," he proclaimed, "we have an organization really and thoroughly expressive of the will and wish of the American people to deal with its fundamental problems." In this new environment, he argued, "the Red Cross may conceive itself as something far broader."[21] Farrand saw a prolonged commitment to both emergency medical relief and constructive health work as essential. Indeed, he anticipated that the ARC must remain in Europe for two or three years, if not more, to achieve its humanitarian objectives in Europe. Farrand's colleagues, many of them veterans of the war years, overwhelmingly agreed with this estimate. In Washington, the ARC's leadership embraced a long-term plan for international health efforts.

Davison may have stepped down as chair of the ARC, but this did not mean he was prepared to stop participating in European social affairs. Far from it. In January 1919, following up on his earlier conversations with Woodrow Wilson, he advanced a proposal intended to revolutionize the International Red Cross Movement. Davison, like Wilson and Axson, had come to believe that the ARC's comprehensive civilian relief activities during the war—its systematic efforts to prevent disease, improve health, and mitigate suffering—had created a viable model for other national Red Cross societies to follow. He regarded the ICRC's founding mission of providing neutral battlefield relief as too narrowly focused, too limited in humanitarian potential. Instead, he proposed to create a more "virile effective international Red Cross" by bringing all national Red Cross societies together to collaborate in peacetime preventive public health work. Such a federation would make permanent the ARC's wartime approach to comprehensive civilian relief and put it on a truly international basis. In Davison's view, this plan could be "the greatest step ever taken" by the ARC, a "fitting climax to its operations during war." Davison had pitched the kernel of his idea to Wilson just days after their initial meeting and noted that Wilson seemed "much taken with subject."[22] Just before the Paris Peace Conference commenced, Wilson wrote Davison to express his full approval.

Davison's campaign to organize this new confederation, which he christened the League of Red Cross Societies, directly coincided with Wilson's efforts to gain support in Paris for his proposed League of Nations, a parallel that suggests much about these men's shared visions for the peacetime international order. Davison stressed the incredible potential of this new movement, not only from the stand-point of health and welfare but as "a practical demonstration of the advantage to be derived from a League of Nations."[23] Wilson, like Davison, understood the LRCS as a complement to his cherished intergovernmental organization. He "saw in it a kind of kindred purpose to that which inspired us with the design of the League of Nations—a purpose to draw all people into action for the welfare of the world."[24] Through international efforts to improve social welfare, Wilson imagined, the LRCS could showcase the power of peaceful cooperation to cre-ate a better world and could "hasten and broaden the spread of fraternal feel-ing among peoples."[25] At the Paris Peace Conference, Wilson therefore made good on his pledge of support. He worked to obtain commitments from the British, French, and Italian Red Cross societies, as well as Russia's and Japan's. Most significantly, Wilson secured an official international endorsement for the LRCS as part of the peace negotiations, formalized as Article Twenty-Five of the League of Nations Covenant. According to its terms, signatories to the Covenant agreed "to encourage and promote the establishment and co-operation of duly authorised voluntary national Red Cross organisations having as purposes the improvement of health, the prevention of disease, and the mitigation of suffering throughout the world."[26] Although the LRCS was to have no affiliation with the League of Nations beyond this original endorsement, its formal inclusion in the peace negotiations gave it an important air of legitimacy and authority.

While Wilson drummed up support at the Paris Peace Conference, Davison began planning a summit to organize the new international body.[27] Held in Cannes, France, in late April 1919, the Cannes Allied Medical Conference brought representatives from twenty-four national Red Cross societies together with an international cadre of medical, scientific, and public health profession-als. Hailing from Europe, South America, Asia, and South Africa, as well as the United States, the convened delegates pledged to "carry the light of science in every dark corner of the world." By May 5, they had drafted and ratified the LRCS Articles of Association and voted to establish its headquarters in Geneva. Returning to the United States in late May 1919, several weeks before the sign-ing of the Treaty of Versailles, Davison held great optimism for the LRCS and its international potential, declaring "its success...as important as any peace treaty."[28] Through the LRCS and its peacetime public health work, Davison hoped, he had breathed new life into the International Red Cross Movement, transforming its founding purposes to better accord with the humanitarian needs of the new international order. In the spring of 1919, before the peace conference had even concluded, former War Council chair Henry Davison had initiated a new phase of the International Red Cross Movement, intended to put the ARC's wartime model for international health and welfare work on a permanent and global basis.

*

In large part, Davison's fellow ARC leaders shared his belief in the importance of continued postwar humanitarian work. They understood, however, that creating a functional and active LRCS would require significant time and resources. Given the tumultuous state of postwar Europe, ARC leaders in the United States and Europe concluded that they could not sit idly by and wait for this new confederation to become established and produce results. And so in late 1918 and early 1919, as Davison labored to build momentum for his new international Red Cross coalition, ARC personnel in Europe simultaneously began to formulate their own designs for health and medical assistance. Responsibility for developing and managing these postwar activities fell to a new Commission to Europe, a central body established just before the Armistice to oversee and coordinate ARC activities on the continent.[29] Leading it was Robert Olds, a Minnesota lawyer who had served as the counselor for the Commission to France throughout the war. Frederick P. Keppel and Ernest Bicknell, the new directors of the ARC's foreign operations, joined Olds in Paris to assist him in his work. Armed with over $127 million in cash and supplies—the remainder from the wartime coffers—these three men devised a slate of health and medical assistance activities to complement Hoover's food relief efforts.

From their headquarters in Paris, Olds, Keppel, and Bicknell fundamentally remapped the ARC's aid infrastructure in Europe. Concluding that France and Italy, the major sites of wartime relief, could address their own health and welfare needs reasonably well without the ARC's help now that the war had ended, they resolved to transfer all ARC activities in those nations to government agencies or private relief societies as rapidly as possible. While the Commission to Europe would not end its assistance to these countries entirely, its leaders rapidly and significantly reduced funding and personnel from wartime levels. In other areas, the Commission to Europe completely terminated relief activities. By mid-1919, the Commissions to Belgium and the Near East had closed their doors, the former restoring control to local Belgian agencies and the latter turning all activities over to the U.S.-based charity Near East Relief. As they shut down work in these areas, the Commission to Europe's leaders turned their attention to new sites, Siberia and Eastern Europe. Interest in these areas predated the Armistice, but geopolitical factors limited the ARC's ability to send personnel there until the last few months of the war, when the arrival of Allied military forces created an opportunity to intervene in a limited manner. In the late summer of 1918, coinciding with the arrival of Allied troops in North Russia, the ARC dispatched two small commissions to Archangel and Siberia to aid civilians in territories not yet occupied by Bolshevik forces. In late October, the defeat of Central Powers forces on the Eastern Front allowed ARC leaders to renew work there as well. But it was not until the Armistice, when France and Italy ceased to be areas of major strategic concern, that ARC leaders and their allies deemed it advisable to significantly expand these fledgling relief activities.[30]

In the winter of 1918 and 1919, the heads of the Commission to Europe redirected the bulk of the ARC's personnel and material supplies to Siberia and Eastern Europe, thus transitioning into the postwar phase of the ARC's humanitarian intervention in Europe. In late 1918, Olds organized a Commission to the Balkan States and put Henry W. Anderson, a Virginia attorney and the wartime head of the ARC's short-lived Commission to Rumania, in charge of the entire region. Over the next few months, dozens of U.S. physicians, public health officers, nurses, and social workers arrived in Serbia, Montenegro, Bosnia-Herzegovina, Croatia, Slovenia, Albania, and Rumania to organize operations. Personnel in the region quadrupled in the first two months of 1919 alone.[31] As relief work grew in the Balkans, ARC leaders also dispatched over five hundred nurses and dozens of physicians to expand the work of the Commission to Siberia. Rudolph Teusler, an American physician and superintendent of St. Luke's Hospital in Tokyo, directed this effort. From his headquarters in Vladivostok, a port and Allied protectorate in far eastern Siberia, Teusler extended operations along the forty-one-hundred-mile stretch of the trans-Siberian railway line (figure 5.1). Complementing the American military's involvement into Russia's Civil War, the ARC had sent its own forces to aid areas not yet under Bolshevik control.[32]

While Siberia and the Balkan States received the lion's share of ARC resources, the Commission to Europe provided assistance to a host of other areas as well. Eventually, relief workers clad in ARC uniforms could be found throughout Poland, Czechoslovakia, Austria, Hungary, Crimea, and the Baltic States, many working in cooperation with ARA personnel. Notably, except for work among prisoners of war, ARC personnel remained conspicuously absent from Germany and Bolshevik-controlled regions of Russia. ARC leaders made no plans to provide civilian aid to either the nation's defeated enemy or to its newest political rival. The war may have ended, but relief remained a fiercely charged political issue.[33]

This postwar refocusing of aid from Western Europe to regions further east represented a clear shift in priorities, from helping major Allies survive the war

Figure 5.1 Members of the ARC Commission to Siberia distribute relief supplies with a reindeer-drawn sleigh. ca. 1919. American National Red Cross Collection, Library of Congress.

to targeting civilians in areas that were deemed to be in the gravest political and social peril. Through their aid, ARC leaders hoped to achieve several objectives. First and foremost, they aspired to improve the health and well-being of individuals in these countries and to help them reconstruct their lives. After they had tended to immediate needs, they planned to overhaul the entire medical infrastructures of these countries and bring them more in line with American standards and expectations. Homer Folks's postwar surveys of these regions revealed that they lagged behind the United States and Western Europe in terms of health, medical knowledge, and the availability of medical care. Compared to either France or Italy, these areas had far fewer hospitals, clinics, and other provisions for child health, as well as higher rates of disease and infant mortality. Doctors were overwhelmed, and trained nursing did not exist as it did in the United States. Hygiene, sanitation, and levels of medical knowledge all failed to meet Folks's expectations.[34] Rectifying these issues was paramount. By relieving immediate suffering and taking steps to make lasting changes to the health care infrastructure, ARC aid stood to foster healthier, more productive, and more orderly societies—and, in so doing, mold a citizenry that was fit to withstand the presumed threats of Bolshevism and anarchy.[35] As it had in the war years, ARC aid promised not only humanitarian benefits but strategic ones as well.

In form and intended purpose, relief efforts in these areas closely mirrored civilian assistance activities in wartime France and Italy. With the approval of local governments and the assistance of local charities, ARC personnel started out by providing material relief and creating job opportunities, all with the stated task of helping "people in their struggle to get back to their normal life"—a concept defined by the ideals and assumptions of the ARC's largely middle-class professional work force.[36] Throughout Siberia and Eastern Europe, ARC workers distributed clothing and household goods to civilians, assisting only those approved by local authorities. They established or funded dozens of orphanage, schools, and homes for the elderly. They also cooperated with ARA personnel to distribute food, helping organize soup kitchens and provide lunches to schoolchildren. Guided by the principle that relief must "not smack of alms or charity," they opened dozens of *ouvroirs* where girls and women sewed garments for orphans and refugees in exchange for wages, and established farms where boys and men labored to produce food for hospitals and for winter storage.[37] To further foster an environment in which aid recipients would be enabled to help themselves, ARC personnel worked to fix crumbled roads, rails, and telegraph lines, many of which had been destroyed or had fallen into disrepair during the years of war and revolution. Such a strategy was essential, as one ARC worker explained, to restore trade and capitalist productivity. "No amount of outside help," she reasoned, "will take the place of economic revival which must come from the people themselves."[38] Going beyond mere material assistance, ARC workers thus aimed to make Russians and Eastern Europeans self-supporting, economically and socially stable, and ultimately no longer reliant on outside aid (figure 5.2).[39]

Yet as in wartime France and Italy, immediate relief represented only the beginning of the ARC's postwar plans. Building upon the models established by

Figure 5.2 ARC workers lauded self-sufficiency among refugees such as these, in Novorossisk, South Russia, who cook for themselves rather than relying on the ARC's soup kitchens. ca. 1919. American National Red Cross Collection, Library of Congress.

Departments of Civil Affairs in various wartime countries, ARC workers soon initiated comprehensive relief projects, intended to make long-term contributions to individual and collective health. Personnel regarded this part of their assistance as crucial. It would "be an error in policy from many standpoints," one argued, "if the activities of the Red Cross are confined to this emergency relief, and no attempt is made to leave some permanent institutions." Otherwise, another concurred, "the larger benefits of this work would be lost."[40] ARC personnel generally assumed that they were not in Eastern Europe and Siberia to simply provide food, jobs, and clothing. Instead, they saw it as their obligation to "promote the development of a...society which will continue after the withdrawal of the ARC and which will have an important part in the national life."[41] From the outset, ARC leaders declared that this work must be a collaborative enterprise. Yet as in wartime Europe, this avowed commitment to cooperation coexisted uneasily with a belief in the superiority of American methods and ideas. Thus while ARC leaders planned to staff all comprehensive relief activities "chiefly with native personnel" and carry them out "in full cooperation with the respective Governments concerned," they put each of these endeavors squarely "under American Red Cross direction."[42] Through the guidance of ARC personnel, they hoped to demonstrate to European aid recipients the value of American medical theories and approaches.

By mid-1919, personnel in Siberia and Eastern Europe had embarked on a series of "constructive health operations" intended to reduce disease and mortality, improve overall health, and teach civilians the principles of hygiene and sanitation.[43] To address immediate health needs, they established hospitals, tuberculosis sanatoria, dispensaries, and mobile health clinics throughout Eastern Europe and Siberia. To influence long-term health outcomes, they provided the "advice of experts in certain branches of public health and public welfare administration" to local governments.[44] ARC personnel recruited local civilians into campaigns for child health and better housing. They built demonstration sites, hoping to illustrate the methods of public health and hygiene that they considered most proper and up-to-date. Throughout the region, they orchestrated large-scale public health campaigns against both tuberculosis and typhus. In addition to educating civilians about how to prevent these diseases, they opened free public baths and built sanitation stations to disinfect clothing. In each of these ways, ARC workers strove to improve European health, the focal point of their postwar crusade.[45]

As ARC workers targeted the health of civilians and sought to increase their understanding of disease and its prevention, they also took steps to plant the seeds of a nursing profession like that found in the United States. In Siberia and Eastern Europe, ARC leaders relied on hundreds of American nurses to staff their hospitals and dispensaries. While these American women treated sick patients, they also took it upon themselves to teach local women about their work. Concerned that "trained nursing is unknown except for a limited number of nurses from the Allied countries," ARC nurses established courses to teach basic skills to Russian and Eastern European women, hoping to generate enthusiasm for this profession.[46] Realizing that they would not be in Europe permanently, American nurses reasoned that they must "teach the natives of any country where we may be operating enough of the underlying principles of nursing and hygiene in order to make them sufficiently intelligent to decide to perpetuate the work."[47] The successful incorporation of American-style nursing, in their minds, not only stood to improve health, but augured the additional benefit of instilling order and morality in local women. Such training was "infinitely worth while," as the head of nursing in Siberia reported, "not only because the standard of nursing care given the patients in our hospitals has been raised but because it has given us a hold on some of the Russian girls."[48] Through instruction, American nurses aspired to make local women self-sufficient, disciplined, and educated, prepared to teach their fellow citizens about modern conceptions of health and to serve as emblems of appropriate moral behavior.

Whether they were administering material aid or taking on comprehensive relief projects, ARC workers and their allies in the State Department recognized the clear diplomatic potential of their efforts. Providing material aid to civilians, one consular official noted, would "create [a] very favorable impression among Russian population toward America."[49] As an ARC leader in the Balkan States put it bluntly, "There is no more practical or effective agency to demonstrate friendship than the American Red Cross."[50] Working in areas assumed to be on shaky political footing, ARC personnel hoped to serve as a living demonstration of the benevolence of the United States and the virtues of democratic governance. Through their assistance, one ARC worker in Siberia reasoned, "America, which had meant nothing more to them than a distant democracy which was vaguely friendly and sympathetic," would take on "a new meaning."[51] ARC workers took care to make the origin of their assistance crystal clear. Using signs, fliers, and other forms of publicity, they worked to ensure that "the people in the villages underst[ood] that these supplies were from the American people."[52] In postwar Eastern Europe and Siberia, ARC assistance represented a critical form of public diplomacy, of enduring value to the Wilsonian state (figure 5.3).

At face value, the relief activities that ARC workers organized in Russia and Eastern Europe—from the provision of emergency aid and employment to such constructive projects as public health campaigns and nursing education—mirrored the efforts that their colleagues had undertaken in wartime France and Italy. Such projects intended to restore order and stability, to improve the health and welfare of European society, and to project a positive image of the United States in these regions. And yet, in spite of the similarities between wartime and postwar aid, the ideological and rhetorical justifications for U.S. postwar assistance differed

Figure 5.3 ARC workers clearly advertise the origins of humanitarian assistance to aid recipients in postwar Russia. ca. 1919. American National Red Cross Collection, Library of Congress.

manifestly from wartime precedents. ARC personnel had largely conceived of their wartime efforts as a mutual exchange with civilized French and Italian peers. To be sure, they had often acted in a manner that undermined such rosy declarations; nevertheless, their personal assessments of Western European individuals generally tended to be positive and collegial. In Russia and Eastern Europe, conversely, the cultural and racial assumptions that ARC workers held about the recipients of their aid tended to be far more negative, far more disparaging. Ultimately, such assessments led many ARC workers to assume a much greater and more blatant level of paternalism in their postwar efforts than they had during the war years. To a much more palpable extent than in France or Italy, ARC civilian assistance in the postwar years began to take on the familiar attributes of a civilizing mission.

Many ARC workers regarded Eastern Europe and Russia as backwards and fundamentally different places, both politically and culturally. One female ARC worker, transferred from Paris to the Balkans after the war and totally unprepared for the culture shock, described it quite simply: "This was really the 'East,'" she confided to her family, "or at least *the* spot that you have always heard described as the one where 'East meets West.'"[53] Henry Anderson, Commissioner to the Balkan States, shared her sentiments exactly. "In considering the situation in the East," as he explained, "it is necessary for us to look at things from a different view point than in considering the situation in the west."[54] Influenced by such

Orientalist mentalities, many ARC workers approached their postwar relief activities with a distinctly imperial mindset. This was no abstract conception. ARC personnel frequently compared their work to the labors of missionaries and colonizers across the non-Western world. Instructing Russian women, as one nurse reported, had prepared her "to teach a group of Hottentots...without so much as the quiver of an eyelash."[55] Aiding and reforming these areas, a fellow physician explained, "is much the same problem...which America faced a few years ago in the Philippines."[56] In Eastern Europe and Siberia, ARC workers saw themselves as medical missionaries, on a quest to uplift populations they deemed politically, culturally, and biologically inferior.

Emboldened by their imperial consciousnesses, ARC workers typically imagined their efforts as having the potential to accomplish something larger than the relief of suffering and improvement of health. Through their aid, they believed, they could nurture a solid commitment to democratic governance and engineer more advanced, enlightened postwar societies. Henry Anderson was convinced of the imperative to do just this. "The future stability of Europe," he proclaimed, "depends upon our ability to establish civilisation" in the region.[57] To turn back the Bolshevik revolution, to create stability in Eastern Europe's new democratic states, and above all to preserve the tenuous peace, he argued, ARC workers must "lay a foundation for a new ideal in their national life" and instill "a sense of obligation and duty which is essential to their own national development, especially in the broad field of international life into which they are now entering." They should aspire to nothing less, he declared, than "laying the foundation of a civilisation different from their present one."[58] Anderson's colleagues in the region largely agreed. They were not in the newly formed nations of Eastern Europe to restore civilians to their prewar positions but to improve them politically, helping "them to go forward toward the higher civilization that their best citizens hope to attain for the nation."[59] In civil-war Russia, likewise, they hoped to bolster civilian resolve against Bolshevism in favor of a republican form of government. ARC workers themselves might not solve the problems causing Russia's war and revolution, but through their assistance they hoped to "make it easier for the people themselves to solve by taking from them as much as we can of their burden in ministering to the sick, clothing the naked, and helping those who are mentally and spiritually groping in the dark to find the light for which they seek."[60] Through relief, the ARC's medical missionaries hoped to bring stability and political progress to tumultuous regions of Europe. In their minds, this would be the most significant legacy of the ARC's postwar humanitarian intervention.

*

Starting immediately after the Armistice and continuing gradually over subsequent months, the ARC's peacetime leaders thus endeavored to sustain America's wartime commitment to European civilian health and well-being while fulfilling the humanitarian and diplomatic goals of the U.S. government and its citizens. By the time Woodrow Wilson returned to the United States in the summer of 1919 to begin lobbying for U.S. ratification of the Treaty of Versailles, the ARC's peacetime leaders had all the essential elements of this new infrastructure in place. ARC workers had built up the new aid infrastructure in Eastern Europe and Russia, while Henry Davison had commenced his quest to modernize the International Red Cross Movement. Yet in the ensuing months, the ARC's international humanitarian aspirations encountered increasing obstacles in both the United States and in Europe. Despite the best efforts of the ARC's postwar leaders, their ability to sustain the major intervention in European health and welfare soon proved unviable.

Problems with the Postwar Program

In late November 1919, as a group of ARC workers in Europe prepared for their return voyage to the United States, their supervisor E. O. Bartlett sent them off with a sober warning of what to expect upon reaching home. In the year since the Armistice, he lamented, some "unfortunate reflexes" had emerged among the American people. While they had been so strongly committed to bettering European welfare during the war years, many U.S. citizens had since come to assume "Now all we have to do is to think about ourselves." The average American seemed to be losing concern for international humanity and becoming the "the sort of man or woman who does not help the world."[61] Bartlett and many of his colleagues bemoaned this shift, for they remained fervent supporters of the ARC and its international relief activities. By late 1919, however, the environment had grown increasingly hostile to their designs. The U.S. public's willingness to support the ARC's postwar operations decreased significantly in the year after the Armistice, as Bartlett well understood, but this was not the only contributing factor. In Europe, ARC fieldworkers began to harbor serious doubts about the postwar program. At the same time, Europeans started to criticize the organization's intrusions and overreach. These issues would only intensify in the months to come. By June 1920, facing rising indifference and outright opposition, ARC leaders saw no choice but to dismantle their postwar program.

This rapid reversal of the ARC's fortunes and the resultant decision to rein in peacetime leaders' extensive plans for Europe coincided with a period of mounting American antipathy toward international political commitments, a parallel that cannot be overlooked. In July 1919, with ARC postwar programs well underway in Europe, a confident Woodrow Wilson returned from Paris to campaign for U.S. ratification of the Treaty of Versailles and American participation in the

League of Nations. Over the next few months, Wilson watched as the political mood in the United States soured on him and his internationalist proposals. On November 19, the Senate voted against the Treaty, modified with fourteen reservations. A second vote in March 1920 again failed to secure ratification, with or without amendments, quashing the matter for good. In a further testament to the climate of the times, Republican Senator and presidential candidate Warren G. Harding garnered wide public acclaim throughout the year for his campaign pledges to return the nation to normalcy and "to stabilize America first, to prosper America first, to think of America first, to exalt America first."[62] On November 2, 1920, such promises helped him win election by a landslide.

As went public enthusiasm for the ARC's peacetime international humanitarianism, so too did it turn against American political internationalism. In a nation ready to reject the extensive overseas commitments of the previous two decades, the ARC's voluntary foreign aid proved as untenable as Wilson's more formal diplomatic initiatives. Many of the ARC's leaders desired to prolong the organization's work in Europe. As a voluntary association, however, the ARC could not administer a major overseas intervention without large financial donations and a willing staff. ARC civilian relief may have served wide-ranging American diplomatic and humanitarian interests during the Great War, but without the support required to maintain its overseas operations, it quickly proved its limits as a form of postwar U.S. foreign relations.

*

Opposition to the ARC's postwar program was not instantaneous. Indeed, in the summer and fall of 1919, a number of indicators pointed to widespread consent to the organization's relief projects. In Europe, many fieldworkers continued to praise the ARC and its new activities. "The Red Cross is doing a wonderful work," as one declared, "and I am surely mighty glad to have the privilege of being associated with it."[63] So did outside observers. "Our Red Cross efforts," an American diplomat conveyed, represented "the most effective help which we have been able to offer Russia during the past year."[64] By providing for "the relief of the sick and needy," Robert Lansing reported to Wilson, the ARC had "called forth from the local officials and the people alike expressions of the most profound gratitude."[65] In the United States, ARC leaders still enjoyed the ardent backing of Woodrow Wilson, who remained a dedicated booster even as he struggled to sell the nation on the merits of his own internationalist visions. In late October 1919, just three weeks after he had collapsed from a debilitating stroke while campaigning for the Treaty of Versailles, and less than a month before the first Senate vote against it, Wilson made a particularly impassioned appeal to the people of the United States in which he encouraged them to join the ARC during its annual membership drive. "Our patriotism should stand the test of peace as well as the test of war," he proclaimed, "and it is an intelligently patriotic program which the Red Cross proposes."[66] That Wilson made such a pitch for the ARC at one of the most pivotal moments in the treaty fight is telling. In his mind, generous civilian assistance and permanent peacetime political commitments complemented one another as critical forms of U.S. engagement with Europe. As Wilson implored U.S. citizens to support League membership without qualification, he urged them just as stridently to fulfill their nation's overseas relief commitments, to remember that supporting international humanitarian aid represented a patriotic duty. By one measure, at least, it appeared as though many Americans still agreed with this logic. By November 11, 1919, the last day of the membership drive and the one-year anniversary of the Armistice, nearly twenty million U.S. adults had again pledged their support for the ARC. The results seemed to bode well for the organization's postwar program.[67]

Beneath the surface, however, a number of cracks had started to appear in this apparent consensus. Even in the early months of 1919, many members of the U.S. public had begun to criticize the ARC's postwar program. Detractors attacked it for its amorphous nature, its extravagant expense, and its extension of ARC authority to unprecedented levels. The inspector general of the Army, for one, voiced profound concern about the organization's "excessive salaries and personnel," which he considered an unnecessary outlay now that the war had concluded.[68] The heads of the ARC's Los Angeles chapter, similarly concerned with the organization's bloated size, expressed their conviction "that there should be no Peace Program" for the ARC, arguing that it must return to its function "in former times," as a humanitarian agency "for emergency only."[69] An attorney from Louisville, Kentucky, spoke for many such critics when he wrote the ARC's national headquarters in early 1919 to denounce the organization's "radical departure" from prewar priorities. While he admitted that it was natural "that people should regret to see the great war organization of the Red Cross dissolve," he argued that such sentiments did not justify sustaining large-scale international relief endeavors. "People will not stay on that exalted level of self-sacrificing devotion in ordinary times," he wrote. "It would be a fatal mistake to count on it."[70]

By the end of 1919, the state of the ARC's finances confirmed this gloomy prediction. Americans may have been willing to join the ARC in large numbers during the November membership drive, but they proved quite disinclined to fund its operations at levels anywhere close to the previous few years. Donations dropped off sharply. Expenditures, however, remained high. Although the ARC had begun the year with a large postwar surplus of cash and supplies, valued at over $100 million, the expansion of relief activities throughout Siberia in Eastern Europe rapidly depleted these reserves.[71] Well aware that the ARC's coffers were drying up, Chair Livingston Farrand appealed to outside agencies to supplement public donations, emphasizing that "the distress in that section of the world is appalling" and "that there is no piece of emergency work comparable to this in importance."[72] Some responded favorably to his request. The heads of the Commonwealth Fund, a newly established health and welfare philanthropy, gave $750,000 to underwrite the ARC's work.[73] In a departure from the government's usual unwillingness to underwrite the ARC's operations materially, Congress unanimously authorized the War Department to transfer $8 million worth of medical and food supplies, previously reserved for the AEF, to the ARC so that it could "relieve and supply the pressing needs of the countries involved in the late war."[74] Despite these subventions, ARC leaders still lacked sufficient funds to maintain far-reaching operations in Europe. In January 1920, a troubled Farrand informed Robert Olds that the Executive Committee could allot just $10 million to the Commission to Europe for the year, a significant decrease from 1919 but a truly tremendous decline from the hundreds of millions of dollars available during the war years. "It would be impossible to make clear to you by letter," Farrand confided to Olds, "the present widespread re-action in the American mind against demands for contributions for European relief or, for that matter, any other projects connected with the war." While Farrand called the situation "discouraging," he conceded that it was "none the less a fact."[75] In the early months of 1920, as Wilson's League of Nations faced its final blows in Congress, the ARC's grand plans for Europe began to erode as well.

While waning support in the United States significantly hindered the ARC's postwar operations, additional complicating factors arose on the ground in Europe. First, even though many ARC personnel remained optimistic about their work and its benefits, more and more began to voice serious doubts about what they could accomplish in Russia and Eastern Europe. The same set of racial and ethnic assumptions that prompted some ARC workers to assume a missionary mentality toward civilians in these regions led others to a very different conclusion: given the presumed backwardness of aided populations, their assistance stood little chance of improving cultural, political, or biomedical conditions. One worker, characterizing Serbians as "the laziest race I have ever known," came to the decision that ARC aid was doing more harm than good. Offering assistance "to these people promotes dishonesty," he reasoned, "because they will lie about the number of people in their families."[76] Frederick Barnum, a physician in Siberia, likewise grew skeptical of the value of humanitarian aid, believing that it encouraged Russian idleness while failing to overcome political radicalism. "These Russians won't work so long as we will clothe and feed them," he confided to his diary. "They are all Bolsheviks—of the lowest layer of the human race... They will ask for bread with one hand and shoot you as soon as you turn around." Although Barnum had joined the ARC with the hope of stabilizing the health and social well-being of Russia, he ultimately concluded that "nothing has been done that could not have resulted just as well if the R.C. had never been in Siberia."[77] Another worker in Siberia concurred. "I don't believe the Red Cross is doing any substantial good," she wrote to her brother. "They are keeping alive a lot of miserable, filthy, backbiting refugees that might as well be dead. Nobody is grateful, nobody appreciates—They think America is rich and might as well give them food and lodging." Russians were not merely unthankful for American generosity; they wholly resented it. "If we saw a pigsty we would say, 'Poor pigs, I'll come to show you how to live, I'll stay a while and clean you up.' That's what we are doing to these Russians and they resent our interference with a deep, dark, wholehearted resentment that spells t-r-o-u-b-l-e."[78] As such scathing and bigoted critiques make clear, many ARC personnel on the ground increasingly rejected the idealistic assumptions about international humanitarianism and its civilizing and diplomatic effects.

In acknowledging European resentment, critics hit on a second impediment to the ARC's postwar agenda. U.S. citizens were not alone in turning against the ARC's relief activities; the lasting American presence on the continent had fueled the antipathy of Europeans as well. This was perhaps most obvious in Russia. By the summer of 1919, the Bolshevik government had grown quite critical of the ARC, regarding it as nothing more than an arm of the U.S. military intervention and its aid, available only to civilians in anti-Bolshevik regions, as propaganda pure and simple. As Bolshevik forces advanced eastward across Siberia through the fall and winter of 1919, Commission to Europe leaders began to fear for the safety of the American physicians, nurses, and other workers stationed in those areas. Consequently, they scurried to evacuate all personnel. By May 1920—coinciding with the withdrawal of the final U.S. troops from the region—ARC leaders had sent all but a few workers back to the United States. While a small number of ARC workers remained in Vladivostok through December to close up operations, the work of the Commission to Siberia was largely complete.[79] The ARC's problems, however, had not only been with the Bolshevik government. An auditor for the work in Siberia wondered, in retrospect, whether ARC workers had been "doing the best by forcing, as it were, the helping hand." Russians, whether they favored the Red Army or the White, had grown frustrated with the ARC's brash interference and with its thinly veiled diplomatic objectives. "If such a suggestion be possible along this line," he advised, "it would be that future work be entirely non-political."[80] Following such a recommendation, of course, was far easier said than done. As diplomatic tensions between the United States and civil-war Russia continued to smolder, the ARC's assistance to non-Bolshevik regions could hardly avoid being seen as a political issue and an intrusion.

Subtler tensions also arose over the ARC's presence in Eastern Europe, where both U.S. aid workers and European aid recipients began to criticize the ARC and question its utility. By late 1919 and early 1920, ARC personnel in the region complained that their commissions suffered "for lack of organization" and an "abundance of personnel." As one worker reported, "authority has broken down all along the line, discontent has developed and, worst of all, gossip has run rampant."[81] Such internal discontent and disorder did little to impress the individuals that the ARC had pledged to help. Moreover, Eastern European physicians, nurses, charities, and government officials voiced their objections to the ARC's continued oversight and excessive meddling. Declaring that "Americans are here to give out food and clothing but not to interfere with our...methods," individuals in these regions pressured the ARC to cede control of its orphanages, hospitals, and other relief activities to local authorities.[82] An ARC nurse in Italy, one of the remaining few stationed in that country, understood the situation all too well. Putting the matter quite simply, she remarked that "Europe really wants us to go home."[83]

By the summer of 1920, this European pressure to withdraw, together with growing dissent among ARC fieldworkers and declining support in the United States, led ARC leaders to come to some sober conclusions about the possibility for future work in Europe. In late June, four years after the first ARC wartime commission had arrived in Paris, twenty-six men and women, including Commissioner to Europe Robert Olds and the heads of the ARC's nine remaining national commissions, convened in Venice, Italy, to discuss the difficulties the ARC faced at home and abroad and to determine a coherent plan for the future. Olds assured the assembled personnel that he and other leaders in Washington "appreciate keenly the existing need and the tremendous value of the effort which is being put forth to meet it." He admitted, however, that "the means at their disposal are extremely limited and that they cannot, therefore, give as much support as they, themselves, might wish to give." Although ARC leaders desired to sustain their international involvement, Olds explained, American public disinterest had constrained their ambitious humanitarian plans. "The atmosphere is not favorable to the making of large demands upon the American people," he lamented. "This is a Presidential year and...many people in our country are saying that America, and not Europe, should engage their attention from now on."[84] Seeing no choice but to yield to the realities of the new postwar climate, Olds announced a slate of sweeping changes to the ARC's European program. Relief work in Albania would close in September, followed by Montenegro and Serbia soon after. Although the ARC would keep some personnel in Poland, South Russia, and the Baltic States until January 1, 1921, ARC leaders had declared their intent to move out of Europe.[85]

This decision to close the ARC's various European commissions, however, did not bring an end to the organization's problems. Back in the United States, it was not only the public that had turned against the ARC; by the summer of 1920, even some ARC leaders had their doubts about postwar work. Beginning in July and continuing over the next few months, the ARC's own treasurer, U.S. Comptroller John Skelton Williams, led a vigorous and public campaign for a thorough audit of the ARC's postwar activities. "Criticisms of Red Cross extravagance or other abuses," he charged, "have reached me from different foreign countries as well as from the United States." Citing "loose and inefficient management" and a "lack of information on the part of high officials of many matters which call for remedy and reform," Williams demanded an investigation and a major change.[86] His charges, amplified by a series of critical accounts of the ARC's European operations in the Hearst newspapers, ultimately prompted a House of Representatives inquiry on the organization's expenditures.[87] Though this investigation eventually exonerated the ARC, such accusations and infighting did little to improve the U.S. public's already tarnished view of the association. The results of the ARC's November 1920 membership drive made this fact abundantly clear. That campaign brought in just 5,772,070 members, nearly a seventy-five percent decline from the previous year.[88] Further testifying to this wholesale evaporation of public support, ARC leaders announced that, due to a steep drop in subscribers and a net loss of profits, the October 1920 issue of *Red Cross Magazine* would be the last. Outside the wartime context, the U.S. public no longer exhibited much interest in the once widely read journal of international humanitarianism.[89] As 1920 drew to a close, both the ARC and its ideological messages had ceased to resonate with large segments of the American public.

Thus, by the time Warren G. Harding won the presidential election in November 1920, both the ARC's sweeping postwar plans for Europe and its widespread popular appeal had dissolved. What, though, had become of Henry Davison and the LRCS during this time? Much like the ARC's peacetime program, Davison's drive to restructure the International Red Cross Movement experienced significant snags. While the LRCS had technically commenced operation in May 1919, shortly after the Cannes Conference, its work rested on shaky foundations. Representatives from twenty-seven of the world's national Red Cross societies had attended that conference, where they vowed to join the LRCS and support it financially. Four years of war, however, had sapped their treasuries and rendered them unable to commit the significant funds that they pledged. The ARC did little better than its sister societies in this regard. In 1919, Livingston Farrand gave $250,000 to help establish the League, but with decreased funding crippling the ARC's own operations, he could provide little more in the months that followed. Adding to these financial burdens, the leaders of the ICRC in Geneva proved quite hostile to Davison's plans. Davison had not sought ICRC approval for the LRCS. Quite understandably, ICRC leaders regarded his attempt to unilaterally modify the traditional mission of the International Red Cross Movement as a gross overextension of authority and an unwarranted American imposition. They objected further still to Davison's apparent indifference to the principles of universalism. In a belligerent postwar climate, Davison had invited only the Red Cross societies of Allied nations to join the LRCS, purposefully excluding the former Central Powers from the new federation.[90] Such partiality and partisanship, directly at odds with the ICRC's founding commitment to neutrality, further fueled the disdain emanating from Geneva. As a result, ICRC leaders refused to formally recognize the LRCS.

And so, even though the LRCS did go on to hold its first general meeting in March 1920 and to launch public health activities in ten national branches across Europe, it did so with only limited financial support and without the ICRC's approval. These conditions severely limited what the LRCS could accomplish in Europe. By the end of 1920, Davison's idea for translating the ARC's peacetime civilian health work into a permanent part of the International Red Cross Movement had materialized but, much like Wilson's League of Nations, it had failed to achieve all that its architect had originally envisioned.[91]

In the early postwar months, Farrand, Olds, and Davison had set out to sustain the organization's intervention in post-Armistice Europe, hoping to address the remaining humanitarian and political challenges facing the continent. Yet by late 1919 and into the following year, in a shift that closely paralleled the wider turn against Wilsonian internationalism, these plans had lost much of their initial steam. While the LRCS continued to lumber along in spite of its setbacks, reluctant ARC leaders found it necessary to terminate their general relief program. The ARC's time in Europe, however, was not yet complete. Even as they made plans to withdraw their postwar commissions from Europe, ARC leaders found it possible to retain their organization's presence on the continent for several more years—albeit on a modified and far more limited scale than they had originally intended—by orchestrating novel health and welfare activities for European youth.

The Future of Europe

In September 1920, the *New York Times* published a lengthy editorial by Frederick Keppel, the ARC's director of foreign operations, which detailed the ARC's dire financial straits as it called attention to the appalling distress still afflicting European civilians. Keppel acknowledged the "growing reluctance on the part of the people to hear anything more about Europe.... To put it brutally," he noted with unreserved disdain, "helping Europe is no longer 'the thing.'" Admonishing the U.S. public for treating foreign aid as nothing more than a passing fad, Keppel pressured Americans to renew their support for the ARC and its overseas relief, stressing that "Europe needs, and will need for some years, the kind of help the American Red Cross is particularly qualified to give." Keppel was impassioned, but he was also pragmatic. Conceding that the ARC "cannot hope ... to meet all the needs," he explained that "there is one field to which the eyes of our workers are turned with eagerness and longing." European youth, Keppel reported, had suffered unduly from "undernutrition during the most critical period of their growth," from the "complete disorganization of educational machinery," and "perhaps most disastrous of them all, from the loss of years of happy home life which is a child's normal heritage." Unchecked, he warned, these developmental setbacks would carry dire consequences, all but guaranteeing that European youth would "come to manhood and womanhood stunted and warped in mind and body." In order for "the children of the war generation ... to have a fair chance in life," Keppel wrote, they needed "far more to make up for what they have lost than Europe alone can possibly provide." Fortunately, he assured readers, "there is much that can be accomplished, if it is done promptly and whole-heartedly by those who know how. The American Red Cross," he declared confidently, "stands ready to concentrate its efforts on such a task."[92]

Keppel's appeal, delivered shortly after the decision to close the ARC's remaining commissions in Europe, demonstrates an important truth about postwar U.S. foreign relations: despite a widespread popular reaction against American international involvement, many U.S. citizens and government officials remained resolutely committed to playing a leading role in European and global affairs—assuming that if they did not, the world would invariably be worse as a result. In the years after the Armistice, Americans continued to lobby for U.S. participation in the League of Nations. They came together with foreign populations at such forums as international peace and women's congresses, the Pan-American Union, and the Washington Naval Conference. Wilson's successor, Warren G. Harding, may have espoused isolationist rhetoric, yet his secretary of state, Charles Hughes, and his secretary of commerce, Herbert Hoover, did not behave accordingly. Strongly committed to the notion that the United States must stay economically and diplomatically engaged with the world, they crafted their foreign policies in light of this worldview. Thus, not all Americans cast aside their worldly commitments in the postwar years. Many remained ardent internationalists, in theory and in practice. The fate of the postwar world, they believed, depended on it.

Among these enduring proponents of U.S. international engagement, the ARC's peacetime leaders proved some of the nation's most fervent. Even as support for their initial postwar plans diminished, Keppel and his colleagues continued to assume a responsibility to intervene in European health and welfare. Yet, keenly aware that the realities of the postwar climate made it impossible for them to pursue their more ambitious designs for Europe, they modified their approach. As their initial postwar plans for Europe crumbled, ARC leaders and personnel pooled their remaining resources behind two novel initiatives, both concentrated solely on European youth. First, relying on the infrastructure of the Junior Red Cross movement that had been built up in the wartime United States, they used funds donated by American schoolchildren to administer a wide array of preventive and positive child health activities across all of Europe. Second, after announcing the closure of their remaining postwar commissions in 1920, ARC leaders collaborated with Herbert Hoover and a new organization, the ARA European Relief Council (ERC), to launch one final postwar project, a comprehensive child health program for Central and Eastern Europe. Knowing that their time in Europe was limited and desiring to establish permanent local enthusiasm for their ideas while overcoming European resentment, personnel in both programs took concerted steps to cooperate with European civilians. Despite their stated intentions, however, ARC workers often exhibited the familiar tendency to behave as guides rather than partners. Unable to sustain their original postwar plans but determined to make a final, lasting contribution to European well-being, the ARC's personnel set their sights on "saving... children who can still be reached and protected" throughout the continent.[93]

Though partly a pragmatic adaptation to the realities of the postwar climate, this decision to concentrate on children also constituted an attempt to achieve specific and long-term diplomatic outcomes. Many ARC personnel, to be sure, felt genuine concern for the well-being of European children. They assumed, moreover, that U.S. citizens would be more likely to respond to appeals to help innocent, vulnerable youth than to more generic calls for aid. But the attention to children's health was motivated by more than compassion and was more than a calculated strategy to rekindle public support. At its heart, it represented a forward-looking quest to bring the next generation of European citizens in line with American medical, social, and political ideals. ARC leaders and personnel recognized, as one physician put it, that "the future of a nation depends on its children," because "the children of today form the citizens of tomorrow."[94] Adhering to this logic, they regarded targeting the health and welfare of European youth as the single most effective way to influence Europe's social and political course. By intervening in this area, another staff member explained, the ARC would not simply "help a few of the millions of children to live," but indeed ensure that they "become useful citizens for the next generation."[95] Such language spoke volumes to the ambitions and assumptions that underlay the ARC's two child health programs. If, through their aid, ARC personnel could ensure that European children grew to be "useful citizens"—defined as educated, industrious, democratic, and healthy—they would play no small role in nurturing permanent economic stability and peace on the continent. Thus conceived, child health relief stood to cultivate the conditions required for stable trade and harmonious cultural exchange while obviating the risk of future war. It promised, moreover, to safeguard the entire United States from external threats. "The theory on which the American Red Cross child health work was based," as ARC leaders put it bluntly, "was this: that the strength of the war-devitalized nations of Europe could be preserved and restored, and that America could be safeguarded from a future influx of undesirable immigration, only by caring for these nations now."[96] Bettering child health in the present augured clear future benefits for both Europe and the United States. In 1920, the United States may have rejected its seat at the League of Nations, but through their two final child health projects in Europe, ARC leaders determined to do what they could to influence continental affairs in both the immediate moment and for years to come.

*

In 1919, the JRC, a program formally tied to the parent organization but largely autonomous in finances and personnel, began to administer a variety of child welfare measures in Europe. Established in the United States in 1917 to involve U.S. schoolchildren in the war effort, the JRC had fast proven a remarkable success, with over eleven million American youths joining it by the end of 1918. After the Armistice, the ARC's peacetime leaders transformed this successful organ into a channel for children's donations to Europe. ARC personnel had long acted according to the belief that they had a special responsibility to ameliorate the suffering of European youth. Now, through the JRC, they labored to instill the same sense of obligation among their own children. "As the children of America answered so valiantly the call to 'make the world safe for democracy,'" the JRC's first postwar director expressed, "let us give them the privilege of demonstrating their determination to help rebuild the world."[97] Although Junior membership dropped off sharply in the years after the Armistice, paralleling the postwar decline in support for the parent organization, at its nadir the JRC still counted four million American children as active members. In schools across the United States, this army of Juniors built furniture and sewed millions of garments for refugees; collected relief supplies from their communities; and raised funds through pig clubs, poultry clubs, and bazaars. To relieve Europe more generously, JRC leaders also established a National Children's Fund, into which they deposited sixty percent of all membership dues.[98] In a period of retrenchment from international commitments, this voluntary, in-school aid program won wide bipartisan support. Throughout both Wilson's and Harding's tenures in the White House, the JRC peace program enjoyed the vocal endorsements of the National Education Association, the U.S. Bureau of Education, and many state and local superintendents and school boards. Speaking for many such supporters, Commissioner of Education P. P. Claxton proclaimed that the JRC stood to "accomplish much for the relief of the needy and suffering throughout the world."[99] John Tigert, his successor, likewise lauded the JRC for "doing a very great and valuable work."[100] American children could not physically participate in rebuilding Europe, but they could support the effort with their pocket change. This was a form of international engagement that many American adults could stand behind.

For four years after the war, hundreds of American child health professionals and lay workers went to Europe as JRC representatives, financed by the donations of millions of U.S. schoolchildren. The first JRC personnel who arrived in Europe in 1919 focused their efforts on material relief, hoping to restore the health and well-being of children whom the war had adversely affected. They worked in France and Italy—areas where the parent organization had already withdrawn most of its resources—but also alongside the ARC's commissions in Russia and Eastern Europe. Using National Children's Fund contributions, they subsidized feeding stations, school lunch programs, and orphanages. To improve the physical condition of weak children, they funded health colonies in the mountains and by the sea that provided children from metropolitan slums with a temporary dose of fresh air, nourishing food, and supervised exercise.[101] Behind these various forms of material relief was a clear diplomatic and pedagogical purpose. As they distributed aid, JRC workers took steps to "establish a very real bond of friendship" between American and European children.[102] European children who received their assistance "got their practice in the three 'R's' in writing post cards to the children of America, telling them of the progress of their work which they have helped to make possible through their generous gifts.... In so doing," one JRC worker in Italy contended, "they are welding links in a chain of international friendship that disputes between the two Governments cannot break."[103] From the beginning, the provision of relief to European children was intended to nurture friendly relationships and forge lasting alliances.

Providing material relief to children defined the JRC's initial approach in Europe, but as ARC leaders began liquidating their postwar efforts in mid-1920, they turned to the JRC to take on more comprehensive social reform efforts, to assume the sphere of activities that the parent organization could no longer afford to finance. After the ARC withdrew its postwar commissions, as Olds pointed out during the Venice Conference, the JRC would be "in a very real sense, the American Red Cross in Europe, and all that the American Red Cross will have in Europe." As long as the JRC remained in action, he declared, "it cannot probably be said that the American Red Cross has pulled out."[104] Working through the Junior division's auspices, ARC leaders realized, they could persist in their effort to influence Europe's social affairs.

Beginning in the summer of 1920, JRC leaders thus fundamentally altered their approach to aid and began to pursue a program they dubbed "educational relief," defined by its focus on long-term positive developmental outcomes. Eschewing the earlier focus on material aid, JRC workers began using National Children's Fund proceeds to provide children with access to libraries, vocational training, health education, and playgrounds. Each of these projects was administered under the approval of, and in cooperation with, local governments and private charities. But, like their colleagues in the ARC, JRC workers also took the opportunity to introduce childrearing practices they deemed superior. As the JRC's director explained, they hoped not simply to restore the prewar status quo but to alter it, to "enrich and above all to *make permanent* our contribution to Europe."[105] This emphasis on enrichment and permanence has much to suggest about the evolving goals of the JRC program. JRC personnel understood their work as a chance to make a constructive and lasting mark on childhood and European society. Utilizing the most up-to-date childrearing methods from the United States, they intended to counter the deleterious effects of war on European childhood development by providing youth with the features of a "normal" upbringing—defined by how closely it aligned with the middle-class professional ideals and expectations of American child health experts.[106] By increasing literacy, teaching hygienic and sanitary knowledge, and fostering a commitment to hard work and democracy, JRC personnel would help make the next generation of Europeans more industrious, more educated, healthier, and more politically stable than their parents. Presuming that European adults lacked both the resources and the knowledge to raise their own children according to American standards, JRC's workers stepped in to do so themselves, intending to lay foundations for an orderly, productive Europe in years to come.

In practice, the JRC's "educational relief" took a variety of forms. One aspect was the promotion of literacy and education. JRC personnel opened and operated dozens of public libraries and mobile book trucks throughout Europe and collected thousands of books from the United States to fill them. They wanted to give European children more than reading material, however. They also sought to "modernize and energize" existing teaching methods by importing "the latest American educational ideas."[107] To achieve this goal, JRC leaders sent teachers and personnel "trained in American library methods in America... to place the libraries on a permanent and scientific foundation."[108] European children, they believed, would reap the greatest intellectual benefits only with the guidance of these knowledgeable American experts. At the same time, European adults would gain new insights into how to educate their children. Fieldworkers praised library projects for fostering local interest in education reform. "Again and again I find them reaching out to modernize and energize their own educational methods, and frequently they seek to learn the latest American educational ideas," reported one field worker in the Balkans. "Dewey and Thorndyke are being slowly transplanted to the alien shores of Jugoslavia [sic] and their teachings are beginning to be absorbed through the medium of the Junior Red Cross."[109]

Libraries and educational reform provided the mental training necessary for informed civic engagement, while agricultural and vocational schools taught the value of hard work, a prerequisite for a capitalist economy to function effectively. Across Europe, the JRC helped establish and maintain over one thousand farm schools, designed for war orphans and children living in poor sanitary environments. Personnel also opened other vocational schools to train children in shoemaking, carpentry, knitting, and other crafts, and to become electricians and mechanics.[110] By preparing thousands of children for "the trades which will enable them to earn a good and honest living," JRC workers aspired to create a disciplined work force in Europe, a necessary step, in their minds, toward reinvigorating the stagnant economies of European countries.[111] Moreover, as the concern with "honest living" suggests, they aimed to prevent children from supporting themselves in ways they considered unsavory. Job training, then, was never the only goal. Of equal importance was the fact that these institutions provided youth with "the moral training of a 'home.'"[112] Worried that poor and orphaned youth had missed the benefits of normal middle-class home life, JRC personnel turned to American-style vocational schools to instill both values and the commitment to industrious labor.

Teaching American ideas of health and sanitation joined literacy and labor as a third foundation of "educational relief." Through an activity called the Health Game, JRC workers transmitted their hygienic ideals to European youth. The Health Game required children to follow fourteen rules of health each day. These included washing one's face, sleeping with windows open, and brushing one's teeth—all activities routinely taught in American schools. Children who met these goals received badges and certificates, while all who participated received hygienic prizes such as toothbrushes and soap.[113] JRC personnel introduced European educators to the Health Game at fairs and demonstrations and urged them to bring it into their classrooms.[114] It soon spread widely in European schools, reportedly reaching over one hundred thousand students in Czechoslovakia alone. Through the Health Game, JRC workers believed, they could win over local teachers to their methods while influencing "a greater number of children with benefits both physical and moral than could be reached in any other way."[115] This form of educational relief stood to foster an appreciation for American hygienic ideals and build character in the process. Healthy and hygienic living was a moral and civic responsibility, according to the worldviews of most JRC personnel, as vital to good citizenship as education and hard work.

Perhaps the most striking of these attempts to shape European moral and physical development was the JRC's mission to teach European children how to play in a manner Americans deemed proper. Influenced by the contemporary organized play movement in the United States, many of the JRC's staff believed that there existed a proper, scientific way to engage in recreation. This vision encompassed team sports, expertly constructed playgrounds, and the oversight of adults trained in play methods. Such organized play, according to its proponents, was a means to combat juvenile delinquency, improve physical fitness, and instill values such as fairness and good sportsmanship. JRC personnel expressed concern that European children were not reaping the benefits of this approach to recreation. It is "a fact that the French children do not know how to play," as one JRC leader asserted, adding, "The contrast between French and American children is marked."[116] Some blamed the disruption of the war years for this disparity, while others faulted European adults for not knowing the correct theories. Regardless of the reason, it seemed that European children had not learned the same play mentalities as their American peers. If children were to derive the moral and physical benefits that organized play offered, JRC personnel believed they would have to introduce it.

In August 1920, to establish a foundation for organized play in Europe, the JRC opened a five-acre demonstration playground designed by an American playground architect in Paris near the city's Porte de Bagnolet. Its purpose was twofold: to teach Parisian children the value of organized play and to train dozens of young adults from all over Europe to be play directors in their home countries. After attending lectures on the theory and history of play and playground management and learning the rules of such team sports as basketball and baseball, these play directors returned to their homes in France, Poland, Austria, Italy, and Serbia to serve as "radiation points for playground and Junior Red Cross propaganda."[117] In the fields of Bagnolet and at other JRC playgrounds soon established throughout Europe, the JRC created opportunities for youth to exercise outdoors under the gaze of professionals trained in American play methods. This guided athleticism intended to improve the general health of children, a central JRC goal. An equally important purpose, however, was to teach children the moral and civic values required of citizens in a democratic society. Through team sports, one JRC worker explained, Europe's children would be "unconsciously imbibing the principles of fair play, consideration of others, care of the younger and weaker, [and] fundamentals of good citizenship."[118] If the recent war was any indication, these values were woefully lacking among European adults. JRC workers saw organized play as a means to teach compassion, justice, and equality to the next generation. With stronger moral and physical constitutions, children would be ready to assume their place as Europe's democratic citizens in the future and avoid the mistakes of their parents. JRC playgrounds were thus sites designed not simply to teach play but to alter the fundamental values of European society. While European children were the primary targets of these reforms, JRC leaders hoped they might positively influence the adults around them as well.

Taken together, the JRC's "educational relief" activities thus aimed to make Europe's future citizens more industrious, educated, healthy, and democratic—characteristics necessary to preserve economic, social, and political stability throughout the continent. At the same time, they aspired to convince European adults of the primacy of American ideals and the merits of the JRC's new philosophy of relief. Yet despite their overarching emphasis on constructive childhood development projects, JRC workers nonetheless reverted on occasion to their earlier approach to assistance, providing material aid in the hopes of demonstrating American sympathy for Europe. Ensuring a merry and gift-filled Christmas struck many JRC staff members as the perfect reason for deviating from the tenets of educational relief. Every fall, the National Children's Fund paid for the shipment and distribution of thousands of Christmas boxes abroad. These packages were intended for "destitute children in European cities" and included toys made by U.S. Juniors, as well as rag dolls, hair ribbons, mittens, rubber balls, picture books, dominoes, tops, and marbles. To distribute the toys, JRC personnel arranged local Christmas parties and invited citizens from nearby towns and villages to celebrate.[119] These parties, together with the toys that American children sent, contained an obvious diplomatic message. As one JRC worker in Italy reported, the gifts "were more than toys—they were a symbol, a personal expression of friendship," that "forged the strong tie between the children of the two countries." Such an act, she concluded, "might be able to do more for the future welfare of the world, perhaps, than any other form of social service."[120] While this JRC worker certainly bordered on the hyperbolic, her point remained a valid one: the exchange of toys provided an easy way to connect American and European children. The men and women who distributed them, in turn, served as a proxy for the entire United States and expressed the country's commitment to international aid and friendship. Though the U.S. government had shunned its political commitments to Europe and the ARC had lost the public support required to support its overseas efforts, the JRC offered a potent way to address childhood suffering, to broadcast American alliance, and to leave a permanent mark on European society.

*

In June 1920, when the ARC's leaders concluded that they must close their postwar commissions in Europe, they turned to the JRC to take their place and to sustain the organization's commitment to comprehensive, long-term relief. Yet to many ARC leaders and personnel, the JRC's educational relief appeared an insufficient mechanism for improving children's lives in Central and Eastern Europe. Playgrounds, libraries, and games might constitute adequate supplementary interventions in France or Italy, countries with a proven commitment to child health and welfare that were on the way to restoring their own health and social services, but assuring the best child health outcomes in Czechoslovakia, Poland, or Yugoslavia necessitated more intensive American interference than the JRC alone could possibly provide. At the Venice Conference, ARC fieldworkers coming from these new nations reported that, in spite of the ARC's postwar efforts, civilians still suffered from hunger, illness, and a persistent lack of material necessities. They also deemed the medical infrastructures in these nations as still woefully inferior by Western medical standards.[121] In addition, and of particular significance, ARC leaders contended that these areas possessed "a type of civilization and culture—if culture it can be called—that differs radically from the conditions under which we are working in Western Europe." ARC personnel sometimes considered French and Italian civilians to be culturally and medically lacking, but they overwhelmingly regarded Slavs, Poles, and Serbians as wholly deficient in these regards. For that reason, they felt "justified . . . in engaging upon activities that we cannot justify in the more established civilizations."[122] Driven by a motivation to better individual health and a strong desire to provide less "established civilizations" with the benefits of Western cultural and medical superiority, the ARC's leaders determined that—funding be damned—they must find a way to do something more for Central and Eastern European children.

In 1920, the ARC was not alone in its concern for the fate of this region's youth. Herbert Hoover, head of the ARA European Children's Fund, exhibited a profound interest in this field of relief as well. Yet ever since the summer of 1919, when he privatized the ARA and began to concentrate feeding efforts solely on children, Hoover had experienced many of the same frustrations as the ARC's leaders. Though his initial appeals had allowed Hoover to distribute over a billion dollars worth of cash and food supplies in Europe, the ARA's cash reserves dwindled markedly by the fall of 1919. Well aware that both economic and agricultural recovery had stalled in Central and Eastern Europe, Hoover believed firmly that the United States must continue to feed children in these regions. Without American aid, he warned, the region would inevitably descend into anarchy and succumb to "the delirium of Bolshevism."[123] Hoover appealed for further federal assistance, but Congress, then engaged in bitter debates over the Versailles Treaty and the value of American international commitments, declined to make further financial commitments. At the same time, private donations—so impressive in the immediate postwar months—dropped off sharply. By the spring of 1920, Hoover thus found himself in much the same place as many ARC leaders and fieldworkers: deeply worried about the welfare of Central and Eastern Europe yet financially unable to provide aid at the level he deemed necessary.[124]

Although Hoover's postwar relief work had focused primarily on responding to European famine, he worried about child health and welfare generally. Since 1919, he had been a strong supporter of the ARC's efforts in this sphere. ARC leaders, in turn, heartily approved of Hoover's child-feeding program and feared what might happen in Europe if it ceased operating too soon. In the summer of 1920, facing shared concerns and constraints, Hoover and ARC chair Livingston Farrand began to discuss the idea of combining their organizational resources. By coordinating their efforts, they imagined, they might raise more funds than either could secure on their own. Eventually, the pair concluded that they should launch a joint program for Europe and a joint appeal for funds. In September 1920, Hoover and Farrand announced the formation of the European Relief Council (ERC), a new umbrella organization comprised of the ARA, ARC, and seven major religious relief agencies—the Young Men's and Women's Christian Associations, the American Friends Service Committee, the Federal Council of Churches, the Jewish Joint Distribution Committee, the Knights of Columbus, and the National Catholic Welfare Council. Together, these agencies planned to undertake a broad fundraising campaign, with the goal of raising $33 million for the children of Central and Eastern Europe. While the bulk of this money would go toward feeding, $5 million would be reserved for the ARC to organize a comprehensive child health program in the region. There was, however, a catch: the ARC's leaders must agree to match the ERC's contribution with funds from their own treasury.[125]

Given their June 1920 decision to close the postwar commissions in Europe and the recent brouhaha over the organization's postwar spending, the ARC's leadership proved bitterly divided on whether to consent to this new financial commitment. William Taft and Mabel Boardman, though they had long supported the ARC and its international humanitarian efforts, strongly objected to Farrand's proposal. They argued that reconstruction work in Europe had already so sapped resources that it had jeopardized the ARC's ability to respond to domestic and foreign disasters, its primary function. To take on further commitments seemed eminently imprudent. "It seems to me," as Taft confided to Boardman, "that they have bitten off more than they can chew in their ambitious plan."[126] Other leaders disagreed completely. Commissioner to Europe Robert Olds, for one, warned his colleagues that the ARC's withdrawal "would amount to world catastrophe." For Olds and other like-minded ARC leaders such as Livingston Farrand and Frederick Keppel, the crisis of European child health *was* a foreign disaster that deserved an ARC response.[127] Hoping to convince the skeptics, Farrand and Keppel called on Hoover himself to testify on their behalf, to express "his belief that the child problem in Europe is the most acute relief problem facing the world today" and that it was "not a problem which the people of Europe can themselves possibly meet unaided."[128] Ultimately, such logic won the day. In November 1920, the ARC Executive Committee pledged "to accept on behalf of the American people peace-time responsibilities far wider and deeper in character."[129] With a $5-million contribution from its decimated reserves, the ARC's leaders agreed to join Hoover on his new postwar relief mission.

The eventual decision to take on this new commitment reflected a mixture of real concern for the fate of Central and Eastern European children, a profound fear of the repercussions that the United States itself would experience if it withdrew too prematurely, and an ardent belief among American humanitarians that the United States was the only nation equipped to carry out this vital work. "The future of America and the world," as one ARC physician put it, "depends upon America saving a certain portion of the children of Europe." It was a job, he declared, that "must be done by America."[130] Farrand, Keppel, and the other supporters of this program, convinced of their medical superiority, believed that they had a singular obligation to improve the health of Central and Eastern European children. Doing so, in their minds, was a matter of vital importance not only to Europe but also to the United States. By tackling epidemic diseases and other child health issues still plaguing the continent, the ARC would address major causes of social disorder while lessening the risk that such diseases might make their way to the United States. By taking long-term steps to ensure that Eastern Europe's next generation grew up to be healthy, productive citizens, their aid promised to bring lasting economic and political stability to the region. ARC leaders did not just adhere to this logic privately; they also used it in their efforts to marshal U.S. public backing. "Have we got a part in this great struggle of humanity, or are we immune from its consequences?" the ARC's general manager, Frederick Munroe, asked an audience in Charleston, South Carolina. Unless Americans resumed their willingness to fund humanitarian aid, Munroe warned, U.S. civilians should invariably expect to see "some of these fellows loose in this country." Such a threat, he declared, "brings the danger home."[131] Playing on sentiments and fears, ARC leaders called to the public to support them and the wider ERC program. Ultimately, such appeals proved successful. By February 1921, the ERC campaign had raised the necessary funds to match the ARC's $5-million contribution. With this, the ARC inaugurated its new program for "desperately needed medical assistance for children," their final contribution to postwar European relief.[132]

To implement their new child health program, ARC leaders called on a veteran of the war years, Homer Folks. Folks had left Europe in early 1919, following his survey of postwar conditions for the ARC's peacetime leaders. Now, ARC leaders charged him to again "go to Europe and co-operate with Colonel Olds in making the program a living reality."[133] In February 1921, Folks arrived and set out on a four-month survey trip of Central and Eastern Europe. He did not like what he found. Folks lamented that there had been only "slight improvement in matters relating to health" in the two years since he had been in the region. If the child health programs were to have any real effect, Folks advised, the ARC must do more than treat children in the short term. To truly improve child welfare required a radical transformation of health practices in the region, an effort to bring health services more closely in line with the best models available in the United States. To achieve this goal, Folks recommended that the ARC recruit a large number of American "expert physicians and thoroughly competent public health nurses and social workers" to "evaluate, standardize and improve" the child welfare activities in the region.[134] Only with a comprehensive, methodical approach, he argued, could the ARC child health program fundamentally alter the state of Central and Eastern European health.[135]

The premium that Folks placed on American expertise and guidance was nothing new, but by 1921, a significant sea change in mentalities had occurred: a number of Folks's colleagues had come to recognize the shortcomings of this strategy. Many ARC leaders had realized that the ineffectiveness of their postwar efforts could be blamed, in large part, on the blatant paternalism and cultural insensitivity that American personnel had exhibited in Europe. Without a more tactful approach, they argued, Americans could never expect Europeans to warm to their ideas. A perceived invasion of ARC personnel might alienate local populations and prompt them to reject the very ideals that Americans hoped to foster. "Mr. Folks came over with full steam up, convinced of the immediate need of a considerable number of Americans," complained Kendall Emerson, a Massachusetts physician and the assistant director of the Commission to Europe. U.S. guidance was important, he admitted, but so was cultural negotiation. Native doctors, nurses, and social workers may have lacked the technical training available to their American counterparts, but they had "a value which our personnel can never achieve; first, in the matter of language, and second, in understanding of what can and cannot be successfully taught the people of their country at the present stage of sanitary and social development." Local professionals were not second-rate replacements for American experts but rather potentially valuable allies whose support was sorely needed. Emerson recognized, moreover, that Central and Eastern

European health professionals were not as enamored with U.S. ideas as Folks and other experts in Washington presumed. "The doctors and health service in some of these countries do not yet look upon American methods as the only successful solution of the problem of preventive medicine," Emerson asserted, "however we may flatter ourselves on our superior wisdom in matters of medical and social service." Unless ARC workers softened their missionary zeal, they risked undermining their efforts to win over Europeans to their methods and practices.[136]

Other ARC leaders concurred with Emerson's critiques. In May of 1921, ARC general manager Frederick Munroe took his own tour of Central and Eastern Europe. He spent several weeks surveying the region and meeting with European physicians and health officials. The trip left Munroe convinced that "the trouble with American politicians and with all western peoples perhaps is that they are unable to detach their point of view and they come to believe that what is good for them is necessarily good for other races." Forcing Czechs, Poles, Serbians, and other Europeans to mimic American biomedical philosophies and practices was a futile enterprise. ARC workers instead had to win their consent by proving the real value of their approaches to improving health and welfare. "Nobody but a fool would try to turn them into Americans," Munroe asserted. By embracing a more cooperative, culturally sensitive approach, he believed that "something of our western technique can be carved on the soul of their race so that they can be made a stronger set economically and culturally."[137] In 1921, many Americans still felt an obligation to commit their expertise and assistance to Europe. Now, however, they understood that they must to do so in a way that prized local autonomy and accepted cultural difference, or else they could never hope to succeed. "The demand must come…from the common people," as Emerson explained, "and it is our job to develop the germ that will produce the demand."[138]

In form, the child health program that the ARC's leaders ultimately developed tried to incorporate this new philosophy of assistance, to provide direction to Europeans in a manner that did not appear coercive. Responsibility for organizing this work fell to new, yet familiar, hands. In June 1921, with the postwar work that they had originally been hired to oversee now concluded, Robert Olds and his deputy, Kendall Emerson, resigned their posts and returned to the United States. Taking their place was Ernest Bicknell, the assistant director of foreign operations and a veteran of the ARC's overseas efforts since 1908. Under Bicknell's watch, ARC personnel in Europe put in place a distinctly cooperative child health program. In partnership with local governments, charity associations, and medical professionals, ARC workers designed and established 471 child health centers in Czechoslovakia, Poland,

Austria, Hungary, and the Balkan States. ARC personnel directed each unit, but they worked side-by-side with local health professionals. Two doctors, two public health nurses, and two social workers—half American and half European—staffed each site and engaged in traveling fieldwork. In an effort to thwart European resentment, ARC leaders instructed all personnel to "keep in mind as to conditions and inhabitants of the community" and "present a sympathetic attitude and not one of open criticism."[139] They also put a firm end date on their intervention, pledging to turn over direction of all health units to local leadership by the end of June 1922. Through their program, ARC leaders would endeavor to provide comprehensive care to thousands of European children while, at the same time, trying to persuade their European colleagues of the superiority of American medical practices via a living demonstration of their value.

During 1921 and 1922, scores of American doctors, nurses, and social workers traveled to Europe to make the child health program a reality. Due to their influence, the program bore a close resemblance to many contemporary community health programs in the United States, combining holistic approaches to health, surveillance by medical experts, and collection of voluminous records. Each individual health center provided free clinical care to children from birth to age fourteen. They offered a wide range of curative and preventative services, including tests and treatment for illnesses, well-child examinations, and vaccinations. Visiting nurses and social workers followed up on clinic appointments with home visits, evaluating whether the hygienic and moral surroundings of young patients were conducive to their proper development.[140] This comprehensive approach was vital, as one ARC social worker explained, for "unless the medical and social work for children is unified, the whole problem of child health cannot be adequately dealt with."[141] ARC workers wanted to not only treat individual bodies but also transform the entire system of care.

Beyond the clinics themselves, ARC personnel also brought new levels of regulation and medical surveillance to the region. Their stated aim was for every child to "be under the eye of the health authorities; every child, be it sick or well or in good social surroundings or bad."[142] To achieve this objective, ARC personnel introduced a system of methodical record keeping. Throughout Central and Eastern Europe, they labored to create complete medical and social records for each child examined and for the national population as a whole. Personnel printed four-page medical and social histories of each patient and installed filing systems in central offices in each country. The health professionals who ran the ARC units considered such surveillance to be an essential part of regulating the public's health. "If our work were to be of lasting benefit to the mothers and children," reasoned Henry

Eversole, a U.S. physician and medical director of the Czechoslovakian health units, "we must have absolutely accurate records of the work for the government."[143] Eversole went on to declare that "the data emanating from such complete records should be of tremendous value" to Eastern Europe as well as "to the world at large."[144] Only with full and precise knowledge of the health situation, he and his colleagues argued, could Central and Eastern Europe's new governments hope to make real and fundamental improvements to the well-being of their young citizens. ARC workers hoped to convince their European counterparts of the same. Fostering local interest in new tools and methodologies was as important to their project as the actual improvement of child health.

ARC personnel believed that the future of Central and Eastern Europe depended fundamentally on the health of its young citizens, but they assumed that this, in turn, required the education of the region's mothers. "We were soon convinced that the people at large were not informed about the simplest rules of health and sanitation," Eversole admitted, adding that if the children "were to be permanently helped, it could be done only through teaching the mother and child."[145] Confident in their expertise and concerned with the presumed local ignorance about scientific childrearing, ARC personnel made providing medical and hygienic education to women a central aspect of their work. In addition to examining children, health unit personnel offered courses to adults on topics such as home hygiene, care of the sick, and infant and child health. They gave demonstrations on feeding and bathing techniques, classes for expectant mothers, and "little mothers" classes for young girls who would presumably be parents themselves one day.[146] By teaching mothers, ARC workers aimed to change not only the standards of professional care and treatment but also everyday approaches to childrearing.

In addition to reforming the mindsets of laywomen, ARC workers sought to educate an elite corps of professional nurses who would take over the Central and Eastern European health units once the ARC withdrew. During the tenure of the child health program, ARC nurses established three training schools for nurses and nurses' aides. In the city of Bajina Basta, Serbia, they offered a four-month training course for nurses' aides. In Warsaw and Prague, ARC personnel took their ambitions further with the construction of two-year training schools.[147] Both of these institutions mirrored newly minted graduate training programs in the United States and were intended to foster "a more rational system of caring" in Poland and Czechoslovakia. Each "modern school of nursing" featured classrooms equipped "for complete and scientific instruction" and offered a curriculum "based as nearly as possible on the standards of the best schools in America." Together, graduate nurses from accredited U.S. training schools and European physicians provided pupils with skilled instruction. ARC workers hoped that this small cadre of Central and Eastern European women, armed with the benefits of an American-style nursing education and childrearing philosophies, could continue shaping the health outcomes of the region's children—and the mindsets of their parents—for years to come.[148]

*

The efforts to engage local women and health professionals in the ARC's child health work were of central importance, for ARC workers knew that their opportunity to personally influence European child health was a fleeting one. While they would do what they could to improve child health during their limited time on the continent, their foremost objective was always to nurture an organic appreciation for their ideals and methods, to fundamentally alter local mentalities so that their lessons would endure long after they departed. On June 30, 1922, that transition began in earnest. On that day, the ARC officially terminated its child health program and turned control of the nearly five hundred health centers over to local staffs and their national governments. JRC personnel remained in Europe for another year, working to organize Junior divisions in the continent's other national Red Cross societies. By July 1, 1923, the date that American JRC workers relinquished control of their remaining activities, nearly two dozen European Red Cross societies had done just that, marking the beginnings of a veritable international JRC movement that would blossom in the decades to come. While a small number of ARC and JRC veterans remained in Europe to work for the LRCS—an organization still struggling to operate without the ICRC's formal endorsement—the ARC's intervention in postwar Europe had largely come to an end. As they returned to the United States, the ARC's doctors, nurses, and social workers could only hope that they had succeeded in their mission to leave a lasting influence on European children, European child welfare, and European social and political organization.

A Return to Normalcy

By the time the final ARC and JRC workers departed Europe, Woodrow Wilson had long been out of office, his dreams for American participation in the League of Nations soundly defeated. Just as Wilson proved unable to convince the United States to accept the permanent international political commitments that League membership entailed, the ARC's postwar leaders failed to persuade most Americans to support a major postwar international humanitarian intervention. By 1920, public disinterest, together with growing discord among both ARC fieldworkers and European aid recipients, forced ARC leaders to scale back their most ambitious plans for relieving and reforming Europe. ARC foreign relief, so crucial to U.S. involvement with Europe during the Great War years, proved far less effectual as a form of postwar foreign relations. Nonetheless, many of the ARC's peacetime leaders and personnel stridently believed in the diplomatic and humanitarian importance of their assistance. They remained convinced that they had a singular responsibility as Americans to help Europe overcome its social dislocations. From 1919 to 1923, these cosmopolitan Americans found it possible to prolong their intervention in European health and welfare by concentrating their efforts on the children of Europe. In so doing, they hoped to leave a lasting mark on European health and European society and politics at large. In a period of American retrenchment from foreign affairs, the ARC remained one key vehicle for internationally minded American citizens eager to interact with and influence the world beyond their borders.

Still, the ARC's overseas influence had clearly diminished since its wartime heyday. Toward the end of the organization's time in Europe, a major change in the ARC's domestic leadership served as a fitting bookend to this international humanitarian moment. Since the early days of the war, Livingston Farrand had been an enthusiast for the ARC's overseas work. As chair of the ARC since 1919, he had been an ardent proponent of its international humanitarian commitments. Yet in the fall of 1921, with the ARC's child health projects firmly underway and the timeline for withdrawal from Europe fixed, Farrand resigned from the ARC to become president of Cornell University. To Warren G. Harding, president of the United States and its Red Cross society, fell the responsibility of appointing Farrand's successor, and therein the opportunity to steer the ARC in very different directions. To replace Farrand, Harding chose John Barton Payne, a Democrat who had served as chair of the U.S. Shipping Board and secretary of the interior during the Wilson administration. Harding appointed Payne, despite his party affiliation, because he considered him an able administrator, a man capable of reducing the ARC's size and expenditures. Payne did not disappoint. Soon after becoming chair in October, he began a major push to contract the ARC, consolidating the number of ARC chapters, reducing the number of paid staff, and rebuffing any further large-scale international commitments.[149] Just as Harding hoped, Payne began returning the organization to a state of peacetime normalcy.

And yet, even as he labored to rein in the ARC, Payne recognized an important truth: "The Red Cross cannot return to pre-war status," he asserted, "because conditions are wholly changed."[150] The United States had become a very different place by the early 1920s, as had the world around it. The ARC, like the nation it served, might not take up the same level of global commitments that it had in the Wilson years but it would not withdraw from international engagements completely. In the ensuing decades, in response to the tumults and travails rippling through the world, the ARC remained a principal instrument through which the U.S. government and people waged their global humanitarian interventions.

6

A World Made Safe?

On October 6, 1922, Ernest Bicknell boarded the *S.S. President Polk* and set sail for the United States. Having lived most of the previous seven years in Europe, Bicknell spent his homeward voyage reflecting on the "vast and significant changes in Europe during this span of time." He also expressed a great "impatience to get in touch with events in my own country." Physically, it did not take long for Bicknell to get back home to the United States. His thoughts, however, remained in a world far beyond U.S. borders. Bicknell soon returned to work at the ARC's headquarters in Washington, where he began "living over the time spent in Europe, thinking of what the American Red Cross has done and wondering just how much has really been settled by this war.... It seems to me," he wrote, "that the great war is only the beginning of our troubles and that no one yet knows whether it is the worst of them. It has shaken loose a good many things in the complicated contrivance which held the world together in a semblance of order and system." To restore and then maintain that global stability, Bicknell judged, would invariably prove "a mighty difficult business."[1]

Ernest Bicknell was in a prime position to know. By 1922, he had taken part in influencing this world order time and again through his involvement with ARC foreign relief projects. Shortly after coming to the ARC as its general manager in 1908, he oversaw the expansion of its humanitarian assistance in places as far afield as Italy, China, Nicaragua, and Mexico. With the eruption of the Great War and the consequent growth of the ARC, Bicknell had devoted his full attention to overseas aid. He worked in Europe from 1915 to 1922 in a variety of capacities, eventually concluding his service as the final ARC commissioner for the entire continent. There would be little rest for the weary. Within a few months of his return to the United States, he was back on the job. In April 1923, Ernest Bicknell became the vice chair of the ARC, in charge of its Department of Insular and Foreign Operations. As the director of the ARC's overseas work until his death in September 1935, he continued to lead the organization's efforts to relieve and reform the world. To his successors fell those same duties at a precipitous moment, just as the world began spiraling headlong into a second global war.

Although the ARC's international activities diminished after the early post-war years, the organization remained an important fixture in U.S. foreign relations throughout the interwar period and beyond. Over the course of these decades, however, the ARC's position and function steadily evolved as its leaders adapted to the changing character of both the American state and the world system. Through the 1920s and the early 1930s, under the direction of Ernest Bicknell and Chair John Barton Payne, the ARC sent assistance abroad in response to earthquakes, hurricanes, famine, and other disasters. In U.S. territories and protectorates, ARC workers undertook health and hygiene reform projects that closely mirrored their predecessors' efforts in wartime and postwar Europe. Through two organizations launched by ARC leaders during the war years, the LRCS and the JRC, U.S. citizens found a means to take part in key agencies of the international community. To these global responsibilities was added another in the mid-1930s. As the international crises that would eventually spawn the Second World War started to mount, the ARC again became an important instrument of wartime civilian assistance. This time though, the American approach to relieving foreign noncombatants differed in pronounced ways from its Great War–era antecedents. Rather than staging another wide-scale humanitarian occupation, ARC leaders sent only a few advisers abroad and limited assistance primarily to emergency, rather than comprehensive, aid. Meanwhile, U.S. government agencies and military departments, together with new international organizations, took up many of the civilian and refugee relief activities that had so occupied the ARC during the First World War and the early 1920s. By the end of World War II, the way the United States administered foreign civilian relief and assistance had changed markedly. Certainly, the ARC did not lose its standing as a major figure in U.S. humanitarian aid, but it did play a far less central role than it once had in American attempts to reconstruct and reorder the world.

Taken together, the ARC's international activities in the interwar years and the Second World War era reflect several important truths about the state of U.S. foreign relations in the quarter century following the Great War. First of all, the ARC's continued involvement in global affairs during the 1920s and early 1930s confirms a point that historians of the period have long sought to establish: contrary to popular belief, these years must not be regarded as an era of U.S. isolationism. By participating in the ARC's work abroad, internationally minded American citizens found a path to intervene in world affairs. Their efforts on behalf of the United States, meanwhile, meshed well with the diplomatic styles of the Harding, Coolidge, and Hoover administrations, which shared the belief that U.S. international involvement was best carried out via partnerships with private agents that shared the government's interests rather than through formal diplomatic channels. In the interwar years, the ARC served as one such vehicle of informal internationalism, giving both U.S. citizens and government officials a means to engage with the world.[2]

If the ARC's pursuits in the interwar years suggest that American isolationism was a myth, the organization's participation in the tumult of the late 1930s, the Second World War, and the war's aftermath calls attention to the changing nature of the U.S. state and of international humanitarianism in that time. During the First World War era, U.S. policymakers relied heavily on the ARC, a voluntary organization, to carry out civilian assistance on the government's behalf. Two and a half decades later, the U.S. government had ceased to depend so heavily on the ARC in its quest to relieve foreign noncombatants. In its place emerged the groundwork for a new foreign aid and development infrastructure, one that would come to dominate in the Cold War era. The growth of the U.S. state and the international community in the 1940s, in short, profoundly altered the approach to American foreign assistance that had arisen and taken hold in the first quarter of the twentieth century.[3]

The post–World War I international relief work of the ARC thus reveals a moment of simultaneous continuity and change, a period in which Americans retained their interest in influencing the wider world even as they revised older methods of doing so. Building on established precedents, U.S. citizens and state officials persisted in their long-standing mission to make the world orderly, safe, and stable through international humanitarianism.

Disasters, Development, and Diplomacy in the Interwar Years

The 1920s and early 1930s, frequently characterized as being as free of international engagement as of legal alcohol, were in fact an important moment in the history of U.S. foreign relations. In the aftermath of a cataclysmic total war, the preservation of international order, peace, and stability represented the overarching goal for most policymakers and private citizens. Having emerged from the Great War financially secure and socially and politically stable—at least relative to the world's other leading powers—the United States stood in a position to exercise tremendous influence in world affairs. And so it did. U.S. international relations in this period sometimes took the form of official diplomacy; international disarmament conferences in Washington and London, leadership in the global movement to outlaw war in the late 1920s, and efforts to improve hemispheric relations and cultivate stronger Pan-American ties all saw State Department officials in action. More often though, the United States exerted its sway in the world in less formal ways, with government officials relying on private initiatives to achieve diplomatic goals. The period saw the Departments of

State and Commerce form official relationships with bankers and investors in an attempt to stimulate European economic recovery and thwart political instability. Tax breaks and other incentives promoted U.S. global trade and helped U.S. communications and transportation industries connect the nation to the world. Hollywood movies, radio broadcasts, and news organizations, underwritten by government subventions, spread U.S. culture worldwide. Across the globe, in both sovereign nations and American territories and protectorates, the U.S. government and people together embarked on a wide array of efforts to nurture global peace, political stability, and economic prosperity.[4]

In these years, in a manner less extensive but no less noteworthy than in the Great War era, the ARC continued to carry out global humanitarian activities on behalf of U.S. citizens and statesmen alike. From 1923 through the mid-1930s, with Ernest Bicknell at its helm, its Department of Insular and Foreign Operations involved the United States in world affairs in three distinct ways. First, as the official voluntary organization of the United States, the ARC provided aid in response to dozens of international disasters. Second, ARC personnel launched an array of new health and hygiene reform projects in U.S. territories and protectorates, complementing American government policies in those regions. Finally, ARC representatives participated in various branches of the evolving International Red Cross Movement, thus connecting the United States to one part of the broader global community. Through each of these foreign initiatives, the ARC remained a principal instrument of U.S. foreign relations. Like many other voluntary and private interests, it provided the United States with a means for securing greater international social and political stability and for nurturing global connections, all without formal governmental commitments.

*

Ever since the ARC's founding in 1881, the duty to respond to natural disasters had constituted a special part of its mission. Since that time, and particularly after the turn of the century, ARC personnel had orchestrated appeals and provided aid in the wake of scores of disasters in foreign countries. In these catastrophic moments, the ARC's provision of foreign assistance on behalf of the United States had offered a way for both the government and the public to demonstrate their concern and compassion. At the same time, these efforts promised to assist in the restoration of normal economic and social conditions in areas of strategic national interest. In the prewar years, the ARC's international disaster relief had proven its diplomatic and humanitarian value to the nation. Throughout the 1920s and 1930s, it would continue to serve in this capacity.

The first major test of the ARC's postwar role in international disaster response came on September 1, 1923, when a tremendous earthquake devastated the cities of Tokyo and Yokohama, Japan. Over 140,000 people died or went missing, while more than 100,000 were injured by the quake or by subsequent fires and typhoons. An additional two million Japanese civilians were left without shelter and food.[5] The catastrophe also came at an auspicious time in U.S. politics, occurring less than a month after Calvin Coolidge became president following Warren G. Harding's death. Coolidge's response would prove an early measure of both his executive ability and his approach to international relief. Coolidge wasted little time in acting. On September 3, he issued an appeal to U.S. citizens, "whose sympathies have always been so comprehensive," asking them to raise a $5-million relief fund for "the people of the friendly nation of Japan." To ensure "the utmost co-ordination and effectiveness in the administration of the relief funds," he recommended "that all contributions, clearly designated, be sent to... the American National Red Cross."[6] Coolidge, like his predecessors, assumed that the U.S. response to the earthquake must take the form of voluntary assistance. And, like them, he regarded the ARC as the appropriate vehicle to administer that aid on behalf of the United States and its citizens. Given the recent public apathy for European relief, the ARC's leaders had good reason to fear a parsimonious response. Their concerns quickly proved unwarranted. By year's end, public donations to the ARC's Japanese relief fund reached $11.5 million, more than double the official request.[7]

After the rapid evaporation of public support for the ARC's postwar program in Europe, ARC leaders delighted in the resurgence of international humanitarian sentiments among U.S. citizens. "The Japan earthquake has proved the thing we have all felt, namely, that there is in all of us a willingness to serve which needs only an appropriate outlet to be translated into action," wrote the ARC's director of domestic operations. "Not since the war days has there been such spontaneity of action and sympathetic response to the Red Cross." The U.S. public, he concluded, had "demonstrated that they are heart and soul with the Red Cross, and always will be."[8] And yet, even as they appreciated the renewal of the public's international sympathies, ARC leaders also took explicit steps to avoid overextending their own commitments. In stark contrast to the ARC's involvement in Great War–era Europe, Chair John Barton Payne opted not to send any ARC personnel abroad. "Japan," as he informed the U.S. ambassador, "was perfectly capable of administering the relief in her own way without American guidance or interference."[9] Relying on local volunteers to distribute American cash and material supplies, Payne imposed strict limits on the ARC's reach. Raising and sending relief funds remained a vital responsibility, but the ARC's peacetime leaders had no intention of staging a major humanitarian occupation abroad.

ARC leaders may have scaled back their physical commitments, but they continued to credit their assistance for its diplomatic value. The earthquake occurred during a critical moment in U.S.-Japanese relations, a juncture when U.S. policymakers struggled to maintain cordial ties with a modernizing and increasingly powerful Japan.[10] The generous outpouring of assistance at this time held the potential to demonstrate U.S. sympathies and garner esteem, an objective not lost on U.S. policymakers. Japanese leaders thanked State Department officials for the ARC's efforts, declaring that the "precious gift of American sympathy... cannot but serve the Peace of the World, in drawing still closer the bond of friendship and trust between the two countries."[11] ARC leaders were quick to take credit for this outcome. The director of the ARC chapter for U.S. citizens in Japan reported that the aid had "so touched the hearts of the Japanese" that he noted "a distinctly new attitude toward all Americans on the part of all classes." He directly attributed this "new cordiality" among the two communities to the ARC's efforts.[12] Whatever esteem the ARC managed to garner in 1923, however, quickly evaporated. In 1924, Congress passed the Asian Exclusion Act as part of a larger series of immigration restriction laws, expressly categorizing Japanese immigrants (among others) as "aliens ineligible for citizenship." Relations between the two countries deteriorated rapidly and continued to sour in coming years.[13] Nonetheless, for a brief moment in 1923, the ARC's leaders believed that their actions "had done more to strengthen the friendship between Japan and America than all the treaties and Washington conferences could ever have achieved."[14]

In many ways, the ARC's response to the 1923 Japanese earthquake exemplified the approach that the organization would take to other foreign disasters in the interwar years. Throughout the remainder of the 1920s and into the early 1930s, the ARC would again act as the official U.S. aid organization following dozens of floods, earthquake, hurricanes, and fires across the globe. In each of these cases, ARC leaders launched appeals for relief funds and distributed assistance on behalf of the United States. Rather than sending their own representatives abroad, they generally relied on local governments and other national Red Cross societies to distribute their aid. Although no other catastrophe would come close to matching the 1923 Japanese earthquake—in terms of the scale of destruction or of the American dollars contributed—each distribution of financial or material assistance stood to demonstrate U.S. concern for the peoples of other nations while helping to restore local stability.[15] In a period that prized informal diplomacy, Ernest Bicknell lauded the importance of such aid efforts. Through its disaster relief, he asserted, the ARC "has done more in late years to build up and maintain the bonds of friendship with other countries than have the efforts of diplomats and statesmen." The citizens of the United States, "in their warm sympathy for neighbors in distress, and with the single desire to help," he concluded, "unconsciously produce a by-product of international goodwill of incalculable value."[16]

*

While responding to foreign disasters represented one way that the ARC intervened in world affairs during the 1920s and early 1930s, so too did the organization's administration of comprehensive health reform efforts on American Indian reservations and in Puerto Rico, the Philippines, and other U.S. territories, protectorates, and zones of occupation. In these years, debates over whether the inhabitants of these areas were ready for political independence or full U.S. citizenship surfaced time and again as major foreign relations issues. While some contemporaries advised scaling back U.S. military and political control over these populations and granting them greater autonomy, others warned of the peril of removing U.S. oversight, arguing that individuals in these regions were not yet prepared to govern themselves.[17] As U.S. politicians, the American public, and the indigenous residents of these sites clashed over this question, ARC leaders claimed that they had the requisite skills and approaches to resolve it. Poor health, inadequate sanitation, and a lack of Western scientific and hygienic knowledge, they argued, had all stunted the physical and mental development of these populations. By taking steps to improve these conditions and address disparities in local health and medical knowledge, ARC personnel declared that they could bring about social and racial progress. Through such reforms, moreover, they promised to make civilians fit for the rigors of industrious labor, raising a family, and civic engagement. Comprehensive ARC interventions, in short, intended to prepare civilians either for participation as full citizens in U.S. society or for their own self-governance. At the same time, through active demonstrations of concern for indigenous peoples' health and well-being, they would improve perceptions of the United States among the nation's wary territorial dependents.[18]

Beginning in the early 1920s, driven by these diplomatic and developmentalist rationales, ARC leaders sent personnel to the far reaches of the U.S. empire—from the Jicarilla and Pine Ridge Reservations in the American West to the nation's territorial holdings in the Caribbean and Pacific—in an attempt to inculcate modernity, construct fit citizens, and to win loyalty and support. ARC activities in these regions focused principally on improving public health. Modeling their efforts on projects first tested in wartime and postwar Europe, personnel initiated a wide array of programs encompassing treatment, prevention, and education. Through parades, festivals, and motion picture screenings, they presented Western ideas of hygiene and sanitation to local residents. They held Baby Days to inform civilians about infant health and hygiene, organized

young girls into Little Mothers' Leagues, and made home visits to interest indigenous peoples in their work. ARC workers built and staffed dozens of station-
ary and mobile clinics that treated thousands of patients per month. Mirroring
European models, the clinics provided not only physical examinations for babies
and young children but also classes for mothers in topics such as home hygiene
and care of the sick. Through their interventions, ARC workers aimed to make
these populations fit for U.S. citizenship.[19]

ARC personnel believed that their immediate assistance was necessary to
remedy disparities in health and hygienic knowledge, yet with a forward-looking
assumption of eventual independence, they stressed that they must also train
local staffs "to carry on the welfare work" themselves in the future.[20] To achieve
this goal, ARC workers created opportunities for indigenous women to train in
health care fields. In Puerto Rico, Hawaii, and the Philippines, for example, ARC
nurses assisted local universities in starting nursing and social work training
courses based on American models. Over time, they also developed autonomous
ARC training schools for these professions. In these and other U.S. insular areas,
the ARC sponsored scholarship programs to bring promising young students to
the United States to study, with the presumption that they would bring contemporary American practices back to their home countries. Personnel also organized annual nursing conferences in the hopes of forging stronger ties between
Americans and imperial populations.[21] In places "where modern sanitation is a
new idea," ARC leaders wanted indigenous women to embrace American ideas
about health and hygiene and then convince their compatriots to do the same.[22]
Fostering autonomous local leadership was intended to spur social and hygienic
modernity.

To reach children, ARC leaders organized JRC divisions alongside adult ARC
chapters, just as they had throughout postwar Europe. By bringing the JRC to
U.S. territories, protectorates, and American Indian boarding schools, ARC
workers aspired for results identical to those they had labored for in postwar
Europe: the promotion of "normal" childhood and the construction of fit, industrious, and democratic youth. Many JRC projects focused on teaching modern
Western hygienic concepts and improving child health. In the classroom, teachers displayed JRC health score charts for each student that listed the percentage
of students of the correct weight and height and the percentage without defects
of posture, teeth, tonsils, and eyes. The JRC also sponsored contests for students
to create posters, plays, and books about the benefits health and hygiene.[23] JRC
personnel not only hoped to transform children themselves but also assumed
that each child would become "a disciple of American ideals," a little ambassador
eager to bring the JRC's medical lessons home to their parents.[24] In addition to
improving health, JRC activities tried to develop a sense of civic responsibility and engagement among children while generating patriotic pride in both

their own nations and in the United States. The JRC's lessons, as staff explained, "intended to build character" and "prepare the children for the good fulfillment of citizenship."[25] To commemorate Decoration Day in 1920s Puerto Rico, Juniors distributed "tiny silk American flags...in memory of the Porto Rican and American Soldiers who lost their lives in the service of their country during the recent war."[26] In the Philippines, in-school activities included an American Flag Ceremony and the singing of both the "Star-Spangled Banner" and the Philippine national hymn. Good citizenship required not just a commitment to healthy living and civic engagement but also cultural and national literacy. As the JRC director in the Philippines explained, "The ideals we are striving to inculcate are American ideals," given "to a people but a short time removed from tribal conditions."[27] In accordance with this mentality, the quest to develop civic and hygienic behaviors went hand in hand.

The ARC's and JRC's efforts among the children and adults of the American empire sought to improve their health and ready them for democratic self-government, but an equally important objective was to mollify political tensions between U.S. government officials and the native inhabitants of these regions. ARC personnel claimed that by addressing health and welfare needs in an apolitical fashion, their humanitarian efforts succeeded where government efforts had failed. In a period when "all other things 'American' are opposed," the ARC's director in the Philippines asserted, "the American Red Cross is accepted without reserve by the Philippine people." The ARC, therefore, stood in a prime position to "solve those problems of misunderstanding that are now troubling the people of the Philippine Islands and the United States," to "help in a very large way to overcome the present bad feeling" and to "cement friendship."[28] In other regions, likewise, personnel saw "the American Red Cross as a means through which the highest spirit of Americanism could be diffused among the people."[29] In the minds of ARC workers, voluntary humanitarian assistance and guidance, as opposed to more militarized or compulsory political oversight, represented the best chance to improve relations and nurture pro-American sentiment.

The lines separating U.S. domestic and foreign interests have often been blurry, and the ARC's interventions in overseas territories and American Indian reservations in the 1920s and 1930s certainly demonstrate the liminal nature of these designations. ARC workers regarded the indigenous populations of these areas as foreign and backward, conceptually, but imagined that through health reforms and other activities, they could make them more modern, more civilized, and ultimately more American. In form, the health and welfare projects that ARC personnel administered in these regions replicated those developed in wartime and postwar Europe. Yet unlike in sovereign nations, where the ARC required the authorization of aided governments to intervene, orchestrating projects throughout the American empire required only the approval of the U.S. Bureaus of Insular or Indian Affairs. American colonial dependents could therefore be "taught and helped to have a better way of living," as one ARC leader put it, without the usual process of achieving and maintaining local consent.[30] In a period of spirited debate about the role of the United States in imperial management, international humanitarianism played an important part in the total system of insular governance, oversight, and uplift.

*

The ARC represented the United States in various countries through its disaster relief and health reform projects, but it also proved an important mechanism for maintaining U.S. involvement in the international community. In the 1920s and early 1930s, the U.S. government remained outside the preeminent international organization of the time, the League of Nations. That did not stop U.S. citizens and government officials from taking part in a wide array of other international movements and agencies. Americans traveled to international conferences for peace, education, science, and health. By the late 1920s, the U.S. government even sent advisers to engage with League of Nations agencies and commissions.[31] In these years, the ARC played a hand in keeping the United States connected to one principal part of global society, the International Red Cross Movement. At this time, significantly, the International Red Cross Movement itself was evolving in important ways. As it did, the ARC and its leaders played an increasing central role in its operations.

While the ARC had, since its founding in 1881, been very much a part of the International Red Cross Movement, it had always remained apart from that movement as well. Like all other national Red Cross societies, it had served the needs of its own government and not simply the mission of the ICRC in Geneva. The ARC's propensity to act autonomously had become especially clear in the Great War and its aftermath. In those years, the organization had engaged in a massive program of civilian assistance that went far beyond the founding mission of the Red Cross movement. In 1919, Henry Davison had led the drive to form the new LRCS, conspicuously doing so without the support of the ICRC's leaders. The new federation of Red Cross societies began to engage in peacetime public health work by 1920, but the lack of ICRC sanction and funding difficulties had together hampered its initial activities.

Ironically, it was just as many Americans turned against the ARC's broad international humanitarian commitments in the early 1920s that Davison's vision began to gain traction in Europe. The ICRC's leaders had objected to Davison's unilateral assumption of authority and to his decision to exclude Central Powers nations from the LRCS, yet they did not disagree with his fundamental goal to commit the world's Red Cross societies to peacetime work. The experiences of the Great War had convinced many of the ICRC's leaders that they must expand their mission beyond aiding the battlefield wounded. In March 1921, at the Tenth International Red Cross Conference, the ICRC's leaders publicly declared their intention to take up peacetime public health work. More importantly, they vowed to cooperate with the fledgling LRCS in this regard. To commemorate this new accord, representatives from both bodies issued a joint Appeal for Peace and began discussing plans for formal fusion. Negotiations, however, temporarily stalled. Over the next few years, the organizations continued to operate independently, with the ICRC embarking on some peacetime efforts and the LRCS's member nations coordinating their own international public health and disaster relief initiatives. Eventually, the push to unite the two societies succeeded. In 1928, the LRCS and ICRC joined as part of a new umbrella organization, the International Red Cross.[32] From this point forward, the organizations cooperated and coordinated quite closely with one another. From Geneva, the ICRC maintained its original functions of recognizing new Red Cross societies, serving as a neutral intermediary between warring countries, and urging governments to adhere to the terms of the Geneva Treaty and other international conventions. It also took steps to alleviate wartime suffering, including making some limited forays into civilian relief. The LRCS, from its headquarters in Paris, took responsibility for stimulating cooperation between the various national Red Cross societies. Additionally, its staff oversaw collaborative Red Cross efforts in public health, nursing work, and disaster response, as well as the activities of the growing international JRC movement.[33]

For many of the ARC's leaders, still ardent proponents of international humanitarianism, these developments were welcome indeed. The U.S. public may have grown apathetic about many of the ARC's international initiatives after the Great War era, but the International Red Cross Movement fulfilled many of the goals and visions that had guided the ARC's leaders in that period. In 1927, Ernest Bicknell lauded the internationalist potential of the worldwide Red Cross. Under its auspices, he asserted, "all countries and people can unite whole-heartedly in measures to preserve and promote public health, to eradicate pestilential disease, to speed relief to those crushed by earthquake or storm or flood." Such work, he went on, "is sweeping away the barriers which have fettered them, freeing their spirits, giving their humane impulses splendid new opportunities to make the world better and keep it better."[34] ARC chair John Barton Payne also recognized the tremendous internationalist potential of this budding collaboration. In 1926 and 1927, he undertook a "Red Cross pilgrimage around the world," a twenty-four-thousand-mile global journey to observe the peacetime work of Red Cross and Red Crescent societies in East and South Asia, the Middle East, and throughout Europe. Payne found much to praise in the actual humanitarian work of the Red Cross Movement, but came away particularly moved by its potential to foster stronger cosmopolitan bonds. "The real wonder," he noted upon his return to the United States, "was the oneness of the Red Cross, and the devotion of the men, women and children who serve under its standard."[35] Not only did ARC leaders appreciate the evolving Red Cross Movement as observers; increasingly, they played a much larger role in managing it. After four years away, Ernest Bicknell would return to Europe from 1926 to 1927, this time as the director general of the LRCS. Payne and several of his successors chaired the federation and served on its board of governors, while many other past and current ARC workers served on the League's staff in Geneva. In addition to personnel, the ARC provided funds to supplement both LRCS and ICRC international efforts. In the International Red Cross, cosmopolitan Americans found an institution capable of accommodating their enduring global commitments.[36]

The ARC's active participation in the International Red Cross Movement manifested itself in two other important ways. First, in a period that found the U.S. government trying to improve its relationships with nations in the Western Hemisphere, ARC leaders came together with their Latin American counterparts at Pan-American Red Cross Conferences. First held in 1923 in Buenos Aires, then in 1926 in Washington and 1935 in Rio de Janeiro, these meetings brought together delegates from Red Cross societies across North and South America to discuss shared approaches to regional health and disaster response. Second, the JRC movement, which flourished both domestically and internationally, offered U.S. children and their overseas peers an important way to engage with one another. In spite of popular apathy toward the parent organization, JRC chapters blossomed in U.S. schools during the 1920s and early 1930s. From a low of 4.4 million students in 1922, American JRC membership increased rapidly throughout the period, reaching over 8 million students by the mid-1930s. Through the JRC's National Children's Fund, U.S. schoolchildren continued to support health and development programs abroad. Starting in the early 1920s, JRC leaders also administered a major program of international interschool correspondence, thereby creating opportunities for children across the globe to communicate with and learn about one another. By the mid-1930s, over fifty national Red Cross societies on six continents had established their own Junior Divisions, uniting millions of children across the world in the JRC's program of international letter writing and cultural exchange.[37] Such potential excited not just ARC leaders, but other internationally minded Americans as well. Administrators of the Laura Spellman Rockefeller Memorial Fund gave tens of thousands of dollars to fund the JRC's global expansion, convinced that uniting children offered "the greatest hope the world now has for peace and understanding between nations."[38] By connecting the world's children and teaching them about each another, the JRC's leaders aspired to build the foundations for a lasting peace in the next generation.[39]

*

"To the people of a foreign country, the American Red Cross is America." Or so Ernest Bicknell told a group of friends and colleagues, gathered in 1928 to commemorate his twenty years of service with the ARC. Throughout his career, Bicknell had developed an appreciation for the ARC's unique diplomatic function. During the 1920s and early 1930s, as vice chair in charge of foreign and insular operations, he had overseen a variety of different humanitarian activities, each of which gave U.S. citizens a chance to help improve world health and welfare or to participate in international initiatives for the same. Such efforts, Bicknell argued, were important for their material benefits as well as for "the electric spark of friendship and understanding which flashes between that country and this" wherever the ARC intervened. Those personal and emotional connections, he concluded, demonstrated "the deeper meanings and vast potentialities of this work in which we are engaged."[40] For Ernest Bicknell, and for his many compatriots who were still committed to the idealistic potential of international humanitarianism, the ARC remained a critical element of U.S. foreign relations.

Politically, the role for the ARC in foreign affairs seemed secure. The organization had become a permanent fixture in the United States, with the federal government reliant on its response to international disasters, war, and other causes of human suffering. During the 1920s, a period marked by a deep-seated popular reaction against the politics of the previous two decades, the ARC's leaders managed to navigate the partisan waters quite successfully. Harding and Coolidge, like Wilson and Taft before them, understood well the diplomatic value of the ARC. Along with their administrations, they gladly endorsed the ARC and assisted its international work because they appreciated its voluntary, nongovernmental approach to international assistance. "Everybody is a friend of the Red Cross because it does not insist on any controversies," as Coolidge explained during his presidential address to the ARC Annual Convention in 1924. "We have not all been able to agree on how to rid society of poverty, but we can all agree with the Red Cross in helping the poor." As Coolidge saw it, the ARC had proven so successful over the years precisely because it was an apolitical structure, a channel for cosmopolitan Americans who wanted to help the world, but one that necessitated no formal state support. Its actions, according to him, were "proof that materialism is not the dominant motive of the people of the United States," its existence "a reliable guarantee of the continuing progress of civilization."[41] ARC overseas assistance projected the benevolence and the humanity of the United States to the rest of the world. In the 1920s, both the nation's enduring internationalists and the many Americans who balked at the extensive international commitments of the previous decade could appreciate this function.

It certainly appealed to Herbert Hoover. On March 4, 1929, the "Great Humanitarian," became president of the United States. On that day, following the custom in place since William Taft's inauguration, he also assumed the presidency of the ARC. Hoover seemed ideally suited to the job. He was, after all, a living symbol of the role that humanitarian assistance had come to occupy in U.S. foreign relations since the dawn of the twentieth century. Trained as an engineer, Hoover had served as the head of the Commission for Relief in Belgium and the U.S. Food Administration during the Great War and had directed the ARA in the war's aftermath. As secretary of commerce under Harding and Coolidge, he had also come to play an important role in the ARC itself; throughout the 1920s, he had served as a member of the organization's governing Central Committee. For much of his adult life, Hoover had prized scientific and social scientific methods as the best means to improve social welfare. He had been committed to the idea, moreover, that it was the civic obligation of American citizens to aid and improve the international community. Assistance was at its best as a voluntary undertaking, he believed, not when controlled by the state.[42] With Hoover in the White House, the environment seemed fertile for the international humanitarian sentiments of the Great War years to resurge.

For this to occur, however, there would have to be willing volunteers and donors. Although public enthusiasm for the ARC could be rekindled temporarily in such times of dire catastrophe as the 1923 Japanese earthquake, Americans in the interwar years proved largely uninterested in making major or sustained contributions to the ARC's foreign aid program. Thus, although the ARC remained an important fixture in U.S. foreign relations in the 1920s and 1930s, public support for the organization and its overseas activities remained relatively stagnant. Adult memberships dropped to just over three million by the mid-1920s. Those counts rose to around four million by the early 1930s, but the increases were largely attributable to the ARC's domestic relief efforts during the 1927 Mississippi Floods and the ensuing Great Depression, and not indicative of any renewed international humanitarian commitments. By the mid-1930s, as the nation reeled from the effects of the Depression, the Dust Bowl, and widespread droughts, the ARC's difficulty in mobilizing public backing for its foreign relief projects only continued to grow. By the time Franklin Delano Roosevelt became president of the United States and its Red Cross society in 1933, most U.S. citizens were looking inward to face their nation's own profound humanitarian crises.

This, then, was the state of the nation's official voluntary aid organization by the mid-1930s. While the ARC continued to represent the United States abroad in a variety of capacities, the public's unwillingness and increasing inability to finance extensive foreign engagements effectively limited the organization's potential to act in the world. Yet it was at precisely this moment that indications of a new global conflict began to surface. In the early 1930s, political tensions and militancy started to escalate in both Asia and Europe. In 1935, at this critical juncture in world affairs, the deaths of John Barton Payne and Ernest Bicknell brought major changes to the ARC's leadership. Both men had been deeply involved with the ARC for decades. During the 1920s and early 1930s, both had organized the ARC's overseas disaster relief and health reform activities and had played personal parts in the evolving International Red Cross Movement. In the hands of their successors, the ARC would continue to represent the United States as the world plunged into a second global conflict. Changes then transpiring in both the U.S. government and in the international system, however, ensured that the ARC's civilian relief activities in the Second World War would differ in tangible ways from the efforts undertaken in the First.

A New International Humanitarian Moment

In the dozen years following the Great War, U.S. citizens and government officials attempted to maintain global order and stability through their economic, cultural, and political influence. In the United States and throughout the world, many hoped that the League of Nations and other international organizations would do the same. During the 1930s, however, a complex series of political events rapidly belied those expectations. In 1931, the world watched as Japan invaded Manchuria and then, in 1933, as it abandoned its seat at the League of Nations. That year, Adolph Hitler came to power in Germany as chancellor, and following Japan's lead, withdrew Germany from the League of Nations. Within two years he had begun rearming Germany and announced a program of universal military training, brazenly flouting the terms of the Treaty of Versailles. The world continued to watch as Italy invaded Ethiopia in 1935, as Spain erupted into Civil War in 1936, and as Japan invaded mainland China in 1937. The following year saw Germany annex Austria and the Sudetenland and then, in 1939, invade Czechoslovakia in March and Poland in September. This last act finally provoked Britain and France to declare war. A momentary lull followed, but by the spring of 1940, German troops marched into Denmark, Norway, the Netherlands, Luxembourg, Belgium, and France. Following France's surrender in June 1940, Hitler turned to Britain with a series of air strikes and terror bombings of civilians in London. The world was once again fully embroiled in war.

The aggression and belligerency that swept the world a second time provoked shock and dismay among many U.S. citizens. Being appalled, however, did not by itself produce support for a second military intervention. In the mid-1930s, large majorities of the U.S. public opposed such a course, preferring a path of strict neutrality. Even by 1940, as Germany stormed through the European continent and reports of Japanese aggression in China flooded into the United States, many Americans resisted Roosevelt's efforts to steer the United States toward some form of intervention or assistance on behalf of the Allies. It would take the bombing of Pearl Harbor in December 1941 before U.S. citizens fully rallied for the war. Once they did, however, the enthusiasm for overseas involvement would be potent. Over the next four years, the United States took active part in its second great war in a generation, again intervening to influence the course of world affairs. By the time the war ended in August 1945, the United States had established itself as a world superpower with the economic, military, and cultural power to influence world affairs profoundly.[43]

In these years of renewed global tumult, from the mid-1930s through the end of the Second World War, the ARC once again mobilized to aid civilians affected by global conflict. The nature and scope of this relief program, however, ultimately diverged in significant ways from its Great War–era precursors. This time, the U.S. government became more deeply involved in the ARC's operations, while the ARC itself played a far more limited role in aiding noncombatants, especially on the ground in Europe. In its place, international and U.S. governmental organizations began to assume much of the responsibility for civilian relief. By the time the war ended in 1945, these shifts had established precedents and patterns for foreign aid that would remain in place for the rest of twentieth century.

*

The onset of the Second World War found the ARC treading a path similar to the one it had taken two decades prior. From 1935 to 1939, with Congress and the U.S. public clinging fiercely to political neutrality, a new generation of ARC leaders began sending funds and supplies to civilians harmed by the period's emerging conflicts. The ARC Central Committee sent assistance to Ethiopia in 1935, to Spain beginning in 1936, and, at the State Department's request, to China following the 1937 outbreak of the Sino-Japanese War.[44] Roosevelt, like Wilson before him, appreciated the ARC's efforts as a key form of voluntary diplomacy. Like Wilson, he too began taking steps to support the ARC's efforts and to establish its position as the preferred U.S. instrument for civilian relief. In early 1938, Roosevelt issued a public appeal asking U.S. citizens to contribute $1 million to the ARC's program of Chinese civilian relief. In December of that year, he also designated the ARC as the U.S. agency responsible for securing and shipping foodstuffs for the American Friends Service Committee to distribute in Spain. With tensions and turmoil mounting throughout the world, both the Roosevelt administration and the ARC's leaders understood the diplomatic and humanitarian importance of the organization's civilian assistance operations and took definite steps to orchestrate them.[45]

And yet most Americans, just as at the start of World War I, proved rather reserved in their response to the humanitarian crises abroad. With Americans still fearful of being drawn into the impending conflict, interest in the ARC's early civilian aid efforts remained sluggish. As late as 1939, adult membership in the organization hovered at roughly 5,500,000, less than five percent of the total population. Contributions to Ethiopia and Spain brought in just tens of thousands of dollars, significantly less than ARC leaders hoped for. Donors gave $600,000 following Roosevelt's public appeal for China, just over half the stated fundraising target. "The meagerness of the response is bound to have unfavorable effects," lamented a concerned Secretary of State Cordell Hull. "The general reputation of the United States abroad for generosity will be adversely affected."[46] As they tried to respond to the world's new military crises, the ARC's leaders also continued to provide assistance following international natural disasters, carry out their health reform projects in American territories and protectorates, and take part in LRCS and JRC activities. Yet without public interest and financial support, their budget for overseas operations was soon stretched quite thin. In the prelude to the Second World War, ARC leaders had begun to implement relief activities for noncombatants, but they had yet to see the resurgence of international humanitarian sentiments necessary to fund them.

A program of civilian assistance offered an alternative to military commitment, just as it had in the early years of the Great War. ARC leaders certainly recognized as much. In August 1939, with war in Europe imminent, they assumed that their organization would play a major role in civilian assistance should any major conflict erupt. "The greatest question to face the Red Cross in the event of a major war in Europe," they argued, "will undoubtedly be that of relief of the suffering which would inevitably develop among civilians who may be injured, driven from their homes, or rendered destitute by military operations." ARC leaders, however, still had to convince a wary public of this point. The ARC's new chair, the career diplomat Norman Davis, understood that "at the present time the overwhelming sentiment of the American people seems to be for non-participation in any foreign conflict." He stressed, therefore, that ARC leaders "should be cautious to see that its course of action could not be interpreted as indicating a belief that the United States ought to be, or inevitably would become, involved in such a war."[47] Davis and his colleagues took care to navigate the contested terrain of neutrality. Nonetheless, these optimistic leaders hoped that, as they had twenty years prior, U.S. citizens would step up to fund assistance efforts should war escalate. It would not take long for them to find out. With England's and France's declaration of war on Germany on September 3, 1939, the ARC faced the reality of a Second World War.

*

From late 1939 to late 1941, as U.S. policymakers and civilians hotly debated the merits of neutrality, preparedness, and military intervention, the ARC's leaders steadily increased their overseas civilian relief activities and labored to build public support for them. Their move into civilian relief, though, was by no means immediate, notwithstanding significant pressure for a large-scale intervention from veteran humanitarian Herbert Hoover. Less than two weeks after the declaration of war, ARC chair Norman Davis solicited Hoover's advice on what the ARC should do to help Europe's noncombatants. Hoover gave his "strong recommendation" that "American participation and American effort in relief of such distress should be conducted under the leadership of the American Red Cross." Davis and his fellow ARC leaders, however, demurred, concluding "that the situation in Europe had not yet developed to the point where it was possible to lay out a general program of relief for the civilian victims of the war." Hoover expressed great disappointment with the "hesitancy on the part of the Red Cross in undertaking one of the greatest obligations that has ever come to them.... Leadership of American effort to allay civilian suffering in the war," he argued, "is a mission which no one can perform so effectively as the Red Cross." In the fall of 1939, however, Davis and his colleagues found it imprudent to make any major civilian relief commitment, concerned that any program of "mass feeding and relief over an extended period" would be far beyond the ARC's capabilities.[48]

Although they tabled a major relief enterprise for the time being, ARC leaders did begin to explore the possibility of administering noncombatant aid. A few weeks after the declaration of war, an ARC commission of three men arrived in Europe. Their task was to make recommendations about the needs of European noncombatants and to "ascertain from the belligerent countries and those likely to be involved what, if any, assistance from the American Red Cross is desired."[49] With their reports, Davis told Hoover, "we will know better what we should do and can do."[50] Initially, these delegates judged the level of civilian suffering less severe than they had feared. Germany's advance through Europe in the spring of 1940, however, soon upset their rosier appraisals. Reports of widespread civilian suffering began flooding the Department of State and ARC headquarters. In turn, ARC leaders decided it was time to launch the concerted response for which Hoover had been clamoring.

On May 10, 1940, the ARC issued a formal appeal for donations to relieve noncombatants. President Roosevelt, like Wilson before him, eagerly lent his voice to the cause, urging Americans to aid "the civilian populations of war-torn countries" as "a concrete example of our inherent and decent generosity."[51] As violence in Europe escalated, such messages gradually began to resonate with the American public. U.S. citizens may have debated entering the war, but they proved willing to increase their commitment to the ARC's international humanitarian endeavors. By 1941, membership had risen to nearly nine million, the highest it had been since 1919. Americans donated tens of millions of dollars to the ARC's War Fund as well.[52] Though good for the ARC, this growing public interest in the world's humanitarian crises also proved beneficial to hundreds of other new and established voluntary relief organizations that were trying to raise funds. The ARC soon faced multiple rivals for financial contributions. Recognizing the ARC's important overseas role and concerned that this competition for resources might limit its effectiveness, the federal government put in place several measures to secure the ARC's position as the nation's preferred choice for overseas assistance. First, when it passed the 1939 Neutrality Acts, restricting trade and travel in belligerent nations, Congress specifically defined the legislation's provisions to exclude ARC relief.[53] Then in March 1941, at the recommendation of Secretary of State Cordell Hull, Roosevelt established a Committee on War Relief Agencies, a body to coordinate and regulate the work of all aid agencies *except* the ARC, in order to ensure "that there should be no duplication or waste" and that other agencies did not "impair" or "restrict" the ARC's program.[54] The Committee's leaders also advised Roosevelt that the ARC's "activities should be extended to include all the functions contemplated under its charter and international agreements," including those functions which "are at present carried out in the field by other agencies."[55] Mirroring its efforts in the First World War, the U.S. government reaffirmed the ARC's role as the nation's official voluntary agency for foreign civilian relief and encouraged the organization to expand its efforts abroad.

In the year and a half after launching its formal fundraising drive for noncombatants, armed with strong public and federal support, the ARC once again served as the nation's principal civilian relief organization. During the remaining months of U.S. neutrality, working in collaboration with the LRCS, the ICRC, and the State Department, ARC leaders sent over $50 million in medical supplies, food, clothing, and funds to eleven belligerent and neutral nations that accepted its offer of assistance.[56] Officially, ARC leaders followed the nation in proclaiming their "impartiality to all countries as far as practicable." In practice, however, their aid was far from universal. No funds or relief supplies went to Axis countries or to Axis-occupied territories. ARC leaders cited the Allied blockades, potential threats to personnel, and the rejection of U.S. assistance as the factors that "prevented the extension of relief in these areas." Regardless of the rationale, the ARC relief program effectively favored the Allied Powers in 1940 and 1941. In a period of official neutrality, such limits on aid sent powerful diplomatic signals and raised questions from some circles about the ARC's inherently political nature.[57] The throes of war, however, soon rendered these issues irrelevant. On December 7, 1941, the Japanese invasion of Pearl Harbor ended any pretenses of American neutrality and brought the United States and its Red Cross society into the war on the side of the Allies.

*

A new international humanitarian moment was on the horizon. Building on the sizeable program of civilian assistance developed before the United States entered the war, the ARC's foreign relief efforts truly exploded following U.S. entry into the conflict on December 8, 1941. In the wartime environment, the ARC benefited from the continually increasing support of both the government and the U.S. public. In July 1942, Roosevelt boosted the ARC's special status among aid organizations further still when he issued Executive Order 9205, establishing the President's War Relief Control Board and making permanent the preferential effects of its predecessor, the Committee on War Relief Agencies.[58] The ARC had the endorsement of the White House and, just as ARC leaders had forecast, found wide support among the American public. By the time the war ended in August 1945, thirty-six million Americans had become members of the ARC and had given hundreds of millions of dollars for domestic and foreign relief. While much of this went to assist U.S. armed forces, wounded soldiers, and prisoners of war, the organization apportioned roughly $130 million in cash and supplies for civilian relief, reaching an estimated fifty million noncombatants in forty-eight allied, liberated, and neutral nations.[59] In these respects, the ARC's relief work for foreign civilians—and its role in the U.S. war effort more broadly—mirrored its work during the Great War.

But for all the resemblance that the ARC's 1940s projects bore to their 1910s counterparts, pronounced differences demarcated the two civilian assistance programs. These differences are important to the ARC's history, but more significantly reveal much about the changing character of international civilian assistance during the Second World War era. During this period, the Roosevelt administration greatly expanded the U.S. government's influence and power, both in the United States and throughout the world. At the same time, the rise of new international organizations shifted the balance of power in the world community. These developments profoundly altered the context in which the ARC had operated a quarter of a century prior. They also affected the ways that both the United States and the international community dealt with the issue of civilian aid. In this new environment arose key patterns and precedents that would characterize both American and global humanitarian and development enterprises, in war and in peace, for decades to come.

The growing size and role of the federal government during the 1940s had profound effects on many areas of U.S. society, and the ARC was no exception. Although the ARC had long benefited from its unique relationship with the federal government, World War II saw the state supporting ARC operations in an unprecedented way: through direct financial contributions. From 1941 to 1943, Congress passed a series of four relief appropriation acts that together allotted $85 million for ARC foreign civilian relief activities.[60] Though private donors continued to fuel the ARC's work, this federal funding marked a significant departure from the Great War era's strict reliance on voluntary donations. It also brought the ARC into a much tighter relationship with federal agencies. Under the terms of the legislation, the ARC worked in close cooperation with the Treasury and Departments of Agriculture, State, and War to purchase foodstuffs, medicine, textiles, and other supplies. The ARC then took charge of distributing these items for "relief of men, women, and children who have been driven from their homes or otherwise rendered destitute by hostilities or invasion."[61] ARC leaders assumed all administrative expenses and continued to staff the organization's operations with their own personnel, thus maintaining a good deal of institutional autonomy. Nonetheless, this federal subvention and collaboration made the ARC's standing as a voluntary, non-state organization more ambiguous.

Not only did the U.S. government make financial investments in the ARC, but also into its own civilian relief infrastructure. Even as the Roosevelt administration helped fund the ARC's noncombatant aid activities, it created new governmental and military agencies to carry out many of the tasks once delegated to the ARC. In 1942, the Department of State established the Office of Foreign Relief and Rehabilitation Operations, an organization charged with assisting civilians in liberated areas.[62] The U.S. Army and Navy, too, formed their own Departments of Civil Affairs to ensure the welfare of civilians, refugees, and displaced persons in liberated territories. Several dozen ARC staff members were assigned to work with the military's new public health and welfare officers in Europe and the Pacific, further increasing the ARC's formal ties with the government. In these various ways, the exponential growth of the U.S. government and military during the war years thus carried into the field of civilian assistance, significantly affecting the ways the ARC had previously operated.[63]

The Second World War heralded changes to the international community just as profound as those in the United States. While the U.S. government played a greater role in administering civilian relief, so too did international organizations old and new. During the First World War, the ICRC had largely avoided civilian relief activities (with the exception of aid for noncombatants interred in occupied territories). The developments that had reshaped the International Red Cross Movement over the ensuing decades, however, left the ICRC and LRCS poised to play a prominent role in civilian relief. In 1939, following the outbreak of war, the LRCS created a special relief department for civilians and refugees, later administered jointly with the ICRC.[64] Unlike in World War I, delegates from the International Red Cross played a major part in civilian assistance efforts, serving as a conduit for the funds of the ARC and other national Red Cross societies throughout the world.[65] In addition to these novel efforts by the International Red Cross Movement, the war also saw the development of new intergovernmental humanitarian agencies, most notably the United Nations Relief and Rehabilitation Administration (UNRRA). Created in November 1943, the UNRRA's founding mission was "to plan, coordinate, administer or arrange for the administration of measures for the relief of victims of war in any area under the control of any of the United Nations through the provision of food, fuel, clothing, shelter and other basic necessities."[66] No longer a problem for volunteers or nation-states to solve alone, the issue of civilian relief had become institutionalized in several major international organizations.

As international organizations and U.S. governmental agencies together took up many of the tasks that had fallen under the ARC's purview in the Great War era, the ARC's on-the-ground efforts contracted relative to their antecedents. The ARC's Central Committee explicitly chose to avoid staging a wide-scale humanitarian occupation of other nations as their predecessors had done in 1917 and 1918. ARC leaders sent small staffs to coordinate the distribution of assistance from Europe to the Middle East to Asia, but ultimately very few U.S. personnel oversaw the ARC's civilian relief program in person. At its peak, the number of staff involved in administering noncombatant aid abroad amounted to just 180.[67] Instead, ARC leaders relied primarily on local volunteers, members of other aid agencies and national Red Cross societies, and delegates from the ICRC and LRCS to distribute the millions of dollars in food, clothing, and other material assistance that they contributed. While thousands of Americans did serve in wartime Europe in an ARC uniform, the vast majority of them were engaged in military, not civilian, relief. Unlike their predecessors, ARC leaders also pledged from the beginning that they would not assume "responsibility for a long time and comprehensive housing, feeding, or clothing program for large populations whose normal means of sustenance have been destroyed or disrupted by the war."[68] Although ARC leaders sent several medical and health professionals to act in an advisory capacity, they overwhelmingly resisted their predecessors' attempts to reform the world as they were relieving it.

The years of the Second World War thus witnessed a major transformation in the way that the ARC, the United States, and the world conducted noncombatant relief. The growing role of international and U.S. governmental organizations in the field of civilian relief—and the relative retraction of the ARC's efforts—became all the more pronounced as the war drew to a close and the period of reconstruction began. In the summer of 1945, ARC leaders announced that they were not yet ready to abandon their commitments to foreign civilians. As the assistant director of wartime civilian relief argued, "the American Red Cross has an obligation and a responsibility for extending assistance on behalf of the American people to victims of the war."[69] Consenting to this logic, ARC leaders committed to "continue carrying on a system of international relief for the civilian populations in countries devastated by war." The ARC ultimately distributed relief supplies purchased with government funds until June 1946; it administered privately funded assistance for several months longer. Yet compared with 1919, such attempts at postwar aid and reconstruction proved far more modest. In Europe and Asia, ARC leaders expressly limited their assistance to the short-term provision of material relief to supplement the needs of local governments, charities, and national Red Cross societies. They did not propose an extended intervention in Europe, nor did they plan major reform projects. Although the ARC's leaders promised to continue serving "as the agency of the American people in expressing their voluntary interest and concern in the well-being of civilians in need in foreign countries," in practice they looked to other organizations to assume much of the administrative burden.[70]

Concurrent with ARC leaders' efforts to scale back commitments in postwar Europe, an international movement for civilian health and welfare was blossoming. By 1946, ARC personnel in Europe noted with approval that they had "witnessed increasing activity and interest in the development of international bodies to meet long-term welfare problems."[71] The early postwar years saw the formation of a host of new humanitarian aid and development agencies within the United Nations. Through their diverse sphere of activities, the Food and Agricultural Organization, the International Children's Emergency Fund, the International Refugee Organization, and the World Health Organization collectively took steps to alleviate hunger, suffering, and ill health while improving the health care, nutrition, and well-being of the world's people. In August 1949, this burgeoning international humanitarianism gained further traction with the adoption of the Fourth Geneva Convention, which established "protection of civilian persons in time of war" as a cornerstone of international law. Together, these endeavors aspired to achieve the objectives that had historically motivated many ARC personnel and their supporters.[72]

The U.S. government, too, continued expanding its investment in foreign relief and development in the post–World War II years. Policymakers had long recognized the diplomatic value of these activities. Now, they began to institutionalize them as a permanent part of the Cold War state. In May 1946, President Harry Truman established a permanent Advisory Committee on Voluntary Foreign Aid, intended to make recommendations to the Departments of State and Agricultural on future foreign assistance needs and to serve as a coordinating body with the ARC.[73] Over the ensuing years and decades, as the U.S. government sought to wage the global Cold War and win the hearts and minds of the world, it increasingly took on responsibilities once considered the domain of the ARC and other voluntary agencies. From the economic and technical assistance programs of the 1940s Marshall Plan and Point Four initiatives to the 1960s relief and modernization efforts of the U.S. Agency for International Development, Peace Corps, and Alliance for Progress, the U.S. government assumed an ever greater role in American efforts to relieve, rebuild, and reorder the world.[74]

*

The ARC, of course, did not disappear from the international scene. It continued and continues to represent the United States in the world during moments of global disaster and disorder. After the Great War era, the organization's voluntary civilian assistance arguably became less essential to U.S. foreign policy. Nevertheless, many of the ideological assumptions that underlay its projects in the early twentieth century reverberated throughout future U.S. humanitarian interventions, modernization efforts, and global development initiatives. The logic and rhetoric of international humanitarian obligation, so prominent during the First World War, presaged visions of one-worldism and U.S. free-world leadership that came to dominate U.S. foreign policy discourses in the aftermath of the Second World War.[75] The social scientists and State Department bureaucrats of the Cold War, in a manner that echoed their counterparts in the Great War–era ARC, strove to stabilize and improve the world through rational planning, professional expertise, and the spread of American biomedical, technical, and social scientific knowledge. In short, the belief that the United States had an obligation to provide foreign aid and assistance—a conviction that the ARC did much to cultivate—remained a central pillar of U.S. foreign relations throughout the American Century. The Great War–era roots of these legacies are worth remembering.

Though ideological and physical continuities persist, the position that the ARC occupied in the United States and the world during the Great War era was nonetheless distinct and very much a product of its time. At a moment when U.S. citizens and government officials grappled with their nation's growing power and influence in the world, the ARC became a principal means for them to engage with world health and welfare issues. Through relief and reform activities—many of them quite comprehensive—the ARC served state diplomatic agendas while offering private citizens a way to fulfill their aspirations to alleviate suffering in the world. In the first quarter of the twentieth century, under the auspices of its Red Cross society, the United States made its first major foray into global relief. Decades before the U.S. government and the international community would take systematic steps to alleviate civilian suffering in the world, the United States had undergone an international humanitarian awakening.

Epilogue: A New Manifest Destiny Revisited

In April 1918, when Edward Devine stood before a crowd of ARC volunteers to proclaim a new Manifest Destiny for the United States, he had proposed a foreign policy of "indefinitely expanding brotherhood" that made the welfare of the world's people the nation's paramount concern.[1] Americans should take part in the world, he had argued, but they must do so in a way that furthered the cause of humanity. Through overseas aid and assistance, they could make this vision a reality. Foreign relief certainly did not supplant other forms of U.S. involvement in the world, but in the late nineteenth and early twentieth centuries, it became an integral part of U.S. foreign relations. Alongside military interventions and occupations, diplomatic maneuvering, financial investments, and the spread of American ideas and commodities, foreign assistance represented an important way that Americans interacted with foreign governments and peoples. But was international humanitarianism the altruistic, benevolent form of foreign relations that Devine made it out to be? Or should it instead be regarded as a gentler variety of American cultural imperialism, just another way that American citizens and government officials exercised power on the global stage? Arguably, it was a bit of both. The Janus-faced nature of the international humanitarian enterprise invites consideration about how to characterize U.S. influence in the world at the dawn of the American Century.[2]

On the one hand, the history of the ARC's foreign aid must be regarded as part of a larger process of American political and cultural expansion in the early twentieth-century world. When ARC supporters and personnel assumed an obligation to intervene in and alter the lives of foreign others, they echoed the logic at the heart of American missionary activity, dollar diplomacy, and territorial governance—the belief that as Americans, they possessed both the responsibility and the unique capability to make the world a better, more civilized place. Through the ARC, Americans engaged with foreign civilians and attempted to reshape their lives. This meant more than ameliorating immediate suffering. Confident in the superiority of American approaches to medicine, charity, and social organization, these humanitarians sought to convince aid recipients to accept not only their relief supplies, but also their ideas about health, welfare, and reform. ARC foreign aid was, in these respects, a missionary enterprise for the new era, with all the familiar power dynamics at work.

Humanitarian assistance was also a profoundly political activity, one that served the needs of the expanding corporate state. The provision of food, clothing, employment, and medical assistance bolstered American military and economic incursions across the globe by creating more stable and orderly conditions in areas of American strategic interest. The avowedly altruistic and voluntary nature of ARC assistance projects, moreover, served as valuable cultural diplomacy, particularly for a nation with only a limited formal diplomatic apparatus in place. As the United States spread its reach in the world as never before, the provision of voluntary assistance helped present this process as a compassionate one, driven by the selfless spirit of the American people. Emphasizing the beneficence of aid effectively masked the more violent and aggressive sides of American involvement in the world and defined U.S. influence as a force for good. The ARC's humanitarian interventions, in short, undergirded the nascent structures of empire and U.S. global power.

While it is vital to not deny or sugarcoat the ways that humanitarian interventionism advanced U.S. national interests, it is equally important to acknowledge its more positive attributes and to appreciate the way that Americans understood it at the time. For many of its practitioners and proponents, ARC foreign assistance represented a distinctly progressive path to American global engagement, especially when compared to contemporary alternatives. The ARC's growing importance in U.S. international relations coincided with a period of rising American military and financial power in the world. The early twentieth century saw U.S. forces occupy Latin American nations on numerous occasions, while U.S. territorial governments—backed by the threat of military intervention—exercised substantial control over foreign civilians. In World War I, the Wilson administration sent U.S. citizens to take up arms in an unprecedented global conflict. Throughout these years, American bankers and capitalists labored to reshape the world economic order, often to the detriment of foreign civilians and their livelihoods. To many contemporary Americans, foreign assistance appeared to offer a real alternative to these incursions, a better way to effect positive change in the world. To be sure, not every ARC supporter discounted other forms of global involvement; indeed, many found it quite feasible—often preferable—to support military and economic interventions and foreign assistance simultaneously. Nevertheless, by electing to fund or participate in foreign aid activities, Americans made the choice to support a nonviolent, compassionate form of engagement with the world.

Through the ARC's foreign aid efforts, Americans also found a potential opportunity to forge cooperative, collaborative, and mutually beneficial relationships with foreign civilians. As an organization, the ARC officially pledged to aid civilians without regard to race, creed, or politics and to be part of a global movement for humanity. Although actual on-the-ground practices often belied these twin institutional missions, many individual ARC workers strove to adhere to these commitments. Biographical sketches of a number of ARC personnel attest to their considerable faith in the capacities, interests, and humanity of the people with whom they worked. Many also demonstrated a strong belief in the importance of international humanitarian engagement and fought hard to keep those ideals alive, even when public support waned. In the early twentieth-century United States, a nation rife with assumptions about the inferiority of certain races and cultures and divided over the merits of American global participation, the ARC could prove a supportive vehicle for Americans committed to pursuing more reciprocal international relationships.

ARC humanitarian interventions, then, rationalized American global expansion even as they offered viable, less violent, and potentially more cosmopolitan avenues for its execution. Historical assessments that center on the inherent politics and power dynamics of humanitarian interventions risk smearing aid as indistinguishable from imperialism. On the other end of the spectrum, analyses focused solely on the virtues of aid tread perilously into apologia or glorification. Neither approach does justice to the practitioners of foreign assistance or to the political and cultural meaning of their activities. Incorporating the ARC's foreign relief into the history of foreign relations thus presents a more complicated, yet ultimately more satisfying, narrative of American global power and influence in the late nineteenth and early twentieth centuries. As Americans grappled with their nation's new role in the international community, their efforts to improve the health and well-being of their fellow world citizens constituted an important means of engaging with the world and defining their place in it.

As the United States contemplates its international identity in today's post-Cold War, globalized world, Edward Devine's vision of foreign assistance as an American obligation is as timely as it was in 1918. In the new millennium, U.S. citizens and government officials continue to wrestle with the question of how to engage ethically and responsibly in international welfare initiatives, and of how to balance the risk of imposing American political and cultural ideals on other populations with the recognition of the poverty, ill health, and suffering that may result should Americans ignore the international community. We debate whether the United States has an obligation to share its material and intellectual resources with the world. Even if we agree that it does, we are left deliberating whether international humanitarianism is the responsibility of the government or of private citizens. We question, moreover, what role both international organizations and the recipients of aid themselves ought to have in shaping and directing U.S. policy. The matter of American international humanitarianism is as vital now as it was in the Great War era. By understanding its history, we can better determine the role that foreign aid should play in U.S. relations with the world today.

NOTES

Introduction: A New Manifest Destiny

1. Edward T. Devine, Address in Paris, April 6, 1918, Box 5, ETD.
2. This book forms part of an emerging field of international humanitarian studies, joining several other recent works in integrating the history of foreign relief and assistance into the history of foreign relations. See, for instance, Gary Bass, *Freedom's Battle: The Origins of Humanitarian Intervention* (New York: Knopf, 2008); Davide Rodogno, *Against Massacre: Humanitarian Interventions in the Ottoman Empire, 1815–1914* (Princeton: Princeton University Press, 2011); Tammy M. Proctor, *Civilians in a World at War, 1914–1918* (New York: New York University Press, 2010); Keith David Watenpaugh, "'A pious wish devoid of all practicability': Interwar Humanitarianism, The League of Nations and the Rescue of Trafficked Women and Children in the Eastern Mediterranean, 1920–1927," *American Historical Review*, 115:4 (October 2010): 1315–1339; Michael Barnett, *Empire of Humanity: A History of Humanitarianism* (Ithaca: Cornell University Press, 2011); Branden Little, "Band of Crusaders: American Humanitarians, the Great War, and the Remaking of the World," Ph.D. dissertation, University of California at Berkeley, 2009; Michael McGuire, "An Ephemeral Relationship: American Non-governmental Organizations, the Reconstruction of France, and Franco-American Relations, 1914–1924, Ph.D. dissertation, Boston University, 2012; Jennifer Polk, "Constructive Efforts: The American Red Cross and YMCA in Revolutionary and Civil War Russia, 1917–1924," Ph.D. dissertation, University of Toronto, 2012; Melanie Tanielian, "The War of Famine: Everyday Life in Wartime Beirut and Mount Lebanon (1914–1918)," Ph.D. dissertation, University of California at Berkeley, 2012; Thomas Westerman, "Rough and Ready Relief: American Identity, Humanitarian Experience, and the Commission for Relief in Belgium, 1914–1917," Ph.D. dissertation, University of Connecticut, 2014.
3. Good syntheses of this period are in Emily Rosenberg, *Spreading the American Dream: American Economic and Cultural Expansion, 1890–1945* (New York: Hill and Wang, 1982), chs. 1–8; Frank Ninkovich, *Global Dawn: The Cultural Foundation of American Internationalism, 1865–1890* (Cambridge: Harvard University Press, 2009); Robert E. Hannigan, *The New World Power: American Foreign Policy, 1898–1917* (Philadelphia: University of Pennsylvania Press, 2002); George C. Herring, *From Colony to Superpower: U.S. Foreign Relations Since 1776* (New York: Oxford University Press, 2008) chs. 7–10.
4. For the culture of voluntary, civic engagement, see Leon Fink, *Progressive Intellectuals and the Dilemmas of Democratic Commitment* (Cambridge: Harvard University Press, 1997), 1–51; Christopher Capozzola, *Uncle Sam Wants You: World War I and the Making of the Modern American Citizen* (Oxford: Oxford University Press, 2008), 3–20; Theda Skocpol, Marshall Ganz, and Ziad Munson, "A Nation of Organizers: The Institutional Origins of Civic Voluntarism in the United States," *American Political Science Review* 94

(Sept 2000): 527–546; and Theda Skocpol, "Patriotic Partnerships: Why Great Wars Nourished American Civic Voluntarism," in *Shaped by War and Trade: International Influences on American Political Development,* eds. Ira Katznelson and Martin Shefter (Princeton: Princeton University Press, 2001).

5. Historians of development and aid have made similar points for the post–World War II period. See, for example, Michael J. Hogan, *Marshall Plan: America, Britain, and the Reconstruction of Western Europe, 1947–1952* (Cambridge: Cambridge University Press, 1989); Elizabeth Cobbs Hoffman, *All You Need is Love: The Peace Corps and the Spirit of the 1960s* (Cambridge: Harvard University Press, 1998); Michael Latham, *Modernization as Ideology: American Social Science and "Nation Building" in the Kennedy Era* (Chapel Hill: University of North Carolina Press, 2000); Nils Gilman, *Mandarins of the Future: Modernization Theory in Cold War America* (Baltimore: The Johns Hopkins University Press, 2007); David Ekbladh, *The Great American Mission: Modernization and the Construction of an American World Order* (Princeton: Princeton University Press, 2009); and Nick Cullather, *The Hungry World: America's Cold War Battle Against Poverty in Asia* (Cambridge: Harvard University Press, 2010). Less has been written on the Great War era, but see Nick Cullather, "The Foreign Policy of the Calorie," *The American Historical Review* 112 (2007): 337–364; David Engerman, *Modernization from the Other Shore: American Intellectuals and the Romance of Russian Development* (Cambridge: Harvard University Press, 2003); Bertrande Patenaude, *The Big Show in Bololand: The American Relief Expedition to Soviet Russia in the Famine of 1921* (Stanford: Stanford University Press, 2002); Branden Little, "Humanitarian Relief in Europe and the Analogue of War, 1914–1918," in *Finding Common Ground: New Directions in First World War Studies*, eds. Jennifer Keene and Michael Neiberg (Leiden and Boston: Brill, 2010): 139–158.

6. Classic—but still valuable—accounts of many of these organizations are found in Merle Curti, *Prelude to Point Four: American Technical Missions Overseas, 1838–1938* (Madison: University of Wisconsin Press, 1954) and *American Philanthropy Abroad* (New Brunswick: Rutgers University Press, 1963). Recently, a new generation of historians has started to examine these organizations in greater detail. See Little, "Band of Crusaders"; McGuire, "An Ephemeral Relationship"; Polk, "Constructive Efforts"; Westerman, "Rough and Ready Relief."

7. See, for instance, *Competing Kingdoms: Women, Mission, Nation, and the America Protestant Empire, 1812–1960,* eds. Barbara Reeves-Ellington, Kathryn Kish Sklar, and Connie A. Shemo (Durham: Duke University Press, 2010); Marcos Cueto, ed., *Missionaries of Science: The Rockefeller Foundation in Latin America* (Bloomington: Indiana University Press, 1994); John Farley, *To Cast out Disease: A History of the International Health Division of the Rockefeller Foundation 1913–1951* (Oxford: Oxford University Press, 2004); many of the essays in Alfred McCoy and Francisco Scarano, eds., *Colonial Crucible: Empire in the Making of the Modern American State* (Madison: University of Wisconsin Press, 2009); Emily Rosenberg, *Financial Missionaries to the World: The Politics and Culture of Dollar Diplomacy, 1900–1930* (Durham: Duke University Press, 2003); Alan Dawley, *Changing the World: American Progressives in War and Revolution* (Princeton: Princeton University Press, 2003); George Nash, *The Life of Herbert Hoover: The Humanitarian, 1914–1917* (New York: W. W. Norton & Company, 1988) and *The Life of Herbert Hoover: Master of Emergencies* (New York: W. W. Norton & Company, 1996); and Kendrick Clements, *The Life of Herbert Hoover: Imperfect Visionary, 1918–1928* (New York: Palgrave Macmillan, 2010).

8. The only book-length study on the ARC's history remains Foster Rhea Dulles's 1950 work, *The American Red Cross: A History* (New York: Harper, 1950). Also influential has been Gustave R. Gaeddert's "The History of the American National Red Cross," an unpublished manuscript in four volumes (Washington, D.C.: American National Red Cross Historical Division, 1950). John F. Hutchinson provides a good sketch of the ARC in his study of the International Red Cross Movement, but limits his focus to the organization's leaders and its work for the U.S. military. He considers neither ARC civilian assistance nor the cultural significance of humanitarian interventionism on American internationalist thought. See his *Champions of Charity: War and the Rise of the Red Cross* (Boulder: Westview Press,

1997). Marian Moser Jones examines the ARC's role in domestic disaster relief. See her *The American Red Cross, From Clara Barton to the New Deal* (Baltimore: The Johns Hopkins University Press, 2013). Branden Little devotes one chapter of his dissertation to the ARC. See "Band of Crusaders," ch. 4. Finally, Caroline Moorhead's popular history of the International Red Cross includes limited information on the American society and its civilian relief efforts. See her *Dunant's Dream: War, Switzerland, and the History of the American Red Cross* (London: Harper Collins, 1998).

9. William Taft, "Proclamation by the President of the United States," 1911, Central Decimal File 811.142/218, DOS.

10. Although the ARC directed time and energy to U.S. soldiers, the organization would spend more than half of the money it raised in 1917 and 1918 to fund projects for civilians overseas. See *Annual Report of the American Red Cross*, for the year ending 1917 and for the fiscal years ending June 30, 1918–1923; and Henry Davison, *The Work of the American Red Cross During the War* (Washington, D.C.: The American National Red Cross, 1919).

11. Although the meaning of the term "Progressive Era" is hotly contested, that has not stopped historians from trying to define it. For an introduction to this historiographic debate, see Glenda Elizabeth Gilmore, ed., *Who Were the Progressives?* (New York: Palgrave MacMillan, 2002); Michael McGerr, *A Fierce Discontent: The Rise and Fall of the Progressive Movement in America, 1870–1920* (New York: Free Press, 2003); Maureen Flanagan, *America Reformed: Progressives and Progressivisms, 1890s–1920s* (Oxford: Oxford University Press, 2006). For the associative state, see Rosenberg, *Spreading the American Dream*, chs. 1–8; Ellis W. Hawley, *The Great War and the Search for a Modern Order: A History of the American People and their Institutions.* New York: St. Martin's Press, 1979). see Michael J. Hogan, "Corporatism: A Positive Appraisal," *Diplomatic History* 10 (1986): 363–372; Thomas J. McCormick, "Drift or Mastery? A Corporatist Synthesis for American Diplomatic History," *Reviews in American History* 10 (1982): 318–330. For discussions of progressivism and social democracy, see James T. Kloppenberg, *Uncertain Victory: Social Democracy and Progressivism in European and American Thought, 1870–1920* (New York: Oxford University Press, 1986), introduction and chs. 5–10; Rogers Smith, *Civic Ideals: Conflicting Visions of Citizenship in U.S. History* (New Haven: Yale University Press, 2009), ch. 12; Capozzola, *Uncle Sam Wants You*, 3–20; Skocpol, Ganz, and Munson, "A Nation of Organizers." For cultures of efficiency, expertise, and professionalism, see Daniel T. Rodgers, *Atlantic Crossings: Social Politics in a Progressive Age* (Cambridge: Harvard University Press, 1998) and John Louis Recchiuti, *Civic Engagement: Social Science and Progressive Reform in New York City* (Philadelphia: University of Pennsylvania Press, 2007).

12. See, for example, Ian Tyrrell, *Reforming the World: The Creation of America's Moral Empire* (Princeton: Princeton University Press, 2010) and *Woman's World/Woman's Empire: The Woman's Christian Temperance Union in International Perspective, 1880–1930* (Chapel Hill: University of North Carolina Press, 1991); Jane H. Hunter, "Women's Mission in Historical Perspective: American Identity and Christian Internationalism" and Ian Tyrrell, "Woman, Missions, and Empire: New Approaches to Cultural Expansion," in *Competing Kingdoms*, 19–42 and 43–68; William R. Hutchinson, *Errand to the World: American Protestant Thought and Foreign Missions* (Chicago: University of Chicago Press, 1987). For the importance of integrating American religious and diplomatic histories, see Andrew Preston, "Bridging the Gap between the Sacred and the Secular in the History of American Foreign Relations," *Diplomatic History* 30 (2006): 783–812.

13. For discussions of "progressive" and "liberal" internationalism, see Ross Kennedy, *The Will to Believe: Woodrow Wilson, World War I, and America's Strategy for Peace and Security* (Kent: The Kent State University Press, 2009); Thomas J. Knock, *To End All Wars: Woodrow Wilson and the Quest for a New World Order* (Princeton: Princeton University Press, 1992); Lloyd Ambrosius, *Wilsonianism: Woodrow Wilson and his Legacy in American Foreign Relations* (New York: Palgrave MacMillan, 2002); Frank Ninkovich, *Modernity and Power: A History of the Domino Theory in the Twentieth Century* (Chicago: University of Chicago Press, 1994), chs. 1–2; Robert David Johnson, *The Peace Progressives and American Foreign Relations* (Cambridge: Harvard University Press, 1995); Leila J. Rupp, *Worlds of Women: The Making of an International Women's Movement* (Princeton: Princeton University Press,

1997); Linda Schott, *Reconstructing Women's Thoughts: The Women's International League for Peace and Freedom Before World War II* (Palo Alto: Stanford University Press, 1997); Dawley, *Changing the World*; Rodgers, *Atlantic Crossings*. Good discussions of American cosmopolitan sensibilities are in Jonathan Hansen, *The Lost Promise of Patriotism: Debating American Identity, 1890–1920* (Chicago: University of Chicago Press, 2003); Martha Nussbaum, "Patriotism and Cosmopolitanism," in *For Love of Country: Debating the Limits of Patriotism*, ed. Joshua Cohen (Boston: Beacon Press, 1996); David Hollinger, "Nationalism, Cosmopolitanism, and the United States," in *Immigration and Citizenship in the Twenty-First Century*, ed. Noah Pickus (Lanham: Rowman & Littlefield Publishers, 1998), 85–99. For debates over the merits of political and informal internationalism, isolation, and non-intervention, see John Milton Cooper, Jr., *The Vanity of Power: American Isolationism and the First World War, 1914–1917* (Westport: Greenwood Press, 1970); Ronald Powaski, *Toward an Entangling Alliance: American Isolationism, Internationalism, and Europe, 1901–1950* (Westport: Greenwood Press, 1991); Christopher M. Nichols, *Promise and Peril: America at the Dawn of a Global Age* (Cambridge: Harvard University Press, 2011).

Chapter One: Making International Humanitarianism American

1. For Bicknell's background, see the Ernest Bicknell Papers, EBHB and EBUI, and his *Pioneering with the Red Cross: Reflections of an Old Red Crosser* (New York: The MacMillan Company, 1935); *In War's Wake, 1914–1915: The Rockefeller Foundation and the American Red Cross Join in Civilian Relief* (Washington, D.C.: The American Red Cross, 1938); *With the Red Cross in Europe, 1917–1922* (Washington, D.C.: The American Red Cross, 1938).

2. See, for instance, Robert M. Crunden, *Ministers of Reform: The Progressives' Achievement in American Civilization, 1889–1920* (Urbana: University of Illinois Press, 1985); T. J. Jackson Lears, *No Place of Grace: Antimodernism and the Transformation of American Culture, 1880–1920* (Chicago: University of Chicago Press, 1994); and Diane Winston, *Red-Hot and Righteous: The Urban Religion of the Salvation Army* (Cambridge: Harvard University Press, 2000).

3. See James T. Kloppenberg, *Uncertain Victory: Social Democracy and Progressivism in European and American Thought, 1870–1920* (New York: Oxford University Press, 1986); Theda Skocpol, Marshall Ganz, and Ziad Munson, "A Nation of Organizers: The Institutional Origins of Civic Voluntarism in the United States," *American Political Science Review* 94 (2000): 527–46; Olivier Zunz, *Philanthropy in America: A History* (Princeton: Princeton University Press, 2011), chs. 1–3.

4. See Leslie Butler, *Critical Americans: Victorian Intellectuals and Transatlantic Liberal Reform* (Chapel Hill: University of North Carolina Press, 2007); Frank Ninkovich, *Global Dawn: The Cultural Foundations of American Internationalism, 1865–1890* (Cambridge: Harvard University Press, 2009); Daniel T. Rodgers, *Atlantic Crossings: Social Politics in a Progressive Age* (Cambridge: Harvard University Press, 2000).

5. My understanding of this turn-of-the-century international humanitarian awakening draws from the work of historians of domestic humanitarianism in the antebellum United States. These scholars have argued persuasively that the impulse to care about the suffering of other sentient beings emerged in response to changing cultural and social norms and sensibilities. See, for example, David Brion Davis, *The Problem of Slavery in an Age of Revolution, 1770–1823* (Ithaca: Cornell University Press, 1975); T. L. Haskell, "Capitalism and the Origins of Humanitarian Sensibility, Part I," *American Historical Review* 90 (1985): 339–361 and "Capitalism and the Origins of Humanitarian Sensibility, Part II," *American Historical Review* 90 (1985): 547–566; Karen Haltunnen, "Humanitarianism and the Pornography of Pain in Anglo-American Culture," *American Historical Review* 100 (1995): 303–334; Elizabeth B. Clark, "'The Sacred Rights of the Weak': Pain, Sympathy, and the Culture of Individual Rights in Antebellum America," *Journal of American History* 82 (1995): 463–493; Robert Abzug, *Cosmos Crumbling: American Reform and the Religious Imagination* (New York: Oxford University Press, 1997); Michael P. Young, *Bearing Witness*

Against Sin: The Evangelical Birth of the American Social Movement (Chicago: University of Chicago Press, 2007).

6. For the ARC's founding, see Folder 110, Box 13, RCNA1. See also Elizabeth Brown Pryor, *Clara Barton: Professional Angel* (Philadelphia: University of Pennsylvania Press, 1987), 204–205.

7. Davis, *The Problem of Slavery in an Age of Revolution*; T. L. Haskell, "Capitalism and the Origins of Humanitarian Sensibility"; Haltunnen, "Humanitarianism and the Pornography of Pain"; Clark, "'The Sacred Rights of the Weak.'"

8. Abzug, *Cosmos Crumbling*; Young, *Bearing Witness Against Sin*.

9. John Duffy, *The Sanitarians: A History of American Public Health* (Urbana: University of Illinois Press, 1997), chs. 7–11; Martin Melosi, *The Sanitary City: Urban Infrastructure in America from Colonial Times to the Present* (Baltimore: The Johns Hopkins University Press, 1999), chs. 4–5.

10. Gary Bass, *Freedom's Battle: The Origins of Humanitarian Intervention* (New York: Knopf, 2008), ch. 7.

11. See, for example, Kathryn Kish Sklar and James Brewer Stewart, eds., *Women's Rights and Transatlantic Antislavery in the Era of Emancipation* (New Haven: Yale University Press, 2007); John Harley Warner, *Against the Spirit of System: The French Impulse in Nineteenth-Century American Medicine* (Baltimore: The Johns Hopkins University Press, 2003).

12. Robert H. Bremner, *American Philanthropy* (Chicago: University of Chicago Press, 1988), chs. 1–4 and *The Public Good: Philanthropy and Welfare in the Civil War Era* (New York: Alfred A. Knopf, 1980).

13. See Duffy, *The Sanitarians*, ch. 7; James Brewer Stewart, *Abolitionist Politics and the Coming of the Civil War* (Amherst: University of Massachusetts Press, 2008); Michele Landis, "'Let Me Next Time Be Tried By Fire': Disaster Relief and the Origins of the American Welfare State 1789–1874," *Northwestern University Law Review* 92 (1998): 967–1034; Michele Landis Dauber, *The Sympathetic State: Disaster Relief and the Origins of the American Welfare State* (Chicago: University of Chicago Press, 2012), chs. 1 and 2.

14. Pryor, *Clara Barton*, chs. 1–5.

15. Duffy, *The Sanitarians*, chs. 8 and 9; Judith Ann Giesberg, *Civil War Sisterhood: The U.S. Sanitary Commission and Women's Politics in Transition* (Boston: Northeastern University Press, 2000).

16. Jacqueline Jones, *Soldiers of Light and Love: Northern Teachers and Georgia Blacks, 1865–1973* (Athens: University of Georgia Press, 1992); Ronald Butchart, *Schooling the Freed People: Teaching, Learning and the Struggle for Black Freedom, 1861–1876* (Chapel Hill: University of North Carolina Press, 2010).

17. See Patricia Hill, *The World Their Household: The American Woman's Foreign Mission Movement and Cultural Transformation, 1870–1920* (Ann Arbor: University of Michigan Press, 1985); Barbara Reeves-Ellington, Kathryn Kish Sklar, and Connie A. Shemo, eds., *Competing Kingdoms: Women, Mission, Nation, and the America Protestant Empire, 1812–1960* (Durham: Duke University Press, 2010); Ian Tyrrell, *Reforming the World: The Creation of America's Moral Empire* (Princeton: Princeton University Press, 2010); and Michael Adas, *Dominance by Design: Technological Imperatives and America's Civilizing Mission* (Cambridge: Harvard University Press, 2009), chs. 1–3.

18. Pryor, *Clara Barton*, chs. 6–10

19. John F. Hutchinson, *Champions of Charity: War and the Rise of the Red Cross* (Boulder: Westview, 1996), ch. 1. David P. Forsythe, *The Humanitarians: The International Committee of the Red Cross* (Cambridge: Cambridge University Press, 2005), ch 1.

20. Hutchinson, *Champions of Charity*, ch. 2.

21. Pryor, *Clara Barton*, ch. 11; Hutchinson, *Champions of Charity*, 224–26.

22. Pryor, *Clara Barton*, ch. 12.

23. James G. Blaine, quoted in Pryor, *Clara Barton*, 203.

24. Hutchinson, *Champions of Charity*, 226–228.

25. John Louis Recchiuti, *Civic Engagement: Social Science and Progressive-Era Reform in New York* (Philadelphia: University of Pennsylvania Press, 2007), chs. 1–2; Cilia Tichi, *Civic Passions: Seven Who Launched Progressive America* (Chapel Hill: University of North Carolina Press, 2009), esp. chs. 1–4; Elizabeth N. Agnew, *From Charity to Social Work: Mary E. Richmond and the Creation of an American Profession* (Urbana: University of Illinois Press, 2003); Zunz, *Philanthropy in America,* chs. 1–3.

26. Tichi, *Civic Passions,* ch. 6; Susan Curtis, *A Consuming Faith: The Social Gospel and Modern American Culture* (Columbia: University of Missouri Press, 2001).

27. George Herring, *From Colony to Superpower: U.S. Foreign Relations Since 1776* (New York: Oxford University Press, 2008), chs. 7–8.

28. Butler, *Critical Americans;* Ninkovich, *Global Dawn;* Jonathan Hansen, *The Lost Promise of Patriotism: Debating American Identity, 1890–1920* (Chicago: University of Chicago Press, 2003).

29. Hutchinson, *Champions of Charity,* chs. 3–4.

30. Clara Barton, *A Story of the Red Cross: Glimpses of Field Work* (New York: MacMillan, 1904), chs. 1–3; Pryor, *Clara Barton,* ch. 13.

31. Barton, *A Story of the Red Cross,* chs. 5 and 7; Pryor, *Clara Barton,* ch. 14.

32. Kristin Hoganson, *Fighting for American Manhood: How Gender Politics Provoked the Spanish-American and Philippine-American Wars* (New Haven: Yale University Press, 1998), chs. 1–4.

33. George M. Sternberg, "The Surgeon Generals' Relations with the American Red Cross," *New York Daily Tribune,* August 30, 1898, 3.

34. William McKinley, "Message of the President to Congress," *FRUS, 1898:* LXIII; Barton, *A Story of the Red Cross,* ch. 8; Pryor, *Clara Barton,* ch. 16.

35. American National Red Cross Charter of Incorporation, 1900 (31 Stat. 277–280); Hutchinson, *Champions of Charity,* 229–231; Pryor, *Clara Barton,* ch. 16.

36. Quotation from Mrs. John A. Logan to the American National Red Cross Society, June 7, 1904, Reel 75, CB.

37. Diary of Clara Barton, December 31, 1902, Reel 5, CB; George B. Cortelyou for Theodore Roosevelt to Mabel Boardman, January 2, 1903, Reel 74, CB.

38. Diary of Clara Barton, December 10, 1902, Reel 5, CB.

39. John T. Forster, Mabel T. Boardman, et. al., Letter to the President of the United States, December 20, 1902, Reel 48, CB.

40. "Red Cross Rows Will Be Stopped," *Chicago Daily,* April 23, 1903, 1.

41. For the text of these letters, see George Cortelyou to Clara Barton, January 2, 1903, in the American Red Cross Annual Report for the Year Ending 1903, Office of the Secretary of War, General Correspondence, 6946, RG 107, NADC; "Miss Clara Barton Writes to Mr. Roosevelt," *New York Times,* February 2, 1903.

42. Clara Barton to Richard Olney, December 3, 1903, Reel 74, CB; "Miss Barton Resigns," *The Washington Post,* May 15, 1904, p. 2.

43. For specific charges, see Boxes 10 and 11, RCNA1; "Red Cross Controversies: Miss Boardman's Correspondence with Mrs. John A. Logan," *New York Times,* March 29, 1903, 2. For more on Boardman and the fight against Barton, see Pryor, *Clara Barton,* 332–366; Marian Moser Jones, *The American Red Cross, From Clara Barton to the New Deal* (Baltimore: The Johns Hopkins University Press, 2013).

44. Theodore Roosevelt, First State of the Union Address, December 3, 1901.

45. See for example Lewis Gould, *The Presidency of Theodore Roosevelt* (Lawrence: University of Kansas Press, 1991, rpr. 2011).

46. Congressional Charter of the American National Red Cross, 1905, (33 Stat. 599–602); Hutchinson, *Champions of Charity,* 231–233.

47. For Taft and Boardman's meeting and friendship, see Jones, *The American Red Cross;* "The Most Intimate Friends of President Taft," *New York Times* May 29, 1910.

48. For Taft's foreign affairs philosophies, see David Burton, *William Howard Taft: Confident Peacemaker* (New York: Fordham University Press, 2004).

49. For these members see the American Red Cross *Bulletins* for the years ending 1906–1908.

50. Theodore Roosevelt, "The Appeal Issued by the President," *The Washington Post*, April 20, 1906.
51. See Recchiuti, *Civic Engagement*, esp. ch. 2.
52. Bicknell, *Pioneering with the Red Cross*, chs. 1, 2, and 5. For a discussion of the San Francisco relief effort, see Kevin Rozario, *The Culture of Calamity: Disaster and the Making of Modern America* (Chicago: University of Chicago Press, 2007), interlude and ch. 2; Ted Steinberg, *Acts of God: The Unnatural History of Natural Disaster in the United States* (Oxford: Oxford University Press, 2006), ch. 2.
53. Ernest Bicknell to Mabel Boardman, October 29, 1906, EBHB.
54. Charles L. Magee to Chicago Bureau of Charities, October 24, 1906, EBHB.
55. Ernest Bicknell to Mabel Boardman, May 17, 1908, EBHB.
56. Graham Taylor, "The Red Cross Director," *Charities and the Commons* (June 1908): 396.
57. See Ruth Crocker, *Mrs. Russell Sage: Women's Activism and Philanthropy in Gilded Age and Progressive Era America* (Bloomington: Indiana University Press, 2006), ch. 11.
58. John M. Glenn to Mabel Boardman, May 20, 1908, Box 8, RCNA1.
59. "Taft Red Cross President," *New York Times*, December 9, 1908.
60. Minutes for the 1908 Annual Meeting, Box 13, RCNA1; American Red Cross to the Russell Sage Foundation, "Report of Progress and Operations of the American Red Cross for the Period from October 1, 1908 to January 1, 1910," Box 8, RCNA1.

Chapter Two: Humanitarian Preparedness

1. William H. Taft, quoted in "Lay Cornerstone of Red Cross Home," *New York Times*, March 28, 1915.
2. Woodrow Wilson, quoted in "Wilson Foresees War of Grimness," *The New York Times*, May 13, 1917.
3. For the similarities of these administrations and their foreign policy approaches, see Ross Kennedy, *The Will to Believe: Woodrow Wilson, World War I, and America's Strategy for Peace and Security* (Kent: The Kent State University Press, 2009); Robert E. Hannigan, *The New World Power: American Foreign Policy, 1898–1917* (Philadelphia: University of Pennsylvania Press, 2002). For "liberal internationalism," see also Thomas J. Knock, *To End All Wars: Woodrow Wilson and the Quest for a New World Order* (Princeton: Princeton University Press, 1992); Lloyd Ambrosius, *Wilsonianism: Woodrow Wilson and his Legacy in American Foreign Relations* (New York: Palgrave MacMillan, 2002); and Frank Ninkovich, *Modernity and Power: A History of the Domino Theory in the Twentieth Century* (Chicago: University of Chicago Press, 1994), chs. 1 and 2.
4. For important discussions of this relationship, see Michael J. Hogan, "Corporatism: A Positive Appraisal," *Diplomatic History* 10 (1986): 363–372; Ellis W. Hawley, "The Discovery and Study of a 'Corporate Liberalism,'" *Business History Review* 52 (1978): 309–320; Thomas J. McCormick, "Drift or Mastery? A Corporatist Synthesis for American Diplomatic History," *Reviews in American History* 10 (1982): 318–330. Emily Rosenberg, *Spreading the American Dream: American Economic and Cultural Expansion, 1890–1945* (New York: Hill and Wang, 1982), chs. 1–8; Rogers Smith, *Civic Ideals: Conflicting Visions of Citizenship in U.S. History* (New Haven: Yale University Press, 2009), ch. 12; and Theta Skocpol, "The Tocqueville Problem: Civic Engagement in American Democracy," *Social Science History* 21 (1997): 455–479.
5. For these individuals, variously described as "progressive internationalists" and "cosmopolitan nationalists," see Daniel T. Rodgers, *Atlantic Crossings: Social Politics in a Progressive Age* (Cambridge: Harvard University Press, 2000); Alan Dawley, *Changing the World: American Progressives in War and Revolution* (Princeton: Princeton University Press, 2003); and Jonathan Hansen, *The Lost Promise of Patriotism: Debating American Identity, 1890–1920* (Chicago: University of Chicago Press, 2003).
6. William H. Taft, Inaugural Address, March 4, 1909.
7. Good accounts of Taft's approach to foreign relations are in David Burton, *William Howard Taft: Confident Peacemaker* (New York: Fordham University Press, 2004); Emily Rosenberg,

Financial Missionaries to the World: The Politics and Culture of Dollar Diplomacy (Durham: Duke University Press, 2003), ch. 3; Hannigan, *The New World Power*, chs. 1–5.

8. William H. Taft, quoted in Secretary of State to Ambassador Griscom, December 29, 1908, *FRUS 1908:* 499.

9. "Italy's Earthquake," *The Washington Post*, December 30, 1908; "Relief of Earthquake Sufferers in Italy," *Congressional Record* 60:2 (January 4, 1909): 452–454; Mabel Boardman, "The American Red Cross in Italy," *The National Geographic Magazine* (1909): 396–397; *FRUS 1908:* 499–501; Salvatore La Gumina, *The Great Earthquake: America Comes to Messina's Rescue* (Amherst, NY: Teneo Press, 2008). Prior to 1908, the U.S. Congress had allocated relief funds to such humanitarian crises as famine and civil strife on a handful of occasions; only rarely had it made appropriations for natural disasters. The amount given to Italy in 1908, moreover, was unprecedented.

10. For U.S.-Italian relations, see Daniela Rossini, *Woodrow Wilson and the American Myth in Italy* (Cambridge: Harvard University Press, 2008), ch. 1.

11. For American assumptions about Italians, see Thomas A. Guglielmo, *White on Arrival: Italians, Race, Color, and Power in Chicago, 1890–1945* (New York: Oxford University Press, 2003), chs. 1–5.

12. Quotation: W. Bayard Cutting Jr., "Early Days of Relief," in *American National Red Cross Bulletin* (April 1909): 42.

13. For further descriptions see Secretary of the American Embassy in Italy to George W. Davis, January 31, 1910, Central Decimal File 811.142, Volume 851, DOS.

14. "E. P. Bicknell Visits London," *Los Angeles Times*, February 25, 1909, 12. See also Ernest P. Bicknell, "Calabria and Sicily Two Months After the Earthquake," *American National Red Cross Bulletin* (July 1909); Bicknell, *Reflections of an Old Red Crosser* (New York: The MacMillan Company, 1935), chs. 11 and 12.

15. Philander Knox to Diplomatic and Consular Officers of the United States, November 1, 1909, *FRUS 1909:* 4–8.

16. William H. Taft, quoted in "Taft Tells of Need of Red Cross Fund," *New York Times*, December 3, 1909. For the status of other Red Cross Societies see John F. Hutchinson, *Champions of Charity: War and the Rise of the Red Cross* (Boulder: Westview, 1996), ch. 5.

17. William H. Taft, quoted in "Taft Tells of Need of Red Cross Fund," *New York Times*, December 3, 1909; *American National Red Cross Bulletin* (January 1910): 61–62.

18. For accounts of these efforts, see *Annual Report of the American Red Cross* (years 1909–1912) and Mabel Boardman, *Under the Red Cross Flag at Home and Abroad* (Philadelphia: J. B. Lippincott, 1915), chs. 9 and 13.

19. Hannigan, *The New World Power*, ch. 4.

20. See, for example, "Chinese Famine A Peril: American Consul Predicts Dangerous Outcome of Terrible Conditions," *New York Times*, January 29, 1907, 8.

21. Randall E. Stoss, *The Stubborn Earth: American Agriculturalists on Chinese Soil, 1898–1937* (Berkeley: University of California Press, 1989).

22. Louis Klopsch, paraphrased in Charles Hurd to Mabel Boardman, April 11, 1907, Box 61, RCNA1.

23. Lebbeus Wilfley, speech to Johns Hopkins University, quoted in *American National Red Cross Bulletin* (July 1908).

24. G. H. Bonfield to Mabel Boardman, November 7, 1911, Box 61, RCNA1.

25. Philander Knox to Minister Calhoun, May 16, 1911, *FRUS 1914:* 95.

26. Huntington Wilson to Minister Calhoun, June 12, 1911, *FRUS 1914:* 96.

27. Preliminary Report of Charles Jameson, in E. T. Williams to Philander Knox, April 28, 1913, *FRUS 1914:* 96–97.

28. For these discussions, see *FRUS 1914:* 95–119, *FRUS 1915:* 212–16, and *FRUS 1916:* 103–114. See also Huntington Wilson, "Report of the International Relief Board," *The American Red Cross Bulletin* (January 1912); Robert Lansing, "Report of the International Relief Board," *Annual Report of the American Red Cross* (1914).

29. Philander Knox to Russian Chargé d'Affaires, February 9, 1911, *FRUS 1911:* 59.

30. W. J. Calhoun to Philander Knox, May 8, 1911, *FRUS 1911:* 62.

31. For ARC correspondence about Strong's work, see Box 6, RCNA1 and *FRUS 1911*: 59–62. See also Eli Chernin, "Richard Pearson Strong and the Manchurian Epidemic of Pneumonic Plague, 1910–1911," *Journal of the History of Medicine and Allied Sciences* 44 (1989): 296–319.

32. William H. Taft, "The Influence of the Red Cross for Peace," Speech at Clark University, December 16, 1915, Box 8, MTB.

33. Taft to Royal Melendy, April 28, 1909, Reel 469, WHT. For Taft's policies in Nicaragua, see Michel Gobat, *Confronting the American Dream: Nicaragua Under U.S. Imperial Rule* (Durham: Duke University Press, 2005), chs. 2–4.

34. ARC Press Release, December 24, 1909, Box 68, RCNA1.

35. Juan Estrada to Department of State, December 30, 1909, Box 68, RCNA1.

36. Department of State to Secretary of the American Red Cross, August 6, 1912, *FRUS 1912*: 1127–1128.

37. George Weitzel to Secretary of State, September 29, 1912, *FRUS 1912:* 1051–1053; George Weitzel to Secretary of State, October 6, 1912, *FRUS 1912*: 1130–1132.

38. Philander C. Knox to Mabel Boardman, March 27, 1911, Central Decimal File 811.142/211, Volume 851, DOS.

39. William H. Taft, "Proclamation by the President of the United States," 1911, Central Decimal File 811.142/218, DOS.

40. Ernest Bicknell to Potential State Delegates, March 7, 1912, Box 6, RCNA1; Bicknell, *Pioneering with the Red Cross*, 203; "The Ninth International Red Cross Conference," in *The American Journal of International Law* 6 (1912): 858–864.

41. Edward T. Devine, "Principles of Relief and the Value of a Trained Personnel," address at the Ninth International Red Cross Conference, Washington, D.C., May 1912, Box 6, RCNA1.

42. See also Ernest P. Bicknell, Address at Ninth International Red Cross Conference, May 17, 1912, Box 6, RCNA1.

43. M. S. Gabriel, Address to the Ninth International Red Cross Conference, May 17, 1912, Box 6, RCNA1.

44. For these comparisons, see *American Red Cross Annual Report* (1912).

45. William H. Taft to Robert W. de Forest, March 19, 1913, quoted in *Annual Report of the American Red Cross* (1913): 12.

46. See Kennedy, *The Will to Believe*, and Hannigan, *The New World Power*.

47. For other accounts see George E. Paulsen, "Helping Hand or Intervention? Red Cross Relief in Mexico, 1915," *Pacific Historical Review* 57 (1988): 305–325.

48. For a survey, see W. Dirk Raat, *Mexico and the United States: Ambivalent Vistas* (Athens: University of Georgia Press, 1992, rpr. 2010), ch. 6.

49. For Wilson's approach to the revolution, see Mark Benbow, *Leading Them to the Promised Land: Woodrow Wilson, Covenant Theology, and the Mexican Revolution, 1913–1915* (Kent: Kent State University Press, 2010).

50. See for example *FRUS 1911*: 416–418; Ernest Bicknell to George Davis, May 16, 1911, Box 63, and Ernest Bicknell to Mabel Boardman, Jan 19, 1914, Box 67, both RNCA1; *FRUS, 1913:* 902–903, 907, 911.

51. Charles Jenkinson to American Red Cross, 1914, Box 67, RCNA1.

52. Charles Jenkinson to Ernest Bicknell, June 20, 1914, Box 67, RCNA1; Charles Jenkinson, "Vera Cruz: What an American Occupation has Meant to a Mexican Community," *The Survey* 33 (1914): 133–140.

53. Letter from Mexican Red Cross, in Acting Secretary of State to Mabel Boardman, May 29, 1915, Box 63, RCNA1.

54. See for example, "Horrors of War are Difficult to Grasp," *American Red Cross Magazine*, October 1914, 239; "Mexico Deserves Sympathetic Aid," *American Red Cross Magazine*, February 1915, 87.

55. These concerns are discussed in correspondence between Charles Jenkinson and leaders of the *Cruz Roja Mexicana*, August to October, 1914, Box 63, RCNA1; and in "Defrays Expenses of Twelve Nurses," *New York Times*, August 9, 1914.

56. Acting Secretary of State to Mabel Boardman, May 29, 1915, Box 63, RCNA1; William Jennings Bryan to Woodrow Wilson, May 26, 1915, *PWW 33*: 258. For an account of the ARC's involvement, see Mabel Boardman to Elliot Wadsworth, August 26, 1916, Box 68, RCNA1.

57. John Eugene Osborne to Woodrow Wilson, June 30, 1915, *PWW 33*: 460–461; Joseph Tumulty to Woodrow Wilson, July 2, 1915, *PWW 33*: 465–466; Charles O'Connor to American Red Cross, August 6, 1915, Box 67, RCNA1; Charles O'Connor, "Report on Relief Work in Mexico City," December 15, 1915, Box 67, RCNA1.

58. Charles O'Connor to American Red Cross, August 6, 1915, Box 67, RCNA1.

59. Charles O'Connor to American Red Cross, July 5, 1915, Box 67, RCNA1.

60. Charles O'Connor to American Red Cross, July 8, 1915, Box 67, RCNA1. See also Secretary of State to the Brazilian Minister to Mexico, July 8, 1915, *FRUS 1915*: 722 and Mr. Parker to Secretary of State, September 4, 1915, *FRUS 1915*: 744–745.

61. Jerome Greene to Ernest Bicknell, September 14, 1915, Box 63, RCNA1.

62. American Red Cross Annual Report, 1916, 3.

63. State Department to American Red Cross, September 30, 1915, Box 67, RCNA1.

64. As explained in Ernest Bicknell to Elbert Baldwin, October 26, 1915, Box 13, RCNA1.

65. See, for example, Stephen Bonsal, "Through Starving Mexico," *American Red Cross Magazine*, July 1916, 219–225.

66. For discussions about intervention, see Mabel Boardman to Woodrow Wilson, August 9, 1916, Reel 169, WHT; William H. Taft to Elliott Wadsworth, September 24, 1916, Reel 542, WHT; and L. S. Rowe to Elliot Wadsworth, September 29, 1916, Box 68, RCNA1.

67. Ernest Bicknell to A. B. C. Dohrmann, May 23, 1917, Box 68, RCNA1.

68. See for example Robert W. Tucker, *Woodrow Wilson and the Great War: Reconsidering America's Neutrality, 1914–1917* (Charlottesville: University Press of Virginia, 2007), chs. 1–3; Kennedy, *The Will to Believe*, ch. 4.

69. Christopher McKnight Nichols, *Promise and Peril: America at the Dawn of a Global Age* (Cambridge: Harvard University Press, 2011), chs. 3 and 4.

70. Woodrow Wilson, Remarks to the American Red Cross Society, December 9, 1914, *PWW 31*: 430.

71. William Jennings Bryan to Walter Hines Page, August 27, 1914, Central Decimal File 811.142/265, and Robert Lansing to whom it may concern, September 11, 1914, Central Decimal File 811.142/295, both Volume 851, DOS. For the State Department's arrangements with European governments, see *FRUS 1914 Supplement, The World War*: 824–831.

72. Secretary of State to the American Diplomatic and Consular Officers, January 23, 1915, Central Decimal File 811.142/579b, Volume 852, DOS.

73. Acting Secretary of State to the American Red Cross, October 8, 1914, *FRUS 1914: Supplement: The World War*, 832.

74. For the State Department's efforts to protect medical supplies, see *FRUS 1914 Supplement, The World War*: 831–836.

75. Robert Lansing, "Report of the International Relief Board," *Annual Report of the American Red Cross* (1914).

76. Robert Lansing to Joseph P. Tumulty, October 23, 1914, Central Decimal File 811.142/337, Volume 851, DOS.

77. "Red Cross Limits War Relief Work," *New York Times*, December 10, 1914; "Policy of Red Cross with Regard to Relief of Non-Combatants," Circular, December 11, 1914, Box 64, RCNA1.

78. John Farley, *To Cast Out Disease: A History of the International Health Division of the Rockefeller Foundation* (New York: Oxford University Press, 2004), chs. 2 and 4.

79. Ernest Bicknell to Robert W. De Forest, October 29, 1914, Folder 734, Box 78, Series 100, RG1, RF.

80. Ernest Bicknell to Mabel Boardman, January 11, 1915, Folder 603, Box 61, Series 100N, RG 1, RF.

81. Jerome Greene to Ernest Bicknell, April 21, 1915, Folder 603, Box 61, Series 100N, RG 1, RF.

82. See Ernest Bicknell, *In War's Wake, 1914–1915: The Rockefeller Foundation and the American Red Cross Join in Civilian Relief* (Washington, D.C.: American National Red Cross, 1936).

83. American Consulate in Saloniki, Greece, to Secretary of State, February 22, 1915, Central Decimal File 811.142/613, Volume 853, DOS.

84. Mabel T. Boardman to Robert Lansing, March 13, 1915, Central Decimal File 811.142, Volume 876, DOS; Secretary of State to Minister in Roumania, Servia, and Bulgaria, March 19, 1915, Central Decimal File 811.142/587, Volume 853, DOS.

85. Richard P. Strong, "Preliminary Report of Richard P. Strong, MD," October 25, 1915, Folder 372, Box 58, Series 2, RG5, RF; Jefferson Kean to Eliot Wadsworth, December 1, 1916, Box 906, RCNA2. For more on this work, see *FRUS 1916, Supplement, The World War*: 913–924.

86. Tucker, *Woodrow Wilson and the Great War*, chs. 4–7, Kennedy, *The Will to Believe*, ch. 5.

87. Nichols, *Promise and Peril*, chs. 3 and 4.

88. Rockefeller Foundation, "Memorandum on the Relation of the American Red Cross to Relief Work in Europe," November 18, 1915, Folder 734, Box 78, Series 100, RG 1, RF.

89. Newton Baker to Mabel Boardman, February 19, 1916, Box 13, RCNA1.

90. Mabel Boardman to Newton Baker, February 23, 1916, Box 13, RCNA1. *91 Annual Report of the American Red Cross* (1915).

92. Robert Lansing to the Ambassadors and Ministers in European Belligerent Countries, July 21, 1915, Central Decimal File 811.142/851, Volume 854, DOS.

93. Mabel Boardman to Robert Lansing, July 16, 1915, 811.142/851, Volume 854, DOS.

94. David Kennedy, *Over Here: The First World War and American Society* (New York: Oxford University Press, 1980), 3–44.

95. Bicknell, *Pioneering with the Red Cross: Reflections of an Old Red Crosser* (New York: The MacMillan Company, 1935), 86.

96. Quotations in this paragraph from ARC Executive Committee to Woodrow Wilson, October 25, 1915, Central Decimal File 811.142, Volume 876, DOS.

97. Cleveland Dodge to Mabel Boardman, September 15, 1915, Box 12, RCNA1.

98. Woodrow Wilson to William H. Taft, October 28, 1915, *PWW 35*: 120.

99. William H. Taft to Mabel Boardman, November 1, 1915; Boardman to Taft, November 4, 1915; Taft to Boardman, November 8, 1915; all Box 8, MTB.

100. William H. Taft, "The Influence of the Red Cross for Peace," speech at Clark University, Worcester MA, December 16, 1915, Box 8, MTB.

101. Woodrow Wilson, public appeal, November 24, 1915, Box 8, RCNA1.

102. William H. Taft to General Arthur Murray, July 30, 1916, Box 8, MTB; William H. Taft to ARC Executive Committee 1916, Central Decimal File 811.142, Volume 857, DOS.

103. For the ARC's relationship with other voluntary agencies, see Boxes 42–55, RCNA1.

104. Secretary of State to Walter Hines Page, November 30, 1915, Central Decimal File 811.142/1176e, Volume 855, DOS; *FRUS 1915, Supplement, the World War*: 1050–1054.

105. Walter Hines Page to Robert Lansing, March 28, 1916, Central Decimal File 811.142/1501, Volume 856, DOS; William H. Taft to British Government, June 10, 1916, Reel 168, WHT; General Arthur Murray to Secretary of State, August 1, 1916, Central Decimal File 811.142/1698, Volume 857, DOS. For more on these discussions, see correspondence between William H. Taft and General Arthur Murray, July and August 1916, Reel 169, WHT, and *FRUS 1916: Supplement, the World War*: 941–959.

106. Yandell Henderson, "Wilson Lets Red Cross Aid Allies Only," *The New York American*, April 25, 1916.

107. O. H. Tittman to Mabel Boardman, September 21, 1916, RCNA1.

108. Boardman to Tittman, September 29, 1916, Box 13, RCNA1.

109. Department of State to Hoffman Philip, June 3, 1916, *FRUS 1916, Supplement, The World War*: 930; Robert Lansing to Henry Morgenthau, January 14, 1916, Central Decimal File 811.142/1294b, Volume 855, DOS.

110. Hoffman Philip to Department of State, March 23, 1916, Central Decimal File 811.142/1504, Volume 856, DOS.

111. Lansing to Hoffman Philip, June 23, 1916, *FRUS 1916, Supplement, The World War*: 931.

112. Abram Elkus to Secretary of State, November 23, 1916, *FRUS 1916, Supplement, The World War*: 940. For more on the U.S. response (and its limits), see Jay Winter, ed., *America and the Armenian Genocide* (Cambridge: Cambridge University Press, 2004).

113. Walter Hines Page to Secretary of State, July 22, 1916, *FRUS 1916, Supplement, the World War*: 922; Austro-Hungarian Ministry of Foreign Affairs to the American Embassy, November 22, 1916, Central Decimal File 811.142/1848, Volume 858, DOS.

114. Wadsworth to Mrs. Slavko Grouitch, December 6, 1916, Box 906, RCNA2.

115. "Copy of Resolution Adopted at American Red Cross Annual Meeting, December 13 1916," Folder 734, Box 78, Series 100, RG 1, RF.

116. Memorandum, "Relations of the Foundation with the American Red Cross, 1914 to 1918" Folder 734, Box 78, Series 100, RG 1, RF.

117. *Annual Report of the American National Red Cross* (1916); Boardman, *Under the Red Cross Flag*, 208–213.

Chapter Three: Mobilizing a Volunteer Army

1. Mabel Boardman, *Under the Red Cross Flag at Home and Abroad* (Philadelphia: J. B. Lippincott & Company, 1915) 86, 317–18.

2. *Annual Report of the American Red Cross* (1919).

3. For a theoretical discussion of this process, see Luc Boltanski, *Distant Suffering: Morality, Media, and Politics* (Cambridge: Cambridge University Press, 1999). See also Olivier Zunz, *Philanthropy in America: A History* (Princeton: Princeton University Press, 2011), chs. 2–3.

4. For a discussion of Great War–era constructions of patriotic duty, see Christopher Capozzola, *Uncle Sam Wants You: World War I and the Making of the Modern American Citizen* (Oxford: Oxford University Press, 2008), 6–8. See also David Kennedy, *Over Here: The First World War and American Society* (New York: Oxford University Press, 1980, rpr. 2004), ch. 1; and Kimberly Jensen, *Mobilizing Minerva: American Women in the First World War* (Urbana: University of Illinois Press, 2008). On civic obligation more broadly, see Linda Kerber, *No Constitutional Right to be Ladies: Women and the Obligations of Citizenship* (New York: Hill and Wang, 1999) and Robert Westbrook, *Why We Fought: Forging American Obligations in World War II* (New York: Smithsonian Books, 2004).

5. For wartime divisions, see Alan Dawley, *Changing the World: American Progressives in War and Revolution* (Princeton: Princeton University Press, 2003), ch. 5.

6. For Wilson's decision to go to war, see John Milton Cooper, *Woodrow Wilson: A Biography* (New York: Vintage Books, 2009), chs. 17 and 18.

7. For a discussion of civilian conditions and European responses, see Tammy Proctor, *Civilians in a World at War, 1914–1918* (New York: New York University Press, 2010); *The Upheaval of War: Family, Work, and Welfare in Europe, 1914–1918*, eds. Jay Winter and Richard Wall (Cambridge: Cambridge University Press, 1988) and Jay Winter and Jean-Louis Robert, eds., *Capital Cities at War: Paris, London, Berlin* (Cambridge: Cambridge University Press, 1999).

8. Woodrow Wilson, War Message to Congress, April 2, 1917, *PWW* 41: 521–527.

9. Woodrow Wilson, Fourteen Points Address to Congress, January 8, 1918, *PWW* 45: 534–539.

10. For Wilsonian internationalism, see Thomas J. Knock, *To End All Wars: Woodrow Wilson and the Quest for a New World Order* (Princeton: Princeton University Press, 1992); Lloyd Ambrosius, *Wilsonianism: Woodrow Wilson and his Legacy in American Foreign Relations* (New York: Palgrave MacMillan, 2002); and Frank Ninkovich, *Modernity and Power: A History of the Domino Theory in the Twentieth Century* (Chicago: University of Chicago Press, 1994), ch. 2.

11. For Wilsonian strategies, see for instance, Lloyd Ambrosius, *Wilsonian Statecraft: Theory and Practice of Liberal Internationalism During World War I* (New York: Rowman and Littlefield, 1991).

12. See Kennedy, *Over Here*, ch. 2, and Ellis Hawley, *The Great War and the Search For a Modern Order* (Boston: St. Martin's Press, 1979), ch. 1.

13. Jerome D. Greene to the Members of the Special Committee of the American National Red Cross on the Promotion of a New and Concerted Movement for the Raising of Funds for War Relief, January 3, 1917, Folder 734, Box 78, Series 100, RG 1, RF.

14. Herbert Hoover and Eliot Wadsworth to Woodrow Wilson, February 5, 1917, Box 18, Correspondence, Pre-Commerce Papers, HHP.

15. Both quotations in Woodrow Wilson, Statement on Coordination of Relief, April 6, 1917, Box 42, RCNA2.

16. William H. Taft, quoted in "Why Red Cross is Neutral," *New York Times*, April 24, 1917

17. Charles Norton, quoted in "Red Cross Neutrality," *The Red Cross Bulletin*, May 31, 1917.

18. See also Henry P. Davison to William H. Taft, July 11, 1917, Reel 181, WHT.

19. Woodrow Wilson, Statement to the Press, May 10, 1917, *PWW* 42: 258.

20. See also The Diary of Colonel House, April 29, 1917, *PWW* 42: 162; Woodrow Wilson to Henry Davison, May 9, 1917, *PWW* 42: 251–252; Woodrow Wilson to William Taft, May 10, 1917, *PWW* 42: 261; Thomas W. Lamont, *Henry P. Davison: The Record of a Useful Life* (New York: Harper & Brothers, 1933).

21. Memo, National Committee on Co-Operation, 1918, Box 42, RCNA2. For corporatization, see Martin J. Sklar, *The Corporate Reconstruction of American Capitalism* (Cambridge: Cambridge University Press, 1988).

22. ARC War Council, Press Release, June 5, 1917, Box 24, RCNA2.

23. "Relations of the Foundation with the American Red Cross, 1914 to 1918," Folder 734, Box 78, Series 100, RG 1, RF.

24. "An Effective Plan for Organizing a Successful Campaign," 1917, Box 24, RCNA2.

25. See Henry P. Davison, *The Work of the American Red Cross During the War: A Statement of Finances and Accomplishments* (Washington, D.C.: The American Red Cross, 1919), ch. 2.

26. Henry P. Davison, *The American Red Cross in the Great War* (New York: The MacMillan Company, 1919), 14, 16.

27. Henry Davison, quoted in "Red Cross Fund Nearly $170,000,000," *New York Times*, June 2, 1918.

28. Woodrow Wilson, Address on Behalf of the American Red Cross, May 18, 1918, *PWW* 48: 56.

29. Insular and Foreign Division to Secretary of State of the United States, November 20, 1917, Central Decimal File 811.142/2697, Volume 861, DOS; Otis Cutler to Robert Lansing, March 20, 1918, Central Decimal File 811/142/2718, DOS; Frank McIntyre to Arthur Yager, May 3, 1918, Document 13483, Box 793, Records of the Bureau of Insular Affairs, RG350, NACP; Francis R. Bellamy, "Our Distant Comrades: An Interview with Otis H. Cutler," *American Red Cross Magazine* (November 1918), 70–76.

30. Quotations in this paragraph from Henry P. Davison to Woodrow Wilson, July 9, 1918, Central Decimal File 811.142, Volume 867, DOS.

31. Davison, *The American Red Cross in the Great War,* 35.

32. Davison, *The American Red Cross in the Great War,* 36; Otis H. Cutler to All Chapter Chairmen, November 26, 1918, Box 78; RCNA2.

33. For this organization, see Marie M. Meloney to Arthur Dunn, April 7, 1924, Box 80; Marie M. Meloney to Mabel Boardman, February 15, 1917, Minutes of the Red Cross War Council, August 22 and 29, 1917, and "Plan of Red Cross Junior Membership and School Activities," August 29, 1917, all Box 81, RCNA2; and "Form Junior Red Cross," *The New York Times*, September 3, 1917, 6.

34. For endorsements see "To List All Youths in Junior Red Cross," *New York Times*, February 11, 1918; Henry MacCracken to Franklin Lane, September 25, 1917 and Henry Davison to P. P. Claxton, January 14, 1918; both File 106, Box 18, Records of the Office of Education, Historical File, 1870–1950, RG 12, NACP.

35. Woodrow Wilson, "Proclamation to the School Children of the United States," September 18, 1917, in *The Washington Post*, September 19, 1917.

36. James N. Rule to Directors of Junior Membership, All Divisions, October 22, 1919; Box 610, RCNA2.

37. William H. Taft to Mabel T. Boardman, December 26, 1917, Box 8, MTB.

38. This mentality resembled the ideal of "cosmopolitan patriotism," as discussed in Jonathan Hansen, *The Lost Promise of Patriotism: Debating American Identity, 1890–1920* (Chicago: University of Chicago Press, 2003).

39. For Wilson's propaganda efforts, see George, Creel, *How We Advertised America* (New York: Harper and Brothers, 1920); Stephen Vaughn, *Holding Fast the Inner Lines: Democracy, Nationalism, and the Committee on Public Information* (Chapel Hill: University of North Carolina Press, 1980); Celia Kingsbury, *For Home and Country: World War I Propaganda and the Home Front* (Lincoln: University of Nebraska Press, 2010); John A. Thompson, *Reformers and War: American Progressive Publicists and the First World War* (Cambridge: Cambridge University Press, 2003). For other discussion of ARC media, see Kevin Rozario, "'Delicious Horrors': Mass Culture, The Red Cross, and the Appeal of Modern American Humanitarianism," *American Quarterly* 55 (September 2003): 417–455.

40. Woodrow Wilson, War Message to Congress, April 2, 1917, *PWW* 41: 521–527.

41. For these debates about wartime involvement, see Knock, *To End All Wars*; Dawley, *Changing the World*, ch. 5; Jonathan Ebel, *Faith in the Fight: Religion and the American Soldier in the Great War* (Princeton: Princeton University Press, 2010), ch. 1; John Dewey, "What Are We Fighting For," *Independent*, June 22, 1918; Walter Lippmann, "The World Conflict in Relation to American Democracy," *Annals* 72 (1917), 1–10; Christopher McKnight Nichols, *Promise and Peril: America at the Dawn of a Global Age* (Cambridge: Harvard University Press, 2011), chs. 3–5.

42. Department of State to Cardinal Gibbons, May 7, 1918, Central Decimal File 811.142/3294, DOS; Mr. Johnson to Ivy Lee, November 15, 1918, Box 142, RCNA2; Homer Folks, address for Chautauqua Lecture on Department of Civil Affairs in France, March 10, 1918, Box 4, HF.

43. William H. Taft, speech on behalf of the Red Cross, April 11, 1917, Box 8, MTB.

44. Edward Bok to William Taft, cable, March 21, 1917, Reel 177, WHT.

45. Woodrow Wilson, "Proclamation of Red Cross Week," May 25, 1917, Box 24, RCNA2.

46. Woodrow Wilson, "Address on Behalf of the American Red Cross," May 18, 1918, *PWW* 48: 53. See also, Wilson, "To the People of the United States," December 11, 1917, and "To the American People," November 26, 1918, both Box 42, RCNA2.

47. "One Hundred Seventy-Five Slogans," pamphlet, 1918, Box 24, RCNA2.

48. Georgene Faulkner, *Red Cross Stories for Children* (Washington, D.C.: The American National Red Cross, 1917); June Richardson Lucas, *The Children of France and the Red Cross* (New York: Frederick A. Stokes, Co., 1918). For films, see American Red Cross, "A Descriptive Catalog of Fifty Motion Pictures," pamphlet, 1921, Box 142, RCNA2.

49. For planning, see Henry Davison to Pierce, May 17, 1918, Volume 864, Central Decimal File 811.142/3391, DOS; Report of the Division of Parades, January 15, 1919, Box 142, RCNA2.

50. For the rise of mass media, see Richard M. Ohmann, *Selling Culture: Magazines, Markets, and Class at the Turn of the Century* (London: Verso, 1996).

51. Henry P. Davison to the Editors of the United States, June 15, 1917, Box 24, RCNA2.

52. William Dana Orcutt, "Report on Organization and Method of Operation of the Red Cross Bureau of Magazines," 1919, and "Periodicals and Newspapers," typescript memo, 1918, both Box 24, RCNA2.

53. C. S. Clark to Mr. Scheitlin, November 19, 1918, Box 24, RCNA2.

54. H.P. Davison to George Creel, December 28, 1917, Records of the Committee on Public Information, Executive Division, General Correspondence of George Creel, Chairman, July 1917–March 1919, Entry 1, RG 63, NACP.

55. "Task of the Red Cross," Committee on Public Information *Official Bulletin*, May 28, 1917, 8.

56. Austin Cunningham, "Opinion and Comment," *The Red Cross Magazine* 10 (January 1915): 27. For the explanation of the change, see "New Name, New Paper, New Department," *American Red Cross Magazine* 8 (April 1913): 5.

57. "An Improved Magazine to Upbuild Red Cross," *The Red Cross Magazine*, 11 (November 1916). See also "Takin' Stock of Our Bloomin' Selves," *The Red Cross Magazine* 11 (August

1916): 290; "About Red Cross Magazine," *The Red Cross Magazine* 12 (August 1917): 340; Ivy Lee, "Report on Red Cross Magazine," November 1918, Box 142, RCNA2; and Ralph Graves, "The Red Cross Magazine," 1919, Box 142, RCNA2.

58. Catherine A. Lutz and Jane L. Collins, *Reading National Geographic* (Chicago: University of Chicago Press, 1993).

59. "Making this Magazine," *American Red Cross Magazine* 13 (October 1918), Frontispiece.

60. Austin Cunningham, "Editorial Comments," *The Red Cross Magazine* 11 (August 1916): 291.

61. Austin Cunningham, "Editorial Comments," *The Red Cross Magazine* 10 (April 1915): 165.

62. Chloe Arnold, "Americans All: Glimpses of War and the Red Cross on the Great East Side of New York," *The Red Cross Magazine* 13 (June 1918).

63. Edward Hungerford, "The Business Side of the Red Cross," *The Red Cross Magazine* 13 (December 1918): 21–25.

64. "The March of the Red Cross," *The Red Cross Magazine* 13 (July 1918): 83.

65. James Hay Jr., "She of the Red Cross," *The Red Cross Magazine* 10 (June 1915): 207.

66. Greville T. Keogh, "With the American Ambulance in France," *The Red Cross Magazine* 12 (August, 1917): 319–327; "What a Man Can Do," *The Red Cross Magazine* 12 (April 1917): 162–166.

67. "Editorial Comment," *The Red Cross Magazine* 10 (April 1915): 165.

68. Woodrow Wilson, quoted in "President Wilson's Appeal," *The Red Cross Magazine* 12 (January 1917).

69. Henry Morganthau, "The Greatest Horror in History," *The Red Cross Magazine* 13 (March 1918): 7.

70. Owen Lovejoy, "Look Out for the Children," *The Red Cross Magazine* 12 (November 1917): 543.

71. M. G. Scheitlin to Homer Folks, June 16, 1919, Box 4, HF.

72. For Hine's images, see Daile Kaplan, *Lewis Hine in Europe: The Lost Photographs* (New York: Abbeville Press, 1988).

73. For photographs and the construction of American sympathies, see Laura Wexler, *Tender Violence: Domestic Visions in an Age of U.S. Imperialism* (Chapel Hill: University of North Carolina Press, 2000), and Boltanski, *Distant Suffering*.

74. See for example "Children of the Warring Nations," photographic essay, *The Red Cross Magazine* 13 (April 1918).

75. "For Our Children's Sake," *The Red Cross Magazine* 14 (May 1919): 3.

76. "The Soul of the Red Cross," *The Red Cross Magazine* 12 (August 1917): 264.

77. H. Addington Bruce, "The Psychology of the Red Cross Movement," *North American Review* 209 (1919): 59.

78. Henry Davison to William H. Taft, June 8, 1918, Reel 195, WHT.

79. Jerome D. Greene to the Members of the Special Committee of the American National Red Cross on the "Promotion of a New and Concerted Movement for the Raising of Funds for War Relief," January 3, 1917, Folder 734, Box 78, Series 100, RG 1, RF.

80. [Untitled Article], *The New Republic* 15 (May 18, 1918): 64.

81. Cardinal James Gibbons to teachers and pupils of parochial schools, January 21, 1918, Box 81, RCNA2.

82. Caroline Van Dyke, quoted in *The Red Cross Magazine* 11 (August 1916): 291.

83. G. F. Ormsby to Department of State, May 29, 1918, Central Decimal Files 811.142/10085 and 811.142/10086, Volume 876, DOS.

84. See John F. Hutchinson, "The Nagler Case: A Revealing Moment in Red Cross History," *Canadian Bulletin of Medical History* 9 (1992): 177–190.

85. Davison, *The Work of the American Red Cross During the Great War*, ch. 2.

86. "The Red Cross Octopus," *Chicago Tribune*, September 7, 1916, 6.

87. Unnamed source, "Independents Ship Through Red Cross," *The New York Times*, August 23, 1917.

88. Grayson Murphy to H. P. Davison, December 13, 1917, Reel 187, WHT.

89. John Skelton Williams to H.P. Davison, September 7, 1917, Reel 183, WHT.

90. See Alice Meggison to Jane Delano, May 10, 1918; W. H. S. Burgwyn to William H. Taft, November 26, 1917; Carolyn C. Van Blarcom to Jane Delano, December 8, 1917; Cora A. Hoyle to Jane Delano, July 29, 1918; Jane Delano to Ella McCobb, May 20, 1918; all Box 95, RCNA2.

91. G. S. V. to Woodrow Wilson, June 13, 1917, Reel 248, Woodrow Wilson Papers, LOC.

92. Davison to Taft, July 11, 1917, Reel 181, WHT.

93. James Warbasse, "The Red Cross and War," *The Class Struggle* 1 (June 1917): 57–62.

94. Martha Lincoln Draper and Elizabeth Hoyt, Report of Mission Abroad, August–October 1917; and Draper and Hoyt, "American National Red Cross Women Workers Other Than Nurses: Information for Applicants, Rules and Regulations," 1917; both Box 830; RCNA2.

95. Daniel T. Rodgers, *Atlantic Crossings: Social Politics in a Progressive Age* (Cambridge: Harvard University Press, 2000); Dawley, *Changing the World*, ch. 5; John Louis Recchiuti, *Civic Engagement: Social Science and Progressive-Era Reform in New York* (Philadelphia: University of Pennsylvania Press, 2007); Richard A. Meckel, *Save the Babies: American Public Health Reform and the Prevention of Infant Mortality, 1850–1929* (Ann Arbor: University of Michigan Press, 1998); Emily S. Rosenberg, "Missions to the World: Philanthropy Abroad," in *Charity, Philanthropy, and Civility in American History* (Cambridge: Cambridge University Press, 2002), 241–258.

96. Homer Folks to George Hastings, September 25, 1917, Box 19, HF.

97. Edward T. Devine, Address to Conference of Delegates, August 19, 1918, Box 5, ETD.

98. Livingston Farrand, quoted in "An International Adventure: What the American Red Cross is Doing for the Civilians of France," 1918, Box 13, HF.

99. Hermann Biggs, "Letter of Introduction for Homer Folks," July 9, 1917, Box 4, HF. Walter I. Trattner, *Homer Folks: Pioneer in Social Welfare* (New York: Columbia University Press, 1968).

100. Howard Dickie to Homer Folks, June 2, 1917, Box 4, HF.

101. Homer Folks, "Allocution de Monsieur Homer Folks a l'Inauguration a Marseilles de l'Exposition Generale de l'Enfance," May 22, 1918, Box 4, HF.

102. Lulu Hunt Peters, "With the Red Cross in Serbia: A Medical Report of the Relief Trip to Milanovatz on the Danube," April 1919, Box 905, RCNA2.

103. Edward Devine to Conference of Delegates, March 20, 1918, Box 5, ETD.

104. See Newton Baker to Woodrow Wilson, August 27, 1917, *PWW* 44: 74; "Conscientious Objectors," *The Stars and Stripes*, February 22, 1918.

105. Homer Folks to Louisa Lee Schuyler, November 15, 1917, Box 19, HF.

106. See, for example, Ellen Fitzpatrick, *Endless Crusade: Women Social Scientists and Progressive Reform* (New York: Oxford University Press, 1990); Regina Morantz-Sanchez, *Sympathy and Science: Women Physicians in American Medicine* (Chapel Hill: University of North Carolina Press, 2000); Patricia D'Antonio, *American Nursing: A History of Knowledge, Authority, and the Meaning of Work* (Baltimore: The Johns Hopkins University Press, 2010); Robin Muncy, *Creating a Female Dominion in American Reform* (Oxford: Oxford University Press, 1994).

107. Clelia Duel Mosher to Dorothy Eaton, Jan 4, 1919, Folder 1.13; Clelia Mosher to Caroline Purnell, October 10, 1917, Folder 1.2; Clelia Duel Mosher, Diary, September 29, 1919, Folder 1.7; all Box 1, Clelia Duel Mosher Papers, HI.

108. John Stewart Van der Veer, unpublished memoirs, John Stewart Van der Veer Manuscript Collection, HB.

109. Carter H. Harrison, *With the American Red Cross in France, 1918–1919* (Chicago: Ralph Fletcher Seymour, 1947).

110. Alice W. Wellington to Smith College Women, 1918, Box 852, RCNA2.

111. Florence M. Marhsall, "Report on Women Personnel in France," April 1, 1918, Box 852, RCNA2.

112. Charles E. Mason to Eliot Wadsworth, June 6, 1918, and Eliot Wadsworth to Charles Mason, June 8, 1918, both Box 2, RCNA2.

113. R. R. Moton to Emmett J. Scott, May 20, 1918, Box 1, RCNA2.

114. Adrian Lentz-Smith, *Freedom Struggles: African Americans and World War I* (Cambridge: Harvard University Press, 2009).

115. Frederick W. Mansfield to Department of State, May 10, 1918, Central Decimal File 811.142/3351, Volume 864, DOS.

116. Charles Bolte to Robert Lansing, June 28, 1917, Central Decimal File 811.142/2197, Volume 859, DOS.

117. Agnes Bill to Woodrow Wilson, July 3, 1917, Central Decimal File 811.142/2220; John Pfalzgraf to Robert Lansing, July 14, 1917, Central Decimal File 811.142/2241; both Volume 859, DOS.

118. Maurice Léon to Robert Lansing, July 3, 1917, Central Decimal File 811.142/2208, Volume 859, DOS.

119. "Tourist Travel Halved," *The New York Times*, July 1, 1915, 3.

120. Diary of Eva L. Hastings, 1919, Eva Lawrence Collection, Box 1, HI.

121. Helen W. Grannis, Diary, November 30–December 19, 1917, December 5, 1917, Helen W. Grannis Papers, HB.

Chapter Four: Relieving Europe

1. Ernest Bicknell, journal entries, June 3, 10, and 20, 1917, in Ernest Bicknell, *With the Red Cross in Europe, 1917–1922* (Washington, D.C.: The American National Red Cross, 1938), 9–17. Quotation on page 9.

2. For an account of this journey, see Charles E.-A. Winslow, Diary, 1917, Box 140, RG749, Series VII, Charles E.-A. Winslow Papers, Yale University Manuscripts and Archives.

3. Henry Davison, "Statement on Arriving from Europe," May 1918, Box 190, RCHI.

4. See Henry P. Davison, *The Work of the American Red Cross During the War* (Washington, D.C.: The American National Red Cross, 1919), 21–61; Henry P. Davison, *The American Red Cross in the Great War* (New York: The MacMillan Company, 1919), chs. 1–11. For discussions of ambulance drivers and military aid, see Arlen Hansen, *Gentlemen Volunteers: The Story of American Ambulance Drivers in the Great War* (New York: Arcade Publishing, 1996); Edward Hungerford, *With the Doughboy in France: A Few Chapters of an American Effort* (New York: The MacMillan Company, 1920); Edwin W. Morse, *The Vanguard of American Volunteers: In the Fighting Lines and in Humanitarian Service, August, 1914–April, 1917* (New York: Charles Scribner's Sons, 1918).

5. For the limits of the ICRC and other Red Cross societies with regard to civilians, see Annette Becker, *Oubliés de la Grande Guerre : humanitaire et culture de guerre, 1914–1918 : populations occupées, déportés civils, prisonniers de guerre* (Paris: Noêsis, 1998); John F. Hutchinson, *Champions of Charity: War and the Rise of the Red Cross* (Boulder: Westview, 1996), ch. 5; Caroline Moorhead, *Dunant's Dream: War, Switzerland, and the History of the American Red Cross* (London: Harper Collins, 1998), 184–186, 253–256; François Bugnion, *Le Comité International de la Croix-Rouge et la protection des victimes de la guerre* (Geneva: International Committee of the Red Cross, 2000), 93–95; Gerald H. Davis, "National Red Cross Societies and Prisoners of War in Russia, 1914–18," *Journal of Contemporary History* 28 (January 1993): 31–52; Matthew Stibbe, "The Internment of Civilians by Belligerent States during the First World War and the Response of the International Committee of the Red Cross," *Journal of Contemporary History* 41 (January 2006): 5–19; Rachel Chastril, "The French Red Cross, War Readiness, and Civil Society, 1866–1914" *French Historical Studies* 31 (2008): 445–476.

6. Commander-In-Chief's Report, Part 8: Activities of G-1 Not Otherwise Covered, Volume 4, Chapter 4, Nov 12, 1918–April 22, 1919, Folder 58, Box 7, Entry 22, AEF.

7. Section II, General Order No. 26, AEF, August 28, 1917, quoted in Commander-In-Chief's Report, Part 8: Activities of G-1 Not Otherwise Covered, Volume 4, Chapter 1, to December 31, 1917, Box 7, Entry 22, AEF.

8. Section IV, General Order No. 31, AEF, Feb 16, 1918, quoted in Commander-In-Chief's Report, Part 8: Activities of G-1 Not Otherwise Covered, Volume 4, Chapter 2, January 1, 1918 to June 30, 1918, Box 7, Entry 22, AEF.

9. Commander-In-Chief's Report, Part 8: Activities of G-1 Not Otherwise Covered, Volume 4, Chapter 1, to December 31, 1917; and Section I, General Order No 139, AEF, August 24, 1918: "Prescribing the organization of the Red Cross in relation to military units of the

AEF," in Commander-In-Chief's Report, Part 8: Activities of G-1 Not Otherwise Covered, Volume 4, Chapter 3, July 1, 1918–Nov 11, 1918; both Box 7, Entry 22, AEF.

10. Bicknell, *With the Red Cross in Europe*, ch. 3. For conditions in France, see Jean-Jacques Becker, *The Great War and the French People* (New York: St. Martin's Press, 1986); Patrick Fridenson, *The French Home Front, 1914–1918* (Providence: Berg, 1992); Smith, Leonard V., Stéphane Audoin-Rouzeau, and Annette Becker, *France and the Great War* (Cambridge: Cambridge University Press, 2003).

11. Homer Folks, "Report of the Director of the Department of Civil Affairs in France," February 1, 1918, Box 13, HF; Paul U. Kellogg, *Four Months in France: Work Done and Plans Underway* (Paris: Office of the Commissioner for Europe, 1917).

12. For prewar conditions in France, see Philip Nord, "Origins of the French Welfare State: The Struggle for Social Reform in France, 1914–1917," *French Historical Studies* 18 (1994): 821–838 and Catherine Rollet, "The Other War I: Protecting Public Health" and "The Other War II: Setbacks in Public Health," in *Capital Cities at War*, eds. Jay Winter and Jean-Louis Robert (Cambridge: Cambridge University Press, 1999), 419–486.

13. "Pershing Combines Work of Red Cross," *New York Times*, June 24, 1917; "Ask Cooperation in War Relief Work," *New York Times*, September 17, 1917. For the American Relief Clearing House, see Merle Curti, *American Philanthropy Abroad* (New Brunswick: Rutgers University Press, 1963), 229–231. For more on American and French aid agencies, see Michael McGuire, "An Ephemeral Relationship: American Non-governmental Organizations, the Reconstruction of France, and Franco-American Relations, 1914–1924," Ph.D. dissertation, Boston University, 2012.

14. James Perkins to Forbes Watson, July 25, 1918, Box 846, RCNA2; H. P. Davison to H. H. Harjes, cable, May 9, 1917, Box 846, RCNA2.

15. See Edith Wharton to James Perkins, December 29, 1917, and Edith Wharton to Homer Folks, January 15, 1918, both Box 850, RCNA2.

16. "Memorandum relating to Mrs. Wharton's Criticisms of the Work of the Bureau of Tuberculosis," 1918; Untitled Statement on Wharton, 1918, Box 850, RCNA2. See also Alan Price, "Edith Wharton at War with the American Red Cross: The End of *Noblesse Oblige*," *Women's Studies* 20 (1991), 121–131.

17. Homer Folks to Grayson Murphy, October 1, 1917, Box 19, HF. For Kellogg, see Clarke A. Chambers, *Paul U. Kellogg and the Survey: Voices for Social Welfare and Social Justice* (Minneapolis: University of Minnesota Press, 1971).

18. See, for example, "Report of the Director, Department of Civil Affairs," February 1, 1918 and "Report on Bureau of Tuberculosis, June 1918," both Box 19, both HF; and "Annual Report of Work for Women and Children in France done by the American Red Cross through its Children's Bureau" August 12, 1918, Box 847, RCNA2. Davison, *The American Red Cross in the Great War*, chs. 2 and 3. For published firsthand accounts of work, see June Richardson Lucas, *The Children of France and the Red Cross* (New York: Frederick A. Stokes Co., 1918); Ruth Gaines, *Helping France: The American Red Cross in the Devastated Area* (New York: E. P. Dutton & Co., 1919); Fisher Ames Jr., *American Red Cross Work Among the French People* (New York: The MacMillan Company, 1921).

19. Davison, *The Work of the American Red Cross During the War*, 65.

20. Herbert Croly, *The New Republic*, March 24, 1917.

21. See N. Gordon Levin, Jr., *Woodrow Wilson and World Politics: America's Response to War and Revolution* (New York: Oxford University Press, 1968), ch. 1; Betty M. Unterberger, "Woodrow Wilson and the Russian Revolution," in *Woodrow Wilson and a Revolutionary World*, ed. Arthur S. Link (Chapel Hill: University of North Carolina Press, 1982).

22. American Red Cross Mission to Russia to H. P. Davison, September 1917, Box 866, RCNA2; Charles E.-A. Winslow, Diary, 1917, Box 140, RG749, Series VII, Charles E.-A. Winslow Papers, Yale University Manuscripts and Archives; Henry Davison, *The American Red Cross in the Great War*, ch. 20. For more on the ARC's work in Russia, see Jennifer Polk, "Constructive Efforts: The American Red Cross and YMCA in Revolutionary and Civil War Russia, 1917–1924," Ph.D. dissertation, University of Toronto, 2012.

23. Branden Little, "Band of Crusaders: American Humanitarians, the Great War, and the Remaking of the World," Ph.D. Dissertation, University of California at Berkeley, 2009, ch. 5; Thomas Westerman, "Rough and Ready Relief: American Identity, Humanitarian Experience, and the Commission for Relief in Belgium, 1914–1917" Ph.D. dissertation, University of Connecticut, 2013; George H. Nash, *The Life of Herbert Hoover: The Humanitarian, 1914–1917* (New York: W. W. Norton & Co., 1988).

24. King Albert of Belgium to Woodrow Wilson, October 18, 1917, *FRUS* 1918, Supplement 2, The World War: 460–461.

25. Bicknell, *With the Red Cross in Europe*, chs. 4–6, 8–12; John Van Schaick, *Little Corner Never Conquered: The Story of the American Red Cross Work for Belgium* (New York: The MacMillan Company, 1922); Henry Davison, *The American Red Cross in the Great War*, ch. 15.

26. Thomas Nelson Page to Grayson Murphy, November 3, 1917, Folder 14; Murphy to Henry P. Davison, November 11, 1917, Folder 28, Box 4, CMB. Paul Kellogg, *Seven Weeks in Italy: The Response of the American Red Cross to the Emergency* (Paris: Office of the ARC Commissioner for Europe, 1918).

27. Account Ledger, Box 1, CMB; "A Brief Survey of the work of the American Red Cross in Italy from its Beginnings up to March 1918," Folder 30, and Chester Aldrich, "Department of Civil Affairs, American Red Cross in Italy, January 1, 1918–March 1, 1919," Folder 21; both Box 4, CMB. Report of the Italian Department of Civil Affairs, July 16, 1918, Folder 3751, Box 95, RCHI. Charles Montague Bakewell, *The Story of the American Red Cross in Italy* (New York: The MacMillan Company, 1920); Davison, *The American Red Cross in the Great War*, ch. 16.

28. For Serbia, see Edward Ryan to Ernest Bicknell, July 25, 1917, Box 906, RCNA2; *FRUS* 1918, Supplement 2, The World War: 597–624; Davison, *The American Red Cross in the Great War*, ch. 19.

29. Bernard Flexner to War Council, November 1, 1917, Box 1, Newton Baker Papers, LOC; Davison, *The American Red Cross in the Great War*, ch. 18.

30. Consul General at Cairo to Secretary of State, August 24, 1918, *FRUS* 1918, Supplement 2, The World War: 562–563; Davison, *The American Red Cross in the Great War*, ch. 19. For conditions in the Near East, see Melanie Tanielian, "The War of Famine: Everyday Life in Wartime Beirut and Mount Lebanon (1914–1918)," Ph.D. dissertation, University of California at Berkeley, 2012.

31. The detailed records of all of these commissions can be found in the Records of the American National Red Cross, RG 200, Series 2, NACP and the American National Red Cross Collection, Accession XX482–9.19/21, HI.

32. For these breakdowns, see Davison, *The Work of the American Red Cross During the War*, chs. 4 and 5.

33. Davison, *The American Red Cross in the Great War*, ch. 17.

34. "History of Russian Commission," January 1921, Box 866, RCNA2

35. Levin, Jr., *Woodrow Wilson and World Politics*, ch. 2 and Unterberger, "Woodrow Wilson and the Russian Revolution."

36. Malcolm Pirnie, Diary, November 16, 1917, Box 1, Malcolm Pirnie Collection, HI.

37. "Personnel of American Red Cross in Russia—First Expedition," August 1, 1918, Box 866, RCNA2.

38. David Francis to Department of State, March 1, 1918, *FRUS 1918, Russia, Volume I:* 389.

39. Henry Davison, via Secretary of State, to Raymond Robins, via Consul at Moscow, May 7, 1918; and David Francis to Department of State, May 16, 1918, *FRUS 1918: Russia, Volume I:* 523–524, 530–531.

40. Sheldon Whitehouse to Secretary of State, August 12, 1918, and September 3, 1918, *FRUS 1918: Russia, Volume I:* 641, 663. See also, William Hard, *Raymond Robins' Own Story* (New York: Harper and Brothers, 1920) and Neil V. Salzman, *Reform and Revolution: The Life and Times of Raymond Robins* (Kent: Kent State University Press, 1991).

41. Grayson Murphy to Henry Davison, November 11, 1917, Folder 28, Box 4, CMB.

42. Frank Billings to Henry Davison, September 4, 1917, Central Decimal File 811.142/2345, Volume 860, DOS; Davison, *The American Red Cross in the Great War*, 275.

43. Harvey B. Carroll to Carl Taylor, November 12, 1917, Box 883, RCNA2.
44. For the U.S. military, see Jennifer Keene, *Doughboys: The Great War and the Remaking of America* (Baltimore: Johns Hopkins University Press, 2001), ch. 1.
45. Paul Kellogg, "Four Months in France," *The Survey*, November 24, 1917, 182.
46. "Report of the Department of Military Affairs, July 1917–July 1918," Box 834, RCNA2.
47. For other discussions of this propaganda work, see Louis John Nigro, Jr., *New Diplomacy in Italy: American Propaganda and U.S.-Italian Relations, 1917–1919* (New York: Peter Lang Publishing, 1999) and Daniela Rossini, *Woodrow Wilson and the American Myth in Italy: Culture, Diplomacy, and War Propaganda* (Cambridge: Harvard University Press, 2008), ch. 4. For U.S.-Italian wartime relations more broadly, see Liliana Saiu, *Stati Uniti e Italia nella grande guerra, 1914–1918* (Florence: L. S. Olschki, 2003).
48. Chester Aldrich to All Delegates, August 27, 1918, Folder 26, Box 4, CMB.
49. Commander-In-Chief's Report, Part 8: Activities of G-1 Not Otherwise Covered, Volume 4, Chapter 1, to December 31, 1917, Box 7, Entry 22, AEF.
50. General Order No. 82, War Department, 1917 (embodied in Special Regulations No. 61, W.D., Oct 8. 1917; see also G. O. No. 17, War Department, as amended by Sec. III G. O. No. 48, W.D., 1918), quoted in Commander-In-Chief's Report, Part 8: Activities of G-1 Not Otherwise Covered, Volume 4, Chapter 1, to December 31, 1917, Box 7, Entry 22, AEF.
51. ARC Commission to Italy, "Suggestions to Delegates," 1918, Folder 26, Box 4, CMB.
52. James Perkins to General John Pershing, November 28, 1917, Box 852, RCNA2.
53. Ernest P. Bicknell, "Remarks on Italy—Continental Hotel in Paris," February 10, 1918, Box 879, RCNA2.
54. G. Barry, "What American Soup has Done for the Italian Army," September 10, 1918, Folder 18, Box 4, CMB.
55. Edward Devine, "Report of the Bureau of Refugees and Relief," August 13, 1918, Box 850, RCNA2.
56. ARC Commission to France, "Housing Refugees," pamphlet, 1918, Box 1, Edward K. Putnam Collection, HI.
57. B. Harvey Carroll to Edward Hunt, 1917, Folder 56, Box 5, CMB.
58. ARC Commission to France, "Housing Refugees," pamphlet, 1918, Box 1, Edward K. Putnam Collection, HI.
59. Edward Ryan to Henry Davison, October 31, 1917, Central Decimal File 811.142/2504, Volume 860, DOS.
60. William Hereford, "The Palermo Canteen," typescript, June 1918, Folder 18, Box 4, CMB.
61. Charles M. Bakewell, "Workrooms," 1918, Folder 70, Box 6, CMB.
62. William Hereford, "A Brief Survey of the Work of the American Red Cross in Italy from its Beginnings up to March 1918," Folder 30, Box 4, CMB.
63. William R. Hereford, "Carrying America's Message to the Italian Front," 1918, Folder 30, Box 4, CMB.
64. Kate H. Horton, "The Big Drive of the American Red Cross," June 18, 1918, Folder 62, Box 6, CMB. See also Rossini, *Woodrow Wilson and the American Myth in Italy*, 88.
65. "Report of Distribution of Funds to the Needy Families of Italian Soldiers in the Provinces of Forli, Pesaro, Ancona, and Macerata April 4th to April 15th 1918," April 15, 1918, Folder 62, Box 6, CMB.
66. William R. Hereford, "Carrying America's Message to the Italian Front," 1918, Folder 30, Box 4, CMB.
67. Preceding quotations in Ernest Bicknell to E. O. Bartlett, April 16, 1918; E. O. Bartlett to Ernest Bicknell, May 1, 1918; Ernest Bicknell to E. O. Bartlett, May 25, 1918; all Box 83, RCHI.
68. "Report on Distribution of Funds for Propaganda at Ancona," April 8, 1918, Folder 62, Box 6, CMB.
69. Memorandum, "Red Cross Personnel in Army Section," June 14, 1918, Box 3665, War Department Decimal .080, Entry 29, AEF.
70. Preceding quotations in Edward T. Devine, "War Relief in Europe," *The Annals of the American Academy of Political and Social Science* 79 (September 1918): 6 and 8.

71. Paul Kellogg to Marion Kellogg, November 16 and 23, December 8 and 26, 1917, Folder 8, Box 39, PUK.

72. Homer Folks to Robert Woods, August 1, 1918, Box 4, HF.

73. Homer Folks, address to Chautauqua Lecturers, March 10, 1918, Box 4, HF.

74. Edward Devine, quoted in Minutes, Annual Meeting of the American Red Cross, December 13, 1917, Box 97, RCNA2.

75. Edna Foley to Clara Noyes, December 9, 1919, Box 881, RCNA2.

76. Edward Devine, quoted in Minutes, Annual Meeting of the American Red Cross, December 13, 1917, Box 97, RCNA2.

77. Paul Kellogg to Members of *Survey* Associates, 1918, Folder 4, Box 47, PUK.

78. See Matthew Frye Jacobson, *Whiteness of a Different Color: European Immigrants and the Alchemy of Race* (Cambridge: Harvard University Press, 1999), ch. 2.

79. Edward Devine, Address to Conference of Delegates, August 19, 1918, Box 5, ETD.

80. For accounts of these inspections, see for example Edward T. Devine, Journal 10, France, 1918, Box 4, ETD; and Clelia D. Mosher, diary, 1917–1918, Folder 1.7, Box 1, Clelia Duel Mosher Papers, HI.

81. Good summaries of these efforts are in Davison, *The Work of the American Red Cross During the War*, chs. 4 and 5, and Davison, *The American Red Cross in the Great War*, chs. 12–20. The ARC's constructive relief projects can be understood as one part of a broader expansion of American culture internationally at this time. Robert Rydell and Rob Kroes offer useful ways to think about this process, examining the ways that American culture influenced Europe while simultaneously analyzing how it was negotiated and contested by those on the receiving end. See their *Buffalo Bill in Bologna: The Americanization of the World, 1869–1922* (Chicago: University of Chicago Press, 2005). See also Victoria De Grazia, *Irresistible Empire: America's Advance Through Twentieth Century Europe* (Cambridge: Harvard University Press, 2005).

82. Homer Folks to Louisa Schuyler, November 15, 1917, Box 19, HF.

83. See for example David Barnes, *The Making of a Social Disease: Tuberculosis in Nineteenth Century France* (Berkeley: University of California Press, 1995); Giorgio Cosmacini, *La peste Bianca: Milano e la lotta antitubercolare, 1882–1945* (Milano: F. Angeli, 2004); Rollet, "The Other War II: Setbacks in Public Health."

84. George E. Vincent to Henry P. Davison, May 21, 1917, Folder 735, Box 78, RF; "Memorandum to Members of the Executive Committee Regarding Washington Interviews: May 26, 1917," Folder 734, Box 78, RF; "Memorandum Regarding Possible Co-Operation between the American Red Cross and the Rockefeller Foundation with Regard to Work for the Prevention of Tuberculosis in France," July 2, 1917, Box 824, RCNA2.

85. R. F. Duncan to Dr. Pearce, quoted in Minutes of a Meeting of the War Council, September 24, 1917, Box 853, RCNA2.

86. For descriptions of this work, see "Annual Report of the Bureau of Tuberculosis of the Department of Civil Affairs," July 1, 1918, Box 850, RCNA2; William Charles White, "General Report of the Commission for Tuberculosis, American Red Cross in Italy," 1919, Box 879, RCNA2; Rockefeller Foundation, *Annual Report* (1918).

87. William Charles White, "The Work of the Bureau of Tuberculosis in France," *American Journal of Medical Sciences* 156 (September 1918): 415–433.

88. Anne de Selincourt, "History of the A.R.C. Children's Bureau in Lyons," 1918, Box 847, RCNA2; Mary S. Gardner, "Report of the Commission for Tuberculosis, American Red Cross in Italy: Supplementary Report of Nursing Section," 1919, Box 879, RCNA2; "Report of the Children's Health Bureau," January 15, 1919, Box 881, RCNA2; Lavinia Dock, *The History of American Red Cross Nursing* (New York: The MacMillan Company, 1922), 810–816. For contemporary American views about scientific education of mothers, see Rima D. Apple, *Perfect Motherhood: Science and Childrearing in America* (Newark: Rutgers University Press, 2006).

89. R. F. Duncan to Dr. Pearce, quoted in Minutes of a Meeting of the War Council, September 24, 1917, Box 853; "Interview with Dr. Livingston Farrand," February 10, 1918, Box 824; Annual Report for the Department of Civil Affairs, for the year ending July 1, 1918, Box 850; all RCNA2.

90. Henry P. Davison to Grayson Murphy, January 2, 1918, Folder 735, Box 78, Series 100, RG1, RF.

91. Morgan to Henry Davison, January 9, 1918, Folder 735, Box 78, Series 100, RG1, RF.

92. George Vincent to the Rockefeller Foundation, May 17, 1918, Folder 591, Box 60, Series 100, RG1, RF.

93. Homer Folks to Charles S. Whitman, April 17, 1918, Box 4, HF.

94. See Alisa Klaus, *Every Child a Lion: The Origins of Maternal and Infant Health Policy in the United States and France, 1890–1920* (Ithaca: Cornell University Press, 1993); Laura Lovett, *Conceiving the Future: Pronatalism, Reproduction, and the Family in the United States, 1890–1938* (Chapel Hill: University of North Carolina Press, 2007).

95. "Sauvons Les Bébés," 1919, Box 847, RCNA2; Philip Platt to "Dear Ones," January 13, 1918, Philip S. Platt Collection, HI.

96. "Sauvons Les Bébés," 1919, Box 847, RCNA2.

97. Anne de Selincourt, "History of the A.R.C. Children's Bureau in Lyons," 1918, Box 847, RCNA2; "General Outline of Exhibit," 1918, Photo Album—ARC Child Welfare Exhibits in France 1918, HB; Philip S. Platt to "Dear Ones," January 13, 1918, Philip S. Platt Collection, HI.

98. Homer Folks, "Remarks at the Opening of the Babies Saving Show at Lyons," April 9, 1918, Box 4, HF.

99. B. Harvey Carroll to ARC Commission to Italy, February 25, 1918, and Carroll to Chester Aldrich, February 26, 1918, both Folder 56, Box 5, CMB.

100. Kate E. Horton, "Solving Italy's Refugee Problem," unpublished manuscript, September 10, 1918, Folder 57, Box 6, CMB. For blueprints, account books, and other documents related to the Pisa Village project, see Boxes 88–93, RCHI.

101. Edward D. Self to Henry P. Davison, November 12, 1919; Chester Aldrich to F. P. Keppel, December 11, 1919, Box 884, RCNA2.

102. James Perkins to Forbes Watson, July 25, 1918, Box 846, RG200, Series 2, NACP.

103. Marion H. to Family, November 13, 1918, Helen W. Grannis Papers, HB.

104. Clelia Mosher to Sarah Mosher, November 13, 1918, Folder 2.11, Box 2, Clelia Duel Mosher Papers, HI.

105. Henry Davison, "Statement on Arriving from Europe," May 1918, Box 190, RCHI,

106. Bicknell, journal entry, July 4, 1917, quoted in *With the Red Cross in Europe*, 22.

107. Mabel Boardman to Mother, April 26, 1918, Box 8, MTB.

108. Edward K. Putnam, "Notes of Visit to American Red Cross Centers in Devastated Regions of France and Belgium," 1918, Box 1, Edward K. Putnam Collection, HI.

109. Orra Blackmore, unpublished report, March 1, 1919, Box 881, RCNA2; Edgar R. Accetta, Personnel Questionnaire, December 20, 1918, Folder 37, Box 5, CMB.

110. John H. Lawson, "The A.R.C. Resthouse for Refugees at Bologna," Folder 18, Box 4, CMB.

111. Clelia Mosher to Eliza Mosher, March 26, 1918, Folder 2.4, Box 2, Clelia Duel Mosher Papers, HI.

112. Edward K. Putnam, "The Seventh Fig," 1918, Edward K. Putnam Collection, HI.

113. June Richardson Lucas to Lee Davison, September 30, 1917, Box 855, RCNA2.

114. Felix Frankfurter to Newton Baker, August 15, 1917, Box 1, Newton Baker Papers, LOC; Thomas Nelson Page to Woodrow Wilson, January 29, 1918, *PWW 46*: 159.

115. Irwin B. Laughlin to Secretary of State, May 24, 1918, Central Decimal File 811.142/3396, Volume 864, DOS.

116. Raymond Poincaré, quoted in Ambassador in France to Secretary of State, December 9, 1918, *FRUS 1919: The Paris Peace Conference, Volume I*: 145; Vittorio Orlando, quoted in ARC Press Release, May 22, 1918, Reel 194, WHT.

117. General John Pershing to Henry Davison, May 24, 1918, reprinted in Commander-In-Chief's Report, Part 8: Activities of G-1 Not Otherwise Covered, Volume 4, Chapter 2, January 1, 1918–June 30, 1918, Folder 58, Box 7, Entry 22, AEF.

118. Raymond Fosdick, "Report on Nonmilitary Organizations Serving with the AEF," Box 3662, War Department Decimal .080, Entry 29, AEF.

119. John Dos Passos, Diary, January 1, 1918, in *The Fourteenth Chronicle: Letters and Diaries of John Dos Passo,s* ed. Townsend Ludington (Boston: Gambit, 1973), 115–116.

120. H. H. Jacobs, Address to the Milwaukee Chapter of the American Red Cross, Mar. 18, 1919, box 881, 954.108, NACP1.

121. Carter Harrison, *With the American Red Cross in France, 1918–1919* (Chicago: Ralph Fletcher Seymour, 1947), 285–286.

122. Ernest Bicknell, journal entry, September 22, 1918, quoted in Bicknell, *With the Red Cross in Europe*, 135.

Chapter Five: Rebuilding Europe

1. Philip S. Platt to Family, November 15, 1918, Philip S. Platt Collection, HI; Marion H. to family, November 13, 1918, Helen W. Grannis Papers, HB.

2. Homer Folks to Henry Davison, November 11, 1918, Box 4, HF.

3. Homer Folks to George F. Canfield, October 24, 1918, Box 4, HF.

4. See, for instance, Lloyd E. Ambrosius, *Woodrow Wilson and the American Diplomatic Tradition: The Treaty Fight in Perspective* (Cambridge: Cambridge University Press, 1990); John Milton Cooper, Jr., *Breaking the Heart of the World: Woodrow Wilson and the Fight for the League of Nations* (Cambridge: Cambridge University Press, 2001); Frank Costigliola, *Awkward Dominion: American Political and Cultural Relations with Europe, 1919–1933* (Ithaca: Cornell University Press, 1984); Emily Rosenberg, *Spreading the American Dream: American Economic and Cultural Expansion, 1890–1945* (New York: Hill and Wang, 1982), chs. 5, 7, and 8; Neil Smith, *American Empire: Roosevelt's Geographer and the Prelude to Globalization* (Berkeley: University of California Press, 2004), chs. 5–7.

5. For detailed accounts, see Frank Surface and Raymond Bland, *American Food in the World War and Reconstruction Period* (Stanford: Stanford University Press, 1931); Paul Weindling, *Epidemics and Genocide in Eastern Europe, 1890–1945* (Oxford: Oxford University Press, 2000), chs. 4–8.

6. See Kendrick Clements, *The Life of Herbert Hoover: Imperfect Visionary, 1918–1928* (New York: Palgrave MacMillan, 2010), chs. 1, 5, and 9; Nick Cullather, "The Foreign Policy of the Calorie," *The American Historical Review* 112 (2007): 337–364; Costigliola, *Awkward Dominion*, ch. 1; Bertrande Patenaude, *The Big Show in Bololand: The American Relief Expedition to Soviet Russia in the Famine of 1921* (Stanford: Stanford University Press, 2002).

7. Robert W. Rydell and Rob Kroes, *Buffalo Bill in Bologna: The Americanization of the World, 1869–1922* (Chicago: University of Chicago Press, 2005), ch. 6; Victoria De Grazia, *Irresistible Empire: America's Advance Through Twentieth Century Europe* (Cambridge: Harvard University Press, 2005), chs. 1–6; Richard Pells, *Not Like Us: How Europeans Have Loved, Hated, and Transformed American Culture Since World War II* (New York: Basic Books, 1998), ch. 1.

8. Alan Dawley, *Changing the World: American Progressives in War and Revolution* (Princeton: Princeton University Press, 2003), chs. 8 and 9; Diana Selig, *Americans All: The Cultural Gifts Movement* (Cambridge: Harvard University Press, 2008); and Akira Iriye, *Cultural Internationalism and World Order* (Baltimore: The Johns Hopkins University Press, 2000), chs. 1 and 2.

9. Woodrow Wilson, Address Nominating Georges Clemenceau as President of the Conference, January 18, 1919, quoted in *London Times*, January 20, 1919.

10. Paul U. Kellogg, "The Expanding Demands for War Relief in Europe," *The Annals of the American Academy of Political and Social Science* 79 (September 1918): 22.

11. George Creel to Henry Davison, November 29, 1918, Records of the Committee on Public Information, Executive Division, General Correspondence of George Creel, Chairman, July 1917–March 1919, Entry 1, RG 63, NACP.

12. *Annual Report of the American Red Cross* (1919).

13. Stockton Axson to Woodrow Wilson, November 27, 1918, *PWW 53*: 232–234.

14. Woodrow Wilson, quoted in "A Memorandum by Stockton Axson," December 2, 1918, *PWW 53*: 303; Woodrow Wilson to Henry Davison, December 3, 1918, *PWW 53*: 306.

15. Henry Davison to Herbert Hoover, January 2, 1919, Box 19, Pre-Commerce Papers, HHP. See also Acting Secretary of State to the Commission to Negotiate Peace, January 2, 1919, *FRUS, The Paris Peace Conference, 1919, Volume 22*: 484.

16. Clements, *The Life of Herbert Hoover: Imperfect Visionary*, chs. 1. and 5.

17. Previous two quotations from Herbert Hoover to Henry Davison, February 22, 1919; Robert Olds to Hoover, February 25, 1919; both Folder 430, Box 430, ARA.

18. Robert Olds, "Memorandum to Form Basis for Instructions to American Red Cross Representatives on the Subject of Co-Operation with American Relief Administration Representatives" 1919, Folder 430, Box 430, ARA.

19. Minutes of the Daily Meetings of the Commissioners Plenipotentiary, Monday March 3, 1919, *FRUS, The Paris Peace Conference, 1919, Volume XI*: 89.

20. Davison to Gibson, Dec 9, 1918, Central Decimal File 811.142/8478a Volume 871, DOS.

21. Livingston Farrand, Address at Publicity Director's Conference, January 29, 1919, Box 142, RCNA2.

22. Davison to Gibson, Dec 9, 1918, Central Decimal File 811.142/8478a, Volume 871, DOS.

23. Davison to Gibson, Dec 9, 1918, Central Decimal File 811.142/8478a, Volume 871, DOS.

24. Woodrow Wilson to H.P. Davison, May 1919, quoted in *The Advocate of Peace* (May 1919): 158.

25. Woodrow Wilson to Henry Davison, quoted in Edward House to Davison, February 16, 1919, *PWW 55*: 201.

26. Article 25, League of Nations Covenant.

27. Henry Davison to Woodrow Wilson, April 13, 1919, *PWW 57*: 330.

28. Henry Davison, quoted in "Red Cross League Will Help Science," *New York Times*, May 23, 1919. For fuller discussions of the LRCS and its planned work, see Henry Davison to George Clemeanseau, Woodrow Wilson, Lloyd George, and Vittorio Orlando, April 11, 1919, *FRUS, The Paris Peace Conference, 1919, Volume X*, 285–289. John F. Hutchinson, *Champions of Charity: War and the Rise of the Red Cross* (Boulder: Westview Press, 1997), ch. 6; Bridget Towers, "Red Cross Organisational Politics, 1918–1922: Relations of Dominance and the Influence of the United States," in *International Health Organizations and Movements, 1918–1939*, ed. Paul Weindling (Cambridge: Cambridge University Press, 1995).

29. "The American National Red Cross Commission to Europe," October 7, 1918, Report Organizing the Commission, Box 193, RCHI.

30. See Minutes of the European Commission, November 14, 1918, Box 193; "Europe Reports—Annual Reports—June 30, 1920," Box 205; both RCHI; Robert Lansing to Woodrow Wilson, November 5, 1918, *PWW 51*: 598.

31. Thomas Farnam to Henry W. Anderson, May 15, 1919, Box 905, RCNA2.

32. Siberian Commission of the American Red Cross, First Annual Report, July 26–December 31, 1918, Box 158, RCHI; Siberian Commission of the American Red Cross, Second Semi-Annual Report, January 1–June 30, 1919, Sarah E. Matthews Collection, Folder 1, HI; Department of Nursing of the Siberian Commission, Semi-Annual Report, July 1, 1919–December 31, 1919, Box 158, RCHI. For more on ARC in Russia, see Jennifer Polk, "Constructive Efforts: The American Red Cross and YMCA in Revolutionary and Civil War Russia, 1917–1924," Ph.D. dissertation, University of Toronto, 2012.

33. For discussions of extending aid beyond Siberia, see Chargé in Sweden to Secretary of State, October 29, 1918, *FRUS, 1918, Russia, Volume 3*: 160; Commission to Negotiate Peace to the Acting Secretary of State, March 24, 1919, *FRUS, 1919, Russia*: 100. For other commission decisions, see Ernest P. Bicknell, "Outline of American Red Cross Activities in Europe," October 8, 1919; Annual Report of the Commission to Europe, for the Year Ending June 30, 1920; both Box 205, RCHI. Discussions of these various commissions are in Ernest P. Bicknell, *With the Red Cross in Europe, 1917–1922* (Washington, D.C.: The American National Red Cross, 1938), Part II.

34. See Homer Folks, "Journal of Homer Folks" on Survey Trip for ARC of Civilian Populations Affected by the War, 1918–1919, Box 4, HF; Homer Folks to Harvey Gibson, "Preliminary Memorandum on Greece," December 10, 1918, Box 19, HF.

35. A fact that the Wilson Administration, the State Department, and the Anti-Bolshevik factions understood well. See, for example, Consul General at Irkutsk to the Secretary of State, December 10, 1918, *FRUS 1918, Russia, Volume II*: 459; Woodrow Wilson to President of the Senate, July 22, 1919, *FRUS, 1919, Russia*: 393. For a useful discussion of public health

and presumed "fitness for citizenship," see Natalia Molina, *Fit to be Citizens? Public Health and Race in Los Angeles, 1879–1939* (Berkeley: University of California Press, 2006).

36. Thomas Farnam to Henry Anderson, April 14, 1919, Box 905, RCNA2.

37. Samuel Mason to Rudolph Teusler, February 21, 1919, Box 157, RCHI.

38. Mrs. J. K. Freeman to Colonel H. W. Anderson, June 13, 1919, Box 905, RCNA2.

39. For descriptions of these activities see, for example, Mary Day Barnes, Journal, 1919, Mary Day Barnes Manuscript Collection, HB; James Mill to Henry Davison, January 1, 1919; D. J. McCarthy to John Carey, January 12, 1919; and H. W. Frantz to Thomas Farnam, May 25, 1919; all box 905, RCNA2.

40. Roger Perkins, "Plans for Fundamental Public Health Work in Connection with Emergency Relief," June 1919, box 905; Henry Anderson to Robert Olds, April 19, 1919, Box 905; both RCNA2.

41. Thomas Farnam to Henry W. Anderson, May 15, 1919, Box 905, RCNA2.

42. Livingston Farrand to The Commonwealth Fund, June 9, 1919, Folder 116, Box 12, Series 18, Commonwealth Fund Collection, RAC.

43. Livingston Farrand to The Commonwealth Fund, June 9, 1919, Folder 116, Box 12, Series 18, Commonwealth Fund Collection, RAC.

44. Thomas Farnam, "Draft for Report of Serbian Commission: The Creation, Organization and History of the Commission," 1919; Box 905, RCNA2

45. See, for example, Roger G. Perkins, "Plans for Fundamental Public Health Work in Connection with Emergency Relief," June 1919, box 905, RCNA2; Siberian Commission of the American Red Cross, Second Semi-Annual Report, January 1–June 30, 1919, Sarah E. Matthews Collection, Folder 1, HI; Department of Nursing of the Siberian Commission, Semi-Annual Report, July 1, 1919–December 31, 1919, Box 158, RCHI.

46. Homer Folks to Harvey Gibson, "Preliminary Memorandum on Serbia," January 22, 1919, Box 905, RCNA2.

47. Clara Noyes to Helen Bridge, December 26, 1919, RCNA1.

48. Helen Bridge to Clara Noyes, November 14, 1919, Box 73, RCNA1.

49. Chargé in Sweden to Secretary of State, October 12, 1918, Central Decimal File 811.142/5947, Volume 869, DOS.

50. Thomas Farnam, "Draft for Report of Serbian Commission: The Creation, Organization and History of the Commission," 1919, Box 905, RCNA2.

51. Roger Lewis, "A Short History of the Red Cross in North Russia," July 1, 1919, Box 867, RCNA2.

52. James Mills to John P. Carey, February 1, 1919, Box 905, RCNA2.

53. Marion H. to family, June 1, 1919; Marion H. to family, June 26, 1919, Helen W. Grannis Papers, HB.

54. Henry Anderson, Address to Conference on Situation in the Balkans, May 28, 1919, Box 1, RCHI.

55. Helen Bridge to Clara Noyes, November 14, 1919, Box 73, RCNA1.

56. Robert Davis to Robert Olds, October 7, 1919, Robert E. Davis Collection, HI.

57. Henry Anderson, Memorandum on Policy of Administration in the Balkan States, January 1, 1919, Box 1, RCHI.

58. Henry W. Anderson, speech to ARC Conference on situation in the Balkans, May 28, 1919, Box 1, RCHI.

59. Thomas Farnam to Henry Anderson, April 14, 1919; Box 905, RCNA2.

60. "The New Year," in "The New Year's Extra," newsletter of the ARC Commission to Siberia, January 1920, Box 1, Benjamin Davis Collection, HI.

61. E. O. Bartlett, Address to personnel, November 28, 1919, Box 86, RCHI.

62. Warren G. Harding, quoted in "Candidates Speak for Phonograph," *New York Times*, June 30, 1920.

63. Carrie Pickett to [her] Folks, June 23, 1919, Box 1, Carrie Pickett Collection, HI.

64. Roland Sletor Morris to Woodrow Wilson, May 22, 1919, *PWW 59*: 410.

65. Robert Lansing to Woodrow Wilson, December 3, 1919, *FRUS, 1920, Volume III*: 437.

66. Woodrow Wilson, quoted in "President Appeals for the Red Cross," *New York Times*, October 26, 1919, p. 5.

67. *Annual Report of the American Red Cross* (1920).
68. Inspector General of the Army to Livingston Farrand, May 8, 1919, Box 9, Newton D. Baker Papers, LOC.
69. ARC Los Angeles Chapter to American Red Cross Headquarters, January 31, 1919, in Livingston Farrand to William H. Taft, February 7, 1919, Reel 204, WHT.
70. Attorney [?] Allen to Keith Spalding, February 1, 1919, Box 81, RCNA2.
71. *Annual Report of the American Red Cross* (1920).
72. Livingston Farrand to The Commonwealth Fund, June 9 1919, Folder 116, Box 12, Series 18, Commonwealth Fund Collection, RAC.
73. M. Fairley of Commonwealth Fund to Livingston Farrand, June 20, 1919, Folder 116, Box 12, Series 18, Commonwealth Fund Collection, RAC.
74. Congressional Statute 1636, Act of July 11, 1919, "Articles of Equipment for Red Cross," reprinted in *Barnes' Federal code: containing all Federal statutes of general and public nature now in force*, ed. Uriah Barnes (Charleston: Virginia Law Book Company, 1919), 392.
75. Livingston Farrand to Robert Olds, April 28, 1920, Box 63, RCHI.
76. R. M. Blakely to Medical Director of the Balkan Commission, June 1, 1919; Box 905, RCNA2.
77. Frederick Lee Barnum, Diary entries for July 31, July 25, and August 15, 1919, Frederick Lee Barnum Collection, Columbia University Rare Book and Manuscript Library.
78. Bessie Lyon to Jim, July 30, 1919 and August 21, 1919, Box 1, Bessie Eddy Lyon Collection, HI.
79. For accounts of this decision to withdrawal, see *FRUS, 1919, Russia*: 206–210, 223, 233; *FRUS, 1920, Volume III*: 527–529; Annie L. Williams, Diary entries for December 25 and 26, 1919, Box 4, Foreign War Relief Collection: Annie L. Williams Collection, HB; Rudolph Teusler to F. P. Keppel, January 15, 1920, Box 144, RCHI; C. McDonald to All Department Heads, March 19, 1920, Box 139; RCHI.
80. E. Alfred Davies to Riley Allen, June 12, 1920, Box 137, RCHI.
81. S. A. Moffatt to Kendall Emerson, May 1, 1920, Box 905, RCNA2.
82. Clara G. Lewis to Thomas Faram, 1919; Edgar E. Hume to Kendall Emerson, February 27, 1920; Edgar E. Hume to Deputy Commissioner to Serbia, January 30, 1920; all Box 906, RCNA2.
83. Edna Foley to Clara Noyes, Dec. 9, 1919; Box 881, RCNA2.
84. Robert Olds, in Minutes of Conference of American Red Cross Commissioners, Held at Hotel Europa in Venice Italy, Morning Session, June 18, 1920, Box 825, RCNA2.
85. Minutes of Conference of American Red Cross Commissioners, Held at Hotel Europa in Venice Italy, June 18–22, 1920, Box 825, RCNA2.
86. John Skelton Williams to Stockton Axson, July 16, 1920, Box 96, RCNA2; Correspondence between John Skelton Williams and Livingston Farrand, July 7–August 2, 1920, in Livingston Farrand to William Howard Taft, July 7, 19, 24, and 29 and August 2, 1920, Reel 219, WHT; John Skelton Williams to F. P. Keppel, November 18, 1920, Folder: American Red Cross, 1917–1920, Box 24, Pre-Commerce Papers, Subject File, HHP.
87. See "War Expenditures: Hearings Before Subcommittee No. 3 (Foreign Expenditures) of the Select Committee on Expenditures in the War Department, House of Representatives, Sixty-Sixth Congress" (Washington, D.C.: Government Printing Office, 1921): 4569–4579; Ernest Bicknell, *With the Red Cross in Europe, 1917–1922* (Washington, D.C.: The American National Red Cross, 1938), ch. 17.
88. *Annual Report of the American Red Cross* (1921).
89. "Announcement of Discontinuance," *American Red Cross Magazine* vol. 15, no. 10 (October 1920): 5; Minutes of Meeting of the Special Committee of the Central Committee, December 9, 1920, Box 9, Mabel T. Boardman Papers, LOC.
90. Henry Davison to Woodrow Wilson, March 14, 1919, *PWW* 55: 526–529.
91. See Boxes 49–52 and 55, RCNA2. See also Hutchinson, *Champions of Charity*, chs. 6 and 7, and Towers, "Red Cross Organisational Politics."
92. Frederick Keppel, quoted in "Red Cross and Europe," *New York Times*, September 19, 1920.
93. Robert Olds to Livingston Farrand, "American Red Cross European Programme Memorandum for the Central Committee," October 30, 1920, Box 196, RCHI. For a

discussion of postwar attention to child health, see John F. Hutchinson, "Promoting Child Health in the 1920s: International Politics and the Limits of Humanitarianism," in *The Politics of the Healthy Life: An International Perspective*, ed. Esteban Rodriguez-Ocaña (Sheffield: European Association for the History of Medicine and Health Publications, 2002): 131–150.

94. R. M. Taylor, Address to Exhibition of Popular Educational Department of Child Health Exhibit, Warsaw Poland, June 19, 1922, Box 106, RCHI.

95. E. F. Allen to Mrs. Leonard Wood, February 24, 1921, Box 837, RCNA2.

96. Report of the Commissioner to Europe, reprinted in *Annual Report of the American Red Cross* (1922).

97. J. W. Studebaker, Address to Department of Superintendence at the National Education Association, Chicago, February 26, 1919, Box 81, RCNA2.

98. J. W. Studebaker, "The European Program," in *Junior Red Cross News* (October 1919).

99. P. P. Claxton to J. W. Studebaker, March 19, 1919, File 106, Box 18, RG 12, NACP.

100. John Tigert to Arthur Dunn, January 26, 1922, File 106, Box 18, RG 12, NACP.

101. For more on earlier projects, see *Junior Red Cross News*, Vol. 1., Nos. 1–9, (September 1919–May 1920); Report on Junior Red Cross Plan of Recuperation Work in the Toulis Sector, 1920, Box 855; Report on Vacations, Junior Red Cross Project No. 3, France, September 30, 1919, Box 855; Mildred Chadsey, Florence Ingersoll, "Report on the Junior Red Cross Cooperation with the French Ministry of Interior in their Children Colonies at Mars and Minden," 1920, Box 855; all RCNA2.

102. "War Orphans in Italy," Junior Red Cross Project No. 12, October 12, 1919, Box 883, RCNA2.

103. "Work Started by American Red Cross in Italy Lives on Today," 1919, Box 880, RCNA2.

104. Robert Olds, in Minutes of Conference of American Red Cross Commissioners, Held at Hotel Europa in Venice Italy, Morning Session, June 18, 1920, Box 825, RCNA2.

105. R. P. Lane to Ernest Bicknell, October 17, 1921, Box 208, RCHI.

106. For discussion of normal childhood development, see James Rule to Directors of Junior Red Cross, All Divisions, Oct. 30, 1920, Box 80, RCNA2.

107. Pattie Day Miller to R.P. Lane, April 25, 1922, Box 906, RCNA2.

108. R. P. Lane to Arthur Dunn, August 10, 1922, Box 885, RCNA2. See also, Press Release, "Libraries in France and Italy Promoted by the Junior American Red Cross," 1921, Box 612, RCNA2.

109. Pattie Day Miller to R. P. Lane, April 25, 1922, Box 906; RCNA2.

110. See, for example, H. J. W., "Work of the Junior American Red Cross in France from its Commencement to January 1, 1921," Box 849; "War Orphans in Italy," October 12, 1919, Box 883; Rhobre Anna Wheldon, "The Belgrade Orphanage Workshop," November 1, 1920, Box 906; all RCNA2. See also Joan Fultz Kontos, *Red Cross Black Eagle: A Biography of Albania's American School* (New York: Columbia University Press, 1981).

111. Hollingsworth Beach, "Report on Italy" January 1, 1922, Box 881, RCNA2.

112. "General Statement in Regard to Farm Schools in France Which are Being Assisted by the Junior Red Cross," February 1, 1921, Box 855, RCNA2.

113. Such activities closely resembled the Modern Health Crusades in the United States. See Nancy Tomes, *The Gospel of Germs: Men, Women, and the Microbe in American Life* (Cambridge: Harvard University Press, 1999), 113–134.

114. "The Junior Red Cross Abroad, from beginning of Operations to Sept. 1920," Nov. 30, 1920, Box 610, RCNA2; Walter Gard, "Playing a Great Game," in *The Junior Red Cross News* (March 1921).

115. Fanneal Harrison, Report on "The Junior Red Cross in Czecho-Slovakia, August 1919 to October 1921," Box 889, RCNA2.

116. A. Ross Hill to John Payne, December 14, 1921, Box 838, RCNA2. For contemporary American ideas about play, see Dominick Cavallo, *Muscles and Morals: Organized Playgrounds and Urban Reform, 1880–1920* (Philadelphia: University of Pennsylvania Press, 1981).

117. Gladys Alberga to R.P. Lane, "Report on Playground Work of Junior American Red Cross in Europe," June 28, 1923, Box 838, RCNA2.

118. H. J. W., "Work of the Junior American Red Cross in France from its Commencement to January 1, 1921," Box 849, RCNA2.

119. See, for example, Jason S. Joy to Arthur G. Rotch, August 12, 1921, Box 610; Helen King to Laura Frazee, January 1, 1920, Box 906; Clara G. Lewis to Thomas Faram, June 25, 1919, Box 906; all RNCA2.

120. Helen J. Way, "Work of the Junior Red Cross in Italy from its Commencement to January 1, 1921," Box 881, RCNA2.

121. Minutes of Conference of American Red Cross Commissioners, Held at Hotel Europa in Venice Italy, June 18–22, 1920, Box 825, RCNA2.

122. R. P. Lane to Kendall Emerson, December 14, 1920, Box 837, RCNA2.

123. Herbert Hoover to Woodrow Wilson, October 1919, Box 20, Pre-Commerce Papers, HHP.

124. Clements, *The Life of Herbert Hoover: Imperfect Visionary*, ch. 5.

125. For these discussions, see F. P. Keppel to Edgar Rickard, November 1, 1920; Christian A. Herter to Herbert Hoover, November 4, 1920; both Folder 728.3, Box 728, ARA. See also "Report on the National Collection by the Control Committee to the European Relief Council" (New York: The European Relief Council, 1920).

126. William H. Taft to Mabel Boardman, November 28, 1920, Box 9, MTB.

127. Robert Olds to F. P. Keppel, August 23, 1920, Folder 6, Box 1, Harry L. Hopkins Papers, Georgetown University.

128. F. P. Keppel to Edgar Rickard, November 1, 1920; Christian A. Herter to Herbert Hoover, November 4, 1920; both Folder 728.3, Box 728, ARA.

129. F. P. Keppel to John S. Williams, November 2, 1920, Box 96, RCNA2.

130. Henry Eversole to Robert Olds, December 20, 1920, Box 203, RCHI.

131. F. C. Munroe, Speech in Charleston South Carolina, 1921, WWI Papers of Frederick C. Munroe, HB.

132. American Red Cross Press Release, January 1921, Folder 728.4, Box 728, ARA. For more on this collaboration, see Livingston Farrand, "Memorandum with regard to the proposed use of funds from the Special Reserve of the American Red Cross," December 8, 1920, Box 837, RCNA2.

133. Ernest Bicknell to Arthur Rotch, March 16, 1921, Box 837, RCNA2.

134. Homer Folks to Livingston Farrand, May 25, 1921, Box 837, RCNA2.

135. See also Homer Folks to Livingston Farrand, February 21, 1921, Box 837, RCNA2; Homer Folks, quoted in Robert E. Olds to Heads of Departments and Field Units in Europe, March 15, 1921, Box 200, RCHI; Homer Folks to Kendall Emerson, May 4, 1921, Box 906, RCNA2; and Homer Folks to Livingston Farrand, May 21, 1921, Box 205, RCHI.

136. Kendall Emerson to Livingston Farrand, February 26, 1921 and June 1, 1921, Box 837, RCNA2.

137. Frederick C. Munroe, "Report on Civilian Relief Survey Trip," typescript, May 5, 1921, WWI Papers of Frederick C. Munroe, HB.

138. Kendall Emerson, quoted in Minutes of Committee on Future Plans, September 28, 1920, Box 196, RCHI.

139. C. H. Halliday to George D. Whiteside, October 10, 1920, Box 865, RCNA2.

140. Henry O. Eversole, "Twenty-One Child Health Centers Organized and Established by the American Red Cross," 1922, Box 889, RCNA2.

141. Elsie Bond to Henry Eversole, 1922, Box 892, RCNA2.

142. Henry Eversole, "Rules and Regulations Governing the Organization and Personnel of the Child Health Centers Known as 'Our Children,'" 1921, Box 891, RCNA2.

143. Henry Eversole, "Our Children: Child Health Work in the Czecho-Slovak Republic," 1922, Box 891, RCNA2.

144. Henry Eversole, "Child Health in Czecho-slovakia," report to Commission to Europe, 1921, Box 68A, RCHI.

145. Henry Eversole, "Our Children: Child Health Work in the Czecho-Slovak Republic," 1922, Box 891, RCNA2.

146. See Stella Mathews, "Report on Classes in Home Hygiene and Care of the Sick," December 31, 1920, Box 862; Mary Gardner, Report on her survey of public health nursing in Europe, 1921, Box 833; both RCNA2.

147. See Helen S. Hay to Clara Noyes, June 28, 1921, Marion G. Parsons File, Box 70, RCNA1; R. R. Reeder, "A School for the Training of Nurses of Serbia," 1921; Sophie C. Nelson to Helen S. Hay, January 20, 1922; R. R. Reeder, "Outline of Plan for Nurses' Aides Training School at Bajina Basta," 1922, Box 905; and Katherine Olmsted, "Report on Visit to Czecho-Slovakia and Poland, December 5–23, 1921," 1921, Box 862; all RCNA2.

148. Helen L. Bridge, "The Warsaw School of Nursing," [1923?], Box 863, RCNA2; Mary Bethel, "American Red Cross Nursing Service, Prague Czecho-Slovakia," report, May 1920, Box 68A, RCHI. See also Clara D. Noyes, "Endowed Training Schools to Meet the World's Need for Nurses," draft article for Johns Hopkins Nurses Alumnae Magazine, April 11, 1921; Clara D. Noyes, "Red Cross Nurses from America: Lifting Nursing to a Higher Plain in Europe," draft article for *The Delineator*, 1921; both Box 3, RCNA2.

149. See John Barton Payne, Box 1, John Barton Payne Collection, HB; John Barton Payne, "Report of the Chairman of the Central Committee," in *Annual Report of the American Red Cross* (1922).

150. John Barton Payne to Margaret E. Fitzgerald, May 1, 1922, Box 80, RCNA2.

Chapter Six: A World Made Safe?

1. Ernest Bicknell, journal entries, October 6 and 15, 1922, in Ernest Bicknell, *With the Red Cross in Europe, 1917–1922* (Washington, D.C.: The American National Red Cross, 1938), 457–461.

2. George Herring has described this foreign relations approach as "involvement without commitment," an apt characterization. See his *From Colony to Superpower: U.S. Foreign Relations Since 1776* (Oxford: Oxford University Press, 2008), ch. 11.

3. The U.S. approach is synthesized in Michael Latham, *The Right Kind of Revolution: Modernization, Development, and U.S. Foreign Policy from the Cold War to the Present* (Ithaca: Cornell University Press, 2011). For concurrent changes in the international community, see Akira Iriye, *Global Community: The Role of International Organizations in the Making of the Contemporary World* (Berkeley: University of California Press, 2004).

4. For good overviews of this period, see for example Herring, *From Colony to Superpower*, ch. 11, and Emily Rosenberg, *Spreading the American Dream: American Economic and Cultural Expansion, 1890–1945* (New York: Hill and Wang, 1982), chs. 5, 7, and 8.

5. See Joshua Hammer, *Yokohama Burning: The Deadly 1923 Earthquake and Fire that Helped Forge the Path to World War II* (New York: Free Press, 2006).

6. Calvin Coolidge, quoted in Press Release Issued by the Department of State, September 3, 1923, *FRUS 1923, Volume II*: 466.

7. American Red Cross to Department of State, January 4, 1924, *FRUS 1923, Volume II*: 497. Ernest J. Swift, "Japanese Earthquake," memo, April 25, 1924; Ernest J. Swift, "The Japanese Earthquake," September 1924; both Box 707, RCNA2.

8. James L. Fieser to Division Managers, September 10, 1923, Box 707, RCNA2.

9. John Barton Payne to Ambassador Wood, cablegram, October 1, 1923, Box 707, RCNA2. See also Ambassador Woods to Secretary of State, September 10, 1923, and Secretary of State to Ambassador Woods, September 11, 1923, *FRUS 1923, Volume II*: 473–474.

10. See Walter LaFeber, *The Clash: U.S.-Japanese Relations Throughout History* (New York: W. W. Norton & Co., 1998), 128–143.

11. Yamamoto Gonbee, in Japanese Embassy to the Department of State, September 9, 1923, *FRUS 1923, Volume II*: 473.

12. Frank McCoy to the U.S. Embassy in Japan, October 17, 1923, Box 707, RNCA2.

13. LaFeber, *The Clash*, 144–160.

14. Howard Ramsey, "Relief Work for Japanese Earthquake Victims: A Narrative Report on American Red Cross Participation in the Recent Catastrophe," October 1923, Box 707, RCNA2.

15. Narrative and financial accounts of these responses are available in the *Annual Report of the American Red Cross* and the *Red Cross Courier* for the months and years in question.
16. Ernest Bicknell, quoted in *Annual Report of the American Red Cross* (1925): 54.
17. A good synthesis of U.S. imperial relations is Frank Ninkovich, *The United States and Imperialism* (Malden: Blackwell, 2001), chs. 2 and 3. For U.S.-American Indian relations at this time, see David W. Daily, *Battle for the BIA: G. E. E. Lindquist and the Missionary Crusade Against John Collier* (Tucson: University of Arizona Press, 2004). For a rich and textured set of essays on various aspects of the American imperial enterprise, see *Colonial Crucible: Empire in the Making of the Modern American State*, eds. Alfred McCoy and Francisco Scarano (Madison: University of Wisconsin Press, 2009).
18. For the place of health and social reform in American imperialism, see Catherine Ceniza Choy, *Empire of Care: Nursing and Migration in Filipino-American History* (Durham: Duke University Press, 2003); Warwick Anderson, *Colonial Pathologies: American Tropical Medicine, Race, and Hygiene in the Philippines* (Durham: Duke University Press, 2006); a number of the essays in Ann Laura Stoler, ed. *Haunted by Empire: Geographies of Intimacy in North American History* (Durham: Duke University Press, 2006).
19. See, for example, Charles Forster, "Report on Organization and Activities Philippines Chapter," 1925, Box 665; Katherine D'Olier, Report on Nursing Service in Porto Rico, July 1, 1922–1923, Box 667; Olympia Torres, "Report on Home Hygiene Classes in Porto Rico, for year 1925–26" 1926, Box 667; all RCNA2. For records of the ARC's work on American Indian Reservations, see boxes 556 and 611; for the Philippines, Boxes 665 and 666; and for Puerto Rico, Box 667; all RCNA2. See also Natalia Molina, *Fit to be Citizens? Public Health and Race in Los Angeles, 1879–1939* (Berkeley: University of California Press, 2006).
20. "Projects of the Service Organization, Insular and Foreign Division," September 24, 1920, Box 215, RCNA2.
21. Ida F. Butler to Clara Noyes, Report on "History of Nursing Service, Insular and Foreign Division, December 1919 to July 1921," June 22, 1921, Box 215, RCNA2.
22. Mary Concannon, "The Organization of Junior Red Cross Dental Clinics in the Philippine Islands," 1927; Box 666, RCNA2.
23. See "Suggested Junior Red Cross Program for Indian Schools, 1924–1925," 1924; "Saving San Lita," A Health Play Written by Seventh Grade of Albuquerque Indian School, 1926; Entries from Albuquerque Indian School in 1925–1926 Contest, "How to Improve My Pueblo/Reservation When I Return Home," 1926; both Box 611, RCNA2.
24. Press Release, "A New Step Toward Solving the American Indian Problem," May 6, 1923, Box 611, RCNA2.
25. Mary Concannon, "Report on Nueva Ecija's Enrollment in Junior Red Cross," 1925, Box 665; Annual Report of the Porto Rican Junior Red Cross, 1929–1930, Box 667; both RCNA2.
26. Annual Report 1920–1921, Puerto Rico Chapter of the Junior American Red Cross, Box 667, RCNA2.
27. Mary Concannon to Arthur Dunn, August 8, 1925, Box 666, RCNA2.
28. "Statement Regarding Resolution of the Executive Committee, Philippines Chapter, Asking $20,000 for Health Activities," March 1927; Charles Forster to Ernest Bicknell, March 13, 1924; Charles Forster to Ernest J. Swift, March 5, 1927; all Box 666, RCNA2.
29. Charles H. Forster, "Report of the Field Representative on Trip to Branches of the Porto Rico Chapter," October 1920, Box 667, RCNA2.
30. "A Proposal that the American Red Cross Extend its Service to the Indians," August 26, 1924, Box 611, RCNA2.
31. See Rosenberg, *Spreading the American Dream*, ch. 6; Akira Iriye, *Cultural Internationalism and World Order* (Baltimore: The Johns Hopkins University Press, 2000), chs. 1 and 2; and Ian Tyrrell, *Reforming the World: The Creation of America's Moral Empire* (Princeton: Princeton University Press, 2010): 209–245.
32. For discussions of this fusion, see Boxes 49–52 and 55, RCNA2.
33. See John F. Hutchinson, *Champions of Charity: War and the Rise of the Red Cross* (Boulder: Westview Press, 1997), ch. 7. Caroline Moorehead, *Dunant's Dream: War, Switzerland, and*

the History of the American Red Cross (London: Harper Collins, 1998), chs. 10–12; David P. Forsythe, *The Humanitarians: The International Committee of the Red Cross* (Cambridge: Cambridge University Press, 2005), 33–50.

34. Ernest Bicknell, "The Worldwide Growth of Red Cross," in *Annual Report of the American Red Cross* (1927): 93–96.

35. John Barton Payne, "The Oneness of Red Cross Service Is a World Wonder," *The Red Cross Courier* (June 1, 1927): 12–13.

36. For discussions of this work, see Reports of the Vice President in Charge of Insular and Foreign Operations, *Annual Report of the American Red Cross,* for the years in question.

37. See A. Schafer to All Junior Chairmen, March 1, 1928, Box 80, RCNA2. See also Arthur W. Dunn, "The Status of the Junior Red Cross as a Factor in Education," *The World's Health* 5 (April 1924); and Dunn, "Education for World Understanding through the Junior Red Cross" in *Progressive Education* (Spring 1925).

38. Sir Claude Hill to Walter Ruml, April 9, 1923, Folder 71, Box 2, Series 3, RG 3.1, Laura Spellman Rockefeller Memorial Archives, RAC. See also Memorandum on League of Red Cross Societies, October 10, 1930, Junior Red Cross Division, Folder 189, Box 23, Series 100, RG 1, RF.

39. For discussions of this work, see *Junior Red Cross News* and Reports of the Vice President in Charge of Insular and Foreign Operations, *Annual Report of the American Red Cross,* for the months and years in question.

40. Ernest Bicknell, "Glamour of Romance to World-Wide Beneficence," *American Red Cross Courier* (June 1, 1929): 27.

41. Calvin Coolidge, Address to the Annual Convention of the American Red Cross, printed in *The American Red Cross Courier,* Vol. 3 (October 11, 1924).

42. George H. Nash, *The Life of Herbert Hoover: The Humanitarian, 1914–1917* (New York: W. W. Norton & Co., 1988); Nash, *The Life of Herbert Hoover: Master of Emergencies, 1917–1918* (New York: W. W. Norton & Co., 1996); Kendrick Clements, *The Life of Herbert Hoover: Imperfect Visionary, 1918–1928* (New York: Palgrave MacMillan, 2010); and Olivier Zunz, *Philanthropy in America: A History* (Princeton: Princeton University Press, 2011), ch. 4.

43. For a thorough synthesis of this period, see David M. Kennedy, *Freedom from Fear: The American People in Depression and War, 1929–1945* (Oxford: Oxford University Press, 2001).

44. *Annual Report of the American Red Cross* (for the years 1936, 1937, and 1938); Cordell Hull to the Ambassador in Spain, March 9, 1937, *FRUS 1937, Volume II:* 490; Cordell Hull to Ambassador in China, September 29, 1937, *FRUS 1937, Volume IV:* 630–31; Cordell Hull to the Spanish Ambassador, September 9, 1938, *FRUS 1938, Volume I:* 369.

45. *Annual Report of the American Red Cross* (for the years 1938 and 1939); Department of State to the British Embassy, December 9, 1938, *FRUS 1938, Volume I:* 381–382; Cordell Hull to Ambassador in China, January 22, 1938, *FRUS 1938, Volume IV:* 572.

46. Department of State to Franklin D. Roosevelt, April 2, 1938, *FRUS 1938, Volume IV:* 574.

47. Norman Davis to ARC Central Committee, "Memorandum Concerning a War Emergency in which the United States is not Engaged," August 28, 1939, Box 1311, RG200, NACP3.

48. Herbert Hoover to Norman Davis, September 15, 1939, Herbert Hoover to Norman Davis, September 20, 1939, and Norman Davis to Herbert Hoover, September 22, 1939, all Box 21, Post-Presidential Series, HHP.

49. Norman Davis to International Red Cross Committee, September 1, 1939, quoted in Ernest J. Swift, "A Report of Operations, September 1, 1939–March 1, 1940," Box 1328, NACP3.

50. Norman Davis to Herbert Hoover, September 27, 1939, Box 21, Post-Presidential Series, HHP.

51. Franklin D. Roosevelt, quoted in "Asks $50,000,000 to Aid Refugees," *New York Times,* June 12, 1940.

52. *Annual Report of the American Red Cross* (1942), 139.

53. Neutrality Act of November 4, 1939, Section 4., 54 Stat. 4; 22 U.S.C. 441–457, Supp. II, 442–452.

54. Cordell Hull to Franklin Roosevelt, March 3, 1941; Norman Davis to All Chapter Chairmen, "Coordination of Foreign and Domestic Relief," March 21, 1941; President's Committee on War Relief Agencies, Press Release, December 11, 1941; Joseph E. Davies to Norman Davis, December 16, 1941; all Box 1323, NACP3.

55. "Digest of the Interim Report of the President's Committee on War Relief Agencies," Box 1323, NACP3.

56. Ernest J. Swift, "A Report of Operations, September 1, 1939–March 1, 1940," Box 1328, NACP3; *Annual Report of the American Red Cross* (1941), 109–110.

57. Norman Davis to Staff Members, "American Red Cross Foreign War Relief," 1940, Box 1311, NACP3; *Annual Report of the American Red Cross* (1941), 110.

58. Executive Order 9205 Establishing the President's War Relief Control Board, July 25, 1942.

59. For a final account of this work, see "Report to the President: Distribution by the American Red Cross of Relief Supplies Purchased with Government Funds," 1946, Box 1310, NACP3. For other field reports see Boxes 1310, 1311, and 1329, NACP3, and *Annual Report of the American Red Cross* (for the years 1942 through 1946).

60. These included the Emergency Relief Appropriation Act (1941), the Third Supplemental National Defense Appropriation Act (1942) the Second Deficiency Appropriation Act (1942), and the Third Deficiency Appropriation Act (1943). Norman Davis to Frederick Lawton, April 19, 1943, Box 1310, NACP3.

61. Norman Davis to Franklin Roosevelt, June 5, 1942; "Report to the President: Distribution by the American Red Cross of Relief Supplies Purchased with Government Funds," 1946; both Box 1310, NACP3.

62. This agency was later consolidated in the Foreign Economic Administration. See Herring, *From Colony to Superpower*, 542–543.

63. "Report to the President: Distribution by the American Red Cross of Relief Supplies Purchased with Government Funds," 1946, Box 1310, NACP3. See also Rosenberg, *Spreading the American Dream*, 222–228.

64. See *Annual Report of the American Red Cross* (1940), 81 and *Annual Report of the American Red Cross* (1941), 100.

65. For the International Red Cross Movement's work in World War II, see Moorhead, *Dunant's Dream*, chs. 13–15.

66. "Agreement for United Nations Relief and Rehabilitation Administration," November 9, 1943, in "Pillars of Peace: Documents Pertaining To American Interest In Establishing A Lasting World Peace, January 1941–February 1946" (Carlisle: Army Information School, 1946). For a history of the UNRRA, see Daniel Cohen, *In War's Wake: Europe's Displaced Persons in the Postwar Order* (New York: Oxford University Press, 2011).

67. "Report to the President: Distribution by the American Red Cross of Relief Supplies Purchased with Government Funds," 1946, Box 1310, NACP3.

68. Norman Davis to Staff Members, "American Red Cross Foreign War Relief, 1940, Box 1311, NACP3.

69. Melvin Glasser to Philip Ryan, "Recommendation for Future Civilian Relief Operations," June 20, 1945, Box 1311, NACP3.

70. G. R. More, "Anticipated Post-war American Red Cross Program for Foreign War Relief," August 10, 1945, Box 1311, NACP3; "Report to the President: Distribution by the American Red Cross of Relief Supplies Purchased with Government Funds," 1946, Box 1310, NACP3.

71. Philip Ryan, "Report on Cooperation with UNRRA and Voluntary Agencies in Foreign Relief," October 15, 1946; Melvin Glasser to James Foley, December 30, 1945; both Box 1311, RG200, NACP3.

72. See Amy L. S. Staples, *The Birth of Development: How the World Bank, Food and Agricultural Organization, and World Health Organization Changed the World, 1945–1960* (Kent: Kent State University Press, 2006); Iriye, *Global Community*, ch. 2; Moorehead, *Dunant's Dream*, 554–557; Forsythe, *The Humanitarians*, 54–55.

73. Charles P. Taft to Norman Davis, Report on Advisory Committee on Voluntary Foreign Aid, July 11, 1946, Box 1311, NACP3.

74. See Michael Latham, *Modernization as Ideology: American Social Science and "Nation Building" in the Kennedy Era* (Chapel Hill: University of North Carolina Press, 2000); David Ekbladh, *The Great American Mission: Modernization and the Construction of an American World Order* (Princeton: Princeton University Press, 2009); and Nick Cullather, *The Hungry World: America's Cold War Battle Against Poverty in Asia* (Cambridge: Harvard University Press, 2010).

75. Wendell Wilkie, *One World* (New York: Simon and Schuster, 1943); John Fousek, *To Lead the Free World* (Chapel Hill: University of North Carolina Press, 2000).

Epilogue: A New Manifest Destiny Revisited

1. Edward T. Devine, Address in Paris, April 6, 1918, Box 5, ETD.

2. On the limits of cultural imperialism as an analytical concept, see Ryan Dunch, "Beyond Cultural Imperialism: Cultural Theory, Christian Missions, and Global Modernity," *History and Theory* 41 (October 2002): 301–325.

BIBLIOGRAPHY

Abbreviations Used in References

ARA   American Relief Administration European Operation Records (Hoover Institution Archives)

AEF   Records of the American Expeditionary Forces, General Headquarters, Commander-In-Chief Reports (National Archives and Records Administration)

CB   Clara Barton Papers (Library of Congress)

CMB   Charles Montague Bakewell Papers (Yale University)

DOS   Records of the Department of State (National Archives and Records Administration)

EBHB   Ernest P. Bicknell Papers (Hazel Braugh Archives Center)

EBUI   Ernest P. Bicknell Papers (Indiana University–Bloomington)

ETD   Edward T. Devine Papers (University of Wyoming)

GU   Georgetown University Special Collections

HB   Hazel Braugh Archives

HF   Homer Folks Papers (Columbia University)

HI   Hoover Institution Archives

HHP   Herbert Hoover Papers (Herbert Hoover Presidential Library)

LOC   Library of Congress

MTB   Mabel T. Boardman Papers (Library of Congress)

NACP   National Archives and Records Administration II—College Park, MD

NADC   National Archives and Records Administration I—Washington, D.C.

PUK   Paul U. Kellogg Papers (University of Minnesota)

PWW   The Papers of Woodrow Wilson

RAC   Rockefeller Archive Center

RCHI   American National Red Cross Collection (Hoover Institution)

RCNA1   Records of the American National Red Cross, Series 1 (National Archives and Records Administration)

RCNA2   Records of the American National Red Cross, Series 2 (National Archives and Records Administration)

RCNA3   Records of the American National Red Cross, Series 3 (National Archives and Records Administration)

RF   Rockefeller Foundation Archives (Rockefeller Archive Center)

WHT   William H. Taft Papers (Library of Congress)

Archival and Manuscript Collections Consulted

Columbia University Rare Book and Manuscript Library, New York, New York
   Homer Folks Papers, 1890–1963
   Frederick Lee Barnum Collection
Georgetown University Library Special Collections, Washington, D.C.
   Harry L. Hopkins Papers, Part III
Hazel Braugh Archives, Lorton, Virginia
   Arleen Cole Manuscript Collection
   Ernest P. Bicknell Papers, 1892–1909
   Foreign War Relief Collection
      Siberian Commission
         Annie L. Williams Collection
         Riley H. Allen Correspondence Collection
         Russian Railway Petrograd Children Correspondence
         Speeches, Correspondence, 1920–1921, Siberian Veterans
   Helen W. Grannis Papers
   Historical Biographies
      Arthur W. Dunn Collection
      James L. Fieser Collection
      Livingston Farrand Collection
   Ida Appenzeller Crom Collection
   Jane Delano Collection
   John Barton Payne Collection
   John Stewart Van der Veer Manuscript Collection
   Lt. L. C. Kelley Manuscript Collection
   Mary Day Barnes Manuscript Collection
   Olive Plank Manuscript Collection
   Photo Album—ARC Child Welfare Exhibits in France, 1918
   Susan Rosentiel Collection
   William Chitlivckz Collection
   WWI Papers of Frederick C. Munroe
Herbert Hoover Presidential Library, West Branch, IA
   Fred Lyman Adair Papers
   The Papers of Herbert Hoover
      Pre-Commerce Period, 1895–1921
      Post-Presidential Series, 1933–1964
   Rosalie Slaughter Morton Papers
Hoover Institution Library and Archives, Palo Alto, California
   Agnes L. Strong Papers
   Alexander F. Edouart Collection
   American Relief Administration European Operation Records
   American National Red Cross Collection
   Bessie Eddy Lyon Collection
   Carrie Pickett Collection
   Chauncey McCormick Collection
   Clelia Duel Mosher Collection
   Edward H. Egbert Collection
   Edward K. Putnam Collection
   Ernest Lloyd Harris Collection
   Eva Lawrence Collection
   Malcolm Pirnie Collection
   Philip S. Platt Collection

Robert E. Davis Collection
Roger L. Lewis Papers
Roger Sherman Boardman Collection
Sarah E. Matthews Collection
Susan L. Dyer Papers
Library of Congress, Manuscripts Division, Washington, D.C.
Clara Barton Papers
Mabel T. Boardman Papers
Newton D. Baker Papers
William H. Taft Papers
Woodrow Wilson Papers
National Archives and Records Administration I, Washington, D.C.
Office of the Secretary of War, RG 107
National Archives and Records Administration II, College Park, Maryland
Records of the American Expeditionary Forces (World War I), Record Group 120
Records of the American National Red Cross, Record Group 200
Series 1: Historical and WWI Nursing Files
Series 2: 1882–1935
Series 3: 1935–1946
Records of the Bureau of Insular Affairs, Record Group 350
Records of the Committee on Public Information, Record Group 63
Records of the Department of State, Record Group 59
Records of the Office of Education, Historical File, Record Group 12
Rockefeller Center Archives, Sleepy Hollow, New York
Rockefeller Foundation Archives
Record Group 1, Series 100
Record Group 1, Series 100N
Record Group 1.1, Series 700
Record Group 1.1, Series 789C
Record Group 5, Series 2
Laura Spellman Rockefeller Memorial Archives
Record Group 3.1, Series 3
Record Group 3.3
University of Indiana—Bloomington, Lilly Library, Bloomington, Indiana
Ernest P. Bicknell Papers
University of Minnesota, Social Welfare History Archives, Minneapolis, Minnesota
Paul U. Kellogg Papers
University of Wyoming, American Heritage Center Archives, Laramie, Wyoming
Edward T. Devine Papers, Accession #3083
Yale University Manuscripts and Archives, New Haven, Connecticut
Charles E.-A. Winslow Papers
Charles M. Bakewell Papers

Government Documents

American National Red Cross Charter of Incorporation, 1900 (31 Stat. 277–280).
American National Red Cross Congressional Charter, 1905 (33 Stat. 599–602).
Congressional Statute 1636, Act of July 11, 1919, "Articles of Equipment for Red Cross," reprinted
in *Barnes' Federal code: containing all Federal statutes of general and public nature now in force,*
ed. Uriah Barnes (Charleston: Virginia Law Book Company, 1919), 392.
Emergency Relief Appropriation Act (1941).
Executive Order 9205: Establishing the President's War Relief Control Board, July 25, 1942.
Foreign Relations of the United States (Washington, D.C.: U.S. Government Printing Office).

The League of Nations Covenant, signed June 28, 1919.
Second Deficiency Appropriation Act (1942).
Third Deficiency Appropriation Act (1943).
Third Supplemental National Defense Appropriation Act (1942).

Newspapers and Periodicals

American Journal of International Law
American Journal of Medical Sciences
American National Red Cross Bulletin
American Red Cross Courier
Annals
The Annals of the American Academy of Political and Social Science
The Advocate of Peace
Charities and the Commons
The Chicago Daily
The Chicago Tribune
The Christian Science Monitor
The Congressional Record
High School Service
The Independent
Junior Red Cross News
The London Times
The Los Angeles Times
The National Geographic Magazine
The New Republic
The New York American
The New York Times
The New York Daily Tribune
The North American Review
Progressive Education
Red Cross Bulletin
Red Cross Magazine
Saturday Evening Post
Stars and Stripes
The Survey
The Washington Post
The World's Health

Published Primary Sources

"About Red Cross Magazine." *The Red Cross Magazine* (August 1917).
American National Red Cross. *Annual Reports*. Washington, D.C.: The American National Red Cross, 1908–1932.
Ames Jr., Fisher. *American Red Cross Work Among the French People*. New York: MacMillan, 1921.
Arnold, Chloe. "Americans All: Glimpses of War and the Red Cross on the Great East Side of New York." *The Red Cross Magazine* (June 1918).
"Ask Cooperation in War Relief Work." *New York Times* (September 17, 1917).
"Asks $50,000,000 to Aid Refugees." *New York Times* (June 12, 1940).
Bakewell, Charles Montague. *The Story of the American Red Cross in Italy*. New York: The MacMillan Company, 1920.
Barton, Clara. *Red Cross: A History of this Remarkable International Movement in the Interest of Humanity*. Washington, D.C.: American National Red Cross, 1898.

————. *A Story of the Red Cross: Glimpses of Field Work*. New York: MacMillan, 1904.

Bellamy, Francis R. "Our Distant Comrades: An Interview with Otis H. Cutler." *The Red Cross Magazine* (November 1918).

Bicknell, Ernest P. "Calabria and Sicily Two Months After the Earthquake." *American National Red Cross Bulletin* (July 1909).

————. "Glamour of Romance to World-Wide Beneficence." *American Red Cross Courier* (June 1, 1929).

————. *Pioneering with the Red Cross: Reflections of an Old Red Crosser*. New York: The MacMillan Company, 1935.

————. *In War's Wake, 1914–1915: The Rockefeller Foundation and the American Red Cross Join in Civilian Relief*. Washington, D.C.: American National Red Cross, 1936.

————. *With the Red Cross in Europe, 1917–1922*. Washington, D.C.: The American Red Cross, 1938.

————. "The Worldwide Growth of Red Cross." *Annual Report of the American Red Cross* (1927).

Boardman, Mabel. "The American Red Cross in Italy." *The National Geographic Magazine* (1909).

————. *Under the Red Cross Flag at Home and Abroad*. Philadelphia: J. B. Lippincott Company, 1915.

Bonsal, Stephen. "Through Starving Mexico." *The Red Cross Magazine* (July 1916).

Bruce, H. Addington. "The Psychology of the Red Cross Movement." *North American Review* 209 (1919).

"Candidates Speak for Phonograph." *New York Times* (June 30, 1920).

"Children of the Warring Nations." *The Red Cross Magazine* (April 1918).

Coolidge, Calvin. Address to the Annual Convention of the American Red Cross. In *The American Red Cross Courier* (October 11, 1924).

Creel, George. *How We Advertised America*. New York: Harper and Brothers., 1920.

Cunningham, Austin. "Editorial Comments." *The Red Cross Magazine* 10 (April 1915).

————. "Editorial Comments." *The Red Cross Magazine* (August 1916).

————. "Opinion and Comment." *The Red Cross Magazine* (January 1915).

Cutting Jr., W. Bayard. "Early Days of Relief." *American National Red Cross Bulletin* (April 1909).

Davison, Henry P. *The American Red Cross in the Great War*. New York: The MacMillan Company, 1919.

————. *The Work of the American Red Cross During the War*. Washington, D.C.: The American Red Cross, 1919.

"Defrays Expenses of Twelve Nurses." *New York Times* (August 9, 1914).

Devine, Edward T. "War Relief in Europe." *The Annals of the American Academy of Political and Social Science* 79 (September 1918).

Dewey, John. "What Are We Fighting For." *Independent* (June 22, 1918).

Dock, Lavinia. *History of American Red Cross Nursing*. New York: The MacMillan Company, 1922.

Dos Passos, John. *The Fourteenth Chronicle: Letters and Diaries of John Dos Passos*, ed. Townsend Ludington. Boston: Gambit, 1973.

Dunn, Arthur W. "Education for World Understanding through the Junior Red Cross." *Progressive Education* (Spring 1925).

————. "The Status of the Junior Red Cross as a Factor in Education." *The World's Health* 5 (April 1924).

"E. P. Bicknell Visits London." *Los Angeles Times* (February 25, 1909).

Faulkner, Georgene. *Red Cross Stories for Children*. Washington, D.C.: The American National Red Cross, 1917.

"For Our Children's Sake." *The Red Cross Magazine* (May 1919).

"Form Junior Red Cross." *The New York Times* (September 3, 1917).

Gaines, Ruth. *Helping France: The American Red Cross in the Devastated Area*. New York: E. P. Dutton & Co., 1919.

Gard, Walter. "Playing a Great Game." *The Junior Red Cross News* (March 1921).

Hard, William. *Raymond Robins' Own Story*. New York: Harper and Brothers, 1920.

Harrison, Carter H. *With the American Red Cross in France, 1918–1919*. Chicago: Ralph Fletcher Seymour, 1947.

Hay Jr., James. "She of the Red Cross." *The Red Cross Magazine*. (June 1915).

Henderson, Yandell. "Wilson Lets Red Cross Aid Allies Only." *The New York American* (April 25, 1916).

"Horrors of War are Difficult to Grasp." *The Red Cross Magazine* (October 1914).

Hungerford, Edward. "The Business Side of the Red Cross." *The Red Cross Magazine* (December 1918).

———. *With the Doughboy in France: A Few Chapters of an American Effort*. New York: The MacMillan Company, 1920.

"An Improved Magazine to Upbuild Red Cross." *The Red Cross Magazine* (November 1916).

"Independents Ship Through Red Cross." *The New York Times* (August 23, 1917).

Jenkinson, Charles. "Vera Cruz: What an American Occupation has Meant to a Mexican Community." *The Survey* 33 (1914).

Kellogg, Paul U. "The Expanding Demands for War Relief in Europe." *The Annals of the American Academy of Political and Social Science* 79 (September 1918).

———. *Four Months in France: Work Done and Plans Underway*. Paris: Office of the American Red Cross Commissioner for Europe, 1917.

———. *Seven Weeks in Italy: The Response of the American Red Cross to the Emergency*. Paris: Office of the American Red Cross Commissioner for Europe, 1918.

Keogh, Greville T. "With the American Ambulance in France." *The Red Cross Magazine* (August, 1917).

Keppel, Frederick. "Red Cross and Europe." *New York Times*. (September 19, 1920).

Lansing, Robert. "Report of the International Relief Board." *Annual Report of the American Red Cross* (1914).

"Lay Cornerstone of Red Cross Home." *New York Times* (March 28, 1915).

Lippmann, Walter. "The World Conflict in Relation to American Democracy." *Annals* 72 (1917).

Lovejoy, Owen. "Look Out for the Children." *The Red Cross Magazine* (November 1917).

Lucas, June Richardson. *The Children of France and the Red Cross*. New York: Frederick A. Stokes, Co, 1918).

"The March of the Red Cross." *The Red Cross Magazine* (July 1918).

"Mexico Deserves Sympathetic Aid." *The Red Cross Magazine* (February 1915).

Morganthau, Henry. "The Greatest Horror in History." *The Red Cross Magazine* (March 1918).

Morse, Edwin W. *The Vanguard of American Volunteers: In the Fighting Lines and in Humanitarian Service, August, 1914–April, 1917*. New York: Charles Scribner's Sons, 1918.

"The Most Intimate Friends of President Taft." *New York Times* (May 29, 1910).

"New Name, New Paper, New Department." *The Red Cross Magazine* (April 1913).

Payne, John Barton. "The Oneness of Red Cross Service Is a World Wonder." *The Red Cross Courier* (June 1, 1927).

———. "Report of the Chairman of the Central Committee." *Annual Report of the American Red Cross* (1922).

"Pershing Combines Work of Red Cross." *New York Times* (June 24, 1917).

"President Wilson's Appeal." *The Red Cross Magazine* (January 1917).

"Red Cross Fund Nearly $170,000,000." *New York Times* (June 2, 1918).

"Red Cross Limits War Relief Work." *New York Times* (December 10, 1914).

"Red Cross Neutrality." *The Red Cross Bulletin* (May 31, 1917).

"The Red Cross Octopus." *Chicago Tribune* (September 7, 1916).

"Red Cross Rows Will Be Stopped." *Chicago Daily* (April 23, 1903).

"Red Cross League Will Help Science." *New York Times* (May 23, 1919).

"Relief of Earthquake Sufferers in Italy." *Congressional Record* 60:2 (January 4, 1909): 452–454.

Roosevelt, Theodore. "The Appeal Issued by the President." *The Washington Post* (April 20, 1906).

"The Soul of the Red Cross." *The Red Cross Magazine* (August 1917).

Sternberg, George M. "The Surgeon Generals' Relations with the American Red Cross." *New York Daily Tribune* (August 30, 1898).

Surface, Frank and Raymond Bland. *American Food in the World War and Reconstruction Period.* Stanford: Stanford University Press, 1931.

"Taft Red Cross President." *New York Times* (December 9, 1908).

"Taft Tells of Need of Red Cross Fund." *New York Times* (December 3, 1909).

"Takin' Stock of Our Bloomin' Selves." *The Red Cross Magazine* (August 1916).

Taylor, Graham. "The Red Cross Director." *Charities and the Commons* (June 1908).

The Papers of Woodrow Wilson, ed. Arthur S. Link et al., 69 vols. Princeton: Princeton University Press, 1966–1994.

[Untitled Article]. *The New Republic* (May 18, 1918).

Van Schaick, John. *Little Corner Never Conquered: The Story of the American Red Cross Work for Belgium.* New York: The MacMillan Company, 1922.

Warbasse, James. "The Red Cross and War." *The Class Struggle* (June 1917).

"What a Man Can Do." *The Red Cross Magazine* (April 1917).

"Why Red Cross is Neutral." *New York Times* (April 24, 1917).

"Wilson Foresees War of Grimness." *The New York Times* (May 13, 1917).

Wilson, Woodrow. "Proclamation to the School Children of the United States." *The Washington Post* (September 19, 1917).

Selected Books, Articles, and Dissertations

Abzug, Robert. *Cosmos Crumbling: American Reform and the Religious Imagination.* New York: Oxford University Press, 1997.

Adas, Michael. *Dominance by Design: Technological Imperatives and America's Civilizing Mission.* Cambridge: Harvard University Press, 2009.

Agnew, Elizabeth N. *From Charity to Social Work: Mary E. Richmond and the Creation of an American Profession.* Urbana: University of Illinois Press, 2003.

Ambrosius, Lloyd. *Wilsonian Statecraft: Theory and Practice of Liberal Internationalism During World War I.* New York: Rowman and Littlefield, 1991.

———. *Wilsonianism: Woodrow Wilson and his Legacy in American Foreign Relations.* New York: Palgrave MacMillan, 2002.

———. "Woodrow Wilson, Alliances, and the League of Nations." *Journal of the Gilded Age and Progressive Era* 5 (April 2006): 139–166.

———. *Woodrow Wilson and the American Diplomatic Tradition: The Treaty Fight in Perspective.* Cambridge: Cambridge University Press, 1990.

Anderson, Warwick. *Colonial Pathologies: American Tropical Medicine, Race, and Hygiene in the Philippines.* Durham: Duke University Press, 2006.

Apple, Rima D. *Perfect Motherhood: Science and Childrearing in America.* Newark: Rutgers University Press, 2006.

Barnes, David. *The Making of a Social Disease: Tuberculosis in Nineteenth-Century France.* Berkeley: University of California Press, 1995.

Barnett, Michael. *Empire of Humanity: A History of Humanitarianism.* Ithaca: Cornell University Press, 2011.

Bass, Gary. *Freedom's Battle: The Origins of Humanitarian Intervention.* New York: Knopf, 2008.

Becker, Annette. *Oubliés de la grande guerre: humanitaire et culture de guerre.* Paris: Noesis, 1998.

Becker, Jean-Jacques. *The Great War and the French People.* New York: St. Martin's Press, 1986.

Benbow, Mark. *Leading Them to the Promised Land: Woodrow Wilson, Covenant Theology, and the Mexican Revolution, 1913–1915.* Kent: Kent State University Press, 2010.

Boltanski, Luc. *Distant Suffering: Morality, Media, and Politics.* Cambridge: Cambridge University Press, 1999.

Bremner, Robert H. *American Philanthropy.* Chicago: University of Chicago Press, 1988.

————. *The Public Good: Philanthropy and Welfare in the Civil War Era*. New York: Alfred A. Knopf, 1980.

Bugnion, François. *Le Comité International de la Croix-Rouge et la protection des victimes de la guerre*. Geneva: International Committee of the Red Cross, 2000.

Burton, David. *William Howard Taft: Confident Peacemaker*. New York: Fordham University Press, 2004.

Butchart, Ronald. *Schooling the Freed People: Teaching, Learning and the Struggle for Black Freedom, 1861–1876*. Chapel Hill: University of North Carolina Press, 2010.

Butler, Leslie. *Critical Americans: Victorian Intellectuals and Transatlantic Liberal Reform*. Chapel Hill: University of North Carolina Press, 2007.

Capozzola, Christopher. *Uncle Sam Wants You: World War I and the Making of the Modern American Citizen*. Oxford: Oxford University Press, 2008.

Cavallo, Dominick. *Muscles and Morals: Organized Playgrounds and Urban Reform, 1880–1920*. Philadelphia: University of Pennsylvania Press, 1981.

Chambers, Clarke A. *Paul U. Kellogg and the Survey: Voices for Social Welfare and Social Justice*. Minneapolis: University of Minnesota Press, 1971.

Chastril, Rachel. "The French Red Cross, War Readiness, and Civil Society, 1866–1914." *French Historical Studies* 31 (2008): 445–476.

Chernin, Eli. "Richard Pearson Strong and the Manchurian Epidemic of Pneumonic Plague, 1910–1911." *Journal of the History of Medicine and Allied Sciences* 44 (1989): 296–319.

Choy, Catherine Ceniza. *Empire of Care: Nursing and Migration in Filipino-American History*. Durham: Duke University Press, 2003.

Clark, Elizabeth B. "'The Sacred Rights of the Weak': Pain, Sympathy, and the Culture of Individual Rights in Antebellum America." *Journal of American History* 82 (1995): 463–493.

Clements, Kendrick. *The Life of Herbert Hoover: Imperfect Visionary, 1918–1928*. New York: Palgrave Macmillan, 2010.

Cohen, Daniel. *In War's Wake: Europe's Displaced Persons in the Postwar Order*. New York: Oxford University Press, 2011.

Cooper Jr., John Milton. *Breaking the Heart of the World: Woodrow Wilson and the Fight for the League of Nations* (Cambridge: Cambridge University Press, 2001).

————. *The Vanity of Power: American Isolationism and the First World War, 1914–1917*. Westport: Greenwood Press, 1970.

————. "Wilson Revisited." In *Reconsidering Woodrow Wilson: Progressivism, Internationalism, War, and Peace*, ed. John Milton Cooper Jr. Baltimore: The Johns Hopkins University Press, 2008: 1–8.

————. *Woodrow Wilson: A Biography*. New York: Vintage Books, 2009.

Cosmacini, Giorgio. *La peste Bianca: Milano e la lotta antitubercolare, 1882–1945*. Milano: F. Angeli 2004.

Costigliola, Frank. *Awkward Dominion: American Political, Economic, and Cultural Relations with Europe, 1919–1933*. Ithaca: Cornell University Press, 1984.

Cullather, Nick. "The Foreign Policy of the Calorie." *The American Historical Review* 112 (2007): 337–364.

————. *The Hungry World: America's Cold War Battle Against Poverty in Asia*. Cambridge: Harvard University Press, 2010.

Crocker, Ruth. *Mrs. Russell Sage: Women's Activism and Philanthropy in Gilded Age and Progressive America*. Bloomington: Indiana University Press, 2006.

Crunden, Robert. *Ministers of Reform: The Progressives' Achievement in American Civilization, 1889–1920*. Urbana: University of Illinois Press, 1985.

Cueto, Marcos, ed. *Missionaries of Science: The Rockefeller Foundation and Latin America*. Bloomington: Indiana University Press, 1994.

Curti, Merle. *American Philanthropy Abroad*. New Brunswick: Rutgers University Press, 1963.

————. *Prelude to Point Four: American Technical Missions Overseas, 1838–1938*. Madison: University of Wisconsin Press, 1954.

Curtis, Susan. *A Consuming Faith: The Social Gospel and Modern American Culture.* Columbia: University of Missouri Press, 2001.

Daily, David W. *Battle for the BIA: G. E. E. Lindquist and the Missionary Crusade Against John Collier.* Tuscon: University of Arizona Press, 2004.

D'Antonio, Patricia. *American Nursing: A History of Knowledge, Authority, and the Meaning of Work.* Baltimore: The Johns Hopkins University Press, 2010.

Dauber, Michele Landis. *The Sympathetic State: Disaster Relief and the Origins of the American Welfare State.* Chicago: University of Chicago Press, 2012.

Davis, David Brion. *The Problem of Slavery in an Age of Revolution, 1770–1823.* Ithaca: Cornell University Press, 1975.

Davis, Gerald H. "National Red Cross Societies and Prisoners of War in Russia, 1914–18." *Journal of Contemporary History* 28 (January 1993): 31–52.

Dawley, Alan. *Changing the World: American Progressives in War and Revolution.* Princeton: Princeton University Press, 2003.

———. *Struggles for Justice: Social Responsibility and the Liberal State.* Cambridge: Harvard University Press, 1991.

De Grazia, Victoria. *Irresistible Empire: America's Advance Through 20th-Century Europe.* Cambridge: Harvard University Press, 2005.

Duffy, John. *The Sanitarians: A History of American Public Health.* Urbana: University of Illinois Press, 1997.

Dulles, Foster Rhea. *The American Red Cross: A History.* New York: Harper, 1950.

Dunch, Ryan. "Beyond Cultural Imperialism: Cultural Theory, Christian Missions, and Global Modernity," *History and Theory* 41 (October 2002): 301–325.

Ebel, Jonathan. *Faith in the Fight: Religion and the American Soldier in the Great War.* Princeton: Princeton University Press, 2010.

Ekbladh, David. *The Great American Mission: Modernization and the Construction of an American World Order.* Princeton: Princeton University Press, 2009.

Engerman, David. *Modernization from the Other Shore: American Intellectuals and the Romance of Russian Development.* Cambridge: Harvard University Press, 2003.

Farley, John. *To Cast out Disease: A History of the International Health Division of the Rockefeller Foundation 1913–1951.* Oxford: Oxford University Press, 2004.

Fink, Leon. *Progressive Intellectuals and the Dilemmas of Democratic Commitment.* Cambridge: Harvard University Press, 1997.

Fitzpatrick, Ellen. *Endless Crusade: Women Social Scientists and Progressive Reform.* New York: Oxford University Press, 1990.

Flanagan, Maureen. *America Reformed: Progressives and Progressivisms, 1890s–1920s.* Oxford: Oxford University Press, 2006.

———. *Seeing with their Hearts: Chicago Women and the Vision of the Good City, 1871–1933.* Princeton: Princeton University Press, 2002.

Forsythe, David P. *The Humanitarians: The International Committee of the Red Cross.* Cambridge: Cambridge University Press, 2005.

Fousek, John. *To Lead the Free World.* Chapel Hill: University of North Carolina Press, 2000.

Fridenson, Patrick. *The French Home Front, 1914–1918.* Providence: Berg, 1992.

Gaeddert, Gustave R. "The History of the American National Red Cross," Unpublished manuscript in four volumes. Washington, D.C.: American National Red Cross Historical Division, 1950.

Giesberg, Judith Ann. *Civil War Sisterhood: The U.S. Sanitary Commission and Women's Politics in Transition.* Boston: Northeastern University Press, 2000.

Gilman, Nils. *Mandarins of the Future: Modernization Theory in Cold War America.* Baltimore: The Johns Hopkins University Press, 2007.

Gilmore, Glenda Elizabeth. *Who Were the Progressives?* New York: Palgrave MacMillan, 2002.

Gobat, Michel. *Confronting the American Dream: Nicaragua Under U.S. Imperial Rule.* Durham: Duke University Press, 2005.

Gould, Lewis. *The Presidency of Theodore Roosevelt*. Lawrence: University of Kansas Press, 1991, rpr. 2011.

Guglielmo, Thomas A. *White on Arrival: Italians, Race, Color, and Power in Chicago, 1890–1945*. New York: Oxford University Press, 2003.

Haltunnen, Karen. "Humanitarianism and the Pornography of Pain in Anglo-American Culture." *American Historical Review* 100 (1995): 303–334.

Hammer, Joshua. *Yokohama Burning: The Deadly 1923 Earthquake and Fire that Helped Forge the Path to World War II*. New York: Free Press, 2006.

Hannigan, Robert E. *The New World Power: American Foreign Policy, 1898–1917*. Philadelphia: University of Pennsylvania Press, 2002.

Hansen, Arlen. *Gentlemen Volunteers: The Story of American Ambulance Drivers in the Great War*. New York: Arcade Publishing, 1996.

Hansen, Jonathan. *The Lost Promise of Patriotism: Debating American Identity, 1890–1920*. Chicago: University of Chicago Press, 2003.

Haskell, T. L. "Capitalism and the Origins of Humanitarian Sensibility, Part I." *American Historical Review* 90 (1985): 339–361.

———. "Capitalism and the Origins of Humanitarian Sensibility, Part II." *American Historical Review* 90 (1985): 547–566.

Hawley, Ellis W. "The Discovery and Study of a 'Corporate Liberalism.'" *Business History Review* 52 (1978): 309–320.

———. *The Great War and the Search for a Modern Order: A History of the American People and their Institutions*. New York: St. Martin's Press, 1979.

Herring, George C. *From Colony to Superpower: U.S. Foreign Relations Since 1776*. New York: Oxford University Press, 2008.

Hill, Patricia. *The World Their Household: The American Woman's Foreing Mission Movement and Cultural Transformation, 1870–1920*. Ann Arbor: University of Michigan Press, 1985.

Hoffman, Elizabeth Cobbs. *All You Need is Love: The Peace Corps and the Spirit of the 1960s*. Cambridge: Harvard University Press, 1998.

Hogan, Michael J. "Corporatism: A Positive Appraisal." *Diplomatic History* 10 (1986): 363–372.

———. *Marshall Plan: America, Britain, and the Reconstruction of Western Europe, 1947–1952*. Cambridge: Cambridge University Press, 1989.

Hoganson, Kristin L. *Fighting for American Manhood: How Gender Politics Provoked the Spanish-American and Philippine Wars*. New Haven: Yale University Press, 1998.

Hollinger, David. "Nationalism, Cosmopolitanism, and the United States." In *Immigration and Citizenship in the Twenty-First Century*. Noah Pickus, ed. Lanham: Rowman & Littlefield Publishers, 1998: 85–99.

Hunter, Jane H. "Women's Mission in Historical Perspective: American Identity and Christian Internationalism." In *Competing Kingdoms*. Barbara Reeves-Ellington, Kathryn Kish Sklar, and Connie A. Shemo, eds. Durham: Duke University Press, 2010: 19–42.

Hutchinson, John F. *Champions of Charity: War and the Rise of the Red Cross*. Boulder: Westview Press, 1996.

———. "The Nagler Case: A Revealing Moment in Red Cross History." *Canadian Bulletin of Medical History* 9 (1992): 177–190.

———. "Promoting Child Health in the 1920s: International Politics and the Limits of Humanitarianism." In *The Politics of the Healthy Life: An International Perspective*, ed. Esteban Rodriguez-Ocaña. Sheffield: European Association for the History of Medicine and Health Publications, 2002: 131–150.

Hutchinson, William R. *Errand to the World: American Protestant Thought and Foreign Missions*. Chicago: University of Chicago Press, 1987.

Iriye, Akira. *Cultural Internationalism and World Order*. Baltimore: The Johns Hopkins University Press, 2000.

———. *Global Community: The Role of International Organizations in the Making of the Contemporary World*. Berkeley: University of California Press, 2004.

Jacobson, Matthew Frye. *Whiteness of a Different Color: European Immigrants and the Alchemy of Race*. Cambridge: Harvard University Press, 1998.

Jensen, Kimberly. *Mobilizing Minerva: American Women in the First World War*. Urbana: University of Illinois Press, 2008.

Johnson, Robert David. *The Peace Progressives and American Foreign Relations*. Cambridge: Harvard University Press, 1995.

Jones, Jacqueline. *Soldiers of Light and Love: Northern Teachers and Georgia Blacks, 1865–1973*. Athens: University of Georgia Press, 1992.

Jones, Marian Moser. *The American Red Cross, From Clara Barton to the New Deal*. Baltimore: The Johns Hopkins University Press, 2013.

Kaplan, Amy and Donald Pease, eds. *Culture of United States Imperialism*. Durham: Duke University Press, 1993.

Keene, Jennifer D. *Doughboys, the Great War, and the Remaking of America*. Baltimore: The Johns Hopkins University Press, 2001.

Kennedy, David. *Freedom from Fear: The American People in Depression and War, 1929–1945*. Oxford: Oxford University Press, 2001.

———. *Over Here: The First World War and American Society*. Oxford: Oxford University Press, 1980.

Kennedy, Ross. *The Will to Believe: Woodrow Wilson, World War I, and America's Strategy for Peace and Security*. Kent: The Kent State University Press, 2009.

Kerber, Linda. *No Constitutional Right to be Ladies: Women and the Obligations of Citizenship*. New York: Hill and Wang, 1999.

Kingsbury, Celia. *For Home and Country: World War I Propaganda and the Home Front* Lincoln: University of Nebraska Press, 2010.

Klaus, Alisa. *Every Child a Lion: The Origins of Maternal and Infant Health Policy in the United States and France, 1890–1920*. Ithaca: Cornell University Press, 1993.

Kloppenberg, James T. *Uncertain Victory: Social Democracy and Progressivism in European and American Thought, 1870–1920*. New York: Oxford University Press, 1986.

Knock, Thomas J. *To End All Wars: Woodrow Wilson and the Quest for a New World Order*. Princeton: Princeton University Press, 1992.

Kontos, Joan Fultz. *Red Cross Black Eagle: A Biography of Albania's American School*. New York: Columbia University Press, 1981.

LaFeber, Walter. *The Clash: U.S.-Japanese Relations Throughout History*. New York: W. W. Norton & Co., 1998.

La Gumina, Salvatore. *The Great Earthquake: America Comes to Messina's Rescue*. Amherst, NY: Teneo Press, 2008.

Lamont, Thomas W. *Henry P. Davison: The Record of a Useful Life*. New York: Harper & Bros, 1933.

Landis, Michele. "'Let Me Next Time Be Tried By Fire': Disaster Relief and the Origins of the American Welfare State 1789–1874." *Northwestern University Law Review* 92 (1998): 967–1034.

Latham, Michael. *Modernization as Ideology: American Social Science and "Nation Building" in the Kennedy Era*. Chapel Hill: University of North Carolina Press, 2000.

———. *The Right Kind of Revolution: Modernization, Development, and U.S. Foreign Policy from the Cold War to the Present*. Ithaca: Cornell University Press, 2011.

Lears, T. J. Jackson. *No Place of Grace: Antimodernism and the Transformation of American Culture, 1880–1920*. Chicago: University of Chicago Press, 1994.

Lentz-Smith, Adrian. *Freedom Struggles: African Americans and World War I*. Cambridge: Harvard University Press, 2009.

Levin, Jr., N. Gordon. *Woodrow Wilson and World Politics: America's Response to War and Revolution*. New York: Oxford University Press, 1968.

Little, Branden. "Band of Crusaders: American Humanitarians, the Great War, and the Remaking of the World." Ph.D. dissertation, University of California at Berkeley, 2009.

———. "Humanitarian Relief in Europe and the Analogue of War, 1914–1918." In *Finding Common Ground: New Directions in First World War Studies*. Jennifer Keene and Michael Neiberg, eds. Leiden and Boston: Brill, 2010: 139–158.

Lovett, Laura. *Conceiving the Future: Pronatalism, Reproduction, and the Family in the United States, 1890–1938*. Chapel Hill: University of North Carolina Press, 2007.

Lutz, Catherine A. and Jane L. Collins. *Reading National Geographic*. Chicago: University of Chicago Press, 1993.

McCormick, Thomas J. "Drift or Mastery? A Corporatist Synthesis for American Diplomatic History." *Reviews in American History* 10 (1982): 318–330.

McCoy, Alfred and Francisco Scarano, eds. *Colonial Crucible: Empire in the Making of the Modern American State*. Madison: University of Wisconsin Press, 2009.

McGerr, Michael. *A Fierce Discontent: The Rise and Fall of the Progressive Movement in America, 1870–1920*. New York: Free Press, 2003.

McGuire, Michael. "An Ephemeral Relationship: American Non-governmental Organizations, the Reconstruction of France, and Franco-American Relations, 1914–1924." Ph.D. dissertation, Boston University, 2012.

Meckel, Richard A. *Save the Babies: American Public Health Reform and the Prevention of Infant Mortality, 1850–1929*. Ann Arbor: University of Michigan Press, 1998.

Melosi, Martin. *The Sanitary City: Urban Infrastructure in America from Colonial Times to the Present*. Baltimore: The Johns Hopkins University Press, 1999.

Molina, Natalia. *Fit to be Citizens? Public Health and Race in Los Angeles, 1879–1939*. Berkeley: University of California Press, 2006.

Moorhead, Caroline. *Dunant's Dream: War, Switzerland, and the History of the American Red Cross*. New York: Carroll & Graf, 1998.

Morantz-Sanchez, Regina. *Sympathy and Science: Women Physicians in American Medicine*. Chapel Hill: University of North Carolina Press, 2000.

Muncy, Robin. *Creating a Female Dominion in American Reform*. Oxford: Oxford University Press, 1994.

Nash, George. *The Life of Herbert Hoover: The Humanitarian, 1914–1917*. New York: W. W. Norton & Company, 1988.

———. *The Life of Herbert Hoover: Master of Emergencies*. New York: W. W. Norton & Company, 1996.

Nichols, Christopher McKnight. *Promise and Peril: America at the Dawn of a Global Age* Cambridge: Harvard University Press, 2011.

Nigro, Louis John. *New Diplomacy in Italy: American Propaganda and U.S.-Italian Relations, 1917–1919*. New York: Peter Lang, 1999.

Ninkovich, Frank. *Global Dawn: The Cultural Foundation of American Internationalism, 1865–1890*. Cambridge: Harvard University Press, 2009.

———. *Modernity and Power: A History of the Domino Theory in the Twentieth Century*. Chicago: Chicago University Press, 1994.

———. *The United States and Imperialism*. Malden: Blackwell, 2001.

Nord, Philip. "Origins of the French Welfare State: The Struggle for Social Reform in France, 1914–1917." *French Historical Studies* 18 (1994): 821–838.

Nussbaum, Martha. "Patriotism and Cosmopolitanism." In *For Love of Country: Debating the Limits of Patriotism*. Joshua Cohen, ed. Boston: Beacon Press, 1996: 3–20.

Ohmann, Richard M. *Selling Culture: Magazines, Markets, and Class at the Turn of the Century*. London: Verso, 1996.

Painter, Nell Irvin. *Standing at Armageddon: The United States, 1877–1919*. New York: W. W. Norton and Company, 1989.

Patenaude, Bertrand. *The Big Show in Bololand*. Palo Alto: Stanford University Press, 2002.

Paulsen, George E. "Helping Hand or Intervention? Red Cross Relief in Mexico, 1915." *Pacific Historical Review* 57 (1988): 305–325.

Polk, Jennifer. "Constructive Efforts: The American Red Cross and YMCA in Revolutionary and Civil War Russia, 1917–1924." Ph.D. dissertation, University of Toronto, 2012.

Powaski, Ronald. *Toward an Entangling Alliance: American Isolationism, Internationalism, and Europe, 1901–1950*. Westport: Greenwood Press, 1991.

Preston, Andrew. "Bridging the Gap between the Sacred and the Secular in the History of American Foreign Relations." *Diplomatic History* 30 (2006): 783–812.

Price, Alan. "Edith Wharton at War with the American Red Cross: The End of Noblesse Oblige." *Women's Studies* 20 (1991): 121–131.

Proctor, Tammy M. *Civilians in a World at War, 1914–1918*. New York: New York University Press, 2010.

Pryor, Elizabeth Brown. *Clara Barton: Professional Angel*. Philadelphia: University of Pennsylvania Press, 1987.

Raat, W. Dirk. *Mexico and the United States: Ambivalent Vistas*. Athens: University of Georgia Press, 1992, rpr. 2010.

Rafferty, Anne Marie. "Internationalising Nursing Education During the Interwar Period." In *International Health Organisations and Movements, 1918–1939*, ed. Paul Weindling. Cambridge: Cambridge University Press, 1995: 266–282.

Recchiuti, John Louis. *Civic Engagement: Social Science and Progressive Reform in New York City*. Philadelphia: University of Pennsylvania Press, 2007.

Reeves-Ellington, Barbara, Kathryn Kish Sklar, and Connie A. Shemo, eds. *Competing Kingdoms: Women, Mission, Nation, and the America Protestant Empire, 1812–1960*. Durham: Duke University Press, 2010.

Rodgers, Daniel T. *Atlantic Crossings: Social Politics in a Progressive Age*. Cambridge: Harvard University Press, 1998.

Rodogno, Davide. *Against Massacre: Humanitarian Interventions in the Ottoman Empire, 1815–1914*. Princeton: Princeton University Press, 2011.

Rollet, Catherine. "The Other War I: Protecting Public Health" and "The Other War II: Setbacks in Public Health." In *Capital Cities at War*, Jay Winter and Jean-Louis Robert, eds. Cambridge: Cambridge University Press, 1999: 419–486.

Rooke, Patricia T. and Rudy L. Schnell. "'Uncramping Child Life': International Children's Organizations, 1914–1939." In *International Health Organizations and Movements, 1918–1939*. Paul Weindling, ed. Cambridge: Cambridge University Press, 1995: 176–202.

Rosenberg, Emily S. *Financial Missionaries to the World: The Politics and Culture of Dollar Diplomacy, 1900–1930*. Durham: Duke University Press, 2003.

———. "Missions to the World: Philanthropy Abroad." In *Charity, Philanthropy, and Civility in American History*. Lawrence Jacob Friedman and Mark Douglas McGarvie, eds. Cambridge: Cambridge University Press, 2002: 241–258.

———. *Spreading the American Dream: American Economic and Cultural Expansion, 1890–1945*. New York: Hill and Wang, 1982.

Rossini, Daniela. *America riscopre l'Italia : l'inquiry di Wilson e le origini della questione Adriatica, 1917–1919*. Roma: Univeristá di Roma, 1992.

———. *Woodrow Wilson and the American Myth in Italy: Culture, Diplomacy, and War Propaganda*. Cambridge: Harvard University Press, 2008.

Rozario, Kevin. *The Culture of Calamity: Disaster and the Making of Modern America*. Chicago: University of Chicago Press, 2007.

———. "'Delicious Horrors': Mass Culture, The Red Cross, and the Appeal of Modern American Humanitarianism." *American Quarterly* 55 (September 2003): 417–455.

Rupp, Leila J. *Worlds of Women: The Making of an International Women's Movement*. Princeton: Princeton University Press, 1997.

Rydell, Robert W. and Rob Kroes. *Buffalo Bill in Bologna: The Americanization of the World, 1869–1922*. Chicago: University of Chicago Press, 2005.

Saiu, Liliana. *Stati Uniti e Italia nella grande guerra, 1914–1918*. Firenze: L. S. Olschki, 2003.

Salzman, Neil V. *Reform and Revolution: The Life and Times of Raymond Robins*. Kent: Kent State University Press, 1991.

Schott, Linda. *Reconstructing Women's Thoughts: The Women's International League for Peace and Freedom Before World War II*. Palo Alto: Stanford University Press, 1997.

Selig, Diana. *Americans All: The Cultural Gifts Movement*. Cambridge: Harvard University Press, 2008.

Sklar, Kathryn Kish and James Brewer Stewart, eds. *Women's Rights and Transatlantic Antislavery in the Era of Emancipation*. New Haven: Yale University Press, 2007.

Sklar, Martin J. *The Corporate Reconstruction of American Capitalism, 1890–1916*. Cambridge: Harvard University Press, 1988.

Skocpol, Theda. "Patriotic Partnerships: Why Great Wars Nourished American Civic Voluntarism." In *Shaped by War and Trade: International Influences on American Political Development*. Ira Katznelson and Martin Shefter, eds. Princeton: Princeton University Press, 2001.

———. "The Tocqueville Problem: Civic Engagement in American Democracy." *Social Science History* 21 (1997): 455–479.

———, Marshall Ganz, and Ziad Munson. "A Nation of Organizers: The Institutional Origins of Civic Voluntarism in the United States." *American Political Science Review* 94 (Sept 2000): 527–546.

Smith, Leonard V., Stéphane Audoin-Rouzeau, and Annette Becker. *France and the Great War*. Cambridge: Cambridge University Press, 2003.

Smith, Neil. *American Empire: Roosevelt's Geographer and the Prelude to Globalization*. Berkeley: University of California Press, 2004.

Smith, Rogers. *Civic Ideals: Conflicting Visions of Citizenship in U.S. History*. New Haven: Yale University Press, 2009.

Staples, Amy L. S. *The Birth of Development: How the World Bank, Food and Agricultural Organization, and World Health Organization Changed the World, 1945–1960*. Kent: Kent State University Press, 2006.

Steinberg, Ted. *Acts of God: The Unnatural History of Natural Disaster in the United States*. Oxford: Oxford University Press, 2006.

Stewart, James Brewer. *Abolitionist Politics and the Coming of the Civil War*. Amherst: University of Massachusetts Press, 2008.

Stibbe, Matthew. "The Internment of Civilians by Belligerent States during the First World War and the Response of the International Committee of the Red Cross." *Journal of Contemporary History* 41 (January 2006): 5–19.

Stoler, Ann Laura, ed. *Haunted by Empire: Geographies of Intimacy in North American History*. Durham: Duke University Press, 2006.

Stoss, Randall E. *The Stubborn Earth: American Agriculturalists on Chinese Soil, 1898–1937*. Berkeley: University of California Press, 1989.

Tanielian, Melanie. "The War of Famine: Everyday Life in Wartime Beirut and Mount Lebanon (1914–1918)." Ph.D. dissertation, University of California at Berkeley, 2012.

Thompson, John A. *Reformers and War: American Progressive Publicists and the First World War*. Cambridge: Cambridge University Press, 2003.

Tichi, Cilia. *Civic Passions: Seven Who Launched Progressive America*. Chapel Hill: University of North Carolina Press, 2009.

Tomes, Nancy. *The Gospel of Germs: Men, Women, and the Micrboe in American Life*. Cambridge: Harvard University Press, 1999.

Towers, Bridget. "Red Cross Organisational Politics, 1918–1922: Relations of Dominance and the Influence of the United States." In *International Health Organizations and Movements, 1918–1939*. Paul Weindling, ed. Cambridge: Cambridge University Press, 1995: 36–55.

Trattner, Walter I. *Homer Folks: Pioneer in Social Welfare*. New York: Columbia University Press, 1968.

Tucker, Robert W. *Woodrow Wilson and the Great War: Reconsidering America's Neutrality, 1914–1917*. Charlottesville: University of Virginia Press, 2007.

Tyrrell, Ian. *Reforming the World: The Creation of America's Moral Empire*. Princeton: Princeton University Press, 2010.

———. "Woman, Missions, and Empire: New Approaches to Cultural Expansion." In *Competing Kingdoms*. Barbara Reeves-Ellington, Kathryn Kish Sklar, and Connie A. Shemo, eds. Durham: Duke University Press, 2010: 43–68.

————. *Woman's World/Woman's Empire: The Woman's Christian Temperance Union in International Perspective, 1880–1930*. Chapel Hill: University of North Carolina Press, 1991.

Unterberger, Betty M. "Woodrow Wilson and the Russian Revolution." In *Woodrow Wilson and a Revolutionary World*. Arthur S. Link, ed. Chapel Hill: University of North Carolina Press, 1982.

Vaughn, Stephen. *Holding Fast the Inner Lines: Democracy, Nationalism, and the Committee on Public Information*. Chapel Hill: University of North Carolina Press, 1980.

Warner, John Harley. *Against the Spirit of System: The French Impulse in Nineteenth-Century American Medicine*. Baltimore: The Johns Hopkins University Press, 2003.

Watenpaugh, Keith David. "'A pious wish devoid of all practicability': Interwar Humanitarianism, The League of Nations and the Rescue of Trafficked Women and Children in the Eastern Mediterranean, 1920–1927," *American Historical Review*, 115:4 (October 2010): 1315–1339.

Weindling, Paul. *Epidemics and Genocide in Eastern Europe, 1890–1945*. Oxford: Oxford University Press, 2000.

————, ed. *International Health Organisations and Movements, 1918–1939*. Cambridge: Cambridge University Press, 1995.

Westbrook, Robert. *Why We Fought: Forging American Obligations in World War II*. New York: Smithsonian Books, 2004.

Westerman, Thomas. "Rough and Ready Relief: American Identity, Humanitarian Experience, and the Commission for Relief in Belgium, 1914–1917." Ph.D. dissertation, University of Connecticut, 2014.

Wexler, Laura. *Tender Violence: Domestic Visions in an Age of US Imperialism*. Chapel Hill: University of North Carolina Press, 2000.

Wilkie, Wendell. *One World*. New York: Simon and Schuster, 1943.

Winston, Diane. *Red-Hot and Righteous: The Urban Religion of the Salvation Army*. Cambridge: Harvard University Press, 2000.

Winter, Jay, ed. *America and the Armenian Genocide*. Cambridge: Cambridge University Press, 2004.

————. and Jean-Louis Robert, eds. *Capital Cities at War: Paris, London, Berlin*. Cambridge: Cambridge University Press, 1999.

————. and Richard Wall, eds. *The Upheaval of War: Family, Work, and Welfare in Europe, 1914–1918*. Cambridge: Cambridge University Press, 1988.

Young, Michael P. *Bearing Witness Against Sin: The Evangelical Birth of the American Social Movement*. Chicago: University of Chicago Press, 2007.

Zunz, Olivier. *Philanthropy in America: A History*. Princeton: Princeton University Press, 2011.

INDEX

CPSIA information can be obtained
at www.ICGtesting.com
Printed in the USA
BVHW042258270722
643220BV00004B/60